The Illustrated Encyclopedia of
ORCHIDS

The Illustrated Encyclopedia of
ORCHIDS

EDITED BY

ALEC PRIDGEON

FOREWORD BY

ALASDAIR MORRISON

CHAIRMAN OF THE ORCHID COMMITTEE, ROYAL HORTICULTURAL SOCIETY

Timber Press
Portland, Oregon

To the memory of Alvin H. Pridgeon,
who cherished Nature and inspired the same
reverence for it in family and friends

A Kevin Weldon Production
Published by Weldon Publishing, Sydney, Australia
a division of Kevin Weldon & Associates Pty Ltd

©Copyright: Kevin Weldon & Associates Pty Ltd 1992
©Copyright design: Kevin Weldon & Associates Pty Ltd 1992

Designed by Ward & Ward from an idea by Prue Smith

Typeset in Garamond by Post Typesetters, Queensland, Australia

Printed in Singapore by Toppan Printing Co (Pte) Ltd

First published in North America in 1992 by Timber Press, Inc.
9999 S.W. Wilshire, Suite 124
Portland, Oregon 97225, USA

ISBN 0-88192-267-6

Photographs:
Endpapers *Vanda* Rothschildiana
Page one *Paphiopedilum barbatum*
Page two *Ophrys apifera*

CONTENTS

FOREWORD

Orchids are widely thought of as special: they have a reputation for glamor. Sometimes people even need reminding that orchids are in the end only plants. While this book will confirm that orchids are plants, it will also illustrate why they are special.

Although some orchids are among the most striking, beautiful and glamorous flowers to be found in nature, many are in fact the weeds of their habitats; but all are interesting to the connoisseur. The size of the orchid family and the unparalleled diversity of form to be found within it constitute a claim on human attention perhaps more fundamental than any claim based on beauty alone. No family of plants is more deserving of encyclopedic treatment.

Orchid-growers will find that Dr. Pridgeon's text and the contributions of his distinguished colleagues form an invaluable work of reference. No other work on orchids has quite the aim of this one, comprehensive yet compact. Few can boast such a solid range of botanical as well as horticultural expertise among their contributors.

The book will not only benefit the convinced orchidophile, but is also admirably designed to attract, to intrigue and perhaps to entice the general reader who as yet knows little or nothing about orchids. A good book to have on one's shelf — and a good book to leave lying about where one's friends may see it, pick it up and see what is within.

There is a serious message too. Nowadays it is unhappily necessary to draw attention to the great environmental pressure which the Orchidaceae are under. This is a fate which they share with much else in the plant, as in the animal, kingdom. It is man's fault, and it is up to all of us to do what we can to minimize or deflect the impact of mankind. Perhaps the orchids, because of their reputation and their glamor, are uniquely fitted to serve as a symbol and a rallying-point for those who are concerned about what we are collectively doing to the only planet that we have.

ALASDAIR MORRISON
Chairman, The Orchid Committee
The Royal Horticultural Society
London

PREFACE

Because of the sheer size of the orchid family, no one volume can ever hope to describe and illustrate every known species. The contributors to this work, all experts in their respective areas of Orchidaceae, have described hundreds of the major species in cultivation as well as many rarely seen, either in cultivation or in books.

Each generic description includes taxonomic authority, common pronunciation(s), distribution, and brief recommendations for successful cultivation. Every effort has been made to ensure that photographs of species are correctly identified and that the text is concise and accurate.

Like the orchids themselves, our knowledge of orchids is constantly and rapidly evolving, engendering the need to continue research and publish the results as quickly as possible, in advance of the rapid degradation of the environment and orchid habitats. I hope that our children and their descendants will be able to see the orchids illustrated here in the wild and not solely in dusty books, relics of another age.

ALEC M. PRIDGEON

THE MAGICAL WORLD OF ORCHIDS

For centuries the orchid in all its sizes, shapes, colors and fragrances has symbolized all that is exotic and mysterious. In one way such a reputation has been beneficial — it has elevated public awareness of orchids and stimulated an exciting industry of hybridization. But in other ways the lore associated with orchids has obscured even more interesting facts about the orchid family:

● With an estimated 25,000–30,000 species worldwide, it is probably the largest flowering plant family, larger than the sunflower family (Asteraceae), grass family (Poaceae), rose family (Rosaceae), and legume family (Fabaceae). Furthermore, since the first artificial orchid hybrid flowered in 1856 in England, the number of hybrids registered is fast approaching 100,000 due to the high degree of compatibility among species.

● Orchids occupy almost every conceivable habitat type except the oceans, from tropical cloud forests to seashore scrub, from tundra to semi-deserts. You can find them in the Andes and Himalayas, the Everglades, ancient Roman and Mayan ruins, even your own back yard.

● Although they probably share ancestors with the lily family (Liliaceae), orchids resemble lilies about as much as the whale resembles its nearest living relative, the hippopotamus. Orchid flowers are some of the most bizarre and diverse on earth. They can be shaped like buckets, slippers, helmets, even flying ducks. Some mimic female bees or wasps so well that males try to mate with the flowers and in doing so pollinate them, a phenomenon known as pseudocopulation.

● Orchid flowers come in virtually every color of the rainbow. Contrary to the orchids of fiction there are no truly black orchids; however, some are so darkly colored that they might appear black. Floral fragrances are equally diverse, from pleasantly sweet to most foul, from the essence of coconuts, to mentholatum, to rotting liver. While some are faintly exhilarating, others are potent enough to empty a room of people and pets.

● Orchids are among the most evolutionarily advanced of all the monocotyledons, having remarkable specializations for pollination, water uptake and storage, and associations with specific fungi for nutritional needs, including those of seed germination.

WHAT IS AN ORCHID?

This is not as silly a question as it might seem, nor is the answer easy. As new evidence is brought to light, taxonomists constantly reassess the limits of the orchid family: some, for instance, place the "most primitive" orchids, *Apostasia* and *Neuwiedia*, in their own family, Apostasiaceae.

In describing a plant family so vast and so diverse, it is almost safe to say that there are no rules, only exceptions. Biologists generally agree, however, that one feature above all others defines the orchid and differentiates it from virtually all other flowering plants — the fusion of the male portion of the flower (stamens) and female portion (pistils). Orchids have three stamens and three pistils, but unlike those of a lily, for example, which are separate from each other, those of the orchid are fused into a structure termed the column or gynostemium, which is located to one side of the flower.

In slipper orchids (*Cypripedium, Paphiopedilum, Phragmipedium, Selenipedium*), only two of the stamens are fertile and produce pollen in aggregated, sticky masses (the sterile stamen is termed the staminode). Most other orchids have only one fertile stamen with pollen massed into "packets" termed massulae or more cohesive units known as pollinia (sing. pollinium). There are thousands, even hundreds of thousands of pollen grains in one pollinium and two, four, six or eight pollinia in a given flower depending on the species. Orchid genera have traditionally been defined (and still are, in part) by the number of pollinia present.

The ovary of the orchid flower is inferior, that is, it appears to be situated below the points of attachment of the other flower parts. It, too, is noteworthy because each at maturity can contain hundreds of thousands if not millions of ovules. After pollinia are deposited on the stigmatic surface of the flower (at the top of the pistil), pollen tubes grow through the styles down to the ovules and toward the embryo sac and egg cell in each.

One sperm cell fertilizes the egg to form the embryo. A second sperm may or may not unite with two other nuclei (polar nuclei) in the embryo sac. In most flowering plants, this fusion product will develop into a tissue called endosperm that nourishes the embryo. In orchids, however, the

Cattleya dowiana var. *aurea* fits the stereotype of the corsage orchid and illustrates the generalized orchid flower. There are three sepals (here at 12:00, 4:00, and 8:00), two petals (9:00 and 3:00), and the showy labellum dominating the flower. The white column with fused stamens and pistils lies at the base of the labellum and just above it.

A ventral view of the column of *Laelia albida* to show (from above) the anther cap, rostellum flap, and the stigmatic cavity.

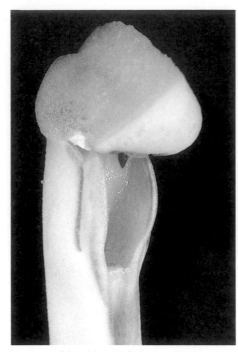

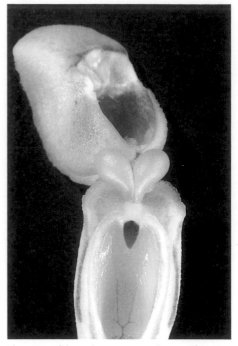

The anther of *Laelia albida* has here been removed to show the pollinia on stalks known as caudicles.

Anatomy of the column of *Aspasia principissa*. The apex of the column as seen in profile, showing the anther cap above the stigmatic cavity. In the flower the column is actually oriented perpendicular to its position here.

The apex of the column in ventral view. The anther cap has been tipped back to show the two pollinia.

development of endosperm is arrested at a very early stage (if it forms at all) so that at maturity seeds will comprise an embryo, a seed coat, and little else. Millions of seeds can fit in the fruit or matured ovary of the flower termed the capsule, commonly called (incorrectly) a "pod."

Without endosperm, then, how is the orchid embryo nourished until it is established and can sustain itself by photosynthesis? As mentioned earlier, on contact with the appropriate fungal strain in nature, the orchid embryo derives carbohydrates and mineral nutrients from a mycorrhizal fungus. This fundamental relationship remained unknown until the turn of the twentieth century, and its discovery had a ripple effect, allowing advances first in scientific laboratories and culminating in the tidal wave of hybridization that continues today.

Another feature that characterizes most orchids is the specialization of the perianth — the sepals and petals. Every orchid flower is bilaterally symmetrical and has an outer whorl of three sepals, one dorsal sepal and two lateral sepals. In some genera such as *Paphiopedilum* the two laterals are fused into a synsepal. Just inside the whorl of sepals is a whorl of three petals. One of these is often different in size, shape, and/ or color, specialized for attracting and perhaps manipulating pollinators in extraordinarily complex and specific ways. This is the labellum, also known as the lip. The labellum is usually lowermost in the orchid flower, with the column just above it. Strangely enough, in the bud the labellum is uppermost, but as the flower develops, the flower stalk or pedicel twists by 180 degrees

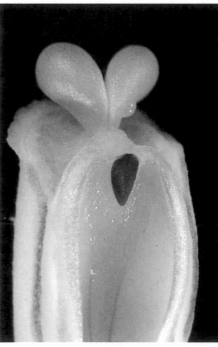

Closer inspection reveals the two pollinia, the brown viscidium, and the stigmatic cavity.

in response to gravity so that by the time the flower opens, the labellum is lowermost. Flowers which undergo this twist are known as resupinate flowers. Some orchid species, however, have flowers that either do not twist at the bud stage (e.g., *Cycnoches*) or else rotate a full 360 degrees (e.g. *Malaxis*). The result is a flower with the labellum uppermost and column lowermost — a non-resupinate flower.

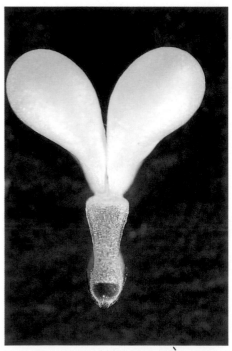

The pollinarium of *Aspasia principissa* consists of (from top to bottom) the two pollinia, a stalk or stipe, and the viscidium. The entire unit is carried on the back of the pollinator.

The labellum is perhaps the most intriguing, even spellbinding element of the orchid flower. As you will see in the accompanying photographs and descriptions in the A–Z Section of the book, the variations seem never-ending. The labellum can be relatively large (*Cattleya labiata*), small (*Disa uniflora*) or minute (*Platystele stenostachya*); gaudy (*Schomburgkia tibicinis*) or dull (*Neottia*

The matured ovary or capsule of *Brassavola nodosa* has been split open to show hundreds of thousands of developing seeds.

A seed of *Phaius* shows the multicellular embryo within already infected with a mycorrhizal fungus. Note the very thin seed coat and complete absence of any nutritive tissue known as endosperm.

nidus-avis); narrow and linear (*Platanthera chlorantha*) or shaped like a bucket (*Coryanthes speciosa*). The margin may be smooth or heavily fringed (*Rhycholaelia digbyana, Dendrobium brymerianum*). The labellum may be extended at the base into a tube called a spur (*Angraecum, Comparettia*), which usually but not always contains nectar. In many genera such as *Stanhopea* the labellum is morphologically and functionally very complex and comprises three distinct parts: the basal hypochile which is often the fragrance source, the middle mesochile, and the apical epichile which is opposite the apex of the column.

The labellum may have other accessory structures as well, generally functioning somehow in the attraction of pollinators or the pollination process itself. Fragrance glands called osmophores may be generalized over the labellum or localized as hairs or small areas of tissue. Osmophores may also occur at the tips of sepals and/or petals (e.g. *Restrepia, Caladenia*). The upper surface of the labellum is frequently furnished with fleshy tissue called the callus, which may have ridges, "warts," bumps or papillae. The shiny, blue callus on the labellum of *Calochilus campestris* demonstrates this very well, as do the papillate calli of many *Oncidium* species.

Orchid flowers are generally on stalks termed pedicels and arranged on unbranched inflorescences called racemes.

In a few species the flowers are not stalked and are borne directly on the main axis of an inflorescence type called a spike. Occasionally, as in some oncidiums, the inflorescences are branched; these are called panicles. Some flowers are solitary on stalks called scapes; examples abound in *Lycaste, Paphiopedilum, Pterostylis*, and *Maxillaria*. *Lockhartia* flowers appear in cymes, inflorescences in which the first flower to open is terminal, but subsequent flowers arise laterally from buds below. Other inflorescence types present in Orchidaceae are the corymb (see Glossary) as in *Corymborkis*, the capitulum as in *Rhizanthella*, and the umbel as in some bulbophyllums (section *Cirrhopetalum*). The vegetative diversity of orchids is one of nature's marvels. Entire flowering-size plants may be as small as a few millimeters or as large as several meters and weighing a ton. They may spend their lives in the Andean treetops at 3,000 meters or most of their lives completely underground in Australia (*Rhizanthella*).

There are two fundamental growth habits of orchids. Sympodial orchids such as cattleyas have a horizontal stem called a rhizome that successively produces new shoots with determinate growth from axillary buds. Monopodial orchids such as vandas lack rhizomes but have upright or pendent stems with indeterminate growth; new leaves develop continuously from the same meristem or growing point.

Cross-cutting these two types of growth habits are two basic ecological habits of orchids: terrestrial and epiphytic. Terrestrial orchids are those that spend most of their

Some orchid species are among the world's smallest flowering plants, while others grow to be quite large. At the small end of the scale is *Platystele stenostachya*, the flower of which fits comfortably on Roosevelt's nose on the United States dime.

Plants of *Grammatophyllum papuanum* from Papua New Guinea may be several meters high and weigh a ton.

Rhizanthella gardneri is one of two Australian species that grow completely underground. Only the inflorescences ever break the soil surface to allow pollination by small flies, beetles, even termites.

lives rooted in the soil. Epiphytes are those that spend most of their lives growing on other plants. There is a third type, actually a subset of the epiphytes, that lives on thin layers of detritus on rocks; these orchids are called lithophytes. Epiphytic orchids, spending their lives on tree branches and separated from the steady supply of water in the soil, have effectively solved the dual

Satyrium bicorne is one of hundreds of terrestrial orchids in Africa that grow in sandy soils. This species, photographed here in the Cape Province of South Africa, flowers from September through November.

problems of uptake and storage of water by the specializations listed below.

Both terrestrial and epiphytic orchids have successfully exploited vastly different ecological microsites around the world because of certain vegetative specializations. Perhaps at the heart of this is the vast array of orchid root systems. Roots of epiphytic and many terrestrial orchids have a specialized epidermis of one or many layers of dead cells called the velamen. Although

the velamen probably has several functions, debated for well over 100 years (Pridgeon, 1987), it seems clear that its primary role is to capture and hold water long enough for it to be absorbed by the cells interior to it. In arid situations it probably also serves as a barrier to excessive, damaging water loss by transpiration, and protects underlying cells from high levels of ultraviolet radiation. Many terrestrial orchids possess fleshy roots or underground storage organs (called tuberoids) with both stem and root tissues. In fact, it was the paired tuberoids of the genus *Orchis* that prompted the botanist of ancient Greece, Theophrastus, to name the genus, after a fancied resemblance of the tuberoids to testicles (Gr. *orchis*, testis). A new tuberoid is formed during each growing season, while the previous year's tuberoid is still present.

Orchid stems may also serve as storage organs. Terrestrial orchid genera such as *Bletia* have underground storage stems termed corms. Sympodial epiphytes often have variously thickened stems commonly called pseudobulbs. Monopodial orchids do not have pseudobulbs but do have fleshy leaves and roots.

The leaves of epiphytes are generally persistent from year to year, but leaves of terrestrials are often shed at the end of the growing season. Leaves may be pleated or plicate (folded many times longitudinally, as in *Bletia* and *Phaius*) or conduplicate (folded only once, in the middle, as in *Cattleya*). Plicate leaves are always thin, but conduplicate leaves may be quite thick, fleshy, and leathery (coriaceous). Some leaves are terete, that is, pencil-like and round in cross-section, as in *Brassavola*, *Luisia*, and some species of *Dendrobium* and *Oncidium*. Epiphytes will generally

The vast majority of orchid species are epiphytes, that is, plants growing on other plants. However, they are not parasites, obtaining water and dilute mineral solutions from condensation and rainfall flowing along tree branches and trunks.

The root of an epiphytic orchid usually has an epidermis of more than one layer of cells that are dead at maturity. This tissue called velamen, which is whitish to gray when dry, quickly absorbs water and holds it long enough for it to enter the living tissues of the root. In the photograph of the plant of *Phalaenopsis violacea* above, note the root with the green tip and the velamen just behind it.

The Australian species *Dendrobium speciosum*, locally known as the rock orchid, usually grows as a lithophyte on granite or sandstone.

have fleshy leaves with some water-storage tissue, although some, such as species of *Taeniophyllum*, *Microcoelia*, and *Chiloschista*, are essentially leafless.

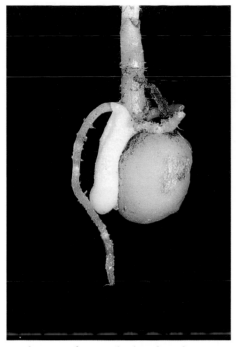

As adaptations for periodic drought and storage of starch, many terrestrial orchids such as *Ophrys* and *Pterostylis* have underground organs called tuberoids. The fancied resemblance of paired tuberoids (one formed during the current growing season and one persisting from the previous year) to testicles gives the genus *Orchis* and the family Orchidaceae their names.

ORCHID DISTRIBUTION

There is hardly one region of the world without orchids, given their success in adapting to and colonizing almost every conceivable niche on land. Some species such as *Cypripedium passerinum*, *Cypripedium guttatum*, and *Coeloglossum viride* flower within the Arctic Circle (Luer, 1975), while *Corybas macranthus* grows in sphagnum bogs on Macquarie Island (Jones, 1988), a scant 1,000 miles from Antarctica. The vast majority of orchid species, however, occur in the tropics, especially the Neotropics. Dressler (1981) estimated that as many as 3,000 species occur in Colombia, 2,500 in Brazil, and 1,500 in Venezuela. Tropical Africa has about 3,100 species and tropical Asia some 6,800. The Malay Archipelago, including Borneo and New Guinea, is also particularly rich in species. The estimate of orchid species in Australasia has risen from Dressler's figure of 600 to about 900 (Clements, 1989; Jones, 1991) in the last ten years. As exploration and research continue, hundreds more are likely to be found worldwide.

Even in the tropics, orchids are distributed differently according to elevation gradients. Diversity is highest in montane cloud forests between roughly 1,000 and 2,000 meters above sea level; as many as 47 different species were found on one tree by the great orchid explorer and taxonomist G. C. K. Dunsterville in Venezuela (Dressler,

The greatest diversity of orchid species is found in montane cloud forests, such as these in the Colombian Andes, between about 1,000 and 2,000 meters above sea level.

Tropical rain forests at lower elevations are relatively poor in terms of numbers of orchid species.

1981). Species richness declines both in warm to hot lowland rain forests and above the timber line. Although orchids are most common in woodlands, they seem to pop up in the most unexpected places: swamps and peat bogs, sandy dunes around salt lakes, semi-desert scrub in blazing sun, savannas, paramo, alpine meadows, elfin forest, your own back yard. It all comes down to this: it is easier to list the habitats in which orchids do not occur than those where they do.

Many orchid genera are pantropical; *Vanilla* is one good example, distributed from Latin America, to equatorial Africa, to southeast

Asia. At the other extreme are hundreds if not thousands of species endemic (restricted) to specific countries, mountain ranges, valleys, or even more localized sites. Consistent with its long, isolated geologic history, Australia's flora has a high degree of endemism; roughly 88 per cent of the terrestrial orchids do not occur elsewhere (Jones, 1988). Because of the high levels of endemism and their sporadic and wide dispersal, many orchid populations suffer with both loss of habitat to agriculture and logging, and also overcollecting. The removal of one tree or a few plants can seriously cripple the reproductive potential

The world's southernmost orchid, *Corybas macranthus*, grows in sphagnum bogs on Macquarie Island, only about 1,000 miles from Antarctica.

Terrestrial orchids such as *Dactylorhiza, Cypripedium*, and *Orchis* flourish in the Dolomites in northeast Italy.

The lovely *Disa uniflora* is commonly found along stream banks in South Africa, as here on one of the flanks of Table Mountain in Cape Town. Roots of the plants are almost always resting in water.

Australian terrestrials quickly seed into sandplain scrub which has been burned. A burned site such as this in Western Australia will support much more orchid diversity than when it is overgrown.

and gene flow of the entire population. For species already endangered, especially those that are self-incompatible, reductions in gene flow can rapidly reduce fitness and adaptability.

ORCHID NAMES AND CLASSIFICATION

All species of the earth's flora and fauna have two Latin names, following Linnaeus's binomial system of nomenclature. The first name listed, always capitalized and italicized or underscored, is the name of the genus, e.g. *Cattleya*. A genus is simply a group of related species. The second name, also italicized, is the species name itself, e.g. *skinneri*. Names of either may commemorate a person, describe some particularly diagnostic aspect of the plant, or refer to the place of its discovery. For example, *Cattleya skinneri* honors George Ure Skinner, a famous explorer and orchid collector in Guatemala, who discovered the species. *Cattleya amethystoglossa* was

named for its amethyst-colored labellum. *Paphiopedilum philippinense* is native to the Philippines.

Through the centuries, botanists have tried to express relationships among orchids by ranking them in hierarchies according to similarities and differences in floral and/or vegetative features. Orchids left no fossil record, as far as we know, so our ideas about the evolutionary history of the family have been largely speculative, based on general trends in flowering plants and on the most parsimonious explanations. As new data become available from the field and laboratory, often as the result of applying new technology, orchid systematists are compelled to reassess relationships, whether at the species level

Granite outcrops in the semi-desert scrub of Australia may appear to be inhospitable to orchids, but genera such as *Pterostylis, Thelymitra,* and *Caladenia* are able to withstand the searing heat and dry soils by utilizing storage products in their tuberoids underground.

or higher. Since the names of plants reflect those relationships, the names may change also, but only in accordance with rules established by the *International Code of Botanical Nomenclature.*

Among other rules and recommendations, this *Code* specifies the various levels of the hierarchy of classification. Closely related genera are grouped into subtribes, names which end in -inae. Following our example of *Cattleya skinneri* above, *Cattleya* is in subtribe Laeliinae along with its relatives such as *Laelia* and *Encyclia.* Related subtribes are grouped into larger taxonomic units called tribes; names of tribes end in -eae. Subtribe Laeliinae is in tribe Epidendreae. Finally, related tribes are grouped into a subfamily, the names of which always end in -oideae. Tribe Epidendreae is in subfamily Epidendroideae.

According to Dressler, whose 1981 classification is followed in this volume, there are six subfamilies in the orchid family: Apostasioideae, Cypripedioideae, Spiranthoideae, Orchidoideae, Epidendroideae, and Vandoideae. Since that 1981 classification was published, Dressler (1986, 1990a, 1990b) has amended the framework more than once at many levels. However, most orchid growers are familiar only with the 1981 scheme, hence its adoption here:

Subfamily Apostasioideae
Subfamily Cypripedioideae
Subfamily Spiranthoideae
  Tribe Erythrodeae
    Subtribe Tropidiinae
    Subtribe Goodyerinae
  Tribe Cranichideae
    Subtribe Spiranthinae
    Subtribe Pachyplectroninae

    Subtribe Manniellinae
    Subtribe Cranichidinae
    Subtribe Cryptostylidinae
Subfamily Orchidoideae
  Tribe Neottieae
    Subtribe Limodorinae
    Subtribe Listerinae
  Tribe Diurideae
    Subtribe Chloraeinae
    Subtribe Caladeniinae
    Subtribe Pterostylidinae
    Subtribe Acianthinae
    Subtribe Diuridinae
    Subtribe Prasophyllinae
  Tribe Orchideae
    Subtribe Orchidinae
    Subtribe Habenariinae
    Subtribe Huttonaeinae
  Tribe Diseae
    Subtribe Disinae
    Subtribe Satyriinae
    Subtribe Coryciinae
  Tribe Triphoreae
  Tribe Wullschlaegelieae
Subfamily Epidendroideae
  Tribe Vanilleae
    Subtribe Vanillinae
    Subtribe Lecanorchidinae
    Subtribe Palmorchidinae
    Subtribe Pogoniinae
  Tribe Gastrodieae
    Subtribe Nerviliinae
    Subtribe Gastrodiinae
    Subtribe Rhizanthellinae
  Tribe Epipogieae
  Tribe Arethuseae
    Subtribe Arethusinae
    Subtribe Thuniinae
    Subtribe Bletiinae
    Subtribe Sobraliinae
  Tribe Coelogyneae
    Subtribe Coelogyninae
    Subtribe Adrorhizinae
  Tribe Malaxideae
  Tribe Cryptarrheneae
  Tribe Calypsoeae
  Tribe Epidendreae
    Subtribe Eriinae

    Subtribe Podochilinae
    Subtribe Thelasiinae
    Subtribe Glomerinae
    Subtribe Laeliinae
    Subtribe Meiracyllinae
    Subtribe Pleurothallidinae
    Subtribe Dendrobiinae
    Subtribe Bulbophyllinae
    Subtribe Sunipiinae
Subfamily Vandoideae
  Tribe Polystachyeae
  Tribe Vandeae
    Subtribe Sarcanthinae
    Subtribe Angraecinae
    Subtribe Aerangidinae
  Tribe Maxillarieae
    Subtribe Corallorhizinae
    Subtribe Zygopetalinae
    Subtribe Bifrenariinae
    Subtribe Lycastinae
    Subtribe Maxillariinae
    Subtribe Dichaeinae
    Subtribe Telipogoninae
    Subtribe Ornithocephalinae
  Tribe Cymbidieae
    Subtribe Cyrtopodiinae
    Subtribe Genyorchidinae
    Subtribe Thecostelinae
    Subtribe Acriopsidinae
    Subtribe Catasetinae
    Subtribe Stanhopeinae
    Subtribe Pachyphyllinae
    Subtribe Oncidiinae

The generic entries in the A–Z section of this volume list the tribe and subtribe to which each orchid belongs. Authors of genera and species are listed immediately after each; usage and abbreviations follow the *Draft Index of Author Abbreviations* published by the Royal Botanic Gardens at Kew.

For purposes of hybridization or awards, specific plants may be given clonal or cultivar names, following the species name and enclosed in single quotes, such as *Cattleya skinneri* 'Many'. Any awards that clone might receive then follow the clonal name, e.g. *Cattleya skinneri* 'Many', CCM/AOS. There are several national orchid societies that grant awards for flower quality or cultural excellence: the American Orchid Society (AOS), the Royal Horticultural Society (RHS), Deutsche Orchideen Gesellschaft (DOG), as well as regional and local societies, about 40 in all. The highest award that the American Orchid Society and Royal Horticultural Society give for flower quality is the First Class Certificate (FCC). The next highest is the Award of Merit (AM). In addition, the American Orchid Society grants a third quality award, the Highly Commended Certificate (HCC). Other societies such as the Deutsche Orchideen-Gesellschaft award Gold (GM), Silver (SM) and Bronze Medals (BM) to flowers. Awards such as the Certificate of Cultural Merit (CCM/AOS) and Certificate of Cultural Commendation (CCC/RHS) recognize superior cultivation of specimen plants.

Orchid Hybridization

In the wild, orchid species rarely form natural hybrids in zones of overlap. The integrity of species is maintained by differences in flowering times, floral morphology, visual and olfactory cues, as well as by genetic incompatibility or inability of the hybrid to establish and reproduce. Once one or more of these barriers or isolating mechanisms are removed, though, for example when orchids are pollinated by hand in the greenhouse, two different species will often produce viable hybrids quite readily. Artificial hybrids are common between species in the same genus, between species of different genera in the same subtribe, more rarely between species in different subtribes (but within the same tribe). In fact, the genes from as many as six different genera are present in some hybrids, leading to the perception of orchids as most promiscuous plants indeed!

The first orchid hybrid to flower (1856) was *Calanthe* Dominyi (*furcata x masuca*), a cross made by John Dominy, head grower for the English firm of Veitch & Sons. Shortly thereafter, a showier hybrid, *Cattleya* Hybrida (*guttata x loddigesii*) flowered, and a new era in orchid cultivation had dawned. Relatively few hybrids were produced in the last half of the nineteenth century, however, because growers were still unaware of the specific relationships between orchids and mycorrhizal fungi that governed the germination of seeds and establishment of seedlings. At the turn of the century, Frenchman Noël Bernard effectively demonstrated that the presence of such fungi was necessary for germination. A practical application of this startling phenomenon was suggested by German Hans Burgeff, who argued that orchid seeds could be germinated on laboratory agar with the addition of the appropriate fungal strain. Finally, in 1922 an American plant physiologist named Lewis Knudson published his discovery: orchids could be germinated on agar not with the fungi themselves but with the sugars normally provided by the fungi along with some mineral nutrients. Hybrids could now be mass-produced in the laboratory simply using nutrient agar in flasks. A veritable explosion of new hybrids ensued, which continues today.

The earliest hybrids were intrageneric, that is, they were crosses between species in the same genus. The generic name of the hybrid remained the same, and a fancy name, not italicized, was given to the cross itself, e.g. *Calanthe* Dominyi. Subsequent more adventurous crosses were made between species of different but related genera, requiring the creation of a new generic name by combining the two. For example, *Cattleya mossiae x Laelia purpurata* became *Laeliocattleya* (abbreviated as *Lc.*) Canhamiana. When a *Laeliocattleya* was then crossed with a species (or hybrid) of *Brassavola*, the hybrid genus name became *Brassolaeliocattleya* (abbreviated as *Blc.*). It was not long before the genes of yet a fourth genus were added, and the former method of simply combining generic names had become unwieldy. Accordingly, the practice of creating generic names ending in *-ara* was adopted for hybrids with genes from multiple genera. Examples are *Vuylstekeara* (*Cochlioda x Miltonia x Odontoglossum*) and *Potinara* (*Brassavola x Laelia x Cattleya x Sophronitis*). One way of distinguishing a natural genus from a hybrid genus is to insert a multiplication symbol before the hybrid name, such as X *Potinara*. Today, the Royal Horticultural Society registers all new orchid hybrids and publishes them regularly in major orchid periodicals and every five years in *Sander's Complete List of Orchid Hybrids*.

Orchid Cultivation

HISTORY

We will never know who first placed the orchid in captivity. The reason may have been medicinal or purely aesthetic. We do know that the Chinese word for orchid, *lan*, appears in herbals 4,000 years ago. Confucius (551–479 BC) commented on the orchid's fragrance. By the third century A.D., references to what we now know as *Cymbidium ensifolium* and *Dendrobium moniliforme* appeared in Chinese botanical manuscripts (Reinikka, 1972).

In the Western world, the Father of Botany, Theophrastus, mentioned *Orchis* in his *Enquiry into Plants* around 300 B.C. Thereafter European orchids appeared in the early herbals, up until the seventeenth century. *Vanilla* even appeared in the *Badianus Manuscript*, the sixteenth-century Aztec herbal. Some of the first orchids in cultivation in the West, brought back from all parts of the world, were maintained at the Royal Botanic Gardens, Kew, England, in the mid-1700s.

It was not until plants of *Cattleya labiata* flowered for Mr William Cattley in 1818, however, that orchids began to be cultivated on a large scale. Pseudobulbs of this orchid had been sent from the Organ Mountains near Rio de Janeiro, Brazil, as packing material for other ornamental plants, and Cattley set the plant in his glasshouse or "stove." When it flowered, he showed it to the famous botanist and orchid taxonomist, John Lindley. Lindley named the genus in his honor and the species for the magnificent labellum. More collectors were then commissioned to find additional plants and species.

Unfortunately, the first attempts at growing orchids in the stoves were tragic failures. Because many of the orchids arriving on British shores were from the warm coastal lowlands, it was assumed that all tropical orchids required the hot and humid climate of rain forests, when in fact many were being collected from the inland cloud forests hundreds of meters in elevation. As a result orchids died by the thousands, prompting the orchid taxonomist and Director of Kew Gardens, Joseph Dalton Hooker, to comment that England had become "the graveyard of tropical orchids." On the advice of John Lindley, who sought climatic information about habitats from collectors, growers such as Joseph Paxton opened up the stoves to allow cooler temperatures and greater air circulation and thereby more closely approximate cloud-forest conditions. By the end of the nineteenth century, orchid growing was a less risky enterprise and a popular Victorian pastime for those who could afford the prices of wild-collected plants. Major firms such as James Veitch & Sons and Sander's maintained a cadre of professional collectors living abroad and sending huge consignments of orchids, sometimes thousands at a time, back to England on a regular basis to meet the demand.

Just after the turn of the twentieth century,

orchids seemed to fall out of fashion in favor of other plants. The costs of collecting and shipping skyrocketed, as did the costs associated with glasshouse maintenance. One by one the professional collectors working in the tropics — Wallis, Arnold, Falkenberg, Degance, Klaboch, Endres — were killed by natives or thieves, died from such diseases as dysentery, malaria, and yellow fever, disappeared in the jungles, or grew too old to travel and died penniless (Reinikka, 1972). Many of Frederick Sander's collectors wrote bitterly to him, complaining about his failure to send letters of credit to firms abroad on their behalf so that they could buy provisions and, more importantly, orchids (letters to F. Sander, Kew). Most of those who lived resigned from his employ.

Orchid growing as a hobby was rejuvenated by the work of Bernard and Burgeff on symbiotic germination of orchid seeds and by the reports from Knudson on asymbiotic germination. Seedlings could now be produced quickly and cheaply. Prices for orchids plummeted, just as an entire industry built around orchid hybridization was finding itself. Following the Second World War, several established firms in England, France, Hawaii and the United States dominated the international orchid trade. The industry received another boost with the discovery in the 1960s that the excised growing point of an orchid, the apical meristem, would proliferate when agitated in nutrient solutions; one plant could produce hundreds of nearly identical copies of itself. Today selected clones of both species and hybrids are reproduced by this laboratory process called meristeming or mericloning. Propagation by meristeming and flasking (raising seedlings on nutrient agar in a glass flask) have made it possible to see orchids selling for a few dollars and entering the pot-plant market once monopolized by African violets, spathiphyllums, and Boston ferns. Orchids have come of age — from wild-collected innocents exploited by a few for the privileged few, to artificially propagated plants raised *en masse* for the general public.

BASICS

Unfortunately, the easily acquired orchid has the unwarranted reputation of being difficult to grow — fussy, unforgiving plants that need a home built like a misty cloud forest, with periodic cloudbursts, insects, and the occasional jaguar. Some people devoted bedrooms or basements to their orchids, while others have constructed elaborate glasshouses with different climatic zones, potting rooms, and Mozart piped in to soothe the soul and presumably fortify the plants.

But you can start simply with orchids, raising a few plants on the window sill, outdoors in spring and summer, or under fluorescent lights, and discover that orchids are not fussy at all. In fact, the very adaptability that has allowed them to colonize all corners of the earth has made them very forgiving and rewarding in cultivation.

In this section we review the fundamentals of light, temperature, watering and fertilizing, humidity, air circulation and potting, and then comment on the pests and diseases which you might encounter in your collection. Refinements in culture of particular species are discussed under individual entries in the A–Z section of this volume. There are many excellent books on orchid culture, such as *Home Orchid Growing* by Rebecca Northen, *You Can Grow Orchids* by Mary Noble, and *Orchid Growing Illustrated* by Brian and Wilma Rittershausen. Many periodicals such as *The Orchid Review* (1893–) and the *American Orchid Society Bulletin* (1932–) provide news of helpful products and techniques, advertisements for plants, and enduring articles of interest for the orchid-growing community. Another very good source of information and plants is your local orchid society; if one does not exist, gather a few friends and start one! The camaraderie and shared experiences enrich the hobby even more.

In orchid growing there are two guiding principles that underlie all else. If you memorize and practice them your success rate will rise exponentially as the months and years pass. First, the most important thing you can do is **buy sensibly**: purchase plants that suit your growing conditions. If you live in a tropical climate, then buy warm-growing plants rather than alpine or cloud-forest plants. Within certain limits and without breaking your budget you can alter the conditions of your growing area to suit the plants, such as by allowing more ventilation, raising the humidity, increasing light intensity or shading. As much as possible try to duplicate the natural growing conditions of the species or, in the case of hybrids, those species in the background of the hybrid. For example, plants of the hybrid genus *Odontioda (Cochlioda x Odontoglossum)* are cool-growing as are both parent genera. The same is true for *Odontonia (Odontoglossum x Miltonia* [actually *Miltoniopsis*]), *Vuylstekeara (Miltonia x Cochlioda x Odontoglossum)*, and a few others. By contrast, hybrid genera such as *Brassidium (Brassia x Oncidium)*, *Miltassia (Miltonia x Brassia)*, *Odontocidium (Odontoglossum x Oncidium)*, and others adapt well to intermediate conditions, defined below under Temperature. Some hybridists have brought the showy, cool-growing orchids down to us from the upper elevations to warmer climates by creating warmth-tolerant masdevallias, cymbidiums, and odontoglossums.

The second principle in orchid growing

Epiphytes are constantly bathed in a fresh, buoyant atmosphere, conditions which the orchid grower should try to approximate in the home or glasshouse.

applies when your plants are already in place in your home or glasshouse and you are responsible for their welfare. Some experienced growers argue that orchids thrive on benign neglect. On the other hand, novices are prone to love their plants to death by overwatering. The Golden Mean between these two extremes is to **observe**. Inspect your plants regularly, not only for the first symptoms of leaf-spotting fungi or the footprints of a scale insect, but for signs of improper culture — yellowing or loss of leaves, failure to flower, gradual decline.

Light
Without light for photosynthesis, most plants will not survive long. If beginners make any mistake at all in judging the amount of light needed, it is in underestimation. A common scenario in the demise of many house plants begins with the plant finding its new home in the bathroom or a dim bedroom. Although the plant brightens the environment for a while, soon the leaves begin to yellow and sag. Misdiagnosing the problem, the owner thinks that the plant needs water and gives it a good drenching. Without sufficient light for photosynthesis, the plant simply cannot use the water. As a result the potting medium remains wet, the roots rot, and soon only compost and a label remain. Orchids are no exception to this scenario. To prevent it, buy only those plants that will adapt to the light conditions of your growing area whether it is a window sill, fluorescent light bench or a greenhouse. Depending on whether species in nature grow in the dim light of the forest floor among the leaf litter or high in the canopy

of cloud forests, the amount of light needed for maintenance and flowering varies somewhat. Phalaenopsis and mottled-leaved paphiopedilums such as *P. callosum* or its famous hybrid, *P. Maudiae*, will accept low-light situations in the home, such as on window sills or trays under fluorescent lights. At the other extreme are the terete-leaved vandas, which require full sun for flowering. Most orchids fall somewhere in the middle, between 2,000 and 3,000 foot-candles of light. If you do not have a light meter, think of it this way: depending on your latitude, full sun on a summer day will likely produce between 10,000 and 12,000 foot-candles. Once the light travels through glass its intensity drops by more than half. Among the different exposures available to window-sill growers in the Northern Hemisphere, the southern exposure is best because of its relatively uniform brightness throughout the day. The second-best exposure is the eastern one, which receives a few hours of strong morning sun. West-facing windows tend to heat up too quickly and can seriously burn leaves, while northern exposures are generally too dim to be effective for flowering. The best exposure for growing orchids in the Southern Hemisphere is of course the northern one. Sun rooms or sun porches are excellent growing areas provided that all other climatic requirements are met. A clear choice for those in cold climates are fluorescent light tubes, from the very simple cool-white to warm-white types to full-spectrum lights and combinations thereof. The most convenient length for fixtures and tubes is 48 inches. Fixtures holding four tubes should be as close as possible to the plants without touching or burning the leaves. Some growers maintain the same day-night cycle (e.g. sixteen hours on, eight hours off) throughout the year with automatic timers, while others vary the "day length" of their setup according to the seasons, longer in summer and shorter in winter. Experimentation under your conditions is the best approach.
Well-grown plants generally have yellow-green leaves. Though they look rich and healthy, dark green leaves usually indicate that more light is needed, especially for flowering. Move the plant to a brighter location in the home or glasshouse or, if it is under fluorescent lights, move it closer to the tubes and/or closer to the center of the tubes where intensity is highest, but do so gradually to prevent burning the leaves. If the leaves are bleached or yellow, the probable cause is excessive light intensity; move the plant to a dimmer location in the home or under lights, or increase shading in the greenhouse.

Temperature
As we have seen, different orchid species grow from sea level (where there may be little variation in temperatures over the course of a day in the tropics) to 3,000

Cloud forest in Monteverde Cloud Forest Preserve, Costa Rica.

meters above sea level (where there may be as much as a 15°C difference between the daytime high and overnight low temperature). It seems intuitive that plants from one extreme will not succeed in the climate of the other extreme. As a result, orchid species and hybrids are customarily categorized as warm-growing (minimum night temperature of 18–21°C), intermediate (minimum of 13–18°C), and cool-growing (10–13°C). Throughout this volume the temperature requirements of species are given to help you decide which are most suitable to your growing conditions.
Remember also that a differential of about 10°C is necessary for most orchids to flower. In the home this can be achieved by opening a window at night or by setting the thermostat down.

Watering
Of all the basics to master, watering is the most difficult because so many other factors interact to affect its frequency: relative humidity, type of potting medium and pot, light intensity, temperature, air circulation. In addition, many orchids such as catasetums have a dormant or "resting period" in their annual cycle when they receive little or no water.
In general, water only when the plants are in active growth, usually beginning in spring when new roots and shoots are initiated. Then reduce watering after flowering. However, orchids without pseudobulbs such as *Phalaenopsis, Paphiopedilum*, and *Masdevallia* should not be allowed to dry out substantially. The best

way to judge if a plant needs water is to feel just below the surface of the potting medium; if it's moist, wait.
Frequency of watering should increase with higher light intensities and temperatures, increased air circulation, lower relative humidity, use of clay pots with good drainage and an open potting medium. The amount of water given on each occasion should be enough to run out amply through the drainage holes in the pot or the bottom of the mount or basket. The goal is to flush out any dissolved salts that have accumulated in the medium so that they do not burn the roots.

Fertilizing
Certain macroelements — nitrogen, phosphorus, and potassium — are necessary for plant growth, metabolism, and reproduction. Fertilizers are sold under different formulations depending on the relative concentrations of these three elements. Balanced fertilizers, those with equal proportions of the three and sold under such formulations as 20–20–20 or 10–10–10, are recommended for tree-fern fiber, osmunda, sphagnum, and inert potting media such as gravel, lava rock, rockwool, etc. Higher concentrations of nitrogen in formulations such as 30–10–10 are frequently sold for plants potted in fir bark, while other products such as 10–30–20 have higher proportions of phosphorus to promote better flowering.
As with watering, some general rules apply. Fertilize only when the plants are in active growth. It is advisable to water plants before fertilizing them so that the fertilizer salts are absorbed more readily by the roots and do not burn them. Another way to prevent this is to fertilize with only half the concentration recommended by the manufacturer (e.g. if the directions call for one teaspoon per gallon or four liters, then use only half a teaspoon). It is far more effective to fertilize at half-strength with every watering than to shock the plant with full-strength fertilizer every so often.

Humidity
Relative humidity in the growing area, which can be measured by a simple instrument called a hygrometer, should be above 50 per cent and ideally 70 per cent. There are a number of ways to raise humidity if necessary. Syringing the plants with a fine mist is the most obvious method but effective only for a few minutes. Be sure that plant surfaces are dry by nightfall to discourage the growth of bacteria and fungi. One very useful technique is to set the plants a few centimeters above water on gravel-filled trays; the water level should be below the top of the gravel layer so that the bottom of the pot is never in direct contact with water. Grouping plants also will raise the humidity in their immediate area. If all else fails, room humidifiers are widely available and very effective.

Air Circulation

Orchids in nature are constantly bathed in breezes and even gusts. Fresh, gently moving air in the home environment benefits plants as well as their owners. Ceiling fans, air-conditioning vents, small fans — all are helpful in preventing stagnant air that favors diseases and in ensuring uniform temperatures throughout the growing area. Be sure, though, that air is not blowing directly on any plants.

Potting

There are several ways to keep different orchids in captivity: pots, slabs of cork or tree-fern, baskets of sphagnum, natural mounts of branches or twigs. Which one of these is best is determined by the growth habit and cultural needs of the species in question. For example, stanhopeas have pendent inflorescences that penetrate the potting medium and emerge below. Potting these in a basket lined with sphagnum moss therefore allows the flowers to be displayed to their full advantage. Vandas and ascocentrums (as well as their hybrid genus, *Ascocenda*) also thrive in baskets, but with coarse bark or charcoal loosely packed around the roots. Those species that prefer to dry out thoroughly between waterings are best suited to cork or tree-fern slabs, while those that prefer moister conditions should go into clay or plastic pots. Plastic pots "breathe" less than clay and therefore retain moisture longer, a factor to consider when watering.

When potting an orchid, the diameter at the top should be no larger than to allow one or two years of growth. Miniature orchids, for example, are very happy in pots five to eight centimeters wide, while standard cattleyas and cymbidiums with five or six growths require pots with much larger diameters. For sympodial orchids, there should be enough space between the youngest shoot and the rim of the pot to allow for two years of growth. Fill the pot about one-third full with stones or even Styrofoam pellets of the sort used as packing material. Add enough potting medium so that the rhizome of the plant will be only about one or two centimeters below the rim, then fill in around the plant with medium, pressing it down firmly in the process. Larger plants may require a rhizome clip or a stake to immobilize them until new roots are initiated and they are well established. Never forget to insert a plant label in the medium, giving the name of the plant and date of repotting.

Monopodial orchids are potted similarly but positioned in the center of the pot instead of to one edge; remember that these types have no rhizome and grow vertically instead of horizontally. The lowest leaf should lie just above the potting medium. When vandas, ascocentrums, and ascocendas outgrow their slotted baskets, the procedure is different. Rather than try to detach the aerial roots from the basket and risk setting the plant back, soak the plant (basket and all) in a bucket of water for a few minutes to make the roots more pliable. Then set the basket within a slightly larger basket, wrap the roots around and set them inside the basket also. Wire the baskets together, add a wire hanger, and attach a new label as above.

Sympodial orchids are very readily propagated asexually by division of the rhizome. When repotting think about whether or not the plant should be divided. Using a new razor blade or a knife or pruning shears sterilized over a flame, cut the rhizome so that each division has three or more growths and preferably at least one actively growing lead. Remove withered pseudobulbs and leaves and snip off dead, brown, and mushy roots. Healthy roots are firm and white with well-defined root-tips. Backbulbs may have dormant buds, so pot them up separately.

Obviously, without a rhizome monopodial plants cannot be divided in this way. However, many such as *Phalaenopsis* species and hybrids produce offshoots called "keikis" at nodes along the inflorescence axis. When the roots of the keikis are a few centimeters long, the plantlets can be potted up in the same way as the parent plants. Older plants that become top-heavy may be severed, the top half with its set of aerial roots moved to a different pot or basket.

A wide array of epiphytes, needing more air around the roots and drier conditions than a pot allows, prefer to be mounted on slabs of cork bark or tree-fern fiber. Simply place the plant on the mount cushioned by a small pad of osmunda or sphagnum moss. Wire the plant through the slab to the back of the mount and tighten. Some growers use staples instead of wire. Attach a hanger and plant label to the top and hang the newly mounted plant in a relatively shady place until it is established on the slab.

Potting Media

Years ago the potting medium of choice for epiphytes was osmunda fiber, the roots of the *Osmunda* fern. When the supply of osmunda failed to meet the demand, however, other media were sought, both organic and inorganic. Today the two most common are tree-fern fiber and fir bark, used in various combinations with perlite or pumice, charcoal, redwood bark, sphagnum moss, lava rock, and cork. Sizes of tree-fern, bark, and charcoal are graded as coarse (for vandas and large sympodials), fine (for seedlings and miniature plants with delicate roots), and medium (for everything else). The potting medium you choose should always be free-draining so that water does not accumulate around the roots.

The mix for terrestrials such as *Orchis* and *Ophrys* usually contains various proportions of loam, coarse sand, and leaf mold with traces of blood and bone meal. More specific recommendations are offered for particular genera and species in the A–Z section of this book.

Epiphytes are constantly bathed in a fresh, buoyant atmosphere, conditions which the orchid grower should try to approximate in the home or glasshouse.

PESTS AND DISEASES

Gardening is impossible without at least cameo appearances by insect and non-insect pests and diseases caused by bacteria, fungi, and viruses. Without vigilance, minor outbreaks can lead to heartbreak when a favorite or expensive plant becomes so infested or infected that it must be discarded. Regular observation of your plants will help you spot and treat problems before they pass the point of no return. A wide selection of pesticides, bactericides, and fungicides is available on the market. Because brand names differ around the world and because chemicals are continually added or removed from the list of approved, registered pesticides, we suggest that you consult your local orchid society, plant nursery, or agricultural agent for recommendations of specific products to control pests and diseases and also ways to improve your growing conditions to prevent future problems.

Safety in the application and storage of all chemicals cannot be overemphasized. Before opening any pesticide container, read and heed the label. One item on the label often disregarded or forgotten is the need for a follow-up spraying a few to several days later to eradicate any juveniles that might have hatched.

Mealybugs appear as white, cottony masses anywhere on the plant but particularly in the leaf axils and underneath the sheaths of pseudobulbs. Small outbreaks can be controlled by removing them with a cotton swab dipped in isopropyl alcohol. Insecticidal soaps are also very effective when used regularly. Larger populations of mealybugs are more easily controlled with chemical preparations.

Scale insects secrete a hard, waxy covering that repels most pesticides unless a wetting agent is added. Their presence is often first noticed by the sticky "honeydew" that they secrete. Large infestations can be very difficult to eradicate, even with highly toxic pesticides.

Aphids — small, green to yellow insects which mass on flower buds or new leaves — are easily controlled, even with soapy water.

They have piercing mouthparts that penetrate plant surfaces, which allows the transmission of some orchid viruses, so it is important that they be eradicated as soon as they are spotted.

Spider mites multiply quickly in dry conditions, leaving pits on the lower surfaces of leaves and giving the leaves a silvery appearance. At least two sprayings several days apart are necessary to kill all adults and juveniles. Raising humidity in the growing area will help prevent outbreaks.

Snails and *slugs* feed on leaves, roots, and flowers in the evening. Pelleted baits have proven to be

Slug damage on an orchid.

the most effective control. Clean up the growing area to remove hiding places.

Bacterial and *fungal diseases* can be difficult to diagnose. The most serious bacterial disease, bacterial brown spot, is caused by a bacterium known as *Pseudomonas*. Water left standing on a leaf or in the crown of a phalaenopsis encourages the growth of bacteria and becomes a watery, brown to black lesion which spreads through the plant rapidly, even overnight. Fungal diseases include black rot, caused by *Phytophthora* and *Pythium*, and affect many different orchid genera. Leafspot fungi such as *Cercospora* cause dark, sunken spots on orchid leaves. For all of these diseases it is important to remove all affected areas then treat with the appropriate product. Increase air circulation and make sure that stems and leaves are dry by dusk. Tilt potted plants so that water does not lodge in leaf crowns.

Several *viruses* are known for orchids in cultivation, chief among them cymbidium mosaic, tobacco mosaic, and bean yellow mosaic. Symptoms are nonspecific and can easily be confused with symptoms of bacterial and fungal diseases or even cultural problems. But plants with yellow to black streaks on the leaves and pseudobulbs or color break in the flowers are suspect and should be examined by a virus-testing laboratory. Infected plants must be discarded. There is no known cure at present, but genetic engineering in progress holds promise for creating virus-free collections.

The only way to control viruses is by prevention — isolation and disposal of infected plants and sterilizing tools between plants when dividing and repotting. Pots should also be sterilized before reuse. Eradicate aphids as soon as they are discovered.

Illustrations depicting pests and symptoms of disease and detailed, authoritative information on the topic are combined in the *Handbook on Orchid Pests and Diseases*, published by the American Orchid Society, 6000 South Olive Avenue, West Palm Beach, Florida 33405 USA.

CONSERVATION

The monumental tragedy of our vanishing tropical forests is well known, although the actual scope of it is hard to comprehend. Amazonian and Malayan rain forests, Andean and Indonesian cloud forests, are all losing ground to uncontrolled population growth in developing countries. Since the turn of the century, 90 per cent of the forests of Madagascar, home to many endemic *Angraecum* and *Aerangis* species, have been cleared for human activity. Thousands of acres are cleared every day for timber and/or agriculture, reducing ecosystems that evolved over the millennia to a pyre of ash and embers.

What of the orchids? As mentioned earlier, the fragmentation of an already widely distributed orchid population compromises its reproductive potential. Geographical isolation, for example in the Andes, that is such a major force in speciation, also contributes to high degrees of endemism. Many orchid species are known only from one mountain or hill. When logging begins, so can extinction. Type localities, from which species new to science were once described, are rapidly becoming pastures, croplands, farmhouses, roads, dams, even tennis courts.

But loss of habitat is not unique to the tropics. In the industrialized countries of North America, Europe, Asia, and Australia developers are constantly proposing new sites for housing and industrial uses — draining or polluting wetlands, bulldozing forests, excavating meadows in the process. Some violations of environmental legislation make the newspapers, usually after the damage is done, but other damage may go unnoticed or unrecognized.

A second threat to orchids is overcollection for the horticultural trade, which has continued since the discovery of *Cattleya labiata* in Brazil. Though the numbers of most species exported today from the orchid-rich countries of the tropics do not approach the vast consignments shipped to Europe at the close of the nineteenth century, species that were once plentiful in countless localities are now gone. In the 1980s thousands of Chinese paphiopedilums — *P. armeniacum, P. micranthum, P. malipoense, P. emersonii* — were shipped to Hong Kong and elsewhere for re-export to the United States and (West) Germany. Some field reports suggest that at least some of these are now extremely rare if not extinct in the wild. As a result, trade in all *Paphiopedilum* species is now prohibited, as is trade in *Phragmipedium* species. These slipper-orchids as well as ten other endangered species in different genera have been placed on Appendix I of CITES (Convention on International Trade in Endangered Species of Wild Fauna and Flora), a treaty instituted in 1975 and now signed by over 100 countries around the world. Trade in threatened (Appendix II) animals and plants is now strictly regulated and requires export permits signed by authorized representatives of the management authorities.

What is being done to halt such abuses of nature? Protection of habitats is clearly ideal, saving not only the orchids but their pollinators and the delicate, profound interrelationships among organisms of all types at all trophic levels and energy levels. Many countries have established national parks or nature reserves, but there are simply not enough, especially near population centers, to guarantee the continued survival of thousands of orchid species. One effective solution by such agencies as The Nature Conservancy, financed largely by donations from individuals, has been to purchase large tracts of land in the United States and abroad for preservation.

Rescue and salvage of tropical orchids from threatened habitats is an option that has not yet been fully maximized, not because of lack of interest, but due to federal bureaucracies and the nuances of international diplomacy. The architecture of workable programs has yet to be drafted. The result is that hundreds of thousands of orchids die *in situ* because counterproductive policies prohibit rescue (removal to similar habitat elsewhere) and salvage (removal to licensed centers such as botanical gardens for cultivation, propagation, and perhaps reintroduction later).

At the forefront of the propagation/reintroduction effort is the Royal Botanic Gardens, Kew, which sponsors the Sainsbury Orchid Project. Seed propagation of some European orchid species has allowed laboratory-grown terrestrials to be reintroduced into nature.

At the local level you can help by assisting your conservation group or orchid society. In the United States, for example, you might contact the Audubon Society; in Australia there is the Australian Conservation Foundation; and in the United Kingdom there is the Nature Conservancy Council. Monitor nearby orchid populations from month to month or year to year and report the data to state or district wildlife agencies. Speak out when critical and sensitive habitats are threatened with development, and make corporate and private interests aware of our natural heritage. Often developers will relent and seek alternative sites when confronted with hard evidence and the prospect of unfavorable publicity.

Second, when you purchase orchids, insist on artificially propagated ones. Doing so removes additional pressure on wild populations and will help reduce the demand for wild-collected plants. Self-pollinate or, better still, cross-pollinate the species in your collection and share seedlings with friends and your local orchid society. Easy-to-follow instructions on flasking seeds in your home are described in several orchid books such as *Home Orchid Growing* by Rebecca Northen, *Orchids From Seed* by P.A. Thompson, *Native Orchids of Australia* by David L. Jones, and volume 2 of *Orchid Biology: Reviews and Perspectives* edited by Joseph Arditti.

We now have the capacity to reproduce orchids by the millions and thereby ensure a place for them in the world of the future, secure against an exploding population and quite unimaginable demands on the earth's natural resources. As an example, *Paphiopedilum delenatii*, once growing in Vietnam, is believed to be extinct in the wild. But through the foresight of the French firm of Vacherot & Lecoufle, which propagated the species early in the twentieth century, its lovely pink flowers are still available for all to enjoy and use in hybridization. We have a responsibility to act as custodians of the orchid and save it in all its diversity and charm for future generations.

One of the many threats to orchids worldwide: deforestation and loss of habitat for crops, lumber or pasturage.

ORCHID POLLINATION

Charles Darwin was not exaggerating when he remarked that the various contrivances and adaptations of orchids "vastly transcend those which the most fertile imagination of the world's most imaginative man could dream up with unlimited time at his disposal." Some have suggested that if his 1862 book, *On the Various Contrivances by which British and Foreign Orchids are fertilised by Insects*, had been published just three years earlier, before *Origin of Species*, then the *Origin* would not have caused such worldwide convulsions. Modifications of Darwinian theory (such as punctuated equilibrium) have since been proposed to explain certain anomalies in the fossil record. Darwin floundered in trying to explain the mechanism of natural selection, but so accurate and cogent were most of his observations and arguments concerning orchid pollination that they provided convincing evidence at the time and can withstand critical scrutiny even today, 140 years later.

This is not to say that all his contemporaries agreed with his ideas on orchid pollination: for instance, scientists laughed at his ideas on how the Madagascan species, *Angraecum sesquipedale*, was pollinated. Although the nectar spur of the flower is up to 30 cm long, nectar fills only the lowermost few centimeters. Darwin reasoned that if the pollinator was to be rewarded for its efforts in visiting the flower, it must have a tongue or proboscis long enough to reach from the mouth of the spur to the apex. This implied that the pollinator was a moth with a tongue about one foot long, a notion his critics found ridiculous. Such a sphinx moth, however, with a tongue of that length, was discovered on Madagascar and named *Xanthopan morgani praedicta* in 1903. Sphinx-moth pollination of other *Angraecum* species on Madagascar has now been recorded and published. Even Darwin's colleagues were skeptical about many of his ideas on pollination. For instance, when he described the pollinia-shooting mechanism of *Catasetum* to his lifelong

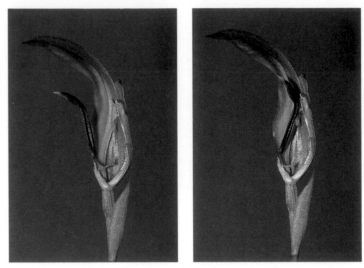

These photographs show how the labellum of a *Pterostylis* flower traps fungus gnats. The flower of *Pterostylis baptistii* is seen here in profile with some parts removed for clarity. In the figure on the left, the labellum lies in the lowered or open position. When a fungus gnat lands on the tip of the sensitive labellum, the labellum quickly closes (right) against the column (note the yellow pollinia). The only exit from the trap is a narrow tunnel between the column and the tip of the labellum. As the gnat squeezes through, pollinia become attached to it.

friend, Thomas Henry Huxley, Huxley said, "Do you really think I can believe all that?"

With the exception of those orchids that are self-pollinated, all are pollinated by animals — bees, wasps, flies and gnats, butterflies and moths, birds, ants — which are attracted (often on a species-specific basis or nearly so) in different ways. Euglossine bees of the Neotropics are attracted to orchids of subtribes Catasetinae, Stanhopeinae, Zygopetalinae, and a few others primarily by floral fragrances secreted from glands called osmophores. Male euglossines work over specific surfaces of the flowers, usually the labellum, and mop up fragrance droplets with brushes on their front feet. They then take off and transfer the droplets to cavities in their hind tibia. Why they do this is still a mystery; the prevailing theory is that fragrances are somehow modified by the male into chemical attractants for females, which do not collect fragrances. The chemical composition of fragrances is sometimes specific enough to attract males of only one bee species. Genetic mutations that result in minor qualitative or quantitative changes in fragrance composition may attract

a different bee species and become fixed in nature over time. Flowers of the genus *Ophrys*, ranging from England to the Middle East, are pollinated by male bees or wasps attracted both by fragrances similar to pheromones secreted by the females and by visual cues such as form, color, and texture. The males are so deceived that they attempt to mate with the flowers (a process known as pseudocopulation) and in doing so remove or deposit pollinia. An equally interesting relationship occurs between many Australian terrestrials and thynnid wasps. Fragrances secreted by the osmophores of *Drakaea, Spiculaea, Caladenia* and other genera attract male wasps in a very species-specific way. The deceit is reinforced by the configuration of calluses on the labellum. The males then try to mate with the labellum or else lift it as they would a female wasp. In the normal sequence of events, the wasp comes into contact with the column of the flower, and is actually hammered onto it in the case of *Drakaea*. Other wasp-pollinated flowers can be found in species of *Cryptostylis, Calochilus, Ada*, and *Brassia*.

Dipterans — flies, fungus gnats,

and their relatives — are attracted to flowers as a food source or a breeding site, which explains the foul odors and dull colors of some flowers. Floral parts often flutter in the slightest breeze to supplement the attraction, as do the banners called paleae on many bulbophyllums and the dangling strings of wax that are secreted from two-celled glands on the sepal margins of *Pleurothallis schiedei*. But there are also secret passageways, intricate hinges, and temporary traps. Why these forms of chicanery? The simple answer is that among the insects, flies are not Rhodes scholars: left to their own devices they are poor pollinators, and special guidance to the column is needed. The labellum is often hinged to the column-foot, so that as the fly lands on the labellum, its own weight pulls it down onto the column. Examples of this hinge type are found in *Bulbophyllum* and *Masdevallia*. In fact, some genera (*Acostaea, Salpistele, Porroglossum, Pterostylis*) have flowers with a sensitive labellum, and as soon as this is touched, it immediately slams shut against the column. In *Pterostylis*, this temporarily imprisons the gnat and forces it to contact the column while it is inside the flower. In some species the sensitive label-

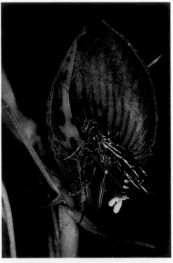

Male ichneumonid wasps attempting to copulate with the non-resupinate flower (labellum uppermost) of *Cryptostylis erecta*. Note the yellow pollinia already attached to the abdomen of the larger wasp.

A male thynnid wasp, thinking that the hinged labellum of this *Drakaea* flower is a female wasp, tries to carry it off to mate with it. That lifting motion repeatedly tosses the wasp onto the column. Following all of this abuse, the wasp flies away with pollinia attached to it and/or has deposited pollinia on the stigma.

One of the Neotropical "bucket orchids", *Coryanthes elegantium*, is visited by male euglossine bees (*Euglossa gibba*) attracted by the fragrance.

The bee pollinator of *Diuris behrii* asleep in the flower.

lum catapults the gnat onto the stigma first.

Brightly colored flowers pollinated by butterflies generally have a landing platform and offer nectar. Good examples of butterfly-pollinated orchids are some species of *Epidendrum*. On the other hand, moth-pollinated flowers such as those of *Brassavola* and *Angraecum* are white, cream or greenish, fragrant at night, and offer nectar in tubular structures such as a spur or a mentum, a "chin" at the base of the flower formed by the column-foot and bases of the lateral sepals.

Bird-pollinated orchids are rarely fragrant and are brightly colored in shades of red or yellow, and often tubular and nectariferous. The best-known examples in the Neotropics are *Comparettia* and some epidendrums, pollinated by

The form, color, fragrance and texture of the labellum of *Ophrys* flowers attract male bees or wasps which attempt to mate with the flower. Here, *Ophrys holoserica* is pollinated by an amorous male bee.

hummingbirds, and the Palaeo-tropical *Dendrobium lawesii* and *Dendrobium mohlianum*, pollinated by sunbirds, honeyeaters, etc.

Pollinia are transferred to pollinators in many different ways. Some pollinia have extensions of anther-derived tissue called caudicles that stick to the pollinators but break once the pollinia are on the stigmatic surface of a flower. Caudicles are found in such genera as *Eria, Laelia, Coelogyne,* and *Bletia*.

An evolutionary advance in orchids was the development of the rostellum, part of the median stigma lobe, which has at least two very important functions. First, it separates the anther from the fertile part of the stigma and prevents self-pollination in most species. Second, part of it, the viscidium, is a sticky pad frequently connected by a stalk to the pollinia. This pollination unit is called a pollinarium (pl. pollinaria). When the viscidium is touched, it quickly adheres so that as the pollinator backs out of the flower the entire pollinarium is removed with it. In many species the stalk dries differentially over time and changes its orientation, promoting outcrossing (Dressler, 1981).

ORCHIDS A—Z

Acacallis cyanea

ACACALLIS Lindley
ak-ah-KAL-is
Tribe: Maxillarieae
Subtribe: Zygopetalinae
Etymology: Gr. *Akakallis*, a nymph

Two showy epiphytic species are known from Colombia, Venezuela, the Guianas, Brazil, and Peru. Both species bear blue-lavender flowers. The pseudobulbs, usually bearing one leaf, are produced along a creeping rhizome. A raceme of up to ten flowers arises from the base of the pseudobulbs. *Acacallis* flowers have four pollinia.
Grow on slab of tree-fern or cork bark. Provide high humidity and temperature (25°–30°C during the day and 20°C at night) and moderate shade.

Acacallis cyanea Lindley

This species, found in lowland forests in Colombia, Venezuela, and Brazil, produces arching inflorescences of up to ten showy flowers from February to August. Sepals and petals are blue-lavender and the lip reddish brown to purple. The flowers maintain a darker shade of blue if not exposed to bright light. In the past most plants collected in the wild survived only one or two years. Recently, however, much hardier plants grown from seeds have been seen in cultivation.

Acampe papillosa

ACAMPE Lindley
ah-KAM-pee
Tribe: Vandeae
Subtribe: Sarcanthinae
Etymology: Gr. *akampes*, rigid

About nine species of *Acampe* are known from Africa, India, southern China, and Indochina. Acampes are vigorous monopodial plants that form large vegetative masses in nature. Lacking pseudobulbs, the plants grow as slow-growing vines noted for their thick, leathery leaves. Few-branched racemes or umbels of proportionately small yellow flowers barred with brown are produced from upper leaf-axils. As a result of their large plant size and small flowers, acampes are rarely cultivated. Acampes are found in exposed tropical habitats and should be given full light and warm temperatures. Though adapted to periodic drought in nature, plants in cultivation benefit from year-round watering and fertilizer. Hanging baskets filled with an open epiphyte compost are suitable although attaching the plants to slabs will work as well if the plants are given sufficient water.

Acampe papillosa (Lindley) Lindley

This vigorous fall-flowering species is known from India, Nepal, and Bhutan through Indochina. Brown flowers marked with darker brown spotting bear frilly white lips, characteristic of the species. Unlike most other species of the genus, the flowers of *A. papillosa* are produced in an umbel.

Acampe rigida (Buch.-Ham. ex J. E. Smith) P. Hunt

Native from mainland Africa, Madagascar, and the Comoro Islands to India and Indochina, extending north into China and south into Malaysia, *Acampe rigida* is notable for its massive plant size. Growths a meter or more in length are not uncommon, and in nature it tends to more or less cover exposed areas of its host tree. Yellow flowers with brown barring, produced during the summer in axillary, few-branched racemes, are notable for being fleshy and rigid, giving the species its name.

ACANTHEPHIPPIUM Blume
a-can-the-FIP-pee-um
Tribe: Arethuseae
Subtribe: Bletiinae
Etymology: Gr. *acantho*, spiny, *ephippion*, saddle

Fifteen species are distributed from the Indian subcontinent to China and the Fiji islands. All species are terrestrial and closely allied to *Calanthe, Pachystoma, Phaius,* and *Spathoglottis*. Prominent, succulent pseudobulbs and plicate leaves characterize the genus, along with the peculiar, cup-shaped, fleshy, usually odiferous flowers on short racemes arising from new growths. Flowers are usually shades of dull yellow to pink and striped or spotted.
Cultivate plants in 60 percent shade and intermediate temperatures in a well-drained sandy compost with plenty of leaf mold. Water and feed plants well when they are in active growth to promote the formation of healthy pseudobulbs. Plants are intolerant of excessive salts and frequent repotting.

Acanthephippium mantinianum Lindley & Cogn.

Endemic to the Philippines, this species

Acanthephippium sylhetense

Acianthus caudatus

Acianthus exsertus

Acanthephippium mantinianum

ACIANTHUS R. Br.

ak-ee-AN-thus
Tribe: Diurideae
Subtribe: Acianthinae
Etymology: Gr. *akis*, point; *anthos*, flower

About 24 species of small, dull-colored orchids, distributed in Australia, New Zealand, Solomon Islands, and New Caledonia. All are deciduous terrestrials with subterranean tuberoids and a solitary, heart-shaped leaf held horizontally above the soil surface. Racemes of few, pinkish or greenish flowers arise from near the center

Acanthephippium striatum

produces up to five flowers on short racemes during June–July. Flowers are highly fragrant, fleshy, dull yellow striped with brownish red. The lip is pale to bright golden yellow. Plants will tolerate temperatures up to 20°C at night.

Acanthephippium striatum
Lindley

Found in the subtropical foothills of the Himalayas, this species bears four to six flowers on short racemes. The flowers, which appear in July, are smaller than those of *A. sylhetense*. Both flowers and bracts are pink with prominent red candy stripes.

Acanthephippium sylhetense
Lindley

This species is distributed through the subtropical foothills of the Himalayas, where it is more prominent and vigorous than *A. striatum*. The flowers are long-lasting, faintly creamy white with purple spots at the tips of the petals. Flowers appear in May–June.

of the leaf. All species have four pollinia attached to a sticky disc. Pollination is by tiny gnats.

Pot in a well-drained soil mix containing wood shavings. Keep moist when in active growth (autumn to spring), dry out as plants die down, keep completely dry and repot over summer. Use fertilizers sparingly.

Acianthus caudatus R. Br.

This unusual Australian species demands attention because of the filamentous tips on the perianth segments which can reach to three centimeters long. The dark purplish flowers, which can be difficult to see in the gloom of a forest floor, release a noticeable smell of decay. Plants grow in colonies but can be difficult to maintain in cultivation.

Acianthus exsertus R. Br.

A robust species from eastern Australia which produces multiflowered racemes from March to August. The small, purplish flowers have a darker labellum, and the petals reflex strongly against the ovary. The cream to white anther is prominent in dull conditions. Adapts well to cultivation and reproduces freely.

Acianthus fornicatus R. Br.

Characterized by its very broad dorsal sepal, this species from eastern Australia grows naturally in moist forest where it can form extensive colonies. Flowers, which are pinkish green with a green labellum, are produced from early autumn to late winter. A robust grower which reproduces well and flowers freely.

Acianthus fornicatus

Acineta superba

Acostaea costaricensis

ACINETA Lindley

ah-si-NEE-ta
Tribe: Cymbidieae
Subtribe: Stanhopeinae
Etymology: Gr. *akinetos*, hollow

Twenty-one species are considered to be valid in the genus and are distributed from Mexico to Peru with most species occurring in Andean South America. Some species seem to be merely color forms, and a critical revision will probably reduce the number. The genus is characterized by the large, sulcate pseudobulbs with two or three apical leaves that are thick but heavily parallel-veined; an elongate, pendent inflorescence; the large, showy, fleshy flowers with the lip divided into a hypochile and an epichile, the hypochile solidly fixed to the column-foot; and the pollinarium of two, hard, yellow, clavate pollinia attached to a subquadrate stipe, with a small round viscidium.
The plants are normally epiphytes but are occasionally found growing as terrestrials on steep embankments at elevations from 800 to 2,000 meters.
Bright light and intermediate night temperatures are required along with adequate moisture at the roots throughout the year. The plants should be grown in baskets so that the pendent inflorescences can exit.

Acineta barkeri (Batem.) Lindley

This attractive species occurs in southern Mexico and has not been reported from nearby Guatemala. It has bright yellow, strongly fragrant flowers marked and spotted with red-brown. The flowers of this species are similar to those of the other members of the genus, differing principally in the dimensions of the lobes of the lip and the shape of the callus.

Acineta superba (H. B. K.) Reichb.f.

This species has larger flowers than the previous one and has been reported from along the Andes from Venezuela to southern Ecuador, where it was originally collected. The flowers are pink, so heavily blotched with purple-brown that they appear dark. The lip is often a lighter pink with fewer spots. Plants are now only rarely found in the wild but campesinos from the region grow them to tremendous size on fruit trees in their gardens.

ACOSTAEA Schltr.

ah-COS-te-ah
Tribe: Epidendreae
Subtribe: Pleurothallidinae
Etymology: Named for Guillermo Acosta, a Costa Rican collector

The four species that constitute this genus range through Central America and the Andes of South America. One species, *A. costaricensis*, is variable morphologically, widely distributed and relatively frequent. The other species (*A. campylotyle, A. tenax* and *A. trilobata*) are restricted in their distribution. All the species are small, tufted plants with a weak, successively flowered raceme. The dorsal sepal is deeply hooded and protects a sensitive labellum. The lateral sepals are connate into a single blade (the synsepal). Upon stimulation the lip snaps up toward the concave, broadly winged column. After some minutes, the lip gradually returns to its previous, exposed position. The motility is caused by changes in the turgidity of the cells in the broad base of the lip folded onto the base of the column-foot. Two pollinia are present. These plants are relatively easy to cultivate in moist, intermediate to cool-growing greenhouse conditions.

Acostaea costaricensis Schltr.

This species is widely distributed from Costa Rica to southern Ecuador. The flowers vary in color from red-purple to yellow. The shape of the lip is also variable. A population with a pair of tiny lobules on the

Acineta barkeri

Ada aurantiaca

Aerangis curnowiana

Aerangis citrata

Ada aurantiaca Lindley

This species, from the central Andes of Colombia, is known for its bright orange, semitubular flowers on nodding inflorescences with the sepals, petals, and lip spreading only above the midpoint. The species belongs with a group that includes the white-lipped *A. lehmannii* Rolfe from northwestern Colombia and the red-flowered *A. bennettorum* Dodson from Peru. All three species are presumed to be pollinated by hummingbirds. The plants grow at high elevations and should be grown in the cool house with members of *Odontoglossum.*

AERANGIS Reichb.f.
ah-er-AN-gis
Tribe: Vandeae
Subtribe: Aerangidinae
Etymology: Gr. *aer*, air; *angos*, vessel

About 60 species of these monopodial epiphytes are known. They are scattered throughout Africa, Madagascar, and the Comoro Islands with one species extending to Sri Lanka and one in Reunion. Many were first described in the genus *Angraecum* from which they are now separated by the prominent rostellum on the column of the flower. The upright or pendent stems bear leaves in two rows and racemes of few to many white, star-shaped flowers which have a long spur at the base of the lip. The flowers are scented in the evening. All have two pollinia.

Most species require deep shade and high humidity in intermediate or warm temperatures. Plants grow best mounted on

callus of the lip is recognized as subspecies *bicornis*. Another with a single lobule is recognized as subspecies *unicornis*. A third subspecies, subspecies *colombiana*, has obscure angles on the margins of the lobes of the lip.

ADA Lindley
AY-da
Tribe: Cymbidieae
Subtribe: Oncidiinae
Etymology: Named for Ada, sister of Artemisia in Caria (historical)

Two species, *A. aurantiaca* and *A. lehmannii*, traditionally have been considered as constituting the genus, but

after Dr. Norris Williams provided convincing evidence and transferred the "glumaceous brassias" to *Ada*, it is now a genus of sixteen species. The genus is characterized by pseudobulbous plants with well-developed foliaceous leaf-sheaths; the lateral, racemose inflorescences with large, inflated floral bracts; the sepals and petals elongate; the spurless flowers with erect lateral sepals; and the two, hard pollinia attached to a heart-shaped stipe and a small, round viscidium.

The plants are normally epiphytes but are occasionally found growing on steep embankments, in very wet cloud forests, at elevations from 1,500 to 2,800 meters. Most of the species thrive under intermediate temperatures and enjoy a drop in night temperature.

Aerangis ellisii

bark or logs and should be sprayed frequently while a new leaf is developing, then kept dry but in humid surroundings for one to two months. Water freely while flower buds are developing.

Aerangis citrata (Thouars) Schltr.

This is one of the smaller species from Madagascar, but well-grown plants are extremely floriferous. The leaves are dark green, shiny, and borne close together on short stems. Many racemes of white or cream flowers are borne in the spring, scented slightly of lemon. This species needs very shady conditions but will tolerate a wide range of temperatures (cool to warm).

Aerangis curnowiana (Finet) Schltr.

This species from Madagascar produces tiny plants with a pair of dark green shiny leaves and few large flowers. It is often confused with *A. punctata* which has similar size and flowers but whose leaves are covered with many minute silver dots and appear grayish. Flowers are white, sometimes tinged pale green or salmon pink, the lip with a long spur.

Aerangis ellisii (Reichb.f.) Schltr.

The largest species in the genus is in Madagascar and has elongated stems bearing large leaves alternating in two rows. Long succulent racemes bear conspicuous bracts and five to 20 large white flowers with long spurs. Strongly fragrant in the evening.

Aerangis fastuosa (Reichb.f.) Schltr.

This is a dwarf species from Madagascar. The plants bear crowded oval leaves on short stems. The short racemes each support two to five large flowers which are somewhat hidden by the leaves. The crystalline white flowers rarely open fully and have a long coiled spur.

Aerangis kotschyana (Reichb.f.) Schltr.

This is one of the larger-growing species, found throughout tropical Africa from Nigeria to Kenya and southward as far as

Aerangis fastuosa

Aerangis kotschyana

Angola and Mozambique. The leaves are dark green with a crispate margin. The flowers are white, tinged salmon pink. The long spur is often coiled like a corkscrew.

Aerangis luteoalba (Kränzlin) Schltr. var. *rhodosticta* (Kränzlin) J. Stewart

This attractive species is one of the smallest of the African species. It is widespread, from Ethiopia to Angola, but nowhere common. The dark green leaves are crowded in two rows on the short stems, but often only a pair of leaves is present. The pretty flowers are borne in long arching racemes, white or cream with a red column. There is no scent. This species is tolerant of a wide range of temperatures but should be kept in a humid environment and sprayed infrequently.

Aerangis punctata J. Stewart

This is a dwarf species from central Madagascar which is easily recognized by its verrucose roots and grayish leaves. It bears large flowers on short inflorescences, and well-grown plants are most attractive despite their small stature.

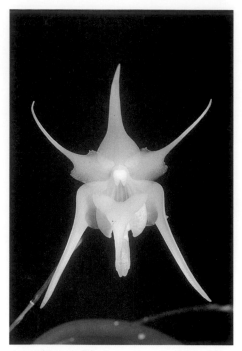

Aeranthes grandiflora

Aerangis luteoalba

AERANTHES Lindley
ah-er-AN-theez
Tribe: Vandeae
Subtribe: Angraecinae
Etymology: Gr. *aer*, air; *anthos*, flower

Nearly 40 species are known in Madagascar and the adjacent islands, and two have been described from Africa. These epiphytic plants are characterized by a fan-shaped leaf growth on short stems and by their flowers which are borne on slender wiry peduncles. The flowers are translucent, in shades of white, green, and yellow. The column has a conspicuous foot which ends in a spur to which the lip is attached. The genus is allied to *Angraecum* and has a similar cleft rostellum. All the species have two porate pollinia, each borne on a separate stipe. These plants grow in tropical forests in deep shade and require shady and humid conditions in cultivation. Temperatures vary depending on the origin of the species. They are most easily cultivated in a moisture-retentive compost in pots which need to be suspended to accommodate the long inflorescences.

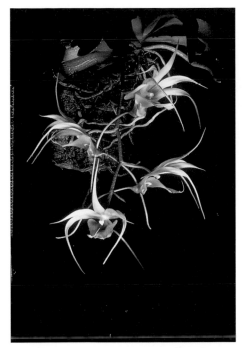

Aeranthes henrici

Aerides lawrenciae

Aerides multiflora

Aeranthes ramosa

Aeranthes grandiflora Lindley

This is one of the larger species and is widespread in eastern Madagascar. The long peduncles are completely covered by overlapping bracts which turn brown or black by the time the flowers appear. Flowers are cream or yellow, the spur inflated at the tip, opening successively.

Aeranthes henrici Schltr.

This species is restricted to a rather narrow range in the humid forests of central Madagascar. It has large dark green leaves and very thick roots. The flowers, green and white, are the largest in the genus and very showy. The sepals and petals are about ten centimeters long and the spur sixteen centimeters.

Aeranthes ramosa Rolfe

This species is widespread in the forests on the eastern slopes of Madagascar. The plants have a stiff fan of dark green leaves and very fine roots. The dark green flowers are borne on very long peduncles, up to one meter long, and are suspended below the plants.

The column-foot has a long slender spur. *Aeranthes caudata* is somewhat similar but has smaller, paler flowers and lighter green leaves. It occurs in the Comoro Islands as well as Madagascar.

AERIDES Lour.
a-er-EE-deez
Tribe: Vandeae
Subtribe: Sarcanthinae
Etymology: Gr. *aer*, air; *eides*, resembling

Aerides comprises nineteen species found from Sri Lanka and southern India north to Nepal and southern China, throughout Indochina, east to Papua New Guinea and north to the Philippines. The genus is prized in horticulture for its showy racemes of fragrant flowers in combinations of white, pink, and purple (rarely yellow). Most species have a distinctive prominent, forward-projecting spur. With the exception of *A. krabiensis*, a diminutive lithophyte, aerides are large epiphytes frequently establishing themselves in disturbed habitats.

Aerides do not have pseudobulbs but they do have leathery leaves that are drought-resistant. Most species grow as vines, producing aerial roots along their stems. They should be established in a basket and allowed to grow more or less unrestrained. Most of the active root system will be aerial, and the plants should not be reworked or disturbed unless necessary. All species like very bright light conditions, frequent watering and heavy feeding. Vining species should be given daily watering.

Aerides lawrenciae Reichb.f.

Endemic to Mindanao in the Philippines, *Aerides lawrenciae* is considered the finest horticultural species because it has the largest flowers in the genus. The summer flowers are typically white with a showy large purple stain on each segment. Several color forms are known, including var. *fortichii* with pure white flowers, var. *punctata* with flowers covered in fine purple spots, and var. *sanderiana* with yellow flowers. Vining plants of *Aerides lawrenciae* should be grown in large baskets.

Aerides multiflora Roxb.

Aerides multiflora is native from Nepal to Indochina. Himalayan plants bear long sprays of rose-pink flowers. Indochinese plants, called var. *godefroyana*, bear shorter racemes of white flowers with bold, dark pink spotting. *Aerides multiflora* is frequently grown under its synonym, *A. affine*. Unlike most other species, *Aerides multiflora* has a short stem and does not become vinelike. Flowers are produced in the late spring and summer.

Aerides odorata Lour.

Aerides odorata occurs throughout tropical Asia from Nepal and northeast India through southeast Asia to Indonesia, Borneo, and the Philippines. Pendent racemes of white flowers stained with five showy purple patches are noted for their strong spicy fragrance. A polymorphic species, flower color grades from pure white to dark purple with various amounts of yellow in the lip. This fall-flowering, vigorous species readily forms specimen plants.

Aerides odorata

Aerides quinquevulnera

Aerides rosea

Aerides quinquevulnera Lindley

Native to the Philippines and Papua New Guinea, *Aerides quinquevulnera* is prized for its long, densely flowered racemes of showy flowers. Closely related to *A. odorata*, flowers of this species have a strong, spicy cinnamon scent. The late summer and fall flowers are typically greenish white with dark purple patches at the segment tips and small purple spots over the whole flower. It is a variable species, and many color forms have been recognized, having flowers from pure white to solid purple.

Aerides rosea Lindley & Paxton

This species is known from northeast India to North Vietnam and southern China. It has been called the "fox-brush" orchid because of its densely flowered, laxly pendent inflorescences that resemble a fox's tail. The flowers in late spring are an even rose-pink overlaid with fine purple spotting. Closely related to *A. multiflora, Aerides rosea* differs by its flat leaves and sharply pointed lip. It has been known for many years in cultivation under the later name, *A. fieldingii.* Native to higher elevations than most *Aerides* species, *Aerides rosea* will not thrive under continuously hot conditions and should be grown at an intermediate temperature.

ALAMANIA La Llave & Lexarza
ah-lah-MAN-ee-ah
Tribe: Epidendreae
Subtribe: Laeliinae
Etymology: Named after Lucas Alamán (1792–1853), a prominent literary and

political figure in early post-independence Mexico, as well as botanical collector

A one-species genus with red-orange flowers similar to *Hexisea*, endemic to southern Mexico. The plants have small, inconspicuous pseudobulbs, with one to three fleshy leaves at the apex, and bear a short one-to-nine-flowered raceme apically. The lip is united to the underside of the column.

Alamania punicea La Llave & Lexarza

Grows in intermediate to high-elevation forests, often embedded in moss at the base of fir trees, on top of which *A. erubescens* also grows. It should be grown together with cold-growing masdevallias, in a cool house with a minimum night temperature of 5°C. Keep humid throughout the year and avoid drying out, but make sure it is well ventilated. The bright red-orange flowers, two centimeters in diameter upon the small plant, make for a very attractive show. The species flowers from April to June. Unfortunately it is not easy to grow

and flower if not given the proper conditions, and thus many plants are lost through incorrect culture.

AMESIELLA Garay
aims-ee-EL-ah
Tribe: Vandeae
Subtribe: Sarcanthinae
Etymology: Honoring Mr. Oakes Ames

This monotypic genus is endemic to the Philippines. *Amesiella* was originally described as an *Angraecum*, a genus of fragrant African orchids which it closely resembles. *Amesiella*, however, has no scent. The miniature plants are almost identical to plants of *Tuberolabium* when not in flower, and the two are often confused when imported from the wild. Lacking pseudobulbs for storage, *Amesiella* should be kept evenly moist. Best grown in small pots with a medium-grade epiphyte compost, plants respond to bright light levels but never direct sunlight.

Alamania punicea

Amesiella philippinensis

Ancistrochilus rothschildianus

Amesiella philippinensis (Ames) Garay

This Philippine plant is noted for its oversized white flowers, which bear long, slender, nectar spurs. The short fleshy racemes of large flowers cover the miniature plant.

ANCISTROCHILUS Rolfe
an-sis-tro-KIE-lus
Tribe: Arethuseae
Subtribe: Bletiinae
Etymology: Gr. *ankistron*, hook; *cheilos*, lip

Two attractive species are currently known in west Africa, one of them spreading across to Uganda and Tanzania. The small, onion-shaped pseudobulbs each bear two deciduous leaves at the apex. Racemes of one to five large flowers arise from the base of the pseudobulb. Both species have eight pollinia.
Provide well-shaded conditions and warm temperatures throughout the year. Keep plants evenly moist while in active growth but allow them to dry off for one to two months once the leaves begin to die off, which is usual after flowering.

Ancistrochilus rothschildianus O'Brien

This pretty species is found from Guinea and Sierra Leone across to Uganda and flowers at various times of year. The flowers are showy, rose pink or lilac with a deep magenta lip.

Ancistrochilus thomsonianus (Reichb.f.) Rolfe

This species has narrower pseudobulbs than the preceding, and the sepals and petals are white. It is recorded only from Nigeria to 'date. Some authorities regard the genus as monotypic, with one rather variable species, in which case *A. thomsonianus* is the earlier name.

ANGRAECUM Bory
an-GRY-kum
Tribe: Vandeae
Subtribe: Angraecinae
Etymology: Malay *angurek*, epiphytic orchid

This is a large genus of about 200 species with green or white flowers, distributed throughout tropical Africa, in Madagascar and the adjacent islands, and in Sri Lanka. The plants have a monopodial growth habit and are mostly epiphytic. Many other African species of similar habit were described originally in this genus, but the whole group of monopodial orchids from this continent has been assigned among a variety of genera following detailed studies of their flower structure. *Angraecum* still remains a large group with a great diversity of growth habit and flowers. All the flowers have a spurred lip which encircles the column at its base, and the rostellum is bifid.
Plants are easy to grow once good roots have been established. They do well on bark and in baskets while some of the larger plants do best in pots. Temperatures and

Angraecum compactum

Angraecum distichum

Angraecum calceolus

light (or shade) appropriate to the origin of the species should be provided. Most species appreciate a decided rest in cooler conditions after flowering.

Angraecum calceolus Thouars

This species has small plants which grow epiphytically or on rocks in Mozambique, Madagascar, and the adjacent islands, and can form large clumps. The flowers are bright green, widely spaced on long branching inflorescences. They are long-lasting. Well-established plants flower almost continuously.

Angraecum compactum Schltr.

This rather uncommon species produces small plants with dark green, thickened leaves. It is restricted to the humid forests of eastern Madagascar. The large white flowers are borne singly or in pairs on short axillary inflorescences and are heavily scented at night. Plants need very shady and humid conditions in cool or intermediate temperatures.

Angraecum distichum Lindley

This dwarf epiphyte often forms clumps of long curving stems which are covered with overlapping compressed leaves. It is distributed from Sierra Leone eastward across tropical Africa as far as western Uganda. The flowers are small, white, usually opposite the leaves like stars along the stems. The plants need high humidity, warm temperatures, and shady conditions in order to grow and flower well.

Angraecum eburneum Bory

The large plants of vandaceous growth habit

of this species grow on rocks and trees along the east coast of Madagascar, in Mauritius, Reunion and the Comoro Islands, and on the coast of Tanzania and Kenya. The thick, leathery leaves are a light yellowish green. The long inflorescences bear many flowers with apple green sepals and petals and a white lip on the upper side of the flower. The var. *superbum* has larger flowers than the type, and those of subspecies *giryamae* (from Africa) are smaller with shorter spurs; variety *longicalcar*, from the highlands of Madagascar, has the longest spurs which may be 30–36 centimeters long.

Angraecum eichlerianum Kränzlin

A large epiphyte with erect or pendent stems, this species often forms large clumps and is distributed throughout western Africa from Nigeria south to Angola. The long stems bear two rows of flattened leaves. The showy, greenish white flowers of medium size are borne singly, opposite the leaves. This is a species of humid warm forests where there is only a short dry season.

Angraecum florulentum Reichb.f.

This is an attractive species which appears to be endemic in the Comoro Islands. It forms clumps of curving upright stems with light green succulent leaves. The short inflorescences bear two to four pure white flowers which have a long spur. They are very sweetly scented in the evening.

Angraecum germinyanum J.D. Hook.

This epiphytic species grows in very humid forests on the cloud-covered slopes of the

Angraecum eburneum

Comoro Islands and eastern Madagascar. The slender stems are sometimes branching and very long, bearing two rows of small shiny leaves. The flowers are borne singly or in pairs. The large shell-shaped white lip is uppermost and has a long spur.

Angraecum infundibulare Lindley

This species is widespread in tropical Africa from Nigeria and the island of Principe in the west across to Uganda and western Kenya. Plants are epiphytic with long branching stems, pendent or upright, rather similar to *A. eichlerianum*. Flowers are much larger with a broad, funnel-shaped greenish white lip and long, narrow sepals and petals.

Angraecum leonis (Reichb.f.) Veitch

This species occurs in the warmer forests of the Comoro Islands and Madagascar. The plants are medium-sized with characteristic curved leaves which are laterally compressed and overlap each other at the base on the short stem. Inflorescences bear

Angraecum eichlerianum

several large, pure white flowers with a large, funnel-shaped lip and a curved spur.

Angraecum magdalenae Schltr. and H. Perrier

This attractive species grows on and among rocks in the highlands of Madagascar, usually in light shade. The grayish green leaves form a broad upright fan. Two or several pure white, rather fleshy flowers are borne near the base of the fan. In the wild plants endure a long, cool, dry season before flowering.

Angraecum florulentum

Angraecum germinyanum

Angraecum infundibulare

Angraecum leonis

Angraecum scottianum

Angraecum sesquipedale

Angraecum scottianum Reichb.f.

A species from the Comoro Islands and Madagascar where it grows on lightly shaded trees in warm, humid forests. The slender stems usually grow in tufts and bear short cylindrical leaves in alternate rows. The flowers are borne singly or on few-flowered inflorescences where they open successively. The lip is large, white, with a long spur and is held on the upper side of the flower.

Angraecum sesquipedale Thouars

The comet orchid from Madagascar is well known because of its large white flowers with very long spur. It grows in the warmer forests at low elevations and is now protected where it still occurs. It grows easily in cultivation and has been raised from seeds on many occasions.

Angraecum sororium Schltr.

This spectacular species grows on and among rocks in the highlands of Madagascar in full sun. The large plants have elongated stems which usually bear a fan of shiny

Angraecum sororium

Angraecum Veitchii

Angraecum magdalenae

leaves at the apex. The fleshy white flowers are large, borne singly or in pairs below or near the base of the leaves. Each has a long spur.

Angraecum Veitchii

This was the first hybrid made between two African epiphytes, *A. sesquipedale* and *A. eburneum*. It flowered first at the Veitch nursery in 1899. The plants are intermediate between the parents as are the flowers. The long inflorescences bear many greenish flowers which fade to a pristine whiteness as they age.

ANGULOA Ruíz & Pavón
an-gyoo-LOW-ah
Tribe: Maxillarieae
Subtribe: Lycastinae
Etymology: In honor of Don Francisco de Angulo, Director-General of Mines in Peru during the eighteenth century

A genus of eleven species from Andean South America. The genus is characterized by having large, sulcate pseudobulbs with three broad, thin, heavily veined leaves at their apices; the erect, single-flowered inflorescences produced from the base of

Anguloa cliftonii

Anguloa clowesii

Anguloa ruckeri

Anoectochilus roxburghii

the pseudobulbs; the flowers with the sepals and petals forming a cup; the erect, balanced lip; and the two hard pollinia on an elongate, rectangular stipe connected to a round viscidium.

The plants are adapted to be epiphytes but are much more commonly found as terrestrials on steep cliffs and embankments at elevations from 1,500 to 2,500 meters. Members of the genus are easily cultivated to form large specimen plants when grown with cool-growing lycastes. All species are pollinated by large male euglossine bees that crawl between the column and the rocking lip and remove the pollinia upon exiting the flower.

Anguloa cliftonii Rolfe

The largest-flowered member of the genus, *Anguloa cliftonii* is seldom seen in cultivation. The butter-yellow flowers are more open than in the other species, and the petals are marked with red-brown becoming more heavily blotched toward their bases. The species occurs in the Andes of northwestern Colombia.

Anguloa clowesii Lindley

This is the best-known species in the genus with its flowers appearing to be large, yellow tulips with an erect lip inside that rocks back and forth. The flowers are evenly golden-yellow and are produced in abundance. The species is found in the central and eastern range of the Andes in Colombia, extending into northwestern Venezuela.

Anguloa ruckeri Lindley

Perhaps the least attractive species in the

genus due to the dark green exterior surface of the sepals and petals and the maroon-red interior. The lip is white shading to yellow on the apical lobe and red on the inner face, pink on the other side. The species occurs in the eastern range of the Andes of Colombia and in Venezuela.

ANOECTOCHILUS Blume
ah-nek-toe-KYE-luss
Tribe: Erythrodeae
Subtribe: Goodyerinae
Etymology: *aniktos*, open; *cheilos*, lip

Primarily known as "jewel orchids," this genus of over 20 terrestrial species ranges from the Himalayas through southeast Asia and China to New Caledonia. All are small herbs inhabiting deep shade and moist surroundings, known chiefly for their glistening, attractive, velvet-like foliage. Flowers are small and insignificant with a usually white, bifurcated lip.

Cultivate plants in 75 percent shade and temperatures of 18–21°C. Use shallow pans with a well-drained compost of equal parts sphagnum moss and osmunda fiber with some sand and charcoal. The pans can be kept in a frame to provide humidity throughout. Feed only with very dilute organic fertilizers.

Anoectochilus roxburghii (Wall.) Lindley

This commonly seen species is found in the tropical forest glades of the Himalayan foothills, flowering October–November. It has a rosette of three to five unequal, velvety leaves with golden yellow veins.

Two to five pale pinkish white flowers are borne in a terminal raceme. Provide warm and humid conditions for healthy growth.

Anoectochilus brevilabris Lindley

Also known as *A. sikkimensis* King & Pantling, *Anoectochilus brevilabris* is found at elevations of 1,000–1,500 meters in Sikkim and Bhutan Himalayas. The plant has four or five nearly rounded leaves about five to six centimeters long and 3.5–5 centimeters broad, of a deep velvety purple-red with prominent golden veins. Racemes are twelve- to fifteen-flowered, the flowers greenish pink with a white lip appearing in September. It tolerates night temperatures up to 10°C.

ANSELLIA Lindley
an-SEL-ee-ah
Tribe: Cymbidieae
Subtribe: Cyrtopodiinae
Etymology: Named in honor of its discoverer, John Ansell

This genus is now considered to be monotypic with only one, rather variable species distributed widely throughout the continent of Africa. Sometimes known as the leopard orchid because the yellowish flowers are variously spotted with brown, this species usually grows epiphytically on branches just below the canopy of large trees or on the trunks. It often grows in areas which are dry for long periods of the year but in cultivation grows well if the roots are kept in a moist medium.

Plants can only be brought into flower if they are grown in good light, particularly

Ansellia africana

Arachnis flos-aeris

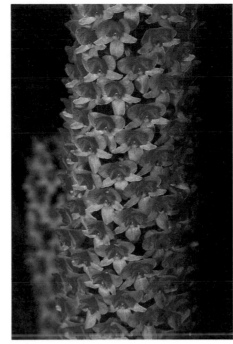

Arpophyllum giganteum

produced once or twice a year, usually in May or June, and again in November. Flowers vary from pale yellow-green with irregular maroon bars and spots to completely deep maroon. A musky fragrance emanates from the dorsal sepal. This fast-growing species thrives in bright light and warm temperatures from 20–34°C.

Arachnis hookeriana (Reichb.f.) Reichb.f.

More compact-growing than *A. flos-aeris*, this is a primarily coastal species, growing on sandy soil and scrambling among the scrub near the sea. Once abundant in Borneo, the Malay Peninsula, and Singapore, it is now rare in the wild. The seldom-branched inflorescence bears cream to yellow flowers that may be finely mottled with purple. It hybridizes readily with *A. flos-aeris* and many vandas and renantheras to produce hybrids desirable for the cut-flower industry. *Arachnis hookeriana* requires full sun and high temperatures.

after the canes have completed their growth. Warm temperatures and high humidity are ideal. They will grow equally well in large pots or baskets.

Ansellia africana Lindley

This vigorous species produces cane-like pseudobulbs up to a meter in length with leaves borne alternately in the upper half. The inflorescence is terminal in the form of a large, branching panicle. On subsequent flowerings subsidiary inflorescences may be produced from the lower nodes on the canes. The flowers are pale yellow with a brighter yellow lip. Sometimes the sepals and petals are unspotted, but usually they are marked with spots or irregular patches of light or dark brown, occasionally so heavily marked as to appear blackish. The flowers may be heavily scented when flowering in sunshine.

ARACHNIS Blume
ah-RAK-nis
Tribe: Vandeae
Subtribe: Sarcanthinae
Etymology: Gr. *arachne*, spider

Seven *Arachnis* species are distributed throughout southeast Asia, New Guinea, and the Solomons. Closely allied to *Vanda* and *Renanthera*, these scandent herbs with long, branching stems scramble up and over supporting vegetation. Long, arching sprays of large, scorpion-shaped blooms are produced on the upper portions of the monopodial stems. The petals and sepals are frequently barred in brown, and the long-lasting flowers have short, thick

columns which bear four pollinia each in terminal anthers.

Bright light is required for flowering, and temperatures should not dip below 18°C. The long stems which can, in some of the species, span the crowns of several forest trees make most *Arachnis* species unsuitable as pot-plants.

Arachnis flos-aeris (L.) Reichb.f.

This tall-growing species is found in the Malay Peninsula, Singapore, Sumatra, and Java. Long, many-branched panicles are

Arpophyllum spicatum

ARPOPHYLLUM La Llave & Lex.
ar-po-FIL-lum
Tribe: Epidendreae
Subtribe: Laeliinae
Etymology: Gr. *arpi*, sickle, scimitar; *phyllon*, leaf

A Neotropical genus of some five or more species, all of which have been cited for Mexico but some ranging as far south as Colombia. The plants have a slender, short stem with one apical, very fleshy-coriaceous leaf, long and sickle-like, though often channeled. They produce a compact, many-flowered, erect spike of non-resupinate reddish purple flowers which can be very attractive. *A. alpinum*, *A. giganteum*, *A. laxiflorum*, *A. medium*, and *A. spicatum* have all been cited recently for Mexico. The species grow at intermediate elevations and require bright light and a night temperature of 15°C. Water throughout the year, although somewhat less after the leaves have fully developed and flowering has finished. Plants require a humid potting medium with very good drainage.

Arpophyllum giganteum Hartweg ex Lindley

This is the largest species of the genus found from Mexico to Costa Rica and Jamaica in the West Indies. Plants grow up to 70 centimeters high, the leaf 50 centimeters long and the spike some 15 centimeters high. Flowering is from January to March.

Arpophyllum spicatum La Llave & Lex.

The original species described, this is easily

Arthrochilus irritabilis

Ascocentrum ampullaceum

Ascocentrum garayi

recognized by the channeled, very hard, sickle-like leaves. It is endemic to the sierras in southern Mexico. The plants are some 30 centimeters tall, and have an attractive spike about six centimeters tall.

ARTHROCHILUS F. Muell.
ar-thro-KYE-lus
Tribe: Diurideae
Subtribe: Caladeniinae
Etymology: Gr. *arthros*, jointed; *cheilos*, lip

Ten highly interesting but inconspicuous species are known from subtropical and tropical Australia and New Guinea. They are terrestrials with a deciduous habit, subterranean tuberoids, wispy racemes of highly insectiform, dull-colored flowers and a rosette of leaves which in many species develops after flowering. The labellum is hinged, and the flowers are pollinated by male wasps which attempt copulation with the flower.

Pot in a well-drained soil mix containing wood shavings. Keep moist over summer, dry out as plants die down, keep completely dry and repot just prior to growth in late spring. Use fertilizers sparingly.

Arthrochilus irritabilis F. Muell.

Found in eastern Australia where it forms colonies in eucalypt woodland, usually in sandy soils. Slender racemes of greenish, inconspicuous flowers appear from late spring to late summer and are followed by rosettes of dull green leaves. A robust species which can be difficult to flower.

ASCOCENTRUM Schltr.
as-koe-SEN-trum
Tribe: Vandeae
Subtribe: Sarcanthinae
Etymology: Gr. *ascos*, bag; *kentron*, spur

About ten species are known from northeast India and Nepal to Borneo, the Philippines, and Taiwan. Most *Ascocentrum* species are showy and widely cultivated. Formerly placed in a broadly defined *Saccolabium*, *Ascocentrum* species typically have brightly colored yellow, orange, red, or cerise flowers in dense upright racemes. One

Ascocentrum curvifolium

diminutive species from Taiwan, *A. pumilum*, has been placed in its own genus, *Ascolabium*, by some authors. All species have a prominent spur, a straplike lip and two pollinia.

With the exception of *A. pumilum*, a cloud forest species that prefers cool conditions, *Ascocentrum* species prefer intermediate to warm temperatures, bright light and plenty of water similar to the culture of their larger relative *Vanda*. The small- to medium-sized plants can be grown in pots or baskets, or mounted on slabs.

Ascocentrum ampullaceum
(Lindley) Schltr.

This compact species is native from Nepal and southwest China to Thailand. Dense racemes of glowing cerise-pink flowers are produced in the spring. They grow in profusion around the base of the plant. An orange-flowered form called var. *aurantiacum* is known from northeast India. Given bright light, dry, or cool conditions the leaves become spotted with distinctive large purple spots. Because of the way the flowers are borne around the base of the plant, *Ascocentrum ampullaceum* should be grown in small pots or mounted on a slab for best effect.

Ascocentrum curvifolium
(Lindley) Schltr.

This species is native to Burma, Thailand, and Laos. *Ascocentrum curvifolium* is one of the largest species in the genus. The upright racemes of dark orange to red flowers have made the species a hybridist's dream. It is the *Ascocentrum* parent of most X *Ascocenda* (*Ascocentrum* x *Vanda*), an important horticultural genus that combines the large flower size and round shape of *Euanthe* (*Vanda*) *sanderiana* with the bright colors and many-flowered racemes of *Ascocentrum*. The species flowers in late spring and early summer. Recently, the red-flowered plants have been treated as a separate species, *A. rubrum*.

Ascocentrum garayi E. A. Christ.

Ascocentrum garayi is native to Indochina where it has been erroneously called *A. miniatum*. *Ascocentrum miniatum* is a rarely grown similar plant from Java. The miniature plant size and the multiple upright racemes of brilliant orange-yellow flowers have made it the most frequently grown ascocentrum. The species is given to producing basal offshoots and plants readily form specimen plants. *Ascocentrum garayi* flowers in the spring.

Aspasia epidendroides

ASPASIA Lindley
as-PAZ-ee-ah
Tribe: Cymbidieae
Subtribe: Oncidiinae
Etymology: Gr. glad, delightful; named for the wife of Pericles

This is a genus of eight species distributed from Guatemala to Brazil. The genus is characterized in part by elongate, flattened, bifoliate pseudobulbs; the lateral inflorescence produced from the leaf-sheaths; the spurless flowers; the spreading lateral sepals; and the two hard, waxy pollinia on a short stipe with a small viscidium.
These are epiphytic plants of lowland tropical forests up to elevations of 1,000 meters. The flowers are large and showy with the lip folded back abruptly from the column at its midpoint. The species are easily cultivated with cattleyas in the intermediate house.

Aspasia epidendroides Lindley

The flowers of this species have a cupped aspect due to the concave petals that tend to hood around the column. The sepals are greenish with transverse bands of brownish lavender. The petals are pale to dark lavender, and the lip is white with purple markings in the center. This species is found from Guatemala to Panama in moist forests.

Aspasia principissa Rcichb.f.

The flowers of this species are a little larger than in the preceding species. The green sepals and petals are spreading and heavily marked with brown. The lip is white with red-brown blotches toward the apex. The species is found from Nicaragua to Colombia in wet forests at middle elevations.

Aspasia principissa

BAPTISTONIA Barb. Rodr.
bap-tis-TONE-ee-ah
Tribe: Cymbidieae
Subtribe: Oncidiinae
Etymology: For Baptista Caetano d'A. Nogueira, a Brazilian philologist and ethnologist

This species contains one Brazilian species often listed under *Oncidium* Sw., to which it is closely related. It differs from this genus mainly in the column which is forward-pointing and curving down at the apex, and not upright as in *Oncidium*. The inflorescence, a dense, often branched raceme of many flowers, arises from the base of the pseudobulbs. Flowers of *Baptistonia*, as other genera allied to *Oncidium*, have two pollinia.
Grows well in suspended tree-fern slabs or in clay pots filled with shredded tree-fern fiber. Provide bright light, warm temperatures (25°–30°C during the day and 20°C at night), and plenty of water; the medium should never be allowed to dry completely.

Baptistonia echinata Barb. Rodr.

This showy epiphyte, endemic to southern Brazil, is rarely found in cultivation. Flowers appear from February to April. Sepals are brownish yellow, petals pale bronze with

Baptistonia echinata

Barbosella australis (Cogn.) Schltr.

This southern Brazilian member of the genus, with a creeping habit, is one of the most attractive. Conspicuous, membranous flowers held above the leaves are distinctive with their oblong lip broadly forked at the apex.

Barbosella cucullata (Lindley) Schltr.

This species of *Barbosella* is the one most frequently found in the Andes from Venezuela into Bolivia. The habit is creeping with a thick rhizome that produces narrow, fleshy, short-stemmed leaves, and a long peduncle that bears its solitary flower with a simple lip far above the leaves. The color of the flower varies from dark purple to pale yellow. Small forms seem to grade imperceptibly into other species, such as the Central American *B. anaristella*.

four to five pale brown transverse lines toward the apex, and the apex of the lip dark maroon, whereas the side-lobes are yellow. The lateral sepals are fused except at the tip.

BARBOSELLA Schltr.
bar-bo-SEL-lah
Tribe: Epidendreae
Subtribe: Pleurothallidinae
Etymology: Named for Brazilian botanist J. Barbosa Rodrigues

This genus consists of about 20 species

found through Central America to southern Brazil and northern Argentina. The species are characterized by a single, long-stemmed flower with a "ball-and-socket" articulation of the lip with the column-foot. Four pollinia are present. Vegetatively they vary from densely tufted plants to long-repent plants with distant leaves. The leaves of all the species are short-stemmed. Prior to the proposal of *Barbosella* in 1918, all the species known at that time had been treated in *Restrepia*.

These plants are relatively easy to cultivate in moist, intermediate to cool-growing greenhouse conditions.

BARKERIA Knowles & Westcott
bar-KER-ee-ah
Tribe: Epidendreae
Subtribe: Laeliinae
Etymology: In honor of George Barker, British horticulturist of the nineteenth century

This is a genus of fifteen species primarily found in Mexico and Guatemala with two species reaching Costa Rica and one found as far south as Panama. The genus is characterized by the cane-like stems, often branching from the midpoint rather than the base, with distichously arranged leaves;

Barbosella cucullata

Barkeria lindleyana

Barkeria elegans

Barkeria spectabilis

the apical inflorescence of the nodding flowers; the spreading, similar sepals and petals; and the column free from the usually flat lip nearly to its base.

The species are usually found growing as epiphytes at intermediate elevations in the forests of Mexico and Central America. They are easily cultivated in the intermediate house but appreciate cool night temperatures with less water during their resting period.

Barkeria elegans Knowles & Westcott

The sepals and petals of this lovely species are dark rose. The lip is pinkish white with a large blotch of reddish crimson toward the apex, the column yellowish dotted with purple. Though producing few flowers, this is one of the best of the genus. It is known only from Guatemala.

Barkeria lindleyana Batem.

The sepals and petals of *Barkeria lindleyana* are rosy pink while the lip is darker pink with a white blotch in the center. The large flowers on elongate inflorescences make this a very showy plant. It occurs from Mexico to Costa Rica and is commonly encountered growing spontaneously on rose bushes in the gardens of San José, Costa Rica.

Barkeria spectabilis Batem.

This species produces the largest flowers of the various members of the genus. The sepals and petals are pale pink, and the lip is white at the base and in the center has a large rose-pink spot at the apex. The whole surface is richly spotted with blood-red dots. The species occurs from Mexico to Nicaragua.

Barlia robertiana

BARLIA Parl.
BAR-lee-ah
Tribe: Orchideae
Subtribe: Orchidinae
Etymology: Barlia, after Sr. Barla

Originally considered to belong to *Himantoglossum* (or *Loroglossum*), the genus has a wide distribution around the Mediterranean and was separated mainly because the outer perianth segments do not converge to form a galea and the bracts exceed the flowers. Tubers are ovoid and comparatively large; leaves are broad, shiny pale green; and stems can grow up to 80 centimeters tall with numerous iris-scented flowers in a dense spike, 8–20 centimeters long.

Like other pot-grown Mediterranean genera *Barlia* plants like plenty of light (but not direct sun), and a free, well-drained compost (with added limestone chips). Repot in the fall and water regularly as the rosette appears. Withhold water after the spike and leaves die away, allowing the "new tuber" a period of aestivation.

Barlia robertiana (Loisel.) Greuter

One of the first of the Mediterranean species to flower (late December–January in Cyprus and Crete, a month or so later farther north), it was for many years considered to belong to a monospecific genus. Recently plants from the Canary Islands have been claimed to belong to a second species, *B. metlesiciana*. Flowers of *Barlia robertiana* are 3.5–4.5 centimeters long; the lip is whitish marked with pink or purple and a narrow to broad greenish or brownish margin. Plants are found on grassy hillsides, among scrub, and in woodland clearings.

BIFRENARIA Lindley
bi-fren-AIR-ee-ah
Tribe: Maxillarieae
Subtribe: Bifrenariinae
Etymology: Latin *bi*, two; *frenum* rein or strap; referring to two caudicles connecting the pollinia to the stipe

This is a genus of 24 South American species. The genus is characterized by ovoid pseudobulbs that are quadrangular in cross-section with one or two apical, lightly veined leaves; the usually few-flowered, lateral inflorescence; and the four hard, flattened, superimposed pollinia.

These are epiphytic plants from wet tropical forests at elevations of 200 to 700 meters.

Bifrenaria harrisoniae

Bifrenaria tetragona

Bifrenaria tyrianthina

Bletia coccinea

recognized by the corms growing near the surface of the soil, the plicate leaves, and the frequently showy flowers in various tones of purple, red, yellow or brown, and green.

Bletia campanulata La Llave & Lex.

Endemic to sierras in central Mexico, at middle elevations, this highland species grows in exposed volcanic flows and grass patches in oak and pine woods. It requires clear-cut dry and wet periods, with heavy rains starting in May and continuing through September, and then diminishing until they practically disappear in February as the dry season starts. The name refers to the bell-shaped flowers, with the sepals and petals forming a hood around the lip.

Bletia coccinea La Llave & Lexarza

This orange-red-flowered species from central Mexico often grows with other

The species from southern Brazil tend to have few large flowers while those of Amazonia are smaller with more flowers. They should be grown under intermediate conditions with uniform watering throughout the year. They should not be allowed to dry out completely. The plants enjoy abundant sunlight but can be shy bloomers. Some authors unite the members of *Rudolfiella* and *Stenocoryne* with *Bifrenaria*, but we feel that the genera are distinct.

Bifrenaria harrisoniae (Hook.) Reichb.f.

This species occurs in southern Brazil. The pseudobulbs have one large apical leaf. The inflorescence carries one or two large flowers. The flowers are six centimeters in diameter, waxy and long-lasting. The sepals and petals are cream-white sometimes flushed with red, and the lip is red-purple.

Bifrenaria tetragona (Lindley) Schltr.

Bifrenaria tetragona occurs in southern Brazil. The flowers are about five centimeters in diameter, fleshy and heavily fragrant. The sepals and petals are greenish

streaked and flushed with red-brown, and the lip is greenish flushed with red-brown toward the base.

Bifrenaria tyrianthina (Lodd.) Reichb.f.

This species occurs in southern Brazil. The flowers are seven to eight centimeters in diameter, waxy and long-lasting. The sepals and petals are violet-purple but paler toward the base, and the lip is violet-purple with a white throat.

BLETIA Ruíz & Pavón
BLE-tee-ah
Tribe: Arethuseae
Subtribe: Bletiinae
Etymology: Honoring Don Luis Blet, a Catalonian apothecary of the eighteenth century, contemporary with the Ruiz and Pavón expeditions to Peru and Chile

A widespread genus in the New World, with some 40 species many of which have been confused. The plants are terrestrial and like to grow on embankments at low to intermediate elevations. Species can be

species of the same genus nearby. It has been observed to form a natural hybrid with *B. campanulata*. It grows in the same conditions as that species.

Bletia purpurea (Lam.) De Candolle

This, the most widespread species of the genus, is found all around the Caribbean basin and South America. Although the flowers are relatively small, it grows with ease in clay soils with good drainage, often among ferns. Keep in a warm house.

BLETILLA Reichb.f.
bleh-TIL-la
Tribe: Arethuseae
Subtribe: Bletiinae
Etymology: Diminutive of *Bletia*, an American terrestrial orchid genus named in honor of Don Luis Blet, a Spanish pharmacist and botanist of the eighteenth century

This is a temperate, terrestrial genus with nine species distributed throughout east Asia, Taiwan, and the adjacent islands. The pseudobulbs are cormlike, each bearing

Bletia campanulata

Bletia purpurea

Bollea coelestis

several stalked and pleated leaves about 30 centimeters long. The erect racemes bear several attractive deep rose to white flowers in the spring and early summer. All species have four mealy pollinia in two pairs. The plants are hardy, with protection required only from severe frost. They grow well in pots or in outdoor beds in well-composted soil with good drainage. Water carefully with the appearance of new shoots, and keep cool and dry after leaves have fallen.

Bletilla striata (Thunb.) Reichb.f.

This is an extremely easy orchid to grow in the temperate region. It is distributed through China, Japan, and eastern Tibet, and found in cultivation under the name *B. hyacinthina*. Up to twelve rose-purple flowers open in succession on erect racemes, mostly in summer. A rare white form with yellow in the throat of the lip also occurs.

Bletilla striata

Bollea lawrenceana

BOLLEA Reichb.f.
BOL-ee-ah
Tribe: Maxillarieae
Subtribe: Zygopetalinae
Etymology: In honor of Carl Bell, German patron of horticulture during the nineteenth century

Bollea is a genus of eleven species, mostly of Andean South America. The genus is characterized by the lack of pseudobulbs; the foliaceous, distichous sheaths forming a fanlike plant; the one-flowered inflorescences produced from the axils of the leaf-sheaths; and the four flattened,

superimposed pollinia, on a short stipe connected to a flattened, cordiform viscidium.
These plants are epiphytic in very wet cloud forest at elevations from 1,000 to 1,800 meters. They should be grown under intermediate conditions with cool nights and should not be allowed to dry excessively. Members of this genus are among the premium orchid species with large colorful flowers.

Bollea coelestis Reichb.f.

The so-called "blue" orchid of the

southwestern slopes of the Andes in Colombia. The flowers are eight to ten centimeters in diameter, very fleshy and long-lived. The widely spreading sepals and petals are violet to blue for the basal half and darker from the midpoint outward with a white apex. The lip has a yellow callus and a dark violet apical lobe. The column is dark violet.

Bollea lawrenceana Reichb.f.

This species is similar to the former with flowers of similar size. It is native to the forests on the western slopes of the western range of the Andes in Colombia and extends into the northwestern area of Ecuador. The sepals and petals are pale cream with a blotch of violet-purple in the upper portion. The lip has an orange-yellow callus, and the apical lobe of the lip is violet-purple.

BONATEA Willd.
bo-NAT-ee-ah
Tribe: Orchideae
Subtribe: Habenariinae
Etymology: Named in honor of M. Bonat, Professor of Botany at Padua in Italy

About ten attractive species have been described in this terrestrial genus which is widespread in eastern Africa, extending from the Cape northward to Ethiopia and into the Yemen. The plants closely resemble the large-flowered species of *Habenaria* but can be distinguished by the hooded midlobe of the rostellum and by the way the lower lobe of the petals and the stigma lobes are adnate to the lip. All the species have green-and-white flowers, often appearing after the leaves have begun to die.
Plants grow from several underground tubers and are not difficult to maintain in cultivation provided they are kept in a well-drained sandy compost. After flowering, when the plants die back, they need to be kept completely dry until the new shoots are a few centimeters high. Then they can be watered and fed generously as growth proceeds. Good light and warm temperatures are desirable.

Bonatea speciosa

Brassavola cucullata

Brassavola flagellaris

Bonatea speciosa Willd.

This is one of the more attractive species from the eastern parts of South Africa which grows on or near the beach and always in very sandy soils. The large green-and-white flowers are borne close together at the apex of the new growth. With care plants can be maintained easily in cultivation and increased by separation of the shoots from time to time. The larger species, *B. steudneri* and *B. lamprophylla*, are also desirable.

BRASSAVOLA R. Br.
bra-SAH-voe-la
Tribe: Epidendreae
Subtribe: Laeliinae
Etymology: In honor of Antonio Musa Brassavola, nobleman and botanist of Venice during the nineteenth century

This is a genus of seventeen species distributed throughout much of the lowland American tropics. The genus is characterized by very small pseudobulbs and a single, fleshy, subterete, apical leaf; the inflorescence produced from the apex of the pseudobulb; the lip usually tightly rolled around the column to form a tube; and the eight laterally flattened, hard pollinia with prominent opaque caudicles. Two atypical species had been traditionally retained in *Brassavola* but have been removed to the genus *Rhyncholaelia* (i.e. *R. digbyana* and *R. glauca*).
These are epiphytes in moist or wet forest trees at elevations from sea level to 1,000 meters. They are easily cultivated under intermediate conditions and provide

Brassavola cordata

Brassavola nodosa

attractive, long-lasting flowers that are highly fragrant at night.

Brassavola cordata Lindley

This species occurs in the West Indies and varies from plants with stiffly erect leaves to slender, hanging leaves. The flowers are similar to other species in the genus but more are produced, and they are smaller.

Brassavola cucullata (L.) R. Br.

This is the first species described in the genus and occurs in the West Indies and

from Mexico to Venezuela. The sepals and petals are long and hang downward while the lip flares at the apex of the column and then becomes a long, slender, spinelike lobe.

Brassavola flagellaris Barb. Rodr.

This Brazilian species has a plant habit similar to *B. subulifolia* with long, slender, terete leaves. The sepals and petals are spreading and yellow-white, the lip white or yellowish white with an emerald-green throat.

Brassavola nodosa (L.) Lindley

This is the most common and widespread species in the genus, distributed from Mexico to Colombia on the Pacific coast and throughout the Caribbean coast and islands. The flowers are among the largest in the genus, reaching eight centimeters in diameter, with cream-colored sepals and a white, heart-shaped lip.

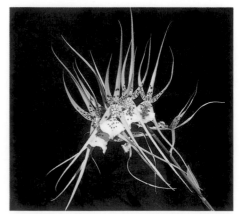

Brassia verrucosa

Brassia gireoudiana

Brassia caudata

BRASSIA R. Br.
BRAS-ee-ah
Tribe: Cymbidieae
Subtribe: Oncidiinae
Etymology: In honor of William Brass, British botanical illustrator during the nineteenth century

Brassia is a genus of 29 species, distributed throughout tropical America. The genus is characterized in part by the pseudobulbs of a single internode; the inflorescences produced from the sheaths at the base of the pseudobulb; the spreading, very elongate, free sepals; and the two hard pollinia attached to a stipe and viscidium. Most of the species are epiphytic in wet forest at elevations from sea level to 1,500 meters. All the species are easily cultivated with cattleyas in the intermediate house.

Brassia arcuigera Reichb.f.

This species long had the name *B. longissima* in horticulture, but it was not validly published until after that of *Brassia arcuigera*. The sepals and petals are very elongate and drooping with the individual sepals reaching 25 centimeters long. The plants have a very flattened pseudobulb with sharp edges and a single apical leaf. The sepals and petals are yellow, heavily marked with red-brown, and the white lip has a few red basal spots and a yellow callus. The species is found from Costa Rica to Ecuador on both sides of the Andes.

Brassia caudata (L.) Lindley

The flowers of *Brassia caudata* are similar to those of the previous species, but the sepals are not quite as elongate. The plants

have a flattened pseudobulb with round edges and a pair of leaves at the apex. The callus of the lip is fuzzy. The species is found from Florida to Brazil and Bolivia.

Brassia gireoudiana Reichb.f. & Warsc.

The plant of this species is similar to *B. caudata* with a pair of apical leaves on the pseudobulb, but is larger in all parts. The inflorescence is more elongate. The stiffly spreading sepals and petals are not as long as in the previous species and are greenish yellow with red-brown spots near the base. The lip is yellow with sparse red-brown spots. The species is known from Costa Rica and Panama.

Brassia lanceana Lindley

This species is similar in plant habit to *B. caudata* with paired leaves. The flowers have much shorter sepals and petals that are similar in shape, the petals often curled around the dorsal sepal. The segments are yellow to almost orange, spotted with dark brown in the lower half, and the lip is whitish yellow spotted with brown near the callus. It is found from Panama to Brazil and Peru.

Brassia verrucosa Lindley

The plants have thick, compressed, egg-shaped pseudobulbs and a pair of leaves at the apex. The base of the pseudobulb is surrounded by foliaceous sheaths. The sepals and petals are pale green spotted with dark green or red-brown. The lip is greenish white to white with black-green warts on the lower half. The flowers are large to extremely large, reaching nearly 20

Brassia arcuigera

Brassia lanceana

centimeters in diameter in the largest forms. The sepals and petals are stiffly spreading. This species is known from Mexico to Venezuela.

BROUGHTONIA R. Br.
braw-TOE-nee-ah
Tribe: Epidendreae
Subtribe: Laeliinae
Etymology: In honor of Arthur Broughton, British botanist of the nineteenth century

Broughtonia is a genus of five species found in the islands of the West Indies. The genus is characterized by the conspicuous, usually flattened, tightly clustered, jointed pseudobulbs; the pair of stiff apical leaves; the several-flowered inflorescence produced from the apex of the pseudobulb, the brightly colored floral segments usually arranged to form a flattened circle; and the eight hard, flattened pollinia.
The species are epiphytes at low elevations. They are easily cultivated under warm conditions with high sunlight and light watering.

Broughtonia sanguinea (Sw.) R. Br.

The pseudobulbs are flattened and nearly round in outline. The flowers are brilliant red, reaching five centimeters in diameter. This species is commonly cultivated in the collections in Florida and less so farther north. It has been hybridized extensively with advanced hybrids of the *Cattleya* complex.

Broughtonia sanguinea

Bulbophyllum barbigerum

BULBOPHYLLUM Thouars
bul-bo-FILL-um
Tribe: Epidendreae
Subtribe: Bulbophyllinae
Etymology: Gr. *bolbos*, bulb; *phyllon*, leaf

Bulbophyllum as currently circumscribed is a diverse, artificial assemblage of 1,000–1,200 pantropical, epiphytic species distributed among several subgenera and sections. Most species occur in the rain forests or cloud forests of southeast Asia, particularly New Guinea, which is believed to be the center of distribution.
Regardless of what characters are used in combination to define the genus, there are exceptions. In general, though, plants are sympodial with one- or two-leaved pseudobulbs spaced closely or at some distance along the rhizome. The fleshy leaves may be more than a meter long or only a few millimeters, depending on the species. Inflorescences arise laterally from the rhizome or the base of the pseudobulb rather than from its apex. Flowers usually have a column-foot which is hinged to the labellum, making the latter quite flexible. Depending on the species, flowers range from several centimeters to a millimeter in diameter, though most flowers are quite small. In fact, entire plants of some *Bulbophyllum* species such as *B. pygmaeum* and *B. minutissimum* are among the smallest in the orchid family. There are two or four pollinia.
Most often the pollinators are flies, attracted by floral fragrances (which may smell like urine, sap, blood, dung or rotting meat) and/or by floral parts moving in the breeze. The floral odor of one species, *Bulbophyllum beccarii*, has been likened to a herd of dead elephants, and that of *Bulbophyllum fletcherianum* makes it

Bulbophyllum falcatum

difficult to walk into the glasshouse where it is being cultivated.
All species are curiosities worth cultivating. Because of the creeping rhizome and sometimes widely spaced pseudobulbs, bulbophyllums are better suited to slabs of wood, cork, or tree-fern than to pots. Water and fertilize plants only when they are in active growth. Plants may generally be grown in diffuse light and under warm to intermediate temperatures, but provide cooler temperatures for those species native to higher elevations. Repot as infrequently as possible; basket or slab culture satisfies this requirement very well. Allow high humidity but also ample air movement to prevent bacteria and fungi from infecting the leaves.

Bulbophyllum barbigerum Lindley

This very unusual African species with one-leaved pseudobulbs occurs up to about 900 meters in forests from Sierra Leone east to Cameroon and Zaire. Multiflowered racemes bearing yellow-green flowers flushed with rose-purple appear variously through the year. The labellum has marginal hairs but also an apical tuft of hairs which flutter in the slightest breeze. Despite its

Bulbophyllum graveolens

Bulbophyllum imbricatum

that give it a reptilian appearance, much like the "rattle" of a rattlesnake. The dark purple flowers open successively over many weeks, and the plant may be in flower throughout the year. From lowland forests, it should be cultivated under warm conditions.

Bulbophyllum lasiochilum Par. & Reichb.f.

Also known as *Cirrhopetalum breviscapum*, this species ranges from Burma and Thailand to Malaya. Pseudobulbs are ovoid and spaced a few centimeters apart on a creeping rhizome. It is distinguished by long hairs along the margins of the labellum and by inrolled lateral sepals which converge at their apices. The dorsal sepal, petals, column, and labellum are dark maroon, while the lateral sepals are a contrasting creamy white spotted with maroon.

Bulbophyllum lobbii Lindley

A variable species from Thailand to Malaysia, Indonesia, and the Philippines, *B. lobbii* is commonly cultivated for its relatively large (to about 6 centimeters across), fragrant flowers of yellow striped with reddish brown. Pseudobulbs are one-leaved and well spaced on a coarse rhizome. Plants in cultivation should be mounted and given intermediate to warm temperatures.

Bulbophyllum longissimum (Ridley) Ridley

One of the most spectacular of the species in section *Cirrhopetalum, B. longissimum* is native to Peninsular Thailand. Pseudobulbs

Bulbophyllum lasiochilum

exotic-looking flowers, it is relatively easy to cultivate in warm, bright conditions.

Bulbophyllum falcatum (Lindley) Reichb.f.

This African species from lowland forests is one of many in which the rachis of the inflorescence is flattened, the tiny flowers opening often simultaneously on both sides. The dorsal sepal is yellowish, and the lateral sepals are a contrasting dark red. Flowering may occur anytime from May to August under warm to intermediate conditions.

Bulbophyllum graveolens (Bailey) J. J. Smith

Native to New Guinea, this charming species produces up to 10 flowers per inflorescence. The sepals and petals are pale green, the labellum a purple-red. Flowers are five to seven centimeters in overall length and are long-lasting. Grow under warm to intermediate conditions.

Bulbophyllum imbricatum Lindley

The wide and flattened rachis of this species has overlapping (imbricate) floral bracts

Bulbophyllum lobbii

Bulbophyllum longissimum

Bulbophyllum putidum

are ovoid and one-leaved. Four to ten flowers are produced in an umbel, each with lateral sepals dangling down to 20 centimeters or more. Sepals are white to cream, veined in red. Petals are the same color but spotted with red, especially at the apex. The labellum is cream to greenish. Grow under warm conditions.

Bulbophyllum medusae (Lindley) Reichb.f.

This eye-catching species was named after Medusa, one of the Gorgons in Greek mythology, in reference to the lateral sepals more than twelve centimeters long. It ranges from Thailand to Borneo and the Philippines. Flowers are borne in umbels from the base of the pseudobulbs anytime between September and March. Sepals and petals are generally straw-colored, and the labellum is yellow. Plants should be grown under warm conditions in baskets to limit disturbance of the roots.

Bulbophyllum putidum (Teijsm. & Binnend.) J. J. Smith

This is a widespread member of section *Cirrhopetalum*, extending from Sikkim to the Philippines. One-flowered inflorescences arise from the base of pseudobulbs. The dorsal sepal and petals are lined toward their apices with threadlike banners termed paleae, which flutter in the breeze. The lateral sepals are connivent except for just above the base and extend about ten centimeters.

Bulbophyllum rothschildianum (O'Brien) J. J. Smith

Another species in section *Cirrhopetalum*,

B. rothschildianum from India has club-shaped paleae on the tips of the dorsal sepals and petals. Inflorescences of three or more foul-smelling flowers are produced from the base of the pseudobulb. The lateral sepals stretch for fifteen centimeters. Flowering occurs from September to March.

Bulbophyllum scaberulum (Rolfe) Bolus

This widespread African species, which flowers from March to July in lowland rain forests and cloud forests up to about 2,000 meters, has two-leaved pseudobulbs and a wide, sometimes thickened rachis bearing

up to about 100 yellow flowers flushed with purple.

Bulbophyllum umbellatum Lindley

This lovely species in section *Cirrhopetalum* ranges from Nepal to Taiwan. From the base of the one-leaved pseudobulbs arise five- to eight-flowered umbels. The sepals and petals are cream-colored spotted with red to lavender. The dorsal sepal is hooded, and the lateral sepals are spreading and inrolled. The labellum is white, heavily marked with lavender. Provide intermediate temperatures. Plants thrive in tree-fern baskets and quickly form specimen plants.

Bulbophyllum scaberulum

Bulbophyllum medusae

Bulbophyllum rothschildianum

Cadetia taylori

CADETIA Gaudichaud
ka-DET-ee-ah
Tribe: Epidendreae
Subtribe: Dendrobiinae
Etymology: After Charles Louis Cadet de Gassicourt

A genus of 55 species of small epiphytes mostly found in New Guinea and the Solomon Islands with outliers occurring in southeast Asia and New Guinea. Each slender stem is topped by a solitary fleshy or leathery leaf. Small white flowers, which are produced in succession from a terminal sheath, may be short- or long-lasting. All species have four pollinia.

Mount on a slab or grow in a small pot of small to medium-sized particles of bark and charcoal. Plants need warmth and high humidity combined with free air movement.

Cadetia taylori (F. Muell.) Schltr.

With its neat, compact growth habit and long-lasting flowers produced freely throughout the year, this species deserves to become more widely grown. A native of Australia and New Guinea, this epiphyte grows in moist forests on trees and rocks in coastal and montane regions. It can be mounted on a slab or grown in a small pot of bark under humid conditions with free air movement.

CALADENIA R. Br.
kal-a-DEN-ee-ah
Tribe: Diurideae
Subtribe: Caladeniinae
Etymology: Gr. *kalos*, beautiful; *adenos*, gland

One of the most distinctive groups of Australian orchids consisting of about 120 species, many of which are still unnamed. A few species also occur in New Zealand, New Caledonia, Indonesia, and Malaysia. They are deciduous terrestrials with subterranean tuberoids entirely or partly enclosed in a fibrous sheath and a solitary, usually hairy leaf. Hairy scapes bear one to four colorful flowers. All species have four pollinia. Grown mainly by specialist terrestrial growers. Pot in a well-drained soil mix containing wood shavings and eucalypt leaf litter. Keep moist when in active growth (winter to spring), dry out as plants die down, and repot carefully over summer. Use fertilizer sparingly.

Caladenia caerulea R. Br.

This is the commonest of a number of blue-flowered species found in the genus. The cheery flowers, which appear in summer, are borne singly atop a very slender, wiry stem to about fifteen centimeters tall. Each flower is about 25 millimeters across, and the petals and lateral sepals project forward in front of the labellum like the fingers of a hand.

Caladenia carnea R. Br.

A very widespread species of eastern Australia which is often erroneously recorded from other countries including

Bulbophyllum umbellatum

Caladenia caerulea

New Zealand, New Caledonia, and Indonesia. Flowers range from white to bright pink, and the labellum and column are heavily marked with transverse red bars. Some variants have a strong musky fragrance. Flowering occurs between late winter and early summer.

Caladenia discoidea Lindley

Commonly known as the bee orchid, this slender species, which is endemic to Western Australia, has dainty, lightly striped flowers and a broad, tremulous labellum which has a prominent marginal fringe of slender teeth. The flowers appear between late winter and midspring, carried on a slender wiry stem to 35 centimeters tall.

Caladenia eminens (Domin) M. Clements & D. Jones

One of the commonest and also most attractive of the amazing Western Australian terrestrial orchids. Commonly grows in open woodland, often in tufts. The large white flowers on stems to 80 centimeters tall are highly visible even from a distance. Because of the depth of the tuberoids in the soil, plants of this species need to be grown in a deep pot.

Caladenia lobata Fitzg.

An amazing orchid which has yellowish green flowers about seven centimeters across. Its most conspicuous feature is a broadly flared labellum. This organ, which has a prominent maroon apex and a fringe of long, slender teeth, trembles in the slightest breeze and has given rise to the local common name of butterfly orchid.

Caladenia carnea

Flowering of this Western Australian orchid takes place throughout spring.

CALANTHE R. Br.
ka-LAN-thee
Tribe: Arethuseae
Subtribe: Bletiinae
Etymology: Gr. *kalos*, beautiful; *anthe*, flower

Calanthe is a popular genus of some 150 terrestrial species distributed throughout tropical and subtropical Africa, Asia, and Australia. It is characterized by pseudobulbous stems; plicate, evergreen or deciduous leaves; lovely, racemose inflorescences arising from the base of the pseudobulb; and flowers with a three- or four-lobed labellum fused to the base and often extended into a spur.

Deciduous calanthes such as *Calanthe vestita* and its many showy hybrids should be potted in a peat/perlite compost and grown under warm, bright conditions. When plants are in active growth (beginning in February or March), they should receive ample water and high-nitrogen fertilizer regularly. When growths

Caladenia eminens

Caladenia lobata

are mature and leaves begin to yellow and abscise, reduce water and fertilizer to absolute minimum levels. Inflorescences will appear from November to January. When new shoots and roots are visible at the base of old pseudobulbs, resume watering and fertilizing as before. Evergreen calanthes should not receive a prolonged rest period. Most species will thrive under intermediate conditions, although a few require cooler or warmer conditions.

Calanthe reflexa Maxim.

This evergreen species is native to Japan, where it flowers from July to September. Racemes ten to fifteen centimeters long carry up to 30 flowers ranging from white to lilac in color. The labellum is deeply three-lobed and lacks a spur. Grow under intermediate conditions.

Caladenia discoidea

Calanthe reflexa

Calanthe triplicata

Calochilus campestris

Calanthe triplicata (Willemet) Ames

Formerly known as *C. veratrifolia*, this lovely evergreen species is distributed from India to Indonesia and the Pacific islands. White flowers appear from May to December (depending on the locality) on inflorescences up to two meters tall. In the rain forests of Australia it flowers in December and so bears the local name of "Christmas lily." The four-lobed labellum has a yellow to red callus at the base. It will grow well in intermediate to warm temperatures.

Calanthe vestita Lindley

One of the most widely cultivated species with many color forms and hybrids, *C. vestita* from southeast Asia is deciduous and should receive a rest period as noted above. Inflorescences about a meter tall bear long-lived, white to red flowers in December–January. The labellum is four-lobed with a yellow to red callus at the base.

CALOCHILUS R. Br.
kal-o-KYE-lus
Tribe: Diurideae
Subtribe: Diuridinae
Etymology: Gr. *calos*, beautiful; *cheilos*, lip

Twelve species comprise this genus of highly interesting terrestrial orchids, the majority occurring in Australia and others found in New Guinea, New Zealand, and New Caledonia. All are deciduous terrestrials with subterranean tuberoids and a solitary, narrow, erect leaf. In most species the flowers have coarse, colorful hairs on the labellum; some also have unusual false

eyes at the base of the column. All species have four mealy pollinia.

These orchids are generally difficult to grow and are mainly the province of dedicated growers. Pot in a well-drained soil mix containing wood shavings and eucalypt leaf litter. Keep moist when in active growth (autumn to spring), dry out as plants die

down, keep completely dry and repot over summer. Use fertilizers sparingly.

Calochilus campestris R. Br.

A robust species which develops sturdy flower spikes to 60 centimeters tall and bearing up to fifteen flowers which open sequentially, each lasting two to four days.

Calanthe vestita

Calochilus robertsonii

Calypso bulbosa

Capanemia superflua

The most striking feature of each flower is the purple hairs which project from the labellum like a bristly beard. A native of eastern Australia, this unusual orchid flowers there from September to January.

Calochilus robertsonii Bentham

The unusual flowers of this orchid, which originates in eastern Australia and New Zealand, always command attention when observed for the first time. The broad labellum is covered with coarse hairs which are mostly purplish or brownish. Flowers open freely from late winter to late spring with the perianth segments expanding very widely on hot, sunny days.

CALYPSO Salisb.
ka-LIP-so
Tribe: Calypsoeae
Etymology: Kalypso, a sea nymph

The genus *Calypso* is monotypic with a wide distribution in Northern Temperate regions which extend from North America via northern Europe and Asia to Japan. It is named after the daughter of the giant Atlas, one of the Titans. Legend has it that her exceptional beauty kept Ulysses for seven years on her island.
In the wild *Calypso* grows in damp places and marshes in coniferous forests, often in wet moss and leaf litter close to rotting tree

stumps. Alpine house conditions are needed in cultivation. Growth starts in the fall, and the plants need an open mix of leaf mold with crushed quartzite grit or, alternatively, living sphagnum moss to survive. During growth, plants need to be kept moist; in the summer they can be allowed to dry out somewhat in a shaded frame.

Calypso bulbosa (L.) Oakes

The short flower-stalk emerges from a small underground tuber (there may be one or two older ones next to it) and is surrounded by a pleated basal leaf which is ovoid in shape, has undulate margins, and is colored dark green. Brownish leaf sheaths surround the reddish stalk which carries a single, dainty, vanilla-scented flower. The erect, spreading sepals are slender, tapered, and between about one and two centimeters long. Colored bright pink, they contrast prettily with the white or pale pink saccate lip. The lip is flat near the front but extended and indented at the rear to make a double spur. It carries purple-brown streaks in the basal half and a yellow or white tuft of hairs at the base of the apical lobe.
As well as the typical variety found in northern Scandinavia, throughout Asia, and in Japan, two others are recognized: var. *americana*, which has a weakly spotted apical lobe and large yellow callus tuft; and var. *occidentalis*, which has a white callus tuft, a purplish mottled apical lobe, and an altogether duller appearance to the flower.

CAPANEMIA Barb. Rodr.
kap-a-NAY-mee-ah
Tribe: Cymbidieae
Subtribe: Oncidiinae
Etymology: For Guillermo Schuch de Capanema, a Brazilian naturalist

Some sixteen miniature epiphytic species are known in Brazil, Argentina, Paraguay, and Uruguay. In all species each small pseudobulb has a single flat or cylindrical leaf ranging, depending on the species, from one to six centimeters long. Racemes of few to many white flowers arise from the base of the pseudobulb. In the past several species were placed in *Rodriguezia* and/or *Quekettia*. All species have two pollinia. Grow in small clay pots. Provide moderate shading, intermediate temperatures (20°–25°C during the day, 15°C at night), and abundant water during periods of active growth, but water less frequently once the minute pseudobulbs are fully developed.

Capanemia superflua (Reichb.f.) Garay

This species, perhaps the largest and showiest of the genus, is endemic to southern Brazil. Racemes of five to ten flowers are produced from March to July. The flowers are white with a yellow spot at the base of the lip, a maroon stripe along sepals and petals, and a maroon spot at the base of the column. Along with *C. australis* and *C. micromera*, this species is most often seen in cultivation.

Catasetum barbatum

Catasetum bicolor

Catasetum integerrimum

CATASETUM Rich.
kat-a-SEE-tum
Tribe: Cymbidieae
Subtribe: Catasetinae
Etymology: Gr. *kata*, down; L. *seta*, bristle

Some 70 species and ten natural hybrids are currently known, ranging from the West Indies to Mexico in Central America, and to Argentina in South America. All species have fleshy pseudobulbs of several internodes with eight to twelve leaves. Racemes of few to many flowers arise from the base of the pseudobulbs. Plants produce inflorescences bearing either male or female flowers; inflorescences with both male and female flowers and/or sexually intermediate flowers are rarely seen in nature or in cultivation. Male flowers are usually colorful and morphologically variable and display a most unusual pollinarium-ejection mechanism. Female flowers are usually yellowish green and fairly uniform in morphology. All species bearing hermaphroditic flowers were transferred to *Clowesia* Lindley and *Dressleria* Dodson. All species have two pollinia.

Most species thrive in well-drained pots or baskets packed with sphagnum moss. Water carefully and provide good ventilation when the new shoot is developing to prevent rotting. When the shoot is mature provide plenty of water and fertilizer. Water sparingly after pseudobulbs shed leaves and repot when a new shoot appears. Large plants will produce female flowers under direct sunlight (provide ventilation to minimize burning of the foliage). Most plants will produce male flowers under moderate shade.

Catasetum cernuum

Catasetum barbatum (Lindley) Lindley

This extremely variable epiphytic species, found in Colombia, Venezuela, Guianas, Brazil, and Peru, produces arching, many-flowered racemes from May to October. Flowers are generally green with maroon spots on sepals and petals. The lowermost lip is variously bearded and has a prominent callus at the base and often a second one at the apex.

Catasetum bicolor Klotzsch

This epiphytic species, found in Panama, Colombia, and Venezuela, produces arching racemes from February to October. Flowers are bronze. The lowermost lip is cream or green with small maroon spots along the margin and internally with two elongate lateral calli.

Catasetum cernuum (Lindley) Reichb.f.

This variable species, found in southern Brazil, produces arching, many-flowered racemes from April to July. Flowers vary

Catasetum discolor

Catasetum expansum

from yellowish green-spotted maroon to almost solid dark maroon. The lip is lowermost, generally three-parted with the longer lateral lobes curving in front of the shorter central lobe.

Catasetum discolor (Lindley) Lindley

This species, found in Colombia, Venezuela, the Guianas, Brazil, and Peru, produces erect, many-flowered racemes from February to July. The flowers are generally yellowish green, with some reddish orange along the dentate margins of the uppermost

Catasetum macrocarpum

Catasetum pileatum

Catasetum sanguineum

lip. The antennae, conspicuous in the male flowers of most other species, are poorly developed in *Catasetum discolor*.

Catasetum expansum Reichb.f.

This showy species, endemic to northeastern Ecuador, produces arching, many-flowered racemes from May to December. Flowers vary from white, green, yellowish white to deep yellow often with maroon spots. The conspicuous triangular callus at the base of the lowermost, cup-shaped lip is usually darker than the rest of the flower.

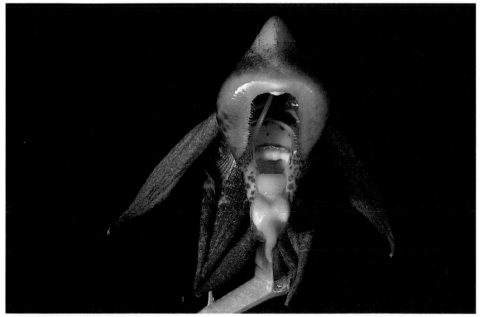

Catasetum maculatum

Catasetum integerrimum Hook.

This robust species, found in Central America from Mexico to Nicaragua, produces erect racemes from April to November. Flowers are deep green to yellowish green often suffused and/or spotted with maroon. The lip is uppermost, shaped like a helmet, with the apical margin entire.

Catasetum macrocarpum Rich. ex Kunth

This showy species, found in Colombia, Venezuela, Trinidad-Tobago, the Guianas, and Brazil, produces erect racemes from July to December. The flowers are deep green to yellowish green suffused and/or spotted with maroon, especially the interior surface of the uppermost, helmet-shaped lip. The apical margin of the lip is typically tridentate. This is perhaps the most common species found in cultivation.

Catasetum maculatum Kunth

This showy species, found in Nicaragua, Costa Rica, Panama, and Colombia, produces erect racemes from May to December. Flowers range from green with maroon spots throughout to almost solid maroon. The margins of the uppermost, helmet-shaped labellum are typically ciliate.

Catasetum pileatum Reichb.f.

This showy species, found in Colombia, Venezuela, Trinidad-Tobago, and Brazil, produces arching, many-flowered racemes from June to November. The flowers are typically ivory-white with a yellow spot at the base of the cup-shaped lip. However, many color forms have been reported, including some bright yellow varieties and others suffused and/or spotted with maroon throughout.

Catasetum saccatum Lindley

This variable species, found in Colombia, the Guianas, Brazil, Ecuador, Peru, and Bolivia, produces many-flowered racemes from June to December. The flowers vary from light green spotted and/or suffused with maroon to dark wine-red. The lip has a small sac toward the base, and the margins vary from dentate to deeply fimbriate.

Catasetum saccatum

Catasetum sanguineum Lindley

This variable species, found in Colombia and Venezuela, produces many-flowered racemes from May to October. Flowers are greenish white to dark green, usually with maroon spots in sepals and petals; the uppermost lip, dark green with the margins and the interior surface dark wine-red, has a three-parted bladelike lobe projecting forward.

Catasetum tabulare Lindley

This curious species, found in Colombia, produces many-flowered racemes from May to October. Flowers are light green, more or less blotched with maroon; the lowermost, boat-shaped labellum has a broad, table-like callus all along the upper surface.

Catasetum tenebrosum Kränzlin

This curious species, confined to southeastern Ecuador and eastern Peru, produces many-flowered racemes from March to October. Sepals and petals are dark wine-red, the lowermost, heart-shaped lip red to yellowish green with a conspicuous basal callus.

Catasetum trulla Lindley

This variable species, found in southern Brazil, produces many-flowered racemes from April to October. Flowers are solid light green or yellowish green to dark green blotched with maroon; the three-parted, lowermost lip has an apical thickening that is orange to dark green, blotched with wine-red. Lateral lobes are ciliate.

Catasetum viridiflavum Hook.

This robust species, found in Guatemala and Panama, produces many-flowered racemes from July to December. Flowers are green, the outer surface of the uppermost, helmet-shaped lip light green to yellowish green, the interior orange.

CATTLEYA Lindley
KAT-lee-ya
Tribe: Epidendreae
Subtribe: Laeliinae

Etymology: In honor of William Cattley, English horticulturist during the nineteenth century

Cattleya is a genus of 48 species distributed throughout mainland tropical America. The genus is characterized by the presence of cylindrical pseudobulbs of several nodes with apical, thick leaves; a racemose inflorescence with a sheath at the base; the usually large and showy flowers; and the four hard, clavate pollinia.

These are epiphytic plants usually of wet forests at elevations from sea level to 1,500 meters. The majority of the species are found in the tops of tall trees in moist to wet forest.

Most of the species can be cultivated in the intermediate house with abundant water provided during the growing season and less water while resting.

This genus, and the man-made hybrids with species of *Laelia, Rhyncholaelia, Sophronitis,* and some lesser genera, have provided the majority of orchid enthusiasts with the prime source of their interest, challenges, victories, and pride in orchid growing. The spectacular flowers of most of the species and the hybrids produced from them have

Catasetum tabulare

Catasetum tenebrosum

dominated the florist market for the last century as the premier flower. Endless hours of gratification, frustration, and envy have resulted from the cultivation of these orchids. Outrageous prices have been paid for particularly choice, awarded clones.

Cattleya aurantiaca (Batem. ex Lindley) P. N. Don

The pseudobulbs are conspicuously swollen above the midpoint and have a pair of leaves at the apex. The erect inflorescence has ten to fifteen flowers that are among the smallest in the genus, usually less than three centimeters in diameter. The sepals and petals are orange, and the orange

Cattleya aurantiaca

Catasetum trulla

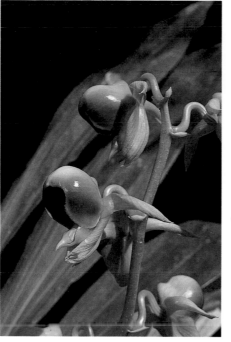

Catasetum viridiflavum

Cattleya dowiana

lip has flecks of red toward the center. Several well-established varieties are known with yellow and white forms that breed true. Crosses with the larger-flowered species and hybrids have resulted in carrying of the genetic material of the brilliant colors to their hybrids. The species occurs naturally from Mexico to Nicaragua, and many of the forms are self-pollinating.

Cattleya bicolor Lindley

The pseudobulbs are cylindrical and bifoliate at the apex. The inflorescence is short with between two and five flowers, each to ten centimeters in diameter. The sepals and petals are green flushed with

red-brown, of very heavy substance and long-lasting. The lip has a long, narrow claw at the base, expanding to an ovate, rich purple-red apex, without lateral lobes. The species is native to Brazil and has been used sparingly in hybrids.

Cattleya dowiana Batem. & Reichb.f.

The pseudobulbs are swollen above the midpoint with a single apical leaf. The inflorescence is erect with five to seven large flowers, exceeding fifteen centimeters in diameter. The sepals are dark yellow, and the petals are rich yellow, usually with red venation and flushing. The lip is a striking, velvety red-purple, with golden yellow veins

radiating from the base to the margins and with three golden yellow streaks down the center. Hybridization with other large-flowered species has produced the spectacular yellow hybrids with red lips that exist in nearly all fine collections. The species occurs from Costa Rica to northern Colombia with the more northern forms of less desirable quality. The Colombian varieties, sometimes known as *C. aurea*, are larger-flowered with more intense coloration.

Cattleya forbesii Lindley

The pseudobulbs are cylindrical and slender, with two apical leaves. The inflorescence is erect with between one and six flowers. The flowers are medium in size, reaching eleven centimeters in diameter. Sepals and petals are pale green or yellowish green often flecked with red-brown. The downcurved, whitish, three-lobed lip is flushed with red on the outside and has a yellow throat with red veins and a dull red midlobe. The lateral lobes of the lip are folded over the column.

Cattleya guttata Lindley

Cattleya guttata is a very large plant with cylindrical pseudobulbs to 1.5 meters tall and a pair of leathery leaves at the apex. The inflorescence reaches 50 centimeters tall with from seven to 30 flowers, each twelve to 20 centimeters in diameter. The flowers are fleshy and long-lasting. The sepals and petals are usually green with red-brown dots and blotches. The lip is three-lobed with pinkish lateral lobes and bright red apical lobe. The lateral lobes of the lip surround the column. This species was

Cattleya bicolor

Cattleya intermedia

or even a synonym of *C. guttata*. The plants are very similar with elongate, canelike pseudobulbs and a pair of leaves at the apex. The inflorescence has six to fifteen flowers. The sepals and petals are brownish or bronzy green, spotted with red. The three-lobed lip is velvety purple. The species is native to eastern Brazil.

Cattleya loddigesii Lindley

The pseudobulbs are cylindrical, slender, to 30 centimeters tall, with a pair of leaves at the apex. The inflorescence has two to six flowers with a small sheath at the base. The flowers reach twelve centimeters in diameter. The sepals and petals are bluish white to white. The lip is lightly three-lobed with the lateral lobes curved over the column and the midlobe light or dark rose with a white disc. The species is native to southern Brazil and reaches Paraguay.

once common near the seashore in southeastern Brazil.

Cattleya intermedia Grah.

The pseudobulbs are cylindrical and have a pair of leaves at the apex. The inflorescence has three to seven flowers, each reaching thirteen centimeters in diameter. The flowers are of heavy substance and are long-lasting. The sepals and petals are usually bluish white, and the three-lobed lip has a rich reddish midlobe. Many naturally occurring varieties are cultivated, the most popular being the splash-petal var. *aquinii*. The *aquinii* varieties have been used extensively in hybridization to produce larger splash-petal types. The species is found in southern Brazil, Uruguay, and Paraguay.

Cattleya labiata Lindley

The plant has club-shaped pseudobulbs to 30 centimeters tall, with a single, thick leaf at the apex. The inflorescence is erect with between one and five flowers and has a sheath at the base that is large and spathelike. The flowers are large, reaching 20 centimeters in diameter in some forms. The sepals and petals are rose-pink to pale pink or white and are spreading. The lip is large, forming a tube around the column, the margin crisped or frilled, and is dark red-purple with a yellow blotch in the throat. The species, in the strict sense, is of Brazilian distribution. A number of taxa has been included as varieties within *Cattleya labiata* (e.g., *C. dowiana, C. lueddemanniana, C. mendelii, C. mossiae, C. percivaliana, C. trianae, C. warscewiczii*, and *C. warneri*). Most growers can readily distinguish them in the greenhouse, and they form stable populations in the wild.

Cattleya forbesii

Cattleya lawrenceana Reichb.f.

The plant has pseudobulbs to 35 centimeters long that are lightly club-shaped with a single, narrow leaf at the apex. They are usually reddish in color. The inflorescence produces five to eight flowers. The flowers reach twelve centimeters in diameter. The sepals are pale rose to white. The lip has a long, slender tube, the blade rose-purple with a white throat. The species is found in inland mountains of the Guyana region of northeastern South America.

Cattleya leopoldii Verschaff. ex Lem.

This species is often considered as a variety

Cattleya loddigesii

Cattleya lueddemanniana Reichb.f.

The pseudobulbs are cylindrical, smooth, with a single, narrow, stiffly erect, grey-green apical leaf. The inflorescence emerges from a conspicuous sheath. The flowers are three to five, reaching 22 centimeters in diameter. The sepals and petals are rose-pink suffused with white, and the petals are very broad. The lip has a narrow, compressed tube at the base and is of similar color to the sepals and petals. The midlobe is round with two blotches of yellow-white on the disc with lines of deep purple radiating outward between them. The species is native to Venezuela.

Cattleya luteola Lindley

The pseudobulbs are cylindrical to ovoid and are compressed with a single leaf at the apex. The inflorescence is shorter than the leaf with two to six flowers. The flowers are small, reaching five centimeters in diameter and are butter-yellow with the margins of the midlobe of the lip white. The inside of the tube of the lip is streaked with purple-red. The species is found in the Amazon basin of Ecuador, Peru, and Brazil.

Cattleya lawrenceana

Cattleya lueddemanniana

Cattleya luteola

Cattleya maxima

Cattleya mossiae

Cattleya maxima Lindley

The pseudobulbs are cylindrical and sometimes club-shaped in the upper part with a single, leathery apical leaf. The inflorescence is erect with five to fifteen flowers. Flowers reach twelve centimeters in diameter. Sepals and petals are pale rose to whitish. The lip is rose with purple-rose, branching veins. The species is native to the coastal dry forests of Ecuador and northern Peru.

Cattleya mendelii Backh.

This species from Colombia has pseudobulbs that reach 25 centimeters long and are club-shaped with a single apical leaf. The inflorescence is short with a large sheath surrounding the base with two to five flowers, each reaching seventeen centimeters in diameter. Sepals and petals are pinkish white with the petals darker. The lip has the apical half dark red-purple sharply separated from the yellow blotch at the disc.

Cattleya mossiae Hook.

The pseudobulbs reach 25 centimeters long and are somewhat oblong and club-shaped with a single apical leaf. The inflorescence has a large sheath at the base and produces two to seven flowers each reaching 20 centimeters in diameter. The sepals and petals are white to light rose. The lip is very broad with a deep cleft at the apex and has a splash of yellow inside the tube and on the disc; the apical portion is dark red-purple. The flowers of this species are variable in color, and it has been used extensively in early hybridization to produce the modern hybrids. The species is native to the Colombian Andes.

Cattleya nobilior Reichb.f.

The pseudobulbs reach eighteen centimeters tall and are oblong with a pair of leathery leaves at the apex. They are usually widely spaced on the rhizome. The inflorescence consists of a short, leafless shoot arising from the base of a pseudobulb with one or two flowers. The flowers are large, to twelve centimeters in diameter, and the segments are held very flat. The sepals and petals are rose-lilac. The three-lobed lip is rose-lilac with a red blotch on the disc. The species is native to Brazil.

Cattleya percivaliana O'Brien

The pseudobulbs are club-shaped with a single apical leaf. The inflorescence has two to five flowers, and is surrounded at the base by an obvious sheath. The flowers are smaller than those of most similar species, reaching twelve centimeters in diameter, and produce a musty, somewhat objectionable odor. The sepals and petals are rose-colored with the petals darker. The midlobe of the lip is red-purple with a pale pink margin; the disc is yellow to orange streaked with red. The species is native to Venezuela.

Cattleya schilleriana Reichb.f.

The pseudobulbs are cylindrical, slightly swollen in the upper portion and to twelve centimeters tall, with a pair of leathery leaves at the apex. The inflorescence has one or two flowers and is very short. The

Cattleya percivaliana

flowers reach eleven centimeters in diameter and are very thick and waxy. The sepals and petals are dark green or brownish green blotched with dark brown. The three-lobed lip is reddish purple; the midlobe has darker red veins and the disc is yellow with a thin yellow stripe extending to the apex of the lip. The species is native to Brazil.

Cattleya skinneri Batem.

The pseudobulbs are club-shaped, to 40 centimeters tall, with a pair of leaves at the apex. The inflorescence has two to twelve flowers and is surrounded at the base by a small sheath. The flowers are small, to nine

Cattleya schilleriana

centimeters in diameter. The sepals, petals, and lip are dark rose-purple with a white spot at the disc of the lip. The species is found from Mexico to northern South America. Some varieties are self-pollinating, and the flowers do not last long.

Cattleya trianae Linden & Reichb.f.

The pseudobulbs are club-shaped, to 30 centimeters long, and with a single, leathery apical leaf. The inflorescence has two to five flowers, each with a diameter to 20 centimeters. Sepals and petals are white to dark purple. The lip is often not widely spreading and is usually dark red-purple with an orange-yellow disc. The arrangement of the colors of the lip is highly variable. The species is native to the upper valleys of the Andes of Colombia.

Cattleya violacea (H. B. K.) Rolfe

The pseudobulbs are spindle-shaped, flushed with red, and have a pair of roundish, red-flushed leaves at the apex. The inflorescence has three to seven flowers and a small sheath at the base. The flowers are very flat and reach twelve centimeters in diameter. Sepals and petals are bright rose-purple. The lip is three-lobed, the lateral lobes are rose-purple, and the midlobe is dark red-purple with a yellow disc with a white blotch on each side. The species is widespread east of the Andes at lower elevations in northern South America.

Cattleya walkeriana Gardn.

The spindle-shaped pseudobulbs are short, to twelve centimeters tall, and have a pair of leathery leaves at the apex. The

Cattleya nobilior

Cattleya skinneri

Cattleya warneri

Cattleya warscewiczii

Cattleya walkeriana

inflorescence consists of a short, leafless shoot arising from the base of a pseudobulb with one or two flowers. The flowers are large, to twelve centimeters in diameter, and the segments are held very flat. Sepals and petals are rose pink to purple. The three-lobed lip is dark red-purple with a yellow-white blotch on the disc. The species is native to Brazil.

Cattleya warneri T. Moore

The pseudobulbs reach 20 centimeters tall with a single, leathery leaf at the apex. The inflorescence is short, with two to five flowers. The flowers reach 20 centimeters in diameter. Sepals and petals are pale rose-

colored shaded with darker rose. The midlobe of the lip is dark rose-red without pale margins, and the disc is pale orange-yellow streaked with lilac. The species is native to Brazil. This species is very similar to *C. labiata* but is distinguished by the color of the lip and the flowering season.

Cattleya warscewiczii Reichb.f.

The club-shaped pseudobulbs reach 40 centimeters tall with a single leathery leaf at the apex. The inflorescence has three to eight flowers and is surrounded at the base by a large sheath. The flowers reach 20 centimeters in diameter. Sepals and petals vary from pale rose to dark pink. The lip is

Cattleya trianae

Cattleya violacea

deeply cleft at the apex, dark red-purple with a yellow disc, and has a white blotch on each side of the disc. The species is native to northwestern Colombia.

Caularthron bicornutum

CAULARTHRON Raf.
kawl-AR-thron
Tribe: Epidendreae
Subtribe: Laeliinae
Etymology: Gr. *kaulos*, stem; *arthron*, joint; in reference to the jointed pseudobulbs

This is a genus of three species from the West Indies, Central America, and South America. The genus is characterized by elongate, cylindrical pseudobulbs of several internodes often inhabited by ants; the apical, fleshy leaves; the apical inflorescence without a sheath at the base; the basal portion of the lip with a pair of hollow calli; and the four laterally flattened, hard pollinia.
The plants grow as epiphytes in seasonally dry forest near sea level. Members of this genus should be cultivated under intermediate conditions but not be allowed to dry out completely.

Caularthron bicornutum (Hook.)
R. E. Schultes

The pseudobulbs are spindle-shaped and hollow and contain stinging ants in the natural habitat. There are two or three leaves toward the apex. The inflorescence is produced from the apex of the pseudobulb, reaches 45 centimeters tall, and has five to 20 flowers. The flowers reach seven centimeters in diameter. Segments are flat and white with a yellow disc on the lip and have a few red spots toward the base. The lip is small and three-lobed. The species is native to Amazonian South America, Venezuela, and the southern Caribbean islands.

CEPHALANTHERA Rich.
kef-a-LAN-ther-a
Tribe: Neottieae
Subtribe: Limodorinae
Etymology: Gr. *kephale*, head; *anthera*, anther

Cephalanthera shares with *Epipactis* the common name of helleborine. It is a genus of largely woodland terrestrial orchids with a preference for calcareous soils. Some fourteen species grow in the North Temperate regions of Europe through Asia into Japan.
Cephalanthera plants have short, creeping rhizomes which remain heavily infected

Cephalanthera damasonium

Cephalanthera longifolia

Cephalanthera rubra

with mycorrhiza even in mature plants. Stems are leafy. Flowers are comparatively large, carried in a lax spike which is usually few-flowered, but *C. epipactoides* and *C. kurdica* from Turkey and farther east can have 20 or more. Petals and sepals are of similar length (circa 15–20 millimeters) and usually connivent to form campanulate flowers. The lip is in two distinct parts: a concave hypochile at the base; an epichile at the apical end, often ridged with a recurved tip. The species from south, central, and western Europe (*C. damasonium, C. longifolia, C. rubra*) are spurless, while *C. epipactoides, C. kurdica,* and *C. cucullata* (endemic to the island of Crete) have short spurs.

With care, plants can be pot grown in a basic terrestrial compost to which limestone has been added. Failure can often be traced to the fact that rhizomes are thin and dry out very rapidly during transference when plants are removed from the soil.

Compost: 3 parts heat-sterilized loam
3 parts crushed grit (6 millimeters) or coarse gritty sand
2 parts sieved beech/oak leaf mold
1 part composted pine bark (6 millimeters)
"Hoof and horn" meal base dressing at 10 milliliters per 10 liters
Limestone chippings (6 millimeters)

Cephalanthera damasonium (Miller) Druce

Usually the commonest of the family in western Europe, *Cephalanthera damasonium* has few broad, short, pointed leaves and from three to twelve rather dingy, creamy white flowers which hardly open. They resemble small hard-boiled eggs about one and a half to two centimeters long. Plants only flower after some ten years of growth, but they can form clumps of up to fifteen or more stems, flowering from mid-May onwards when established under beech or pine on calcareous soils in a temperate wood or garden.

Cephalanthera longifolia (L.) Fritsch

An orchid of mainly deciduous woodland and scrubby woodland margins, *Cephalanthera longifolia* can also be found growing in open pine woods or on sand dunes, often in dwarf form because of exposed conditions. It can survive on less calcareous soils then either *C. rubra* or *C. damasonium* but is more dependent on soil moisture content. Flowers appear from mid-May to July and are clear white, opening wider than those of *C. damasonium*. An inflorescence can have up to 20 blooms. *Cephalanthera longifolia* has a wider distribution than others in the genus, extending southward through Europe to north Africa and eastward to the Himalayas and China.

Cephalanthera rubra (L.) Rich.

Slender, flexuous stems and rather short lanceolate leaves give this species a delicate appearance. The bright magenta-pink flowers, opening widely in June or July, are reminiscent of some exquisite miniature *Cattleya*. Although very rare in Britain, where it just hangs on at the edge of its western range, the species is fortunately much more easily encountered in the Massif Central of France and the woodlands of southern Germany, Austria, and Switzerland. It has a reputation for capricious behavior with sudden appearance or disappearance of flowering plants in places where it has been known to thrive.

CERATOSTYLIS Blume
se-rat-oh-STY-lis
Tribe: Epidendreae
Subtribe: Eriinae
Etymology: Gr. *kerato*, horn; *stylis*, style

The genus *Ceratostylis* comprises approximately 100 epiphytic species

Ceratostylis retisquama

distributed from Nepal to New Guinea, with a concentration of species in Indonesia and New Guinea. *Ceratostylis* is noted for having small, insignificant flowers; few species are cultivated. Plants typically have short, nearly terete pseudobulbs and a solitary, linear to terete leaf much like a Neotropical *Octomeria*.

Plants are either caespitose or trailing. Caespitose species may be grown in small pots, but most species should be mounted on slabs. All species grow in intermediate to warm conditions and should be kept lightly moist at all times. Medium light levels should be provided.

Ceratostylis retisquama Reichb.f.

This species, the showiest in the genus, is endemic to the Philippines. The species has been long known in horticulture under the synonym *C. rubra*. The trailing plants are unusual in having a persistent brown sheath around the rhizome and small pseudobulbs. Proportionately large orange-red flowers are produced at the base of new growths periodically throughout the year. Plants of *Ceratostylis retisquama* may be grown in pots but are shown to best advantage when mounted on slabs. Medium to bright light should be provided. Excessive light levels will stunt the plant, and too little light will limit flower production.

CHAUBARDIA Reichb.f.

shaw-BAR-dee-ah
Tribe: Maxillarieae
Subtribe: Zygopetalinae
Etymology: In honor of Chaubard, a French botanist during the nineteenth century

Chaubardiella tigrina

Chiloglottis formicifera

Chaubardia is a South American genus of three species from east of the Andes from Surinam to Bolivia. The genus is characterized by the small, unfoliate or leafless pseudobulbs surrounded by foliaceous leaf-sheaths; the one-flowered inflorescences produced from the axils of the leaf-sheaths; the prominent, radiate callus, the narrow column winged at the midpoint, not surrounding the callus; and the four hard, superimposed pollinia attached to a small stipe and a flattened viscidium.

The plants are epiphytes in lowland wet forests from sea level to 1,200 meters.

Members of this genus should be cultivated under intermediate conditions but never be allowed to dry out completely. Flowering occurs in succession throughout most of the year.

Chaubardia heteroclita (Poepp. & Endl.) Dodson & Bennett

The pseudobulbs are inconspicuous, rectangular, flat, with a single apical leaf, surrounded by several distichous sheaths, each leaf-bearing. Sepals and petals are greenish, heavily washed, and striped with red-brown. The lip is pink. The species is distributed along the eastern slope of the Andes from Colombia to Peru. This species was originally described as a *Maxillaria* and was transferred to *Huntleya*, but its affinities are with *Chaubardia*.

CHAUBARDIELLA Garay

shaw-BAR-dee-el-ah
Tribe: Maxillarieae
Subtribe: Zygopetalinae
Etymology: Gr. *iella*, similar to, referring to the genus *Chaubardia*

This is a genus of eight species distributed along the slopes of the Andes from Surinam to Peru and is also found in Costa Rica. The genus is characterized by the lack of pseudobulbs; the conduplicate leaves in a fan shape; the one-flowered inflorescences creeping along the surface of the substrate; the non-resupinate flowers; the concave base of the lip with the apical half flattened and truncate or obtuse; the short and thick column; and the four hard, superimposed pollinia attached to a small stipe and a flattened, elongate viscidium. The plants are epiphytes in very wet cloud forest at

Chaubardia heteroclita

Chiloglottis trapeziformis

Chiloglottis valida

elevations from 500 to 1,200 meters. All of the species produce similar flowers with the species characterized by the shape of the lip, the nature of the callus, and the size and color of the flowers.

Members of this genus should be cultivated under intermediate conditions but never be allowed to dry out completely. Flowering occurs in succession throughout most of the year.

Chaubardiella tigrina (Garay & Dunsterv.) Garay

Chaubardiella tigrina occurs from Surinam to Peru. This was the first species described and was originally placed in the genus *Chaubardia*. The flowers are pale cream-colored but so heavily spotted as to appear brown. The column is nearly white. The lip in this species is somewhat obtuse at the apex rather than rounded as in other species, and the horseshoe-shaped callus is smooth rather than ribbed.

CHILOGLOTTIS R. Br.
kye-lo-GLOTT-is
Tribe: Diurideae
Subtribe: Caladeniinae
Etymology: Gr. *cheilos*, lip; *glottis*, the mouth of the windpipe

Twenty-one interesting species are currently known, all endemic to Australia and New Zealand. They are deciduous terrestrials with paired leaves and subterranean tuberoids. All species reproduce vegetatively and grow in colonies. The flowers are generally dull-colored and have a strongly mimicking, insect-like arrangement of calli on a hinged labellum. Pollination is achieved when male wasps attempt to mate with the labellum. All species have four pollinia.

Generally easy to grow but mainly found in the collections of terrestrial enthusiasts. Pot into a well-drained soil mix containing wood shavings and leaf litter. Keep moist while in active growth (late summer to spring), dry out as plants die down, and keep dry over summer. Annual repotting may be necessary for vigorous species.

Chiloglottis formicifera Fitzg.

A vigorous, free-flowering species from eastern Australia and also once recorded from New Zealand. Plants reproduce freely, and the small, ant-like flowers appear throughout spring. These are greenish to brownish with prominent black, shiny calli on the labellum.

Chiloglottis trapeziformis Fitzg.

A vigorous Australian species which forms extensive colonies in moist forests. Plants have attractive dark green leaves, and the small greenish to brownish flowers are produced freely throughout spring. The labellum has a small, compact, crowded group of calli near the base.

Chiloglottis valida D. Jones

The most robust species in the genus and the one with the largest flowers. It occurs naturally in New Zealand and southeastern Australia. The flowers, to four centimeters across, appear from early spring to midsummer and have a remarkable resemblance to a young bird waiting to be fed. They are dark reddish brown to purplish green, and the labellum, which is hinged at the base, trembles in the slightest breeze.

CHILOSCHISTA Lindley
kye-low-SHIS-ta
Tribe: Vandeae
Subtribe: Sarcanthinae
Etymology: Gr. *cheilos*, lip; *schistos*, cleft

Chiloschista is a genus of about twenty epiphytic species distributed from Sri Lanka to Nepal and east to tropical Australia. Formerly included in a broadly defined *Sarcochilus*, *Chiloschista* differs in its leafless habit as well as technical characters of the flowers.

Chiloschista lunifera

Chondrorhyncha bicolor

Chondrorhyncha chestertonii

Because *Chiloschista* plants are leafless (or with small, ephemeral leaves) they need to have their photosynthetically active roots exposed to sunlight. For this reason they must be grown mounted on slabs and seem to prefer branches with relatively smooth surfaces. All species should be given very bright light and frequent watering.

Chiloschista lunifera (Reichb.f.) J. J. Smith

Chiloschista lunifera is native to Burma, Thailand, and Laos. Pendent racemes in the fall bear flowers that are yellowish with solid brown patches in the center of each segment. This species has been frequently confused with *C. parishii*, a species which differs by having flowers covered with fine brown spots.

CHONDRORHYNCHA
Lindley
kon-dro-RIN-ka
Tribe: Maxillarieae
Subtribe: Zygopetalinae
Etymology: Gr. *xhonseoa*, cartilage; *rhynchos*, nose or beak; referring to the beak-like rostellum

This is a genus of 31 species distributed from southern Mexico, through Central America and northern South America, to Bolivia. The genus is characterized by the lack of pseudobulbs; leaves in a fan shape; the one-flowered inflorescences produced from the axils of the leaf-sheaths; the inrolled lateral sepals; the sides of the non-saccate lip surrounding the column; the unwinged, club-shaped column without a ventral keel; and the four flattened,

superimposed pollinia on a short stipe connected to a flattened, heart-shaped viscidium.

There are two major groups in the genus, distinguished by the lacerate-fringed margin of the petals and lip in the subgenus *Chondroscaphe*, and the entire margins of the same structures in the subgenus *Chondrorhyncha*. All members of the fringed-lip group occur in Andean South America.

The plants are epiphytes occurring in wet cloud forests from 500 to 2,000 meters elevation. Members of this genus should be cultivated under intermediate conditions but never be allowed to dry out completely. Flowering occurs in succession throughout most of the year.

Chondrorhyncha bicolor Rolfe

Chondrorhyncha bicolor is known from Costa Rica and Panama and belongs to the subgenus *Chondrorhyncha*. The flowers are white with chocolate-brown blotches around the disc of the lip. The lip margin is entire.

Chondrorhyncha chestertonii Reichb.f.

The species occurs in northwestern Colombia. The flowers are bright yellow with red-brown markings inside the lip and around the column. The margins of the petals and the lip are heavily frilled. Careful study reveals several unrecognized species making up the concept of *Chondrorhyncha chestertonii* in Colombia and Ecuador. The characters that distinguish the species are found in the form of the column and the callus of the lip. The callus of *Chondrorhyncha chestertonii* is bilobed at the apex, but an additional callus farther out

on the lip is triangular, giving the aspect of a three-lobed callus.

Chondrorhyncha flaveola (Linden & Reichb.f.) Garay

This species has been called *C. fimbriata* Reichb.f. but examination of the type specimens reveals that *Chondrorhyncha flaveola*, described earlier, is the same. The type specimens of both species were collected near the same locality in northeastern Colombia. The population extends into northwestern Venezuela. The flowers of this species are yellow with red-brown spotting at the base of the lip. The margins of the lip and the petals are fringed.

Chondrorhyncha rosea Lindley

The species is found in northeastern Colombia and western Venezuela. The flowers of *Chondrorhyncha rosea* have the sepals spreading with the petals held alongside the lip. The lip is tubular and entire on the margin with a small three-ribbed callus at the midpoint and three low lamellae extending to the apex. The sepals are green and the petals yellow-green. The

Cirrhaea dependens

Chysis bractescens

lip is greenish at the base turning to yellow in the throat and red for the outer half with a yellow margin. Many distinct South American species have been confused with *Chondrorhyncha rosea*.

CHYSIS Lindley
KYE-sis
Tribe: Epidendreae
Subtribe: Bletiinae
Etymology: Gr. *chysis*, melting, referring to the fusing of pollinia prior to opening of the flowers in autogamous forms

Chysis consists of about five species distributed from Mexico to Peru. The genus is characterized by the pendent, elongate pseudobulbs of several internodes, with thin, strongly veined leaves; the multi-flowered inflorescence produced with the new growth; and the soft and mealy pollinia.

The plants are epiphytic and grow on tree-trunks in shady, damp habitats in wet forest from 500 to 1,000 meters. Cultivation of the species of *Chysis* is relatively easy in the intermediate house growing on plaques or in baskets. The pseudobulbs are pendent and need space for development. The plants should be watered heavily from the time that the new growths emerge until the development of the pseudobulb is complete. Afterwards less water should be applied.

Chysis aurea Lindley

This species occurs from Venezuela to Colombia. The flowers are yellow with a whitish lip marked with red-brown. The lip has five parallel keels of equal length extending from the base to the midpoint. The flowers are four to five centimeters in diameter. The pseudobulbs of this species are relatively slender when compared with other species.

Chysis bractescens Lindley

Chysis bractescens occurs from Mexico to Nicaragua. It is distinguished by the waxy, white flowers with a yellow disc on the lip and the enlarged floral bracts. The lip, which may have red lines near the apex, has five or seven parallel, fleshy lamellae between the side-lobes. The flowers reach seven centimeters in diameter.

Chysis laevis Lindley

The species is found from Mexico to Nicaragua. It is similar to *C. aurea* with yellow flowers, the segments turning orange toward the apical half. The lip is yellow marked with red-brown. It is distinguished by the presence of five to seven parallel keels of which the three middle keels are nearly twice as long as the laterals. The flowers reach six centimeters in diameter.

CIRRHAEA Lindley
suh-RYE-ah or suh-REE-ah
Tribe: Cymbidieae
Subtribe: Stanhopeinae
Etymology: Latin *cirrus*, tendril, in reference to the prolonged rostellum

This is a genus of six species found in central and southern Brazil. The genus is characterized by the elongate, ribbed, tightly packed pseudobulbs with a thin, heavily veined leaf at the apex; the elongate, pendent, multiflowered inflorescence produced from the base of the pseudobulb; the ovary twisted so as to face the flower toward the outside of the inflorescence; and the two hard pollinia on an elongate stipe attached to a round viscidium.

The plants grow as epiphytes in forests at lower elevations. The species should be cultivated in the intermediate house under conditions similar to those of *Gongora*.

Cirrhaea dependens Reichb.f.

The species is distinguished by the fact that the flowers do not open fully, the narrow and flat midlobe of the lip; and the lateral lobes of the lip folded back and parallel. The flowers reach five centimeters in diameter. They vary from apple-green to red-brown, spotted and barred with dark brown or orange-red.

Cirrhaea loddigesii Lindley

Cirrhaea loddigesii occurs in southeastern Brazil. It is distinguished by the flat, narrow midlobe of the lip, the flowers with spreading segments, and the lateral lobes of the lip folded back and parallel. The flowers reach six centimeters in diameter and vary in color from green-white to red-brown speckled with darker red-brown, with the midlobe of the lip barred with red-brown.

Cirrhaea saccata Lindley

This species occurs in southeastern Brazil. It is distinguished by the broad, shell-shaped midlobe and the spreading lateral lobes of the lip. The colors vary from green to red-brown.

CISCHWEINFIA Dressler & N. Williams
ci-SWINE-fee-a
Tribe: Cymbidieae
Subtribe: Oncidiinae
Etymology: In honor of Charles Schweinfurth, American botanist of the twentieth century, whose name is abbreviated to "C. Schweinf." and appears

Cirrhaea saccata

Chysis laevis

Chysis aurea

Cischweinfia dasyandra

Cischweinfia rostrata

after many species that he proposed, composite of *Ci* (C.), *schwein.* (abbreviation of last name), *ia* (of)

This is a genus of seven species occurring from Costa Rica to Bolivia. The genus is characterized by the pseudobulbs of one internode with subtending foliaceous sheaths and oblong, conduplicate leaves; the axillary, several-flowered inflorescences; the spurless flowers less than two centimeters in diameter; the green sepals and petals; the lip surrounding the column for the basal half; the footless column with a pronounced hoodlike extension at the apex and an auricle on each side below the stigma; and the two hard pollinia attached to a stipe and an oval viscidium.

The plants are epiphytic in very wet cloud forest at elevations of from 500 to 1,000 meters. Cultivation of all the species should be under intermediate conditions with watering remaining constant throughout the year.

Cischweinfia dasyandra
(Reichb.f.) Dressler & N. Williams

The species occurs from Costa Rica to western Ecuador and is distinguished by the relatively small flowers with green sepals and petals and a pink lip that is not broadly spreading.

Cischweinfia rostrata Dressler & N. Williams

Cischweinfia rostrata occurs from southwestern Colombia to west-central Ecuador. The species is similar to *C. dasyandra*, but the flowers are much larger and the rosy pink lip is broadly spreading.

CLOWESIA Lindley
klo-WEES-ee-ah
Tribe: Cymbidieae
Subtribe: Catasetinae
Etymology: In honor of Rev. Clowes, English cultivator of orchids during the nineteenth century

This is a genus of six species distributed from Mexico to Ecuador. The genus is characterized by the fleshy pseudobulbs with thin, heavily veined, deciduous leaves; the pendent inflorescence produced from the basal nodes; the bisexual flowers with a saccate lip; and the two hard pollinia attached to an elongate stipe which is attached to a round viscidium.

The plants are epiphytic in moist or dry forest at elevations from 200 to 1,500 meters. Members of this genus should be cultivated under intermediate conditions along with its close allies in *Catasetum*.

Clowesia rosea

Clowesia russelliana

They should be watered and fertilized heavily during their growth period but should be allowed a rest period when not actively growing.

Clowesia rosea Lindley

This species is found naturally in southwestern Mexico only, though it has been reported from much of tropical America. The flowers are pink, and the lip is heavily frilled around the margin. Several spectacular hybrids have been produced by crossing this species with large, flat-flowered catasetums.

Clowesia russelliana (Hook.) Dodson

This species has been reported to occur from Mexico to Venezuela and Colombia. The flowers are apple-green with darker, parallel, green lines. The lip is deeply saccate at the base, and the margin of the apical lobe is wavy.

Clowesia thylaciochila (Lemaire) Dodson

Clowesia thylaciochila is found in

Cochleanthes amazonica

southwestern Mexico. The flowers are apple-green with darker green lines, similar to C. russelliana, but the lip is slipper-shaped rather than deeply saccate at the base. The margin of the apical lobe of the lip is wavy.

Clowesia warscewiczii (Reichb.f.) Dodson

This species is distributed from Costa Rica south to coastal Ecuador and eastward to Colombia, Venezuela, and Brazil. The flowers are green with darker green lines,

and the margin of the apical lobe of the lip is frilled.

COCHLEANTHES Raf.
kok-lee-AN-theez
Tribe: Maxillarieae
Subtribe: Zygopetalinae
Etymology: Gr. *cochlos*, snail shell; *anthos*, flower; referring to the shell-like flower

Cochleanthes is a genus of fifteen species distributed from Costa Rica to Peru. The foliaceous, distichous sheaths form a fanlike plant with narrow leaves. The single-flowered inflorescences are produced from the axils of the leaf-sheaths. The callus is fanlike at the base of the lip, usually consisting of radiating ribs nearly divided to the surface of the lip. There are four hard, flattened, superimposed pollinia attached to a short stipe connected to a flattened, cordiform viscidium.
The plants are epiphytes from low to intermediate elevation cloud forest from 500 to 1,500 meters. Members of this genus should be cultivated under intermediate conditions but never be allowed to dry out completely. Flowering occurs in succession throughout most of the year.

Cochleanthes amazonica
(Reichb.f. & Warsc.) R. E. Schultes & Garay

This species occurs in the Amazon drainage in Colombia, Ecuador, Peru, and Brazil. It produces the largest flowers in the genus, reaching seven centimeters in diameter. The flowers are white with blue vein-lines on the disc of the lip.

Clowesia warscewiczii

Cochleanthes discolor (Lindley)
R. E. Schultes & Garay

Cochleanthes discolor occurs from Costa Rica to Venezuela and in the West Indies. Sepals and petals are apple-green, and the lip is dark purple-red or green with a blotch of purple-red on the disc and with a yellow callus. Petals are held forward over the column and surround the tube of the base of the lip. Flowers reach five centimeters in diameter.

Cochleanthes flabelliformis (Sw.)
R. E. Schultes & Garay

This species has been reported from Mexico to Costa Rica, from the West Indies and from most of northern and northeastern South America. The sepals and petals are greenish white, and the lip is violet or purplish violet with darker-colored veins. The callus is almost square.

Cochleanthes discolor

COCHLIODA Lindley
kok-lee-OH-da
Tribe: Cymbidieae
Subtribe: Oncidiinae
Etymology: Gr. *kochliodes*, spiral or snail-shell, reference to the snail-like appearance of the linear calli of the lip

This is a genus of five species from the Andes of Ecuador, Peru, and Bolivia. The genus is characterized by the presence of unifoliate or bifoliate pseudobulbs of a single internode subtended by distichous leaflike sheaths; the inflorescence produced from the axils of the sheaths, the flowers without a spur; the column without a foot; and the two, hard pollinia attached to a stipe connected to a viscidium.
The plants are epiphytes or lithophytes in cloud forest at elevations from 2,000 to 3,500 meters. Cultivation of members of this genus should be in cool conditions as for members of the Andean genus *Odontoglossum*.

Cochlioda noezliana (Mast.) Rolfe

This species occurs from central Peru to northern Bolivia. The flowers are brilliantly colored with broad, red sepals and petals, and the three-lobed lip is red with a yellow callus composed of four long, pubescent keels. The lobes of the lip are broad. The flowers reach a diameter of five centimeters.

Cochlioda rosea (Lindley) Benth.

Cochlioda rosea occurs in southern Ecuador and northern Peru. The flowers are bright red with a white callus on the three-lobed lip. The lateral lobes of the lip are rhombic and the midlobe is narrowly oblong. The flowers are about three centimeters in diameter.

Cochlioda rosea

COELIA Lindley
SEE-lee-ah
Tribe: Arethuseae
Subtribe: Bletiinae
Etymology: Gr. *koilos*, hollow

Five attractive species are currently known, ranging from the West Indies to Mexico, Guatemala, Honduras, El Salvador and Panama. Four of these, *C. macrostachya, C. bella, C. guatemalensis* and *C. densiflora*, were previously placed in the genus *Bothriochilus*. The pseudobulbs of all species have several leaves at the apex. Racemes of few to many white to rose-colored flowers arise from the base of the pseudobulb. All species have eight pollinia. Provide bright light and intermediate temperatures (15°C at night). Keep plants evenly moist when in active growth, but water less frequently once pseudobulbs have developed. All species are intolerant of excess salts at the roots.

Coelia triptera (Smith) G. Don ex Steud.

This vigorous species, found from the West Indies to Mexico and Guatemala, produces many-flowered racemes from February to April. Flowers are white, with a green spot at the base of the lip. The fragrance is reminiscent of lily-of-the-valley. *Coelia triptera* will tolerate warmer temperatures than the other species, up to 20°C at night. Along with *C. macrostachya* and *C. bella*,

Coelia triptera

Coeloglossum viride

COELOGLOSSUM Hartmann
see-lo-GLOSS-um
Tribe: Orchideae
Subtribe: Orchidinae
Etymology: Gr. *koilos*, hollow; *glossa*, tongue

The single species in this genus is at once one of the most widespread of all temperate terrestrial orchids and also one of the most unprepossessing because of its often small stature and greenish coloring. Preferring calcareous soils, but not confined to them, plants are found throughout central and northern Europe, in mountain regions of southern Europe, temperate Asia, and North America, and in the frozen wastes of Greenland and Iceland. It is one of the few orchid genera found within the Arctic Circle.
Cultivation is either in alpine house conditions using the basic compost described for *Ophrys* and *Orchis* with the addition of extra dolomite or limestone. It is also a candidate for a well-drained rockery with calcareous soils. Flowering, dependent on elevation, is from June to August.

Coeloglossum viride (L.) Hartmann

Below ground there are two deeply rooted, palmately lobed, ovoid tubers. Particularly vigorous plants might reach some 20 centimeters in height but usually grow no more than a few centimeters. At the base of the stalk there are two blunt-ended, elliptical leaves with two narrow, pointed ones carried higher on the stem. The inflorescence is greenish with irregularly twisted, faintly scented flowers. Petals and sepals curve to form a helmet over an extended, hanging lip which is obscurely three-lobed at its apex. Flowers on plants from montane regions are often suffused with a rich purplish brown which extends to the lip and produces flowers attractive in extreme close-up.

this species is most often seen in cultivation.

COELIOPSIS Reichb.f.
see-lee-OP-sis
Tribe: Cymbidieae
Subtribe: Stanhopeinae
Etymology: Gr. *opsis*, appearance, in reference to a resemblance to the orchid genus *Coelia*

Coeliopsis is a monotypic genus found in Costa Rica and Panama.
It is characterized by the egg-shaped, flattened pseudobulbs with three or four apical, thin, heavily veined leaves; the subpendent, capitate inflorescence produced from the base of the pseudobulb; the waxy, fleshy white flowers with an orange-brown spot in the throat; and the two hard, yellow pollinia attached to a short stipe connected to a round viscidium.

Coeliopsis hyacinthosma Reichb.f.

These plants grow as epiphytes in mid-elevation cloud forests from 500 to 1,200 meters. They should be cultivated in baskets or on plaques in intermediate conditions that provide space for the short, pendent inflorescences to emerge.

COELOGYNE Lindley
see-lo-GUY-nee or see-LODGE-eh-nee
Tribe: Coelogyneae
Subtribe: Coelogyninae
Etymology: Gr. *koilos*, hollow; *gyne*, female

More than 100 species of sympodial epiphytes comprise this genus distributed from India through China and Indonesia to the Fiji Islands. Pseudobulbs with one or two plicate leaves may be closely or distantly spaced on the rhizome. Racemes of often very showy flowers arise from the apex of the pseudobulb or simultaneously with new growths. The dorsal sepal is usually concave and nods above the labellum, which often has a series of lamellae

Coeliopsis hyacinthosma

Coelogyne cristata

running the length of the midlobe. There are four pollinia.

Species having tightly clustered pseudobulbs may be grown in pots; others should be mounted on slabs to minimize root disturbance. Provide bright light, but avoid direct sun which can easily burn the leaves. Intermediate- to warm-growing species include *C. asperata, C. mayeriana, C. massangeana,* and *C. pandurata.* These may be watered and fertilized uniformly throughout the year. Cool-growing species, however, such as *C. cristata, C. flaccida, C. fimbriata,* and *C. nitida* require a rest when the new growths mature and until new roots appear.

Coelogyne cristata Lindley

From the Himalayas, this cool-growing species quickly forms magnificent specimen plants. The flowers, which appear from February to April on pendent racemes, are pristine white with yellow-orange lamellae extending from the base to just below the apex of the midlobe of the labellum.

Coelogyne dayana Reichb.f.

From Thailand to Indonesia, this warm-growing species produces pendent racemes of long-lived, cream to beige flowers. The

Coelogyne fimbriata

labellum has erect lateral lobes and brown markings with white lamellae on the midlobe. It flowers principally from April through June.

Coelogyne fimbriata Lindley

From Nepal to China, *C. fimbriata* is a lithophyte with ovoid, two-leaved pseudobulbs. It produces yellow to light brown flowers variously through the year depending on locality. The midlobe of the labellum is finely fringed along the margin and has two yellow to brown lamellae. Grow under cool to intermediate temperatures.

Coelogyne mayeriana Reichb.f.

This rarely seen species from Malaysia and Indonesia has two-leaved pseudobulbs spaced very widely on a creeping rhizome. The green and purple-black flowers are very similar to those of *C. pandurata,* except that the labellum is not fiddle-shaped. Grow under warm conditions on long slabs to accommodate the long internodes of the rhizome.

Coelogyne massangeana Reichb.f.

This warm-growing species from Thailand to Indonesia produces striking pendent racemes of fragrant, yellow-and-brown flowers with several warty lamellae on the midlobe of the labellum. Flowers mainly in summer.

Coelogyne pandurata Lindley

This very distinctive species from Malaysia and Indonesia has widely spaced pseudobulbs on a creeping rhizome and green flowers with dark purple to blackish areas on the labellum. The midlobe of the labellum is pandurate (fiddle-shaped) and has two conspicuous lamellae with numerous warty papillae. Hybridized with *C. asperata,* it forms *C.* Burfordiense, which is sometimes seen in cultivation. Grow

Coelogyne dayana

Coelogyne massangeana

Coelogyne parishii

Coelogyne mayeriana

Coelogyne pandurata

Coelogyne speciosa

under warm conditions on slabs or in baskets with sphagnum moss.

Coelogyne parishii J. D. Hook.

Very similar in coloration to *C. mayeriana* and *C. pandurata*, this species is known only from Burma but may occur in Thailand also. Erect inflorescences of two to four flowers arise from the apex of the pseudobulbs from March through June. Provide warm to intermediate temperatures.

Coelogyne speciosa Lindley

A spring- to summer-flowering species from Indonesia, *C. speciosa* is distinguished by its yellow-green flowers with thin, recurved petals and a brown labellum with three dark brown lamellae (two long and one short). The closely spaced pseudobulbs make it suitable for pots or baskets under intermediate to warm conditions.

COMPARETTIA Poepp. & Endl.
kom-pah-RET-ee-ah
Tribe: Cymbidieae
Subtribe: Oncidiinae
Etymology: In honor of Andreo Comparetti, Italian botanist during the nineteenth century

This is a genus of ten species, found mostly in the Andes, with one species widespread in tropical America. The genus is characterized by the presence of small, terete, unifoliate pseudobulbs of a single internode without leaflike sheaths at the base; the inflorescence produced from the base of the pseudobulb; the sepals with an elongate, slender spur-sheath at the base; the spur of the lip double and inserted in the sepaline spur-sheath; and the two hard pollinia attached to a stipe connected to a viscidium.

The plants are epiphytes often found in guava trees at elevations from 800 to 1,500 meters. The species should be cultivated in intermediate conditions; they seem to do best when grown on pieces of wood or on plaques of tree-fern. They should be watered uniformly throughout the year.

Comparettia falcata Poepp. & Endl.

This species is widely distributed from Mexico to Peru, Venezuela, and the West Indies. It is recognized by the dark rose-red flowers with an elongate spur. The diameter of the flower reaches 2.5 centimeters but is usually smaller.

Comparettia speciosa Reichb.f.

Comparettia speciosa occurs from east-central Ecuador to northeast Peru. The large orange to orange-yellow flowers immediately distinguish it. The flowers reach a diameter of five centimeters in large forms. It is often found dangling by a single root.

COMPERIA C. Koch
com-pe-REE-a
Tribe: Orchideae
Subtribe: Orchidinae
Etymology: After Komper

Although there are superficial links with genera such as *Barlia*, *Himantoglossum*, and *Orchis*, this monotypic genus with its spectacular flowers clearly belongs on its own. Like the genera mentioned, *Comperia* has two tubers below ground, and the perianth segments form a hood; only the tips are free. It is the convex lip which is remarkable, with three lobes the ends of which are prolonged into four filiform processes; hidden by the galea, the other two petals also end in processes. Restricted

Comparettia falcata

in Europe to a few Greek islands (recorded from Kos, Lesbos, and Rhodes) and Russia (Crimea), its distribution is Middle Eastern: Turkey (southern Anatolia), northern Lebanon, northern Iraq, and Iran. Never more than local in Turkey, it is now becoming rare because of the collection of orchid tubers for a national beverage, salep, and for salep ice cream.

Comperia comperiana (Steven) Asch. & Graebn.

A tall species growing from 30–70 centimeters in height, it has three to six glossy green basal leaves and a stout stalk with a few flowers. The galea formed by sepals and petals is 1.5–2.0 centimeters long, but the extended length of the lip can be as much as four centimeters. As the flower opens from the bud it is fascinating to watch the processes, which untangle from tight coils to reveal a whitish lip marked with pink. Darker flowers are suffused with reddish brown, and the processes are brownish; in paler flowers they are green. In the wild *Comperia comperiana* grows in deciduous and coniferous woodland, on scrubby hills, always on limestone and often where conditions are dry. On the Greek islands

Comparettia speciosa

Comperia comperiana

flowers can appear from late April to early May: elsewhere, at higher elevations, June is the best time to see it. The most successful attempts to grow this species have employed alpine house conditions and a compost such as that recommended for *Ophrys* and *Orchis* plants.

CONSTANTIA Barb. Rodr.
kon-STANT-ee-ah
Tribe: Epidendreae
Subtribe: Laeliinae

Etymology: For Constança Barbosa Rodrigues, wife of the author

Four species are currently known, all endemic to southern Brazil. The small, tightly packed, roundish pseudobulbs typically bear two leaves. A single flower is produced in a short peduncle from the apex of the pseudobulb. This genus was considered a synonym of *Sophronitis* for some time because of similarities in flower morphology. *Constantia* species, however, are distinguished by the much smaller size of the plants and the bifoliate pseudobulbs. All species have eight pollinia.

Constantia species are difficult to cultivate, due perhaps to their specialized habitat (branches of *Vellozia* bushes). Best results have been obtained when plants are grown on their original substrate and provided with moderate temperatures and humidity under full sunlight. Much experimentation with growing media and domestication is needed before these plants can be successfully cultivated.

Constantia cipoënsis Campos Porto & Brade

This delightful miniature, endemic to Serra do Cipó, Minas Gerais, Brazil, blooms in cultivation from September to December. Flowers are creamy white with a yellow spot at the base of the labellum.

Constantia cipoënsis

CORYANTHES Hook.
ko-ree-AN-theez
Tribe: Cymbidieae
Subtribe: Stanhopeinae
Etymology: Gr. *korys*, helmet; *anthos*, flower; in reference to the helmet-like apical portion of the lip

Coryanthes is a genus of 30 species distributed throughout lowland tropical America. It has large, ribbed pseudobulbs with two or three thin, heavily veined leaves. Inflorescences are produced from the base of the pseudobulb. The lip forms a bucket with two water "faucets" dripping from the base of the column. Two hard pollinia are attached to a broad stipe connected to a viscidium.

The plants grow as epiphytes in ant nests in very wet forest from sea level to 800 meters elevation. The species are very specifically

Coryanthes elegantium

Coryanthes leucocorys

Coryanthes bicalcarata

pollinated by male euglossine bees that are attracted to the powerful fragrances produced by the flowers. The bees scratch around the hypochile and fall into the water-filled bucket. The only exit is a tunnel from the apex of the lip that passes under the stigma and anther of the flower, depositing pollinia on the back of the wet bee.

The species should be cultivated under intermediate to warm conditions in baskets that permit the inflorescences to hang. A very acid medium is required with copious fertilizer to match the ant nest conditions in which the plants grow. Under natural conditions the plants reach flowering age in twelve to eighteen months.

Coryanthes bicalcarata Schltr.

This species occurs in northeastern Peru near Moyobamba. The flowers are usually cream with flecks of red scattered throughout.

Coryanthes elegantium Linden & Reichb.f.

Coryanthes elegantium occurs in western Ecuador and Colombia. It is characterized by the hypochile being either flat or convex.

The flower color varies from light yellow-brown to dark red-brown and has dark red-brown flecks.

Coryanthes leucocorys Rolfe

This species is known from northeastern Peru and southeastern Ecuador. The very large hypochile is white and extends to the back of the red epichile. The flowers smell strongly of mint.

Coryanthes macrantha (Hook.) Hook.

This species is known from Trinidad and around Iquitos in northeastern Peru. The flowers from the two populations are very similar but may represent distinct species. The sepals and petals are yellow or red-brown and the lip is light red-brown or red. All the segments are speckled with red. The hypochile is round while the epichile has four or five obvious, shelflike plates that extend outward.

Coryanthes speciosa (Hook.) Hook.

This species occurs in Central America, the West Indies, and northeastern South America. Recently several valid species have been recognized that were formerly considered as part of this "variable" species. The flowers are yellow with small flecks of red-brown on the hypochile and mesochile. The hypochile is hood-shaped and deeper than wide. The mesochile is rodlike and bent outward at the midpoint.

Coryanthes macrantha

CORYBAS Salisb.
KOR-ee-bus
Tribe: Diurideae
Subtribe: Acianthinae
Etymology: A Corybant or dancing priest of the goddess Cybele in Phrygia.

About one hundred species of these tiny, fascinating orchids are currently known, ranging from northern India, southern China, Malaysia, Polynesia, various Pacific Islands, New Zealand, New Guinea, and Australia. There is even a single species on Macquarie Island — the most southerly occurring orchid in the world. All species are deciduous terrestrials with tiny pseudobulbs and unusual small flowers which are dominated by the dorsal sepal and labellum. Pollination is achieved by tiny gnats.
Grown mainly by specialist terrestrial growers. Pot in a well-drained soil mix containing wood shavings and leaf litter. Keep moist when in active growth (autumn

Corybas aconitiflorus

Coryanthes speciosa

Corybas pruinosus

sheltered forests of New South Wales, Australia, usually grows in small colonies under bracken fern and shrubs. The ground-hugging leaves are green on both surfaces. Between mid-autumn and midwinter, small gray-and-reddish purple flowers are borne on some plants. These flowers have a prominent hooded dorsal sepal and coarse, spreading teeth on the margins of the labellum.

CRYPTOCENTRUM Benth.
krip-toe-SEN-trum
Tribe: Maxillarieae
Subtribe: Maxillariinae
Etymology: Gr. *kryptos*, hidden; *kentron*, spur

Ten to fourteen species are currently known in tropical America, ranging from Costa Rica to Peru. Plants, typically without pseudobulbs, vary from miniature tufts of cylindrical leaves less than five centimeters tall to large rosettes over 25 centimeters tall. A basal scape, covered with several bracts, bears a single star-shaped, green, yellowish green, or greenish tan flower; the lateral sepals form a conspicuous spur that is usually covered by the uppermost, rather large bract of the scape. All species have four pollinia.

Most species grow well mounted on tree-fern slabs or in small clay pots filled with osmunda or equal proportions of shredded tree-fern fiber and sphagnum moss. Provide moderate shade and constant humidity.

to spring), dry out as plants die down, and repot over summer. The small tuberoids are easily overlooked at repotting time. Use fertilizers sparingly.

Corybas aconitiflorus Salisb.

An attractive species from Australia which is the type of the genus. It grows in colonies in sheltered situations, and the ground-hugging heart-shaped leaves are purplish beneath. Helmet-shaped pink to purplish flowers are produced on some plants between early spring and midwinter.

Corybas fimbriatus (R. Br.) Reichb.f.

This species has heart-shaped to orbicular leaves which are green on the upper surface and sparkling silvery beneath. A native of eastern Australia, it forms large colonies in protected situations under shrubs. The dark reddish flowers, borne between mid-autumn and late winter have prominent marginal teeth in a coarse fringe.

Corybas pruinosus (Cunn.) Reichb.f.

This vigorous species, found in moist

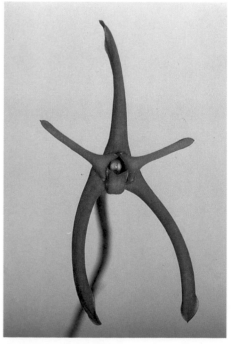

Cryptocentrum gracillimum

Corybas fimbriatus

Cryptopus elatus

CRYPTOSTYLIS R. Br.
crip-toe-STY-lus
Tribe: Cranichideae
Subtribe: Cryptostylidinae
Etymology: Gr. *cryptos*, hidden; *stylos*, style or column

About 20 species are currently known, distributed from southeast Asia, Taiwan, Malaysia, various islands of the Pacific region to Australia and New Zealand. Except for *C. hunteriana*, which is a leafless saprophyte, all have prominent, leathery leaves. The spreading roots are fleshy and

Cryptocentrum gracillimum
Ames & C. Schweinf.

This inconspicuous species, found in Costa Rica and Panama, produces flowers year round, but flowering peaks between October and December. The scapes are shorter than the leaves, bearing a typically dull olive-green flower.

CRYPTOPUS Lindley
KRIP-toe-pus
Tribe: Vandeae
Subtribe: Angraecinae
Etymology: Gr. *kryptos*, hidden; *pous*, foot

Two species of *Cryptopus* are known in Madagascar and a third in Reunion and Mauritius. They are all epiphytic plants with slender branching stems and long roots which are often curved and twisted. Both the labellum and the petals of the white

flowers are deeply lobed at the apex, giving them an attractive and quite distinctive appearance. They grow in humid forests and are usually lightly attached to the branches or trunks of trees, the stems growing upright with apparently very little support.

Plants need deep shade and very humid conditions but plenty of fresh air. They do best in intermediate temperatures where the moisture supply is constant.

Cryptopus elatus Lindley

This attractive species from Mauritius and Reunion has long inflorescences up to 60 centimeters long and bearing many flowers. The petals are four-lobed at the apex, and the lip is also four-lobed. In *C. paniculatus* from Madagascar the inflorescence is a panicle, and the lip is three-lobed. *Cryptopus brachiatus* from Madagascar has a shorter, simple inflorescence, and the petals are T-shaped.

Cryptostylis subulata

do not develop into tuberoids. The flowers are dominated by a large, colorful labellum which may be variously adorned by patterns of lines, false glands or hairs. The Australian species of this genus are pollinated by male ichneumonid wasps which attempt to mate with the flower.

Pot in a well-drained soil mix containing wood shavings and leaf mold. Keep plants evenly moist throughout the year and water regularly over spring and summer. Resents disturbance and should be left alone until repotting becomes absolutely necessary. Flower stems require staking. Liquid fertilizers are beneficial.

Cryptostylis subulata (Labill). Reichb.f.

A common species from eastern Australia which grows in a range of habitats including moist to wet soils. Tall racemes are produced from late winter to midautumn. Flowers are reddish to reddish brown. The labellum has a prominent lobed, dark purple callus near the apex.

Cycnoches chlorochilon

CUITLAUZINA La Llave & Lex.
kweet-law-ZEE-nah
Tribe: Cymbidieae
Subtribe: Oncidiinae
Etymology: In honor of Cuitlahuatzin, Aztec horticulturist and Governor of Iztapalpo

This is a monotypic genus from western Mexico. The genus is characterized by the large, flattened pseudobulbs with two apical, leathery leaves; the elongate, pendent inflorescence produced from the base of the developing pseudobulb of the new growth; the highly fragrant, white or pinkish white flowers with a kidney-shaped lip without a callus; and the two hard pollinia attached to a stipe and a round visicidium.

The plants are epiphytic in trees at intermediate elevations. This species should be cultivated in baskets that permit the pendent inflorescences to hang downward. The plants can be grown under intermediate conditions but benefit from cool night temperatures and a rest period after the growths are completed.

Cuitlauzina pendula La Llave & Lexarza

The inflorescences are produced from inside the newly developing growths and hang downward with the weight of the flowers. The flowers are waxy, very fragrant, and reach five centimeters in diameter. The sepals and petals are usually white or pale pink while the lip is bright pink with a yellow claw at the base. The lip is without a callus and is kidney-shaped.

CYCNOCHES Lindley
Sik-NOE-keez
Tribe: Cymbidieae
Subtribe: Catasetinae
Etymology: Gr. *kyknos*, swan; *auchen*, neck; in reference to the slender, arched column of the male flower

Cycnoches is a genus of 23 species distributed throughout much of tropical America. The genus is characterized by the fleshy pseudobulbs of several internodes with thin, heavily veined, deciduous leaves; the inflorescence produced from the apical nodes; and the unisexual flowers. The three or four female flowers are very fleshy, and the column is short and thick with a club-shaped apex with three broad hooks. The five to 30 male flowers are thinner in substance with the column much longer and more slender, and with an apparatus for throwing the pollinarium onto the pollinator. The two hard, round pollinia are attached to an elongate stipe connected to a round viscidium.

These are epiphytic plants from lowland moist or wet forest from sea level to 600 meters. Specific kinds of male euglossine bees are attracted to the powerful fragrances

Cuitlauzina pendula

Cycnoches aureum

Cycnoches haagii

Cycnoches egertonianum

Cycnoches loddigesii

Cycnoches ventricosum

produced from the lip of the flower. While visiting the male flowers the pollinia are thrown onto the end of the abdomen of the bee and are stripped by the hooks of the column of the female flower on subsequent visits.

The plants should be cultivated under warm to intermediate conditions with extensive water and fertilizer applications during active growth followed by a relatively dry resting period.

Cycnoches aureum Lindley & Paxt.

This species occurs in Costa Rica and Panama. It is distinguished by the medium-sized (to eight centimeters in diameter), yellow, male flowers often flecked with red-

brown, and the lip having marginal processes that are forked at the apex.

Cycnoches chlorochilon Klotzsch

Cycnoches chlorochilon occurs in southeastern Panama, Colombia, and Venezuela. It has long and persistently been confused with C. warscewiczii. Both of them are sometimes placed as varieties of C. ventricosum but are easily distinguished. Cycnoches chlorochilon has male flowers that are longer than broad, reach fifteen centimeters in diameter, and lack a claw at the base of the lip.

Cycnoches egertonianum Batem.

Cycnoches egertonianum is distributed from

Mexico to Costa Rica. The male flowers are small, reaching five centimeters in diameter, but many flowers are produced on the pendulous inflorescence. The margin of the lip of the male flowers is provided with finger-like projections that are slightly lobed at the apex. The male flowers are usually wine-red but may be green with wine-red spots.

Cycnoches haagii Barb. Rodr.

This species is found from Venezuela and the Guianas, through Colombia, Ecuador, and Peru to Bolivia and Brazil. The male and female flowers are similar, differing only in the length of the column. The margin of the lip does not have projections in the male flowers and the flowers are about six centimeters in diameter. The lip is white to pink with small red-brown spots.

Cycnoches loddigesii Lindley

Cycnoches loddigesii occurs in Colombia, Venezuela, and the Guianas and extends into Brazil. The male flowers of this species are large, reaching twelve centimeters in diameter, and the sepals are brown with dark red-brown spots. The petals are light brown, and the blade of the lip is white, with a large, flattened claw at the base.

Cycnoches ventricosum Batem.

Cycnoches ventricosum occurs from Mexico to northern Costa Rica. The male flowers reach nine centimeters in diameter. The species is distinguished from *C. chlorochilon* and *C. warscewiczii* by the presence of an elongate claw at the base of the lip, and the petals held backwards toward the ovary.

Cycnoches warscewiczii Reichb.f.

Cycnoches warscewiczii occurs from central Costa Rica to Central Panama. The male flowers reach ten centimeters in diameter. The species is distinguished from *C. chlorochilon* and *C. ventricosum* by the intermediate length of the claw of the lip and the flatly held petals. The male flowers have floral segments of equal length and are broad so that the flower is well balanced. This is the most attractive of the species and is commonly labelled as *C. chlorochilon* in collections as well as misidentified in even the most modern of literature.

CYMBIDIELLA Rolfe
sim-bid-ee-EL-ah
Tribe: Cymbidieae
Subtribe: Cyrtopodiinae
Etymology: Diminutive of *Cymbidium* in which the species were once classified

There are three species of this attractive

Cycnoches warscewiczii

genus which is confined to Madagascar. They all have pseudobulbs bearing many leaves, arranged close together or distantly along a basal rhizome. The inflorescence arises from the base of the pseudobulb and bears many flowers which are yellowish green with a differently colored lip. The plants of two of the species somewhat resemble those of the genus *Cymbidium* with which they were once classified. Each species needs rather different treatment in cultivation depending on its growth habit in the wild (see below), but all need warm, humid conditions with good light.

Cymbidiella pardalina (Reichb.f.) Garay

This vigorous species is an epiphyte which is nearly always associated in the wild with the fern, *Platycerium madagascariense*. It has robust inflorescences with large, pale green bracts, and its fleshy flowers are very showy. The four-lobed lip is bright red with black markings. *Cymbidiella flabellata* has rather similar but smaller flowers. It is a terrestrial plant of heathland with a long rhizome growing over sphagnum moss. *Cymbidiella falcigera* grows on the trunks

of *Raphia* palms and has the largest pseudobulbs bearing many leaves. Its flowers are pale green, and the side lobes of the green lip are strikingly marked with purplish black.

CYMBIDIUM Sw.
sim-BID-ee-um
Tribe: Cymbidieae
Subtribe: Cyrtopodiinae
Etymology: Gr. *kymbos*, boat-shaped cup

Cymbidium is a genus of 44 species distributed throughout the old world tropics. Species may be epiphytic, lithophytic, terrestrial, and occasionally saprophytic. Cymbidiums are easily recognized by their prominent pseudobulbs covered by numerous linear leaves and fleshy white roots. The frequently showy flowers bear three-lobed lips with a central, ridged callus. All species have two notched pollinia.

Large-flowered hybrids, derived primarily from Indian and Chinese species, are an important component of the orchid cut-flower trade. Better able to withstand shipping and storage stress, cymbidiums have largely replaced cattleyas as corsage orchids. Large-flowered species and hybrids are strongly winter–spring flowering.

All cymbidiums are vigorous growers. When in growth, the plants should be given copious water and fertilizer. All species prefer bright light to full sun and intermediate temperatures when in growth. A variety of composts may be used, but some moisture-retaining components should be included to maximize water availability during active growth.

Cymbidiums may be roughly divided into

Cymbidiella pardalina

Cymbidium eburneum

Cymbidium insigne

three basic horticultural groups: (1) Large-flowered species (and hybrids) from the Himalayas and China require a pronounced chilling period in order to initiate flower spikes. Following their growth cycle fertilizer should be withheld, watering reduced, and the plants should be kept with a maximum night temperature of 12°C. Because of their large plant size, large-flowered species are normally grown in large pots or tubs. (2) Small-flowered terrestrial species from the Himalayas, China, and Japan do not require a substantial chilling period to initiate flowers and can be maintained at cool to intermediate temperatures year round. Bearing upright inflorescences, these species are best grown in pots. (3) Small-flowered tropical species should be kept continuously warm, as they prefer no chilling period. The tropical species mostly produce pendent inflorescences and should be grown in baskets or in hanging pots.

Cymbidium canaliculatum R. Br.

This species is native to tropical Australia. It is a warm-growing epiphytic species, producing variably colored flowers, from greenish yellow with dark red-brown spots to solid dark maroon. The dark-flowered form is sometimes known as var. *sparkesii*. The small flowers are borne on long, floriferous, arching to horizontal inflorescences.

Cymbidium dayanum Reichb.f.

Cymbidium dayanum is widely distributed from northeast India and China through Indochina to Sumatra, Borneo, and the Philippines. A warm-growing epiphytic species, it bears few-flowered, arching

Cymbidium finlaysonianum

inflorescences shorter than the leaves. The flowers are white with a central reddish brown stripe down the center of each segment and a reddish lip.

Cymbidium devonianum Paxton

The species is native from Nepal and northeast India to Thailand. Numerous flowers are produced on pendent inflorescences in late spring. The flowers are light brown with a reddish lip and have a fuller shape than most pendent species. The leaves are proportionately wide as in *C. lancifolium* and *C. tigrinum*. A lithophytic and epiphytic species, *Cymbidium*

devonianum prefers intermediate to cool temperatures.

Cymbidium eburneum Lindley

Cymbidium eburneum is native to Nepal, northeast India, northern Burma, and southwest China. The species is unusual because it bears solitary flowers. The large, pure white flowers with a bright yellow throat are similar to those of *C. insigne*. It is a cool-growing epiphyte that flowers in midwinter.

Cymbidium ensifolium (L.) Sw.

This species has one of the widest ranges in

Cymbidium lowianum

Cymbidium tigrinum

the genus and is recorded throughout tropical Asia from Sri Lanka and southern India to New Guinea and the Philippines. A terrestrial species, it bears erect inflorescences with flowers that range from clear greenish white to greenish yellow striped with brown.

Cymbidium erythrostylum Rolfe

Cymbidium erythrostylum is endemic to Vietnam. A terrestrial, lithophytic or epiphytic plant, it produces erect, few-flowered inflorescences. The large, pure white flowers are contrasted with the bright yellow lip striped with red. An unusual feature of the flower is the forward projection of the petals, yielding an *Iris*-like appearance.

Cymbidium finlaysonianum Lindley

The species is native from Indochina through Indonesia as far as Sulawesi and north to the Philippines. A warm-growing epiphytic species, it produces long, pendent inflorescences in the summer. The numerous small flowers are greenish yellow suffused with variable amounts of brown. The lip is white with a dark reddish brown base.

Cymbidium floribundum Lindley

Cymbidium floribundum is native to southern China and Taiwan. A lithophytic or epiphytic species, it produces an arching inflorescence with numerous small flowers. Flower color is variable from green to dark brown, the lip white or marked with bright rose spots. The species flowers in the fall and periodically throughout the year. This species has long been known in horticulture as *C. pumilum*. Under that name it has been used to create a class of hybrids known as "miniature" cymbidiums produced by crossing *Cymbidium floribundum* with standard large-flowered species and hybrids.

Cymbidium goeringii (Reichb.f.) Reichb.f.

Cymbidium goeringii is native from northwest India through China and Taiwan to Japan and Korea. The species is sometimes found under the name *C. virens.* A small-growing terrestrial plant, the species is unusual for producing solitary flowers on short scapes amid the leaves. The flowers are typically green with white lips marked with a few purple spots. *Cymbidium goeringii* is one of the classic orchids of Chinese and Japanese horticulture and art.

Cymbidium insigne Rolfe

The species is native to northern Thailand, Vietnam, and Hainan, China. A large, cool-growing terrestrial species, it produces erect inflorescences that bear several large white flowers with purple stripes and spotting on the lip. This extremely showy species is one of the parents of most modern hybrids.

Cymbidium lowianum (Reichb.f.) Reichb.f.

Native to Burma, southwest China, and northern Thailand, this is a large, cool-growing lithophytic or epiphytic species. Long, arching inflorescences bear numerous large green to pale brown flowers with white to yellow lips. The typical variety has a prominent dark red blotch at the tip of the lip. A concolor green form is known. *Cymbidium lowianum* is one of the parents of modern hybrids.

Cymbidium madidum Lindley

Cymbidium madidum is endemic to eastern Australia. A warm-growing epiphytic species, it is noted for its extremely leathery leaves. Numerous waxy yellow flowers with red-marked lips are produced on long pendent inflorescences during the winter. The petals are characteristically parallel and project forward. The species is closely related to *C. chloranthum*, which has an erect inflorescence, and to *C. suave*, which lacks a defined pseudobulb.

Cymbidium parishii Reichb.f.

Endemic to Burma, this is a rare, cool-growing epiphytic species. The inflorescences are two- to three-flowered and much shorter than the leaves. The pure white flowers with lips marked yellow and purple are reminiscent of *C. insigne.*

Cymbidium tigrinum Parish ex J. D. Hook.

Native to northeast India and Burma, *C. tigrinum* is one of the smallest species in the genus. The flowers, produced on a few-flowered arching raceme, are greenish brown with a stark white lip punctuated with short, purple, horizontal barring. Flowers are produced in late spring. The leaves are proportionately broad as in *C. devonianum* and *C. lancifolium.*

Cymbidium tracyanum L. Castle

Cymbidium tracyanum is native from southwest China to northern Thailand. A large, cool-growing epiphytic or lithophytic species, it produces long, arching racemes and numerous flowers. The flowers are greenish yellow with variable dark brown markings, appearing almost solid brown in some individuals. The lip is white with brown spotting and striping. This showy species is in the parentage of many modern hybrids.

CYNORKIS Thouars
sin-OR-kiss
Tribe: Orchideae
Subtribe: Habenariinae
Etymology: Gr. *kynos*, dog; *orchis*, testicle

This is a genus of more than 100 species. Most occur in Madagascar and the adjacent islands of the western Indian Ocean, but about 20 are found in Africa. They may be terrestrial or epiphytic and nearly always grow so that the tubers are embedded in moss. The genus is related to *Habenaria* but differs in having lilac, white or pink flowers, the outer surfaces of which are more or less densely covered with pin-shaped glandular hairs. These hairs are also usually present on the peduncle. The stigmatic processes are usually adnate to the side lobes of the column, and the rostellum is four- or five-lobed.

Plants are easily maintained in a well-drained moist compost in shallow pans. Temperatures should be chosen to suit individual species.

Cynorkis compacta (Reichb.f.) Rolfe

This is a terrestrial species known only from a few localities in Natal, South Africa, where it grows among rocks. There is a solitary leaf in spring, in the axil of which the inflorescence arises. The flowers are white with a few purplish spots. *Cynorkis kassneriana*, which has lilac flowers with

Cynorkis fastigiata

Cynorkis compacta

darker spots, is the only other species in South Africa and is also distributed throughout the forested areas as far north as Kenya.

Cynorkis fastigiata Thouars

This species occurs in Madagascar and the Comoro Islands. It is a robust grower with a single leaf and tall inflorescence. The flowers are lilac with a pale yellow four-lobed lip. In many greenhouses this species has become a weed as the fruits ripen and shed their seeds very rapidly.

CYPRIPEDIUM L.
sip-re-PEE-dee-um
Subfamily: Cypripedioideae
Etymology: Gr. *Kypris*, Aphrodite; *pedilon*, shoe

The generic name refers directly to the inflated, cloglike lip which is the hallmark of a genus admired by botanists and sought after by collectors, often to the point of destruction. In Britain where *C. calceolus* once grew in northern woods, collecting has reduced the population to one or two wild plants. Chinese species found in the last decade have been rendered extinct in the wild within two years of discovery, and Italian hotels have decorated tables with bunches of blooms. Such is the thoughtlessness of those who collect and those who provide the market for their spoils.

There are around 50 species mainly distributed through the North Temperate regions of North America, Europe, and Asia to Japan and south into Mexico.

Members of the genus have creeping rhizomes and stems with two to four leaves. Flowers tend to be solitary, more unusually two or three in number. Perianth segments are spreading; the dorsal sepal is erect and ranges from ovate to elliptical, while the laterals are fused for most of their length and point downward behind the lip. Petals are thong- or strap-like, often with a spiral twist. The lip is large, concave, and saccate with inrolled margins to produce the inflated structure which protects the reproductive organs. These latter comprise a short column and three stamens. Two of these are fertile; the third is sterile and forms a large petalloid staminode which surmounts the column.

Most *Cypripedium* species are protected within the country of origin, and thus comparatively few are seen openly advertised by orchid growers. A few have been successfully propagated both vegetatively and from seed and are beginning to appear commercially in increasing numbers.

Much has been published on the cultivation of these plants. To date there are three

Cypripedium acaule

reliable methods of cultivation, but inevitably enthusiasts will recommend innumerable variations on the basic theme:
1. Using a slightly acid to neutral loam, Case (1987) has had great success with many of the North American species.
2. The "Holman Bog": R. T. Holman (1976) and a further modified form by C. E. Whitlow (1977). In structure, this is a trench some 200 millimeters deep lined with a polyethylene sheet (providing for a waterlogged medium). Above stands a wooden frame about 150 millimeters deep. The liner is attached halfway up this, allowing the top 75 millimeters to drain into the liner or the surrounding soil. The trench is filled with soil (free of fertilizers) mixed with about 25 percent sphagnum peat to within 75 millimeters of the top of the frame. Holman topped this with a layer of black lake-bottom peat. Cribb and Bailes (1989) suggest that this is not critical and that the potting mix suggested above for *Cephalanthera* could be used just as well. Whitlow modified the method, mainly by lowering the zone of saturation from 150 to 250 millimeters below the surface by experimenting with the depth of the plastic liner. He also used a general fertilizer at one-tenth its recommended strength and conditions of open shade. A bog with garden soil and peat to provide a slightly acid/neutral pH suited *C. calceolus, C. calceolus* var. *parviflorum, C. candidum, C. macranthum, C. reginae,* and *C. speciosum.* By creating more acidic conditions using pine duff and quartzite grit, he grew *C. arietinum, C. cordigerum, C. formosanum* and *C. guttatum.*
3. Pot-growing using the woodland terrestrial mix mentioned for *Cephalanthera.*

Cypripedium arietinum

Cypripedium acaule Aiton

Popularly known as the moccasin flower, this is the most common of the slipper orchids in North America and enjoys a distribution in many north/northeastern and eastern seaboard states into eastern and central Canada. It is widespread and locally common. It often grows in layers of pine needles in the higher and drier parts of coniferous woods, but it also occurs in some bog sites. The base of the flower-stalk is virtually cupped, at ground level, by two substantial elliptic leaves. A large, inflated, rose-purple pouch dominates the flower. The lip is distinctly pleated in front, and the petals and sepals are maroon. Occasionally, a white-lipped form is found in the wild.

Cypripedium arietinum R. Br.

Three to four elliptic, pleated, spreading leaves grow on the middle part of the stem of this softly pubescent species which grows to around 30 centimeters high. Its common name, ram's-head slipper orchid, derives from the side view of the flower which is solitary and small (about 3–4 centimeters) with distinctive deflexed lateral sepals. The lip is a deeply cleft, heavily veined pink pouch which comes to a reflexed conical point at its base. It flowers from May to June, usually in sphagnum bogs with *Thuja,* but also in shady places on thin, drier soils over limestone or calcium-rich sand. Although cited as "rare" it can be locally abundant. The distribution extends from Manitoba, southwest Quebec, locally to Minnesota, Michigan, New York, and Massachusetts.

Cypripedium calceolus

Cypripedium calceolus L.

Although *Cypripedium calceolus* is the most widespread member of the genus, with a range that extends throughout Europe and temperate Asia to North America, its fame throughout most of Europe is due to its being by far the largest and showiest of all orchid species found there. Its obvious beauty and size has contributed in no small way to its downfall through collecting. Although nearly extinct in Britain, it is now carefully protected on the European mainland and survives in large numbers on reserves in Italy, France, Germany, and Switzerland. Flowers of the typical variety have dark maroon petals and sepals (6–9 centimeters long) and bright yellow lips. They are usually carried singly (more rarely two or three) on stems 15–20 centimeters tall with three or four elliptic or ovate, sparsely pubescent leaves. The staminode is yellow but spotted with red down each side. Var. *pubescens* differs in having one or two rather larger flowers with long greenish or pale brown perianth segments, a yellow unspotted staminode and densely pubescent leaves (capable of causing irritation in sensitive skin). Flowering until August, it is locally common in Canada and the eastern United States, but rarer in the west.

Cypripedium californicum

Cypripedium californicum A. Gray

In the wild this species is a distinctly rare native of the mountains of northern California and southern Oregon. Established plants in favorable conditions (in coniferous forests by rocky streams and springs) can comprise clumps of numerous flowering stems reaching a meter or so in height. From four to ten flowers are borne on stems with five to ten pleated leaves. Flowers are small (up to 3.5 centimeters) but are very attractive because of the pure white, almost globular lip framed by hairy, yellow-green sepals and petals. In cultivation in temperate climates it has proved to be surprisingly hardy and can be established in a raised peat bed with plenty of added leaf mold and grit for drainage.

Cypripedium irapeanum La Llave & Lex.

A widespread species in the Sierras of southern Mexico and Guatemala, it grows in grassy patches and mixed pine and oak forests at 1,500–3,200 meter elevations. The plant reaches up to 1 m in height and produces two to six flowers, 6–13 centimeters across in July to August. To survive it is dependent on mycorrhizal fungi to the extent that cultivation outside its natural habitat has proven impossible unless a very large amount of soil is taken with the plant and cultivated under conditions identical to those in nature.

Cypripedium japonicum Thunb.

A pair of elegantly pleated, fan-shaped leaves borne on a slender pubescent stalk enables this species and its variety *formosanum* to be identified even in the absence of flowers. Many enthusiasts consider the flowers to be the finest in the genus, closely rivaled by *C. reginae*. They can be ten centimeters across. Sepals and petals are pale green with a light pink spotting near the base. The large lip is mottled with pink and white with a distinctive corrugated apical margin. In the wild this species can form large colonies growing in deep leaf litter in lightly shaded woods. It can be successfully pot-cultivated, using the "woodland" mix, in lightly shaded but frost-free conditions.

Cypripedium macranthum Sw.

The name is an apt description of the size of the flowers, often eight centimeters or more across. The typical variety is a striking plant, robust in form, around 30–45 centimeters tall with broad, pleated, downy leaves and flowers with deep purple-magenta lips. Broad sepals and petals are heavily veined in deep purple, and the lip itself can have a "chequered" appearance. In the wild it favors light stony soils in woodland clearings or margins in mountain regions to well over 3,000 meters. Its distribution is wide, from Japan through China to Russia and just within Europe at the western end of its range. Plants are hardy in cultivation and can be readily established in a shady peat bed to which plenty of leaf mold has been added, again with grit for drainage. Several color varieties appear in cultivation, from a white "albino" to the light pink var. *speciosum*.

Cypripedium reginae Walt.

While certainly the finest of the North American species, *Cypripedium reginae* could only have *C. japonicum* as a serious

Cypripedium macranthum

contender for the prize of finest in the genus. Well-established plants can produce sizeable clumps with numerous flowering stems from 30 to 100 centimeters tall, each carrying from one to four flowers. The large flowers have white sepals and petals to set off a pink lip and a staminode flushed with yellow and spotted red. Bog margins and an association with the fern *Osmunda regalis* offer a typical wild habitat. Its distribution is wide in northern and eastern North America across the Great Lakes. A cool shady site with a compost of peat, leaf mold and loam mixed with gritty sand provides the setting for efforts to establish this plant in the garden. Flowers appear in June and early July.

CYRTOPODIUM R. Br.
ser-toe-POH-dee-um
Tribe: Cymbidieae
Subtribe: Cyrtopodiinae
Etymology: Gr. *kyrtos*, curved; *podion*, little foot

Some 30 species are currently known, occurring in Florida, the West Indies, Central America, and South America to

Cypripedium irapeanum

Cyrtopodium punctatum

Cyrtopodium andersonii

Argentina and Bolivia. Cigar-shaped, fleshy pseudobulbs bear eight to 20 leaves. Racemes or panicles of many yellow flowers, often spotted maroon, arise from the base of the developing new shoot. All species have two juxtaposed pollinia. Most species thrive in large, well-drained clay pots packed with a mixture of rich organic soil, shredded osmunda, and chopped tree-fern fiber in equal proportions. Follow watering and fertilizing instructions for *Catasetum*. Plants will do best if kept in bright sunlight during periods of active growth provided that good ventilation is available to avoid burning of the foliage.

Cyrtopodium andersonii (Lamb. ex Andrews) R. Br.

This showy species, found in the West Indies, Venezuela, the Guianas, and Brazil, produces many-flowered panicles from January to June. Flowers are greenish yellow, the lip bright yellow with a reddish, inconspicuous basal callus.

Cyrtopodium punctatum (L.) Lindley

Another showy species, found in Florida, Cuba, and northern South America, produces many-flowered panicles from January to June. Flowers are greenish yellow with maroon spots throughout and warts along the margin of the lip. This species, usually an epiphyte, is often confused with *C. paniculatum*, a terrestrial species found in Central and South America.

CYRTORCHIS Schltr.
sert-OR-kiss
Tribe: Vandeae
Subtribe: Aerangidinae
Etymology: Gr. *kyrtos*, swelling or curve; *orchis*, orchid

About fifteen species of this monopodial epiphyte occur throughout Africa, some widespread, others with a rather narrow range. They all have white flowers which are easily recognized by their regular starry shape and by the fact that they turn orange as they fade. The sepals, petals, and lip are all similar and curve back on themselves. They are borne on horizontal inflorescences with large pale green bracts which turn black as the flowers mature.
The plants are easy to maintain in

cultivation and are best grown in baskets or mounted on cork oak bark so that drainage is very good. They may produce copious roots. All the species need bright light to flower well.

Cyrtorchis arcuata (Lindley) Schltr.

This is the most widespread species, occurring in forests and woodland throughout Africa. Several different subspecies are recognized in different parts of its range, the largest of them, ssp. *whytei*, is found in Malawi. It is easily cultivated under any greenhouse conditions or in shade houses which are frost-free.

CYRTOSTYLIS R. Br.
sert-oh-STY-lis
Tribe: Diuridae
Subtribe: Caladeniinae
Etymology: Gr. *cyrtos*, curve; *stylos*, style or column

About five species of relatively small, dull-colored orchids restricted to Australia and New Zealand. They are deciduous

Cyrtorchis arcuata

Cyrtostylis robusta

terrestrials which have small subterranean tuberoids and a solitary oblong to heart-shaped ground-hugging leaf. Slender stiff racemes carry relatively few pinkish or greenish flowers, each with a relatively large labellum projecting like a landing platform and narrow, relatively inconspicuous sepals and petals. All species have four separate pollinia. Pollination is by tiny gnats.
Pot in a well-drained soil mix containing wood shavings. Repot over summer when dormant and keep dry until growth begins in autumn. Keep moist when plants are in active growth (autumn to spring) and dry out as plants die down. Use fertilizers sparingly.

Cyrtostylis robusta D. Jones & M. Clements

A slender, vigorous species from southern Australia which grows in dense colonies under shrubs. The attractive bright green leaf, which grows to six centimeters x four centimeters, appears first and later supports a slender, wiry raceme which bears up to seven small, pinkish to reddish flowers. Grows readily in a pot and reproduces freely.

Dactylorhiza elata

Dactylorhiza maculata

DACTYLORHIZA Necker ex Nevski
dak-til-o-RISE-a
Tribe: Orchideae
Subtribe: Orchidinae
Etymology: Gr. *dactylos*, finger; *rhiza*, root

The curious generic name refers to the finger-lobing of the tubers. Taxonomically this is a very confusing genus. Distinctions between so-called species are blurred, and they hybridize readily. Changing habitat conditions can favor the survival of a hybrid swarm rather than either parent, adding further problems to identification.
The genus is distributed throughout Europe, into the Middle East, through temperate Asia with a single North American species, *D. aristata*. Currently at least 33 species are recognized in Europe and the Middle East alone.

Dactylorhiza elata (Poiret) Soó

Tall magenta spikes of this species present an imposing sight in wet flushes and ditches in the limestone regions of France's Massif Central. Leaves are usually unspotted and held nearly erect. The raceme is dense with numerous magenta flowers arranged cylindrically. Lateral sepals spread (10–13 millimeters in length). The lip ranges from entire to three-lobed with side-lobes deflexed to give the lip a folded appearance. The spur is cylindrical or slightly conical and about as long as the ovary. Plants can be pot-grown using the compost recommended for *Orchis* and

Ophrys as long as it is kept moist throughout the growing season. Clumps can be established as marginal plants or in a peat bed.

Dactylorhiza maculata (L.) Soó

This is commonly called the spotted orchid, and several distinct subspecies occur throughout its range in northern and central Europe. Most of them have spotted leaves and pale pink flowers variously marked with lines and spots of purple. Flowering depends on latitude but starts in June and goes on through to August. One of the commonest subspecies, subsp. *ericetorum*, is a frequent British moorland plant. Flower lips have rounded side-lobes and small midlobe. It hybridizes readily with other species and in cultivation is tolerant of a wide range of growing conditions. It is one of the few European orchids that grow in acid bog conditions, and certainly the most common.

Dactylorhiza praetermissa (Druce) Soó

This species is closely related to *D. elata* and replaces it farther north in Europe (eventually being itself replaced by *D. purpurella*). Widely known by its common name, southern marsh orchid, it forms substantial colonies in marshes, dune slacks, and wet meadows. It has broad, lanceolate, unspotted leaves on stems, growing to 50 centimeters and more, topped by a dense raceme of magenta flowers. Flowers have a lip with midlobe longer than the side-lobes. The species can be cultivated in a peaty compost with added

leaf mold which must be kept moist throughout the growing season.

Dactylorhiza purpurella (T. & T. A. Stephenson) Soó

Known as the northern marsh orchid, this species is found in northern Britain and parts of Scandinavia. With its broad, folded, unspotted leaves, it is superficially similar to *D. praetermissa*. The species has deeply colored flowers with lips that are almost entire and marked with darker red or purple. Flowering begins in mid-June, and cultivation is the same as for *D. praetermissa*. Both *D. praetermissa* and *D. purpurella* have been treated as subspecies of *D. majalis*, a variable and widespread European species.

Dactylorhiza traunsteineri (Reichb.f.) Soó

True *Dactylorhiza traunsteineri* is a slender species with narrow, unspotted leaves and comparatively few flowers in a loose raceme. The flower is a distinctive light magenta. Lateral sepals spread while petals curve to form a loose hood. The lip is distinctly three-lobed, all lobes of the same width. An important feature, however, is that the side-lobes are rounded while the midlobe is pointed and extends noticeably beyond them. This species is known from a handful of lime-rich fen sites in Britain and similar locations in temperate and Boreal Europe (Germany, Austria etc.). Flowers appear from late June to August. In cultivation use the compost suggested for *D. praetermissa*, with added limestone chips. Keep moist throughout the growth period.

Dactylorhiza praetermissa

Dactylorhiza purpurella

Dactylorhiza traunsteineri

DENDROBIUM Sw.

den-DRO-bee-um
Tribe: Epidendreae
Subtribe: Dendrobiinae
Etymology: Gr. *dendron*, tree; *bios*, life

A large genus of over 1,000 species, ranging from India and Sri Lanka then eastward to Japan and southward through the Philippines, Malaysia, Indonesia, and New Guinea to Australia and through the Pacific Islands to New Zealand. The genus *Dendrobium* is extremely variable; Rudolf Schlechter in 1914 divided the genus into four subgenera and 41 sections to make determination of the species less difficult.

These are mostly epiphytes and lithophytes with fleshy or wiry pseudobulbous stems, of erect to pendulous habit, with one to many leaves from linear to almost round to terete. Single- to many-flowered racemes are borne laterally or terminally. Flowers are tiny to quite large and showy and of every color conceivable, except black; all have the lateral sepals joined to the column-foot to form a mentum. Four pollinia are present in two closely appressed pairs.
Growing conditions vary from cool to warm, from considerable shade to almost full sun, so a study of the plants' natural habitat is essential. Generally the two most important factors are good air movement and good light. When in active growth keep plants

evenly moist; during the dormant period (generally the cold winter months) plants do not require watering but need to be in a humid atmosphere or to receive just enough water to stop the pseudobulbous stems from shriveling.

Dendrobium amethystoglossum
Reichb.f.

Attractive canelike plant from the mountains of the Philippines. Pseudobulbous stems are up to 90 centimeters long with deciduous leaves. Racemes with densely set pendulous clusters of delicate flowers, white with an amethyst-purple lip, appear generally in winter and are long-lasting. It needs cool temperatures, humidity and good air movement, with a minimum winter temperature of 6°C.

Dendrobium anceps Sw.

Flattened, leafy-stemmed plant from India, Burma, Thailand, and Vietnam. Stems, to 60 centimeters, have imbricate fleshy leaves. Small, greenish-yellow, solitary flowers from axils of leaves, are seen in the spring. Slab culture in a warm humid atmosphere with a minimum winter temperature of 15°C is recommended.

Dendrobium anosmum Lindley

A large, pendulous, widespread species found in Borneo, Indonesia, Laos, Malaya, New Guinea, Philippines, Sumatra, and Vietnam. Pseudobulbous stems, up to two meters long, are leafless at flowering. Fragrant flowers, borne in twos along the length of the stem and up to ten centimeters across, are a rich magenta purple through to a rare white form. It

Dendrobium amethystoglossum

Dendrobium anosmum

Dendrobium aphyllum

Dendrobium antennatum

grows well in an open medium, with ample water while in full growth, then followed by a rest in winter with a minimum temperature of 15°C.

Dendrobium antennatum Lindley

This mostly large plant, with pseudobulbous stems to 130 centimeters long, is found from New Guinea to the Solomon Islands and in the north of Queensland in Australia. The raceme carries up to fifteen well-spaced, fragrant, long-lasting flowers approximately 6 centimeters long, with white to greenish sepals and greenish, narrow and twisted petals with a purple- to violet-veined lip. The species flowers at any time of the year but mostly during winter and spring. It needs lots of light and humidity and a minimum winter temperature of 15°C.

Dendrobium aphyllum (Roxb.) C. Fischer

Long, slender plant from India, Burma, Thailand, Indochina, and Malaya. Pendulous pseudobulbous stems are up to a meter long, the leaves soon deciduous. Fragrant, fragile flowers are borne in twos or threes along the length of the old stems. They are five centimeters in diameter, and white to rosy mauve with a mostly primrose yellow lip. It produces a spectacular display in the spring, if watered and fed well after a fairly dry winter with a minimum temperature of 12°C.

Dendrobium atroviolaceum Rolfe

Erect, compact plants found in the eastern New Guinea islands. Pseudobulbous stems are 30 centimeters long, swollen in their

upper half, two- to four-leaved at the top. Racemes are mostly erect, seldom longer than the leaves, carrying up to 20 very long-lasting cream flowers, usually heavily marked with violet spots. The lip is recurved and heavily veined with violet. It is popular with hybridists despite its nodding flowers; many of its progeny flower continuously. It likes a warmish, humid atmosphere with plenty of air movement and a minimum winter temperature of 10°C.

Dendrobium bellatulum Rolfe

A dwarf plant found in India, Burma, Thailand, China, Laos and Vietnam. Tufts of pseudobulbous stems up to ten centimeters

long with between two and four leathery, greyish green leaves. The long-lived, fragrant flowers are borne in late winter to early spring at the top of the stem and are creamy white, the broad lip having a yellow midlobe and scarlet throat. Slab culture suits it best in a humid atmosphere and a cool, dry winter with a minimum of 10°C.

Dendrobium bifalce Lindley

This species is found in Timor, New Guinea, the Bismarck Archipelago, the Solomon Islands, and north Queensland, Australia. Erect racemes carry up to twelve green to yellow, long-lasting flowers, marked with purplish brown spots. It needs

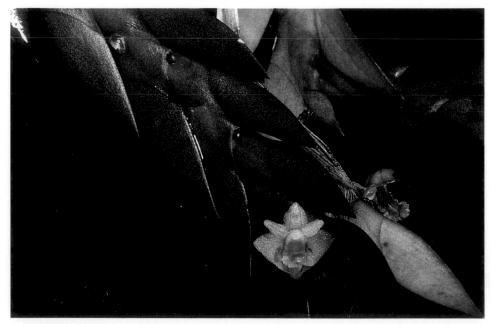

Dendrobium anceps

Dendrobium atroviolaceum

Dendrobium bracteosum

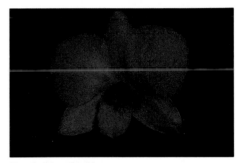

Dendrobium bigibbum

Dendrobium bellatulum

a warm, sunny position, as it requires high light, and a decided rest after flowering. Minimum winter temperature 15°C.

Dendrobium bigibbum Lindley

A variable species of two subspecies, one occurring in northeastern Australia with three varieties and the other (subspecies *laratensis*) in the Tanimbar Islands. *Dendrobium bigibbum* var. *bigibbum* is also found in the Torres Strait islands and New Guinea. Slender, pseudobulbous stems, often quite purplish, are up to 60 centimeters long. Racemes bear about 20 rosy, mauve to purple flowers, very occasionally white or bicolored, long-lasting and between three and seven centimeters across the petals. Essentials for good culture

are excellent drainage, high light intensity, plenty of water while in full growth, good air movement and a good rest after flowering. Minimum winter temperature 12°C.

Dendrobium bracteosum Reichb.f.

Widely distributed in lowland New Guinea and islands to the east, from sea-level up to 1,200 meters, this species produces dense clusters of long-lasting flowers. Each flower is approximately two centimeters long, and may be colored deep reddish purple, pale pink through mauve to creamy-yellow or greenish white; all of the color variations exhibit the orange lip. Plant size is variable with small specimens flowering quite freely; others may have stems 50 centimeters or

more long. The large floral bracts are a distinctive feature for which *D. bracteosum* is named. Culture requires intermediate temperatures (15°–20°C minimum at night).

Dendrobium brymerianum Reichb.f.

A striking species from Burma, Thailand, and Laos. Pseudobulbous stems are slightly swollen in the middle, and up to six leaves are borne near the apex. Short racemes carry one to five quite large, yellow to golden yellow flowers with a most impressively branched fringe on the lip. The var. *bistrionicum* is inferior and frequently self-fertilising. Provide an open medium with good light. Minimum winter temperature 10°C.

Dendrobium bullenianum Reichb.f.

This very attractive species is found in the Philippines and Western Samoa. Its slender pseudobulbous stems are up to 60 centimeters long. The densely flowered, short racemes arise from the nodes of leafless stems and carry numerous yellow to orange flowers with red striations. It is easy to grow if given plenty of light and grown in a humid atmosphere with a minimum winter temperature of 12°C.

Dendrobium canaliculatum R. Br.

A variable species found in northern Australia and New Guinea. It is widespread

Dendrobium chrysotoxum

Dendrobium brymerianum

Dendrobium bullenianum

Dendrobium canaliculatum

in a variety of habitats, from swamplands to open forest grassland to semi-arid areas, mostly on the trunks of trees in clusters of four to seven small pseudobulbous stems with up to eight thick, semi-cylindrical leaves. Numerous racemes, carrying 50 or more tricolored, fragrant flowers, are frequently seen. They are white to pale yellow on the basal half and yellow at the tips; the lip has mauve to purple markings. It prefers slab culture. In its natural habitat its growing season is the "wet season," which is from late spring to early fall, when rain falls nearly every day. Rest plants in late autumn to early winter, keeping drier than most dendrobiums and giving maximum light. Minimum winter temperature 15°C.

Dendrobium chrysotoxum
Lindley

This stout-clustered, pseudobulbous plant comes from India, Burma, Thailand, China, and Laos. In spring it produces a many-flowered arching raceme of golden to yellow-orange flowers that are quite waxy in appearance. It requires high light in the winter to encourage flowering and only a short resting period, during which only enough water should be provided to ensure that the pseudobulbous stems do not shrivel.

Dendrobium crepidatum Lindley

Found in India, Burma, Thailand, China,

Laos, and Vietnam, this species has fairly thick, mostly pendulous, pseudobulbous stems with few leaves. The waxy flowers are borne in the early summer from the nodes of leafless stems. They are up to 4.5 centimeters across and are white tinted with pink; the basal half of the lip is orange-yellow. It is easy to grow if careful attention is paid to watering, particularly when the new growth first appears. Minimum winter temperature 10°C.

Dendrobium cruentum Reichb.f.

A lowland plant found in Thailand. Erect, slender pseudobulbous stems up to 35 centimeters tall carry flowers in the upper part, in ones or twos. Long-lasting flowers, 5

Dendrobium cruentum

Dendrobium crumenatum

Dendrobium crepidatum

centimeters across, are a pale green to yellowish cream with blood-red markings on the lip. It prefers a warm moist atmosphere with good air movement and a very open medium. Minimum temperature of 15°C.

Dendrobium crumenatum Sw.

The well-known "pigeon orchid" is found in India, Thailand, China, Malaysia, Indonesia, and the Philippines. The pseudobulbous stems, to 1.5 meters long, are narrow at the base, then swollen for a few internodes, and the rest of their length is narrow and stalklike. The short-lived

flowers are borne on the top, leafless part of the stem. Flowering is initiated by a sudden fall in temperature, producing numerous white flowers, sometimes suffused with pink, all opening at the same time. It does not appear to require a definite rest and needs watering throughout the year, provided that it is grown in warm humid conditions with a minimum winter temperature of 15°C.

Dendrobium cucumerinum
Macleay ex Lindley

The "cucumber orchid" found in eastern Australia receives its name from its gherkin-

shaped leaves which are attached to a creeping rhizome. The slightly perfumed, 2.5 centimeter flowers appear on a short raceme in late spring and are a greenish white with reddish purple streaks on the basal half of the segments. Quite difficult to grow, slab culture suits it best. It prefers about 60 percent shade and moist conditions with plenty of air movement. Minimum winter temperature 1°C.

Dendrobium cunninghamii
Lindley

The only *Dendrobium* from New Zealand. Its occurrence on Stewart Island represents the southernmost occurrence of the genus in its world distribution. Wiry, hard, and brittle stems, profusely branching, are up to 120 centimeters long. Summer flowers, mostly borne in pairs, are white with pink to purple markings on the side-lobes of the lip. It is best grown with slab culture and should have plenty of moisture, high humidity and air movement plus 60 percent shade. Minimum winter temperature 1°C.

Dendrobium cuthbertsonii
F. Muell.

Acclaimed as the most beautiful orchid from New Guinea, *D. cuthbertsonii* is characterized by diminutive plants, about five centimeters high, finely papillate-rough leaves and very long-lasting flowers (up to ten months) about 2.5–4 centimeters long. This species has been known for many years in cultivation under the name of *D. sophronites*, now regarded as a synonym. Red is the predominant color, but there are many other brilliant color forms — purple, pale yellow, pink, orange — as well as

Dendrobium cuthbertsonii

Dendrobium cucumerinum

Dendrobium dearei

pseudobulbous stems are generally about six centimeters long with leaves throughout their length. Young stems bear racemes in the fall with about ten small graceful flowers, greenish white to pale yellow with reddish purple striations on the lip, the midlobe conspicuously fringed. Bring up new growths quickly, and give little water in the winter. Minimum winter temperature 10°C.

bicolored and tricolored variations (e.g. purple with white petal tips and yellow lip). The blunt lip apex is usually marked with short brown veins. A high-elevation species from about 1,800–3,000 meters, *D. cuthbertsonii* is cool-growing and cultivated successfully either on slabs or in pots with night temperatures down to 10°–15°C. High humidity combined with good air movement is essential.

Dendrobium dearei Reichb.f.

A robust plant found in the Philippines. Erect, pseudobulbous stems are up to 90 centimeters long with leathery leaves. The

rather short racemes are borne on the upper part of the stem in spring or summer and carry few to many, 7.5 centimeter snow-white, long-lasting flowers with a green or yellow area at the base of the lip. This most beautiful species is relatively easy to grow, provided that it is given a warm, humid atmosphere with high light in the winter and a minimum temperature of 15°C.

Dendrobium delacourii Guillaumin

A small plant found in Burma, Thailand, Laos, and Vietnam. The short and yellowish

Dendrobium discolor Lindley

A large and robust plant found in northeastern Australia, the islands of the Torres Strait, and New Guinea. It is frequently common and in very large clumps in its native habitat. The pseudobulbous stems are up to five meters high. Racemes, from the upper nodes, are many-flowered and often numerous, carrying 20–40 creamy, yellowish to golden brown flowers with mauve markings on the lip. It is free-flowering, and the flowers are long-lasting. It is best grown in a bright, humid atmosphere with a minimum winter temperature of 15°C.

Dendrobium draconis Reichb.f.

A common, widespread species from Burma, Thailand, Laos, Vietnam, and Cambodia. The stoutish pseudobulbous stems, up to 45 centimeters long with leathery leaves, carry ivory-white flowers, approximately seven centimeters across, in fascicles of between two and five. The long lip has orange-red stripes at the base. It is easy to grow in an open medium with high humidity, good air movement and cool conditions in the heat of summer. Minimum winter temperature 12°C.

Dendrobium engae T. M. Reeve

Named after the Enga Province in the Highlands of Papua New Guinea (where it is the floral emblem), this species grows high up on *Nothofagus* trees at 2,000–2,700 meters elevation. With yellowish stems up to 50 × 3.3 centimeters and thick, leathery leaves, *D. engae* is one of the largest-flowered, cool-growing species belonging to section *Latouria*. The racemes are three-to-eighteen-flowered, the flowers approximately 5–6 centimeters in diameter, lasting up to two months and strongly but sweetly scented. It has not proved an easy subject to cultivate, as it is very sensitive to poor drainage.

Dendrobium farmeri Paxton

A widespread species from India, Burma, Thailand, Laos, Vietnam, and Malaysia. Mostly erect pseudobulbous stems, up to 30 centimeters long, are four angled in the upper part. Dense, pendulous racemes on leafless stems bear numerous white to pale pink flowers with a golden lip. Fairly shady conditions with high humidity, a minimum temperature of 6°C, and a good winter rest will produce spring flowers.

Dendrobium fimbriatum Hook.

A large, frequently pendulous plant from India, Burma, Thailand, Indochina, and Malaya. Narrow, many-leaved pseudobulbous stems up to two meters long bear many shortish racemes of six to

Dendrobium delacourii

Dendrobium draconis

Dendrobium discolor

Dendrobium engae

Dendrobium fimbriatum

Dendrobium forbesii

Dendrobium johnsoniae

Dendrobium farmeri

Dendrobium finisterrae

fifteen flowers, usually on leafless stems. Flowers, five to eight centimeters in diameter, are a golden yellow with a slightly darker fringed, round lip. In var. *oculatum*, which is most commonly seen in collections, there is a dark maroon blotch at the base of the lip. Minimum winter temperature 6°C.

Dendrobium finisterrae Schltr.

Unusual but attractive is often a first impression when the large, hairy flowers of this species are seen. Known only from the mountains of Papua New Guinea, at 900–2,100 meters, *D. finisterrae* requires intermediate to cool temperatures in cultivation. Stems are two-leaved at the apex and up to 70 cm tall. Inflorescences are few-flowered, and the slightly scented flowers do not open widely.

Dendrobium forbesii Ridley

Another New Guinea member of the section *Latouria*, this floriferous species is known for its white to creamy-white flowers, about four centimeters long, and its wide petals. In the wild, *D. forbesii* occurs as an epiphyte from 800–1,700 meters, and sometimes plants may be detected from a distance by their strong honey scent. Cultivation requirements are for intermediate to cool temperatures, down to about 15°C at night.

Dendrobium formosum Roxb.

A stoutish plant from the lowlands and highlands of India, Burma, Thailand, and Vietnam. Pseudobulbous stems up to 45 centimeters long bear leaves in the upper two-thirds and one- to five-flowered

racemes from near the apex. Large, showy white flowers, with yellow on the lip, up to twelve centimeters across, appear mostly in late winter and early spring. It needs strong light, a moist atmosphere, regular feeding after the new growths appear, and a minimum winter temperature of 12°C.

Dendrobium gouldii Reichb.f.

This large section *Spatulata* species is found mainly in New Ireland and the Solomon Islands (from Bougainville to Malaita and Guadalcanal). It occurs from sea level, often right by the sea and on branches overhanging the sea, up to about 700

meters. Closely allied to *D. lineale*, it differs mainly in the longer, more twisted, somewhat pointed petals and in the longer lip. The common color is white with a purple or violet-veined lip, but there are also striking pale yellow or golden yellow variants often with darker petals. Warm growing conditions are required.

Dendrobium gracilicaule F. Muell.

This very slender, long pseudobulbous-stemmed plant comes from Australia, Lord Howe Island, Fiji, and New Caledonia. There are up to six lanceolate leaves at the top of the stem which, in spring, bears

Dendrobium harveyanum

Dendrobium gracilicaule

Dendrobium gouldii

racemes of up to 40 fragrant flowers, one to two centimeters across, from yellow to green-yellow with red-brown blotching on the outside. The lip is yellow with few red-brown markings. Good drainage is essential if grown in a pot. Minimum winter temperature 2°C.

Dendrobium harveyanum
Reichb.f.

A rare plant from Burma, Thailand, and Vietnam. Shortish, slender pseudobulbous stems have leaves clustered together near the apex. Few-flowered racemes from the upper nodes in spring bear canary to golden yellow five-centimeter flowers with darker blotches on the lip. The petals and lip are marginally fringed. Give a prolonged winter rest. Minimum temperature 10°C.

Dendrobium infundibulum
Lindley

A slender plant from the mountains of Burma and Thailand. Erect pseudobulbous stems are up to a meter long with persistent leaves on the upper part. Flowers are similar to but smaller than those of *D. formosum.* They are white with orange to red markings in the throat of the lip. It requires coolish treatment to correspond to the high elevations and lower temperatures of its native habitat.

Dendrobium johnsoniae F. Muell.

The large, pure white flowers, which are beautifully marked with purple on the lip, make this section *Latouria* species one of the most attractive orchids from New Guinea and the Solomon Islands. In addition, the showy flowers are carried on

Dendrobium infundibulum

Dendrobium kingianum

Dendrobium lichenastrum

Dendrobium lineale

Dendrobium lasianthera

relatively small plants for this section, up to 30 centimeters high. *Dendrobium johnsoniae* occurs from 500–1,200 meters in nature and is suitable for cultivation in intermediate glasshouses with night temperatures down to 15°–20°C. As for most dendrobiums, good light and air movement are required.

Dendrobium kingianum Bidw.

This compact, popular species from Australia has pseudobulbous stems from five to 55 centimeters long with three to seven leaves at the top. Racemes carry up to fifteen slightly fragrant, mostly pink to deep mauve (and occasionally white) flowers with generally darker markings on the lip. It prefers to grow in shallow containers in an open medium with plenty of light, fresh air and humidity. It does not like "wet feet." Minimum winter temperature 2°C.

Dendrobium lasianthera J. J. Smith

These very large, erect plants from the lowlands of New Guinea are safe in their remote habitat, guarded by crocodiles and leeches. Pseudobulbous stems extend to three meters tall, with leathery leaves in the upper portion. Arching racemes, up to 60 centimeters, bear numerous beautiful, eight-centimeter-long flowers with twisted petals and variously colored in red, mauve and bronze. Warm and very humid conditions

with ample light are necessary. Minimum winter temperature 15°C.

Dendrobium lawesii F. Muell.

Common between 400 and 1,600 meters in the lower mountains of New Guinea and Bougainville, this section *Calyptrochilus* species exhibits a great range of variation in the color of the flowers. Bright purple or pink-red are the main colors, but orange, creamy-yellow or white are other variants. In addition, the tips of the sepals and petals as well as the hooded lip apex may be colored differently (e.g. white or yellow). In the wild, *D. lawesii* is often found as a low epiphyte in full shade, pendulous in habit, but always where there is good air movement. Consequently, it is best cultivated on slabs (remembering the pendulous to semi-pendulous habit of growth) under intermediate temperatures.

Dendrobium leonis (Lindley) Reichb.f.

A common lowland plant from Thailand, Laos, Vietnam, Cambodia, Malaya, Sumatra, and Borneo. Pseudobulbous stems up to 25 centimeters long, usually pendulous, bear flattened leaves. Fragrant flowers are borne singly or in pairs. They are 15 millimeters across, pale greenish cream with purple-red markings on the outside. The lip has a reddish purple blotch. Provide warm conditions and high humidity with a minimum winter temperature of 15°C.

Dendrobium lichenastrum (F. Muell.) Kränzlin

A small plant with a creeping rhizome,

Dendrobium lawesii

Dendrobium leonis

Dendrobium lindleyi

found on trees and rocks in northeastern Australia. Fleshy leaves, alternating along the rhizome, are oval to almost round. Single six-millimeter flowers on a short stem are greenish to cream to pinkish with reddish striations. Slab culture suits it best in a humid atmosphere with plenty of moisture and a minimum winter temperature of 6°C.

Dendrobium lindleyi Steudel

A small plant from India, Burma, Thailand, Laos, Vietnam, and China. The strongly ribbed pseudobulbous stems generally lie flat on their host and may be up to ten centimeters long, bearing one leaf. Wiry racemes carry many golden flowers, with the lip darker toward the base. Cool, humid conditions, with a decided dry rest during the winter months, ensure spring flowers. Minimum temperature 6°C.

Dendrobium lineale Rolfe

Common in lowland New Guinea and adjacent islands, *D. lineale* grows from sea level (will also tolerate splashing by the surf) up to about 700 meters. It is a robust species requiring warm conditions, and plants may grow up to two meters tall or more. Flowers are usually white with a purple-veined lip, but the petals vary in color. The petals are only half twisted or not twisted at all, with the tips rounded or blunt, and the lip midlobe is oblong with a wavy margin. *D. veratrifolium*, a synonym, was the name previously used for this species.

Dendrobium loddigesii Rolfe

A dwarf plant from Laos and China. Freely

branching, slender, pseudobulbous stems up to ten centimeters long, prostrate or pendulous, produce aerial growths freely. The fragrant, long-lasting, solitary flowers are five centimeters across. They are pale rose-purple, and the broad lip is rose-purple, edged with an orange disc. It is easy to grow but needs a fairly dry rest in winter to ensure plenty of flowers in spring and summer.

Dendrobium macrophyllum A. Rich.

This species was among the first to be discovered (1823) and named (1834) from

New Guinea. It has a wide distribution from the Philippines and Java through New Guinea, the Solomon Islands, Vanuatu, New Caledonia, Fiji, and Samoa, and is found from sea level up to 1,700 meters. As the name indicates, the leaves are very large, up to 31 × 9 centimeters, usually with three leaves at the apex of the yellowish green stems. The flowers are variable in color and size; the most common form is greenish white to yellow with purplish markings. The outer surfaces of the sepals and ovary are covered with bristles or hairs. Warm to intermediate temperatures are required. *D. musciferum*, a synonym, is a name that has been used widely in the past.

Dendrobium loddigesii

Dendrobium macrophyllum

Dendrobium moschatum

Dendrobium moniliforme

Dendrobium nobile

Dendrobium parishii

Dendrobium pendulum

Dendrobium mohlianum Reichb.f.

Brilliant scarlet (vermilion) or orange flowers characterize this charming section *Calyptrochilus* species from the Pacific Islands of the Solomons, Vanuatu (New Hebrides), Fiji, and Samoa. Sometimes the hooded apex of the lip is colored with violet. The plants have slender canes up to 60 cm or more, with lanceolate leaves 5–12 × 0.8–1.8 centimeters, and the flowers are 2–3 centimeters long. *D. mohlianum* occurs in the wild from 700 to 2,000 meters, so it requires intermediate to cool temperatures.

Dendrobium moniliforme (Lindley) Sw.

A small plant from China, Taiwan, Korea, Japan, and the Ryukyu Islands. Slender pseudobulbous stems to 40 centimeters long often grow into large clumps. Fragrant flowers in ones or twos, borne in spring on old leafless stems, are white or pink with the base of the lip greenish yellow with a few red-brown spots. It grows best in a cool greenhouse with good air circulation and a dry winter rest with a minimum temperature of 6°C.

Dendrobium moschatum (Willd.) Sw.

A robust plant found in India, Burma, Thailand, and Laos. Pseudobulbous stems, up to more than 1.5 meters long, are leafy throughout. Pendulous racemes bear seven to fifteen pale yellow to apricot, eight-centimeter flowers with pale purplish veins. The lip has two purplish blotches at the base. The flowers last only up to seven days. It is easy to grow providing it is in a well-drained medium. Minimum winter temperature 6°C.

Dendrobium nobile Lindley

A widely distributed and variable plant from India, Burma, Thailand, Laos, Vietnam, and China. This most popular and widely grown dendrobium has many botanical and horticultural varieties. Pseudobulbous stems may be up to 60 centimeters tall. Large, long-lasting, waxy flowers are seven centimeters across in short racemes of between one and four. The color varies; it is mostly white with varying degrees of mauve to purple and a deeper blotch in the lip, rarely pure white (var. *virginalis*). It is easy

to grow, but it is necessary to keep plants dryish in winter to ensure a good flowering in spring.

Dendrobium parishii Reichb.f.

A smallish plant from India, Burma, Thailand, Laos, Vietnam, Cambodia, and China. Pseudobulbous stems to 35 centimeters long have deciduous leaves. Inflorescences, from the leafless stems, bear between one and three fragrant flowers, five to six centimeters across. They are light rose-purple, and the lip has a dark purple blotch on each side of the throat. It needs warm, humid conditions with a good rest in winter, slightly on the dry side and in good light, to produce spring flowers.

Dendrobium pendulum Roxb.

A knobbly-stemmed plant from India, Burma, Thailand, Laos, and China. Curved, mostly pendulous pseudobulbous stems, much swollen at each node, have deciduous leaves. Inflorescences arise from leafless stems. One to three fragrant flowers, up to seven centimeters across, are white with purple tips. The lip is white with a

Dendrobium pseudoglomeratum

Dendrobium scabrilingue

yellow basal half and a purple tip. Provide bright light and a good winter rest with a minimum temperature of 10°C.

Dendrobium polysema Schltr.

Somewhat shy in flowering, this species exceeds most others in section *Latouria* for the number of flowers in each raceme (under good conditions). From New Guinea, where it grows between 600 and 1,900 meters, it is one of a group of hairy-flowered species allied to *D. macrophyllum,* but *D. polysema* is readily distinguished by the tapering lateral lobes of the lip. Flowers are medium to large in size, creamy to yellow and heavily spotted/striated with maroon. Intermediate temperatures favor this species, and possibly relatively drier conditions may stimulate more flowering. High humidity and good air movement should be maintained.

Dendrobium pseudoglomeratum T. M. Reeve and J. J. Wood

A beautiful New Guinea section *Pedilonum* species found from sea level up to about 1,800 meters. *Dendrobium pseudoglomeratum* has bright mauve-pink flowers with an orange lip. A pleasing feature of the flowers is that they are often widely opening. Clusters of flowers arise from leafless stems which occasionally grow up to one meter in length. There are two varieties which differ only in the size of the flowers, although this feature will vary even on the same inflorescence. The main variety has flowers 2–4 centimeters long and has been incorrectly known as *D. glomeratum.* The smaller-flowered form, which is identical in morphology, has flowers 1.2–2.5

Dendrobium polysema

Dendrobium sanderae

centimeters long and has sometimes been referred to as *D. chrysoglossum.* *Dendrobium pseudoglomeratum* prefers plenty of light and warm to intermediate temperature conditions.

Dendrobium rhodostictum F. Muell. & Kränzlin

An erect epiphyte found in New Guinea and the Solomon Islands. Pseudobulbous stems are very slender at the base and then ovoid in the upper third with two to four leathery leaves. Racemes are erect, bearing two to eight nodding, large white flowers with

Dendrobium rhodostictum

purple markings on the lip. High light, humidity, good air movement and a minimum winter temperature of 10°C are its requirements.

Dendrobium sanderae Rolfe

A robust species from the mountains of the Philippines. Pseudobulbous stems up to 80 centimeters long have two rows of leaves. Slender racemes carry six to twelve large, pure white flowers with the base of the lip streaked with purple. Two forms are known: the larger-flowered one, var. *major,* flowers in the spring; and the smaller, var. *parviflorum,* flowers mostly in the fall. It needs good air movement, humidity and a decided rest in winter. Minimum winter temperature 6°C.

Dendrobium scabrilingue Lindley

A compact plant found in the high areas of Burma, Laos, and Thailand. Pseudobulbous stems to 30 centimeters long produce four to six leaves and short, two- to three-flowered racemes. Very fragrant, long-lasting, waxy flowers are 3.5 centimeters across, ivory-white with a yellow-and-green

Dendrobium senile

lip. It requires coolish conditions with good light, a moist atmosphere and a minimum winter temperature of 8°C.

Dendrobium secundum (Blume) Lindley

Tall canelike plants from Burma, Thailand, Sumatra, Laos, Java, Cambodia, Vietnam, Borneo, Philippines, and some Pacific islands. Pseudobulbous stems to 120 centimeters long bear racemes from the upper nodes with numerous densely packed, small waxy flowers, frequently all pointing to one side. They are pink to mauve-purple, rarely white, and the lip is orange to yellow. The long-lasting flowers appear in the winter months. Provide a very open medium in small pots in a warm humid atmosphere, and keep fairly dry in the winter.

Dendrobium senile Parish ex Reichb.f.

A dwarf species from Burma, Thailand, and Laos. Pseudobulbous stems to eight centimeters long, covered with long, white, woolly hairs, bear two to three leaves at the apex. Flowers occur in ones or twos and are five centimeters across, pale yellow, the lip slightly darker and greenish in the basal half. It is not easy to grow, needing high light, a decided rest in winter and good air movement to produce spring flowers.

Dendrobium smillieae F. Muell.

A robust, erect plant found mostly in the lowlands of New Guinea and northern Australia. Pseudobulbous stems to a meter long produce thin leaves that are soon deciduous. Racemes that are very short and densely flowered are carried on the leafless stems. Odorless, almost tubular flowers are waxy and pastel-colored from greenish white to pink with a bright green tip to the lip. A warm, humid atmosphere in a fairly shaded position and a decided rest in winter with higher light will ensure spring flowers. Minimum winter temperature 15°C.

Dendrobium speciosum Smith

A widespread, mostly robust species found along the east coast of Australia. It is an extremely variable species, comprising six varieties. Pseudobulbous stems are from five centimeters to a meter long, often in large masses. Racemes carrying up to 100 or more white to yellow flowers with dark purple markings on the lip appear in the spring. They vary in length from 1.5 to eight centimeters. Culture varies: most southern forms prefer cool conditions and minimum temperatures of 2°C; northern forms need some warmth, a decided rest and high light in winter to ensure good flowering.

Dendrobium spectabile (Blume) Miq.

A widespread, robust species from the lowlands and lower mountains of New Guinea, Bougainville, and the Solomon Islands. Pseudobulbous stems to 60

Dendrobium stratiotes

Dendrobium smillieae

centimeters long have three to six leathery leaves. Racemes to 30 centimeters long bear many large, grotesquely beautiful flowers with twisted, undulate, and pointed segments. They are cream with rich red-brown to maroon markings. Give warm conditions in an open medium with a minimum winter temperature of 12°C.

Dendrobium stratiotes Reichb.f.

A large canelike plant from the Moluccas. Pseudobulbous stems to a meter long have many persistent, leathery leaves. Racemes to 30 centimeters long bear up to eight or more large, long-lasting flowers. Sepals are white; petals are long and twisted, yellow-green; and the lip is white with violet veins. In a bright, moist, and airy situation it flowers more than once each year. Minimum winter temperature 15°C.

Dendrobium strebloceras
Reichb.f.

A large canelike plant from the Moluccas with pseudobulbous stems up to 1.5 meters tall. Racemes are up to 40 centimeters long with up to eight long-lasting, fragrant flowers, pale yellow-green with brown suffusions. The lip has violet veins. It requires the same conditions as *D. stratiotes*.

Dendrobium striolatum Reichb.f.

The most southern *Dendrobium* species in Australia, this small plant with a creeping rhizome often grows into large masses on rocks. The terete leaves appear like succulent grass. One or two small, fragrant flowers appear on each raceme. They are

green yellow to yellow with brown-purple striae. The lip is white. Slab culture suits it best with plenty of moisture in the hottest months, plus a misting at dusk. Minimum temperature 1°C.

Dendrobium subclausum Rolfe

Dendrobium subclausum is the most common member of section *Calyptrochilus* from New Guinea where it is found from about 1,500 to 3,200 meters. Plant form is very variable. Stems may be quite slender and much branched to reasonably thick.

Dendrobium secundum

Dendrobium striolatum

Most varieties grow as epiphytes, sometimes pendulous in habit, but others in the wild are found growing terrestrially. Cool temperatures are required for cultivation except for the yellow-flowered variety *pandanicola* which should be grown under intermediate conditions. *Dendrobium subclausum* is usually quite floriferous with flowers 1.5–2.5 centimeters long (3–4 centimeters long in the rare variety *speciosum*). Flowers are usually bicolored orange and yellow or red and yellow, but also may be entirely yellow, orange or reddish pink. The plant illustrated is a typical form of the variety *subclausum*. The species has been known under the synonyms *D. dichroma*, *D. mitriferum*, and *D. phlox*.

Dendrobium taurinum Lindley

A large, cane-like, lowland plant, widespread in the Philippines. Pseudobulbous stems are up to two meters tall. Racemes to 45 centimeters long bear up to 30 large, long-lasting, waxy flowers. Sepals are white tinged with green. Petals

Dendrobium subclausum

Dendrobium speciosum

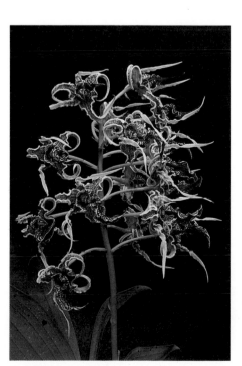
Dendrobium spectabile

Dendrobium strebloceras

Dendrobium tetragonum

Dendrobium taurinum

are twisted and reddish brown to purple. The lip is whitish, heavily suffused and veined with reddish brown to rose-purple. It needs a warm, humid atmosphere with bright light and a minimum winter temperature of 15°C.

Dendrobium teretifolium R. Br.

This is the "bridal veil" orchid of the low elevations in eastern Australia. Tough, branching, wiry, pendulous stems frequently form large, long masses with cylindrical leaves up to 65 centimeters long. Numerous racemes bearing up to sixteen spidery white to cream, fragrant flowers, with red to purple markings on the lip, appear in late winter early spring. Hang in a shady, sheltered position with ample air movement and a minimum winter temperature of 2°C.

Dendrobium tetragonum Cunn.

A variable species from eastern Australia with three varieties. Mostly pendulous, pseudobulbous stems are up to 50 centimeters long, very wiry at the base and thicker and distinctly four-sided in the top half, with up to five thin, leathery leaves. Short racemes produce from one to nine spidery flowers up to twelve centimeters long, greenish to yellowish with reddish markings. Slab culture is best. Allow good air movement and a shady position with minimum temperature of 2°C in winter. Low-elevation forms of the var. *giganteum* need extra warmth in winter.

Dendrobium thyrsiflorum
Reichb.f.

A large but compact plant from India,

Dendrobium trigonopus

Burma, Thailand, Laos, Vietnam, and China. Upright, pseudobulbous stems to 60 centimeters long bear five to seven persistent leaves. Crowded racemes, pendulous with many white four- to five-centimeter flowers with a golden yellow lip, appear in the spring but last only for a week. It is easy to grow in good light and ample air movement, with a minimum winter temperature of 5°C.

Dendrobium trigonopus Reichb.f.

A compact plant from Burma, Thailand, Laos, and China. Pseudobulbous stems to 25 centimeters long bear few leaves at the top. One to three waxy, golden yellow flowers with some red lines on the lip, about five

centimeters across, are seen in the spring. It prefers slab culture with good light and humidity and a minimum winter temperature of 10°C.

Dendrobium vexillarius J. J. Smith
variety **uncinatum** (Schltr.) T. M. Reeve & P. Woods

One of the largest-flowered species belonging to the spectacular section *Oxyglossum*, *D. vexillarius* exhibits a very large range of flower color — almost every color of the rainbow. Six varieties are recognised, three of them — variety *vexillarius*, variety *albiviride*, and variety *retroflexum* — growing in New Guinea at very high elevations, usually over 3,000 meters and therefore requiring cool temperatures for cultivation. Variety *uncinatum* occurs widely in the Highlands of New Guinea, from 1,600 to 2,800 meters. Usually it is pinkish purple or cerise in color, but there are also dark crimson and yellow forms. The flowers last several months. Sufficient air movement, very good drainage, and cool temperatures are required for success in cultivating these orchids.

Dendrobium victoriae-reginae
Loher

A pendulous plant from the mountains in the Philippines. Pseudobulbous stems to 60 centimeters long have slightly swollen nodes and thinnish leaves. Summer flowers develop in clusters from two to six (occasionally more) and are a waxy bluish purple on the apical half to two-thirds and white near the base. The lip is similarly colored. Occasionally white or pink flowers

Dendrobium teretifolium

Dendrobium thyrsiflorum

Dendrobium victoriae-reginae

Dendrobium vexillarius

are seen. Allow cool conditions with plenty of moisture. Minimum winter temperature 5°C.

DENDROCHILUM Blume
den-droe-KYE-lum
Tribe: Coelogyneae
Subtribe: Coelogyninae
Etymology: Gr. *dendron*, tree; *cheilos*, lip

Dendrochilum is a genus of more than 120 epiphytic species. Native from southeast Asia to New Guinea, the genus is particularly well represented in Borneo and the Philippines. Two generic segregates are sometimes recognized, *Acoridium* and *Platyclinis*. Most species are known as "golden chain" orchids because of their arching-pendent racemes of fragrant, yellowish flowers. The flowering habit is reminiscent of *Pholidota*. All cultivated species have rather small, tightly clustered pseudobulbs topped by a single lanceolate leaf. Inflorescences arise from the top of the pseudobulb and tend to be persistent after flowering.

Dendrochilum plants can be grown mounted on slabs but do best when grown in small pots. They prefer to be potbound, and care should be taken not to disturb the roots during repotting. Most species enjoy bright light levels, intermediate to warm temperatures, and an evenly moist compost.

Dendrochilum cobbianum
Reichb.f.

Endemic to the Philippines, this is one of the showiest species in the genus. The peduncles are stiffly erect before arching

and producing a laxly pendent raceme of flowers. The highly fragrant flowers are greenish with an orange-yellow lip. Flowers are produced in the fall.

Dendrochilum glumaceum
Lindley

Dendrochilum glumaceum is endemic to the Philippines. Arching sprays of white flowers are highlighted by contrasting orange-yellow lips. The species is easily recognized by its partially closed flowers and large floral bracts nearly half the length of the flower. Flowers appear in the spring.

Dendrochilum cobbianum

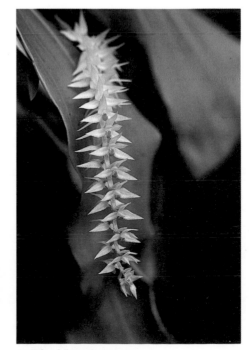

Dendrochilum glumaceum

Dendrophylax funalis

DENDROPHYLAX Reichb.f.
den-droe-FYE-lax
Tribe: Vandeae
Subtribe: Angraecinae
Etymology: Gr. *dendron*, tree; *phylax*, guard

Dendrophylax is a genus of about five species endemic to the Caribbean. These epiphytes are unusual in that they have no leaves; the plants consist of large root masses. *Dendrophylax* is closely related to other leafless Neotropical orchids such as *Harrisella* and *Polyradicion* (*Polyrrhiza*). The green to white flowers have prominent nectar spurs.

Because photosynthesis occurs in the roots of *Dendrophylax*, the plants must be grown mounted on a slab. Keep them frequently watered but do not allow water to remain around the roots — similar to the treatment given *Tolumnia* (equitant oncidiums). The plants should be grown in intermediate to warm temperatures and given bright light.

Dendrophylax funalis Fawcett

This species is endemic to Jamaica and closely related to the Cayman *D. fawcettii*. The winter flowers have light green sepals and petals offset by a white lip with a long greenish nectar spur. The blade of the lip is prominently bilobed. The several large flowers are borne on wiry individual scapes.

DIAPHANANTHE Schltr.
dye-a-fah-NAN-thee
Tribe: Vandeae
Subtribe: Aerangidinae

Etymology: Gr. *diaphanes*, transparent; *anthos*, flower

This genus of epiphytic orchids with monopodial stems contains about 50 species which are confined to Africa, mostly within the tropics. Their chief characteristic is the almost transparent flowers which range from white through pale green, yellow or pinkish colors. They are mostly rather small and are borne in few or many flowered, pendent inflorescences. There is a spur at the base of the lip and very often a callus at the mouth of the spur.

All species can be cultivated in intermediate or warm conditions. They are best mounted or established in well-drained compost in a basket. Many will flower several times a year and can withstand a prolonged dry period.

Diaphananthe pellucida (Lindley) Schltr.

This is one of the largest species in the genus with succulent pale green leaves 30–60 centimeters long alternating along the upright or pendent stem. It occurs throughout west Africa and as far east as Uganda. The pale yellow flowers are borne in long inflorescences, usually several at the same time, with up to 60 or 80 flowers each. The lip is broader than long, and its crystalline, fringed margin has a frosted appearance.

Diaphananthe rutila

Diaphananthe rutila (Reichb.f.) Summerh.

This is one of the most widespread species in Africa, but the plants are easily recognized by the reddish purple color of the stems and lower surface of the wide leaves. The flowers are also usually a rather reddish green. Inflorescences often appear repetitively from the same site on the stem, usually several times a year. The flowers are small but produced in great abundance.

DICHAEA Lindley
die-KEE-ah
Tribe: Maxillarieae
Subtribe: Dichaeinae

Diaphananthe pellucida

Etymology: Gr. *diche*, twofold; in reference to the leaves in two ranks

Dichaea is a poorly known genus of more than 100 species from throughout tropical America. The genus is characterized by the lack of pseudobulbs; the elongate, monopodial stems with closely arranged, strictly distichous leaves; the one-flowered inflorescences arising opposite the leaf axil; the free sepals and petals; the anchor-shaped lip; the column with a ligule beneath the stigma; the four hard pollinia attached to a stipe connected to a viscidium; and the smooth or echinate ovary. The species are placed in one of four groups depending on the presence or absence of deciduous leaves and echinate or smooth ovaries.

The species are epiphytic and occur in wet forests at elevations from 100 to 2,800 meters. As many as thirteen species have been found growing together in particularly rich habitats. All species appear to be pollinated by male euglossine bees, and some species produce powerfully fragrant flowers.

Cultivation of members of this genus is usually in intermediate conditions with abundant water throughout the year. The pendent species are often grown on plaques so that they can grow downward. The erect-growing species can easily be grown in pots.

Dichaea glauca (Sw.) Lindley

This species occurs from Mexico to Costa Rica and in the West Indies. The plants grow stiffly erect and the deciduous leaves are gray-green. The flowers reach 1.5 centimeters in diameter and are grayish

Dichaea hystricina

white spotted with lavender, especially on the lip. The ovary is smooth.

Dichaea hystricina Reichb.f.

This species is native from Guatemala to Ecuador and Venezuela and in the West Indies. The stems are sprawling to suberect. Leaves are deciduous, and the margins of the leaflets are ciliate. The flowers are cream-colored with red-brown spots. The lip has a pair of swollen calli at the base of the blade, and the ovary is echinate.

Dichaea morrisii Fawc. & Rendle

This species is the largest in the genus with flowers reaching three centimeters in diameter. It is native to the West Indies, Central America and most of tropical South America. The stems may be erect but usually curve downward, and the leaves are broad and articulated at the sheaths. The sepals and petals are usually green or yellow marked with red-brown. The lip is blue or white spotted with blue. The ovary is echinate.

Dichaea muricata (Sw.) Lindley

Dichaea muricata is distributed from the West Indies, through the Andean countries, and in Brazil. It is characterized by the pendent stems with the entire, non deciduous leaves slightly overlapping toward the base; the echinate ovaries; and the blue, anchor-shaped lip. Several species have been confused with *Dichaea muricata*, particularly in Central America where the species does not occur.

Dimerandra emarginata

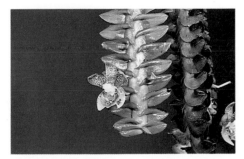

Dichaea muricata

DIMERANDRA Schltr.
die-mer-AN-dra
Tribe: Epidendreae
Subtribe: Laeliinae
Etymology: Gr. *di*, twice; *andra*, stamens; in reference to the reflexed lobes of the clinandrium of the column

This is a genus of nine species distributed throughout lowland tropical America. The genus is characterized by the presence of canelike stems with flat leaves at the nodes; the sessile inflorescences apical on the cane, with flowers produced singly in succession; the pink flowers with a white spot in the lip; and the eight hard pollinia. These are epiphytic plants of dry forests at elevations from sea level to 300 meters. The plants grow well in warm to intermediate conditions with abundant water during the growing season.

Dimerandra emarginata
(G. F. Meyer) Hoehne

This species is very similar to the other species in the genus, differing only in characters of the callus and column. The flowers are pink with a white spot at the base of the lip. The species is distributed from Mexico to Brazil and the West Indies.

Dimorphorchis lowii

DIMORPHORCHIS
(Lindley) Rolfe
die-morf-OR-kis
Tribe: Vandeae
Subtribe: Sarcanthinae
Etymology: Gr. *di-*, twice; *morphe*, shape; *orchis*, orchid

Three species have been described for this very unusual genus, which is endemic to the island of Borneo. *Dimorphorchis lowii* has been placed at various times in the genera *Arachnis, Renanthera,* and *Vanda.* The epiphytic, pendent stems usually branch at the base to form clusters. The unbranched inflorescences are limp, long, pendulous, hairy and many-flowered. Two forms of flowers occur in each inflorescence, hence the generic name. The terminal anther contains four pollinia in two pairs.

Dimorphorchis lowii (Lindley) Rolfe

Dimorphorchis lowii grows on branches of trees along rivers and other wet areas. Its long, pendulous sprays of large, fragrant flowers are extremely striking. The basal one to three flowers are yellow spotted with purple, while the remaining flowers are heavily blotched with maroon. Warm and humid growing conditions are required. Plants do best in shade and do not tolerate disturbance of the roots. This species has done well in captivity, but its size, with 70-centimeter-long leaves, makes it a rarity in collections.

DIPLOCAULOBIUM
(Reichb.f.) Kranzlin
dip-lo-call-O-bee-um
Tribe: Epidendreae
Subtribe: Dendrobiinae
Etymology: Gr. *diplous*, double; *kaulos*, stem

This genus of some 100 epiphytic species extends from Malaysia to Australia and the Pacific islands, with the most species from New Guinea. The one-leaved pseudobulbs are clustered or at some distance from one another on a creeping rhizome. The single-flowered inflorescences arise in succession from the apex of the pseudobulb. The flowers, often brightly colored but ephemeral, have rather filamentous sepals and petals and a three-lobed labellum fused to the column-foot. The lateral sepals are also fused at the base to the column-foot to form a mentum. There are four pollinia. Plants should be grown on slabs with bright light, high humidity, intermediate temperatures, and no rest period.

Diplocaulobium regale (Schltr.) A. Hawkes

One of the largest species in the genus, *D. regale* may grow into clumps 40 centimeters across with stems up to one meter high. The flowers are beautiful and last from one to three days, even longer at high elevations. The red flowers last the longest, but the white, pink and mauve forms are also very striking. In common with other members of this genus, the roots must be well drained as too much moisture can quickly kill the plants. In the wild, plants are often found growing in full sunlight, but some shade is helpful. Intermediate to cool conditions are required for this New Guinea species which occurs in nature from 1,000 to 2,300 meters.

Diplocaulobium regale

Dipodium ensifolium

DIPODIUM R. Br.
di-POE-dee-um
Tribe: Cymbidieae
Subtribe: Cyrtopodiinae
Etymology: Gr. *dis, di*, two; *podion*, little foot

About 25 species occur in this genus, adopting a range of growth habits including saprophytes, leafy terrestrials and climbing epiphytes. They occur in Malaysia, Solomon Islands, New Hebrides, New Caledonia, New Guinea, and Australia and range from temperate to tropical regions. Racemes of white to pink, often spotted or blotched flowers arise from axils on the stems. All species have four pollinia. Pollination is achieved by small bees.
The saprophytes are impossible to grow. Epiphytes should be attached to weathered hardwood or cork and grown in tropical conditions. Leafy terrestrials need to be potted in a soil-based mix. Keep plants evenly moist throughout the year and provide bright light. A dip in temperature in late winter/early spring may be necessary to induce flowering.

Dipodium ensifolium F. Muell.

Whereas many species of terrestrial *Dipodium* are leafless saprophytes, this species develops leafy growths which in old plants may become long and straggly. In their natural habitat these long growths are normally rejuvenated by bushfires. Long racemes bear large, showy flowers which are pink or mauve with prominent dark spots and blotches. *Dipodium ensifolium* will tolerate temperatures as low as 6°C at night.

DIPTERANTHUS Barb. Rodr.
dip-ter-AN-thus
Tribe: Maxillarieae
Subtribe: Ornithocephalinae
Etymology: Gr. *dipteros*, fly; *anthos*, flower; in reference to the resemblance of the flower to a fly

Dipteranthus planifolius

Disa cardinalis

Disa crassicornis

Dipteranthus is a genus of twelve species from South America. The genus is characterized by the presence of tiny pseudobulbs; a thick apical leaf; the inflorescence produced from the axils of the leaf-sheaths; the spurless yellow flowers; the long-beaked anther; and the four hard, ovoid pollinia attached to an elongate stipe connected to a flattened viscidium.

The plants grow as epiphytes in dry or wet forest at elevations from sea level to 1,000 meters. They are usually cultivated on plaques, so that the pendent inflorescences are shown to advantage. They may be grown under intermediate conditions but should not be allowed to dry severely.

Dipteranthus planifolius
(Reichb.f.) Garay

This species occurs from Venezuela to Bolivia. It is distinguished by the fan of tiny leaves surrounding the very small pseudobulbs and the erect column and rostellum directly in line with the lip rather than twisted. The flowers are yellow.

DISA Bergius
DYE-sa
Tribe: Diseae
Subtribe: Disinae
Etymology: Queen Disa, in Swedish mythology

The genus *Disa* consists of some 125 terrestrial species, grouped into fifteen sections and distributed throughout Africa, with the greatest concentration in south central Africa and South Africa. Only six species — *D. cardinalis, D. uniflora, D. racemosa, D. tripetaloides, D. venosa*, and

D. caulescens — are amenable to cultivation. All of these are from the western and southwestern Cape, South Africa, and have similar wet, stream-side habitats. All are cross-fertile and form the basis for 85 registered, highly desirable *Disa* hybrids. Seed, flasks, and plants are available from licensed growers. The other *Disa* species have a different habitat, defy cultivation, and are protected.

Cultivation demands strict adherence to basic rules. Provide a well-drained medium (coarse sand alone or with peat and sphagnum), and never allow it to dry out. Water from above or below (hydroculture). The water should have a pH of 4.5–6.0 with very few dissolved salts (less than 200 ppm). Disas are singularly intolerant of salt build-up. Maintain a relative humidity above 50 percent with abundant air circulation. Sunlight should be filtered and the fertilizer dilute and balanced. Propagate by division, new tubers, or from seed. Although seed germinates well on damp moss, flasking yields quicker results. Peak flowering season is midsummer, after which the old stem dies and gives rise to a new tuber or additional tubers via stolons.

Disa cardinalis Linder

This species grows in dense, stream-side colonies, producing long inflorescences 30–70 centimeters tall with up to 25 bright red flowers with a sparkling texture from November through February. Plants are easily grown from seed or divisions. The species has value as a long-lasting cut-flower and parent of outstanding *Disa* hybrids.

Disa crassicornis Lindley

This stunning, robust species from Natal, Transkei and the Eastern Province of South

Africa can reach one meter tall with a sturdy inflorescence of from five to 30 flowers. The colors vary from purple mottling on a pale cream background to striking deep pink mottling on a pink background. There is a strong, almost overwhelming sweet fragrance. The flowers have a characteristic decurved, cylindrical spur arising from the dorsal sepal, which is deeply hooded and triangular in side view. Petals are prominent, wing-shaped and extend beyond the hood. The lateral sepals are larger than the petals. The labellum is fairly long. This species from section *Hircicornes*

Disa Diores

Disa Kewensis

Disa racemosa

has an entirely different habitat from that of the other disas illustrated — grasslands, usually in damp places. Many attempts to grow this large disa with gladiolus-like flowers have succeeded for a year or two, but most often plants eventually die out in cultivation. This protected orchid is unavailable in nurseries, and all attempts to cross it with the other disas and their hybrids have failed.

Disa Diores

This famous hybrid (Veitchii x *uniflora*), originally registered by Veitch in 1898, has been frequently remade by *Disa* growers in the Cape. It is taller and more robust than *D.* Veitchii, having up to ten or more blooms, each the size of *D. uniflora*. Flowers are well-spaced and have a wide color range, usually lavender-lilac to magenta, but some have red, pink, yellow, and pastel tones. There are many awarded clones of this hybrid, which is excellent as a cut-flower and as a parent of many advanced hybrids.

Disa Kewensis

An important primary hybrid (*tripetaloides* x *uniflora*) first registered in 1893, *Disa* Kewensis has been frequently remade in the Cape, South Africa. The long inflorescences, up to 60 centimeters, bear up to 20 well-spaced flowers, about one-half the size of *D. uniflora* with an overall width of 40–45 millimeters. Color range varies from pale pink to deep cerise and magenta to pale lavender if the white or pink *D. tripetaloides* is used. Using yellow *D. tripetaloides* produces yellow to orange hybrids. Like *D.* Diores, there are many awarded clones of this key *Disa* hybrid.

Disa Kirstenbosch Pride

This primary hybrid (*cardinalis* x *uniflora*), registered in 1980, produces sturdy inflorescences of 60 centimeters or more, supporting fifteen cardinal red flowers often 60–70 millimeters wide. It makes a long-lasting cut-flower and produces hybrids with orange-red or rich red colors.

Disa racemosa L.F.

An important species in *Disa* hybridization, *Disa racemosa* is difficult in cultivation; in nature it occupies seepage marsh habitats and flowers only after fires. On an

Disa Kirstenbosch Pride

inflorescence of up to one meter, two to twelve pale pink-mauve to rosy magenta flowers are well spaced. Although vein markings are absent in the dorsal sepal, the petals have striking magenta margins and bars. The main value of this species lies in its contribution to important *Disa* hybrids.

Disa tripetaloides (L.F.) N. E. Br.

This species grows in dense colonies along stream banks in the Cape (flowering November–December) and Natal (flowering July–August). Attractive inflorescences 10–60 centimeters, bear up to 25 flowers, 20–30 millimeters wide, either white, white suffused with pink, or rosy pink or pure yellow, depending on locality. The deeply hooded dorsal sepal has numerous rosy purple stipples or spots. The best clones make stunning hybrids of wide color range when crossed to *D. uniflora* and other species.

Disa uniflora Berg.

By far the most striking and important species and parent, *Disa uniflora* is greatly cherished for the large, vibrant red colors and long bloom season, December–March. Mature plants produce flowering spikes up to one meter, depending on habitat, and bear up to three or more large flowers, ranging from red, carmine, orange, pink, and even yellow. The dorsal sepal is upright, hooded and veined, with a nectar-bearing spur inferiorly. The broad lateral sepals, slightly reflexed at the tips, form an equilateral triangle with the dorsal sepal. Two diminutive petals lie within the dorsal sepal. The long, narrow lip lies inferiorly. Flowers are long-lasting as cut-flowers and are even fragrant. Many fine clones of this

Disa tripetaloides

Disa Veitchii

Disperis fanniniae

species, the "Pride of Table Mountain," have been awarded and used as a key parent for numerous hybrids.

Disa Veitchii

This was the first *Disa* hybrid (*racemosa* x *uniflora*) to be made and registered by Veitch in 1891. The cross has been frequently remade, chiefly to make advanced crosses such as *D.* Diores, *D.* Betty's Bay, and *D.* Foam. Inflorescences up to one meter tall bear ten or more flowers about two-thirds the size of those of *D. uniflora.* They have a similar shape but are

Disa uniflora

colored pink, rosy magenta, or rosy purple. Yellow colors have recently been added by making the reciprocal cross.

DISPERIS Sw.
DIS-per-is
Tribe: Diseae
Subtribe: Coryciinae
Etymology: Gr. *dis*, twice; *pera*, pouch or sac

At least 70 or 80 species have been recognized in this genus, mostly African but a few extending into Madagascar and others eastward into Asia. About half of them are forest plants, growing in the humus-rich floor or in a thick blanket of moss on the lower branches of trees. Others grow in damp grasslands, where they are not easy to find, and disappear from view for many months. The flowers are extremely complex, with spurs or pouches on the lateral sepal and sometimes the dorsal sepal as well, while the lip and its appendage are usually hidden inside the flower. Several species have very attractive leaves. Many of the species can be easily maintained in a suitable compost in shallow pans. The species from forest habitats require heavy shade. Careful attention must be paid to the compost when the plants are dormant as overwatering can easily result in loss.

Disperis fanniniae Harvey

This terrestrial species occurs on the floor of forests and plantations throughout South Africa and Swaziland. It flowers in the summer months and is locally known as

'granny bonnets' from a fancied resemblance of the deeply saccate dorsal sepal. The plants are easily recognized by having three cordate, lanceolate leaves below the flowers and bracts, while the somewhat similar *Disperis lindleyana* with which they sometimes grow has only a single large leaf.

DIURIS Smith
die-URE-is
Tribe: Diurideae
Subtribe: Diuridinae
Etymology: Gr. *dis*, double; *oura*, tail

A colorful genus of about 55 species with one occurring in Timor and the remainder endemic to Australia. All species are deciduous terrestrials with subterranean tuberoids. Racemes of few to many attractive flowers provide an impressive floral display. These are commonly in bright hues and are often patterned or suffused with darker markings. All species have four pollinia and are pollinated by small bees. A very rewarding genus to grow because most species are adaptable and flower readily. Pot in a well-drained soil mix containing wood shavings and eucalypt leaf litter. Keep plants evenly moist when in active growth (autumn to spring). Dry out as plants die down and keep dry over summer. Repot every two or three years when dormant. Use fertilizers sparingly.

Diuris lanceolata Lindley

An attractive species from eastern Australia which commonly grows in moist, grassy situations. Flowers, which range from pale

Diuris lanceolata

Doritis pulcherrima

Dracula bella

yellow to bright yellow, are produced between late winter and midspring and often have a semi-nodding habit. Adapts well to cultivation and flowers readily.

Diuris punctata Smith

One of the most attractive of the Australian terrestrial orchids, this majestic species from the eastern states often grows in extensive colonies. Plants can have flower stems in excess of one meter tall and bear two to ten flowers each about six centimeters across. Colors are mostly mauve to purple and often have darker markings and suffusions.

Diuris punctata

The fragrance is pleasant and refreshing. Grows well in a pot and flowers readily.

DORITIS Lindley
doe-RYE-tis
Tribe: Vandeae
Subtribe: Sarcanthinae
Etymology: Gr. *dory*, spear; perhaps *Doritis* (Aphrodite)

Doritis is a genus of three terrestrial species native to southeast Asia. Closely related to *Phalaenopsis*, *Doritis* differs by its terrestrial habit, stiffly erect inflorescences, tiny lip side-lobes, and four pollinia.
Doritis has been hybridized with *Phalaenopsis* to make the genus X *Doritaenopsis*. This hybrid genus adds dark cerise color, upright inflorescences and a summer flowering time to *Phalaenopsis*. *Doritis* species should be given warm conditions similar to *Phalaenopsis*. Lacking pseudobulbs, they should be kept evenly moist throughout the year. Unlike *Phalaenopsis* species, *Doritis* species can tolerate medium to bright light levels.

Doritis pulcherrima Lindley

Native from northeast India and China to Borneo, this is a diploid species, having two sets of chromosomes. A closely related species, *D. buysonniana*, is a tetraploid, with four sets of chromosomes. With larger, paler flowers, *D. buysonniana* has been considered a variety of *Doritis pulcherrima* in horticulture. The flowers of *Doritis pulcherrima* are variable in color with typical plants bearing intensely pigmented cerise flowers. Pure white, white with

colored lip, and bluish strains are common in cultivation. All *Doritis* species have stiffly erect inflorescences in the summer.

DRACULA Luer
DRA-cu-la
Tribe: Epidendreae
Subtribe: Pleurothallidinae
Etymology: L. *dracon*, a dragon

Prior to 1978, the fabulous species that are now included in the genus *Dracula* were treated in *Masdevallia*. Presently about 90 species are recognized. They are distributed in the moist forests from southernmost Mexico to Peru, where only one species is known. Most occur in western Colombia and Ecuador. Some species are frequent, but many are rare and local. Vegetatively they are characterized by short-stemmed, thin leaves with a distinct midrib. The usually large, colorful flowers are produced by elongated stems that emerge from low on the leaf-stem. The sepals are variously connate (united) toward the base to form a flat or cup-shaped flower. The tips of the three sepals are attenuated into long, slender tails. The short, thick petals are warty at the apex, like a pair of eyes to either side of the nose (the column) and above the toothy lip. The apex of the lip is variously developed into a separate portion that is usually inflated with an assortment of lamellae or ridges, and larger than the basal portion. The column is thick with two pollinia.
Plants of this genus are relatively easy to cultivate in moist, well-ventilated, shady, cool greenhouse conditions. Most should

Dracula benedictii

Dracula chestertonii

Dracula chimaera

be planted in well-drained, hanging baskets because the inflorescences descend and emerge from the bottom of the container. During the last quarter of the nineteenth century the species then known were popular in cultivation in Europe. Today they are popular in the Americas, Europe, Australia, and New Zealand.

Dracula bella (Reichb.f.) Luer

This spectacular species is one of the most attractive of the genus. It is found locally only in the remaining virgin forests of the Western Cordillera of Colombia. The large, widely expanded, pendent flowers are shortly pubescent and densely spotted with red-brown on the yellowish background of the inner surfaces. The broad, kidney-shaped, white lip, traversed within by numerous ridges, dangles from the center.

Dracula benedictii (Reichb.f.) Luer

Also known affectionately by the later name *troglodytes*, which means cave-dweller, this species is found in both the Western and the Central Cordillera of Colombia. Although the small, cup-shaped flower is whitish on the outside, the deep interior appears black. In the depths of the flower the tiny column, petals, and lip appear like some mysterious thing lurking in the dark.

Dracula carderi (Reichb.f.) Luer

This species is found infrequently in the remaining virgin forests of the Western Cordillera of Colombia. It is easily recognized by the small, cup-shaped flowers that are densely pubescent within. The flowers with diverging tails are white, but variously marked with purple, from a

few dots to large, coalescing spots. The tiny lip within the cup is concave at the apex without ridges or teeth.

Dracula chestertonii (Reichb.f.) Luer

This species with grotesque flowers occurs locally in forests of the Western Cordillera of Colombia. The yellowish green, purple-warted sepals are widely spread to expose a proportionately huge, pinkish, mushroom-like lip complete with gills. Even a scent reminiscent of a fungus is emitted. Tiny gnats, recently identified as "fungus-gnats," frequent the flowers as well as those of any other species in open greenhouses in South America. Spontaneous hybrids frequently develop in nearby containers.

Dracula chimaera (Reichb.f.) Luer

This relatively frequent species from western Colombia is one of the largest-flowered of the genus. First discovered by Benedict Roezl in 1871, it is the first species of the genus to be described. The bizarre flowers can be more than 30 centimeters long between the tips of the sepaline tails. The fleshy sepals are hairy and variously colored, although densely purple-spotted forms are the most frequent. The orange, inflated, toothed lip protrudes from the center.

Dracula cutis-bufonis Luer & Escobar

This species from the Central Cordillera of Colombia is similar to *D. chestertonii* of the Western Cordillera. The name, which implies the skin of a toad, refers to the warty sepals. In contrast to the fixed lip of

D. chestertonii, the proportionately smaller lip of *Dracula cutis-bufonis* is loosely hinged from within the flower.

Dracula erythrochaete (Reichb.f.) Luer

This species is frequent, morphologically variable, and widely distributed in the forests of Central America. Four epithets have been applied to various forms. The flowers vary from small to medium in size, with forms more or less cup-shaped to widely expanded. They are shortly pubescent within. The basic color is a

Dracula erythrochaete

creamy white variously dotted, mostly at the base, with red to purple. The petals and lips with dilated, ridged apices are the same in all forms.

Dracula felix (Luer) Luer

This floriferous, small-flowered species is frequent in the Andean forests of northwestern Ecuador and adjacent Colombia. To compensate for size, the pale, little, cup-shaped flowers are produced in profusion on short stems. Apparently many flowers are self-fertilized because fruits are often encountered in the wild, and capsules also develop in the greenhouse.

Dracula gigas (Luer & Andreetta) Luer

One of the most robust of all species of *Dracula, Dracula gigas* is still found occasionally on the mountainous slopes of northwesternmost Ecuador where it once was abundant. Instead of descending, the strong inflorescence rises, sometimes to over 60 centimeters in height, to bear a succession of large, pinkish flowers with deep, pointed chins.

Dracula gorgona (Reichb.f.) Luer

This beautiful flower with large, rounded, long-tailed sepals is found uncommonly in the Western Cordillera of Colombia. The cream-colored sepals are densely long-pubescent on their inner surfaces, which are usually spotted with purplish brown. However, the coloring is usually absent on the lower, inner quadrants of the lateral sepals. The margins of the inflated apex of the lip are not rolled in.

Dracula nycterina

Dracula iricolor (Reichb.f.) Luer & Escobar

This species with small, short-tailed, lilac-colored flowers is found locally in the forests of western and central Colombia and northern Ecuador. The flowers are borne in slow succession on erect stems that reach as high as the leaves. The apex of the lip is smooth without forming ridges.

Dracula nycterina (Reichb.f.) Luer

This species from the Central Cordillera of Colombia resembles *D. bella* from the Western Cordillera. Both species produce similarly colored, widely expanded, long-tailed, pendent flowers, but those of *Dracula nycterina* are considerably smaller with a much smaller lip.

Dracula orientalis Luer & Escobar

No species of *Dracula* is yet known from Venezuela, but this species occurs farther east than any other known member of the genus, growing almost in the shade of mountains in Venezuela. The white flowers, dotted with dark brown and minutely pubescent within, have very long, slender tails. The apex of the lip is toothed with a few interrupted ridges.

Dracula platycrater (Reichb.f.) Luer

This species is found relatively frequently in both the Western and the Central Cordillera of Colombia. The flowers are easily recognized by the widely spread, narrow, oblong sepals with white tails no longer than the blades. The blades of the sepals are white and diffusely dotted with red-purple. The little lip is pink and ridged but convex instead of concave.

Dracula orientalis

Dracula psyche (Luer) Luer

This species is found infrequently in one forested valley in northwesternmost Ecuador. Small, delicate flowers are produced successively on erect stems about half as long as the narrow leaves. The cup-shaped flowers are white and streaked in red, with the red extending onto the slender tails. The tails of the lateral sepals are held more or less parallel.

Dracula radiosa (Reichb.f.) Luer

This species occurs in both the Western and

Dracula gorgona

Dracula platycrater

Dracula psyche

the Central Cordillera of Colombia in the north, and also in southern Colombia nearly to the Ecuadorian border. The somewhat fleshy, cup-shaped flowers are orange externally, and except for a prominent white band across the back the round, concave sepals are diffusely dotted with blackish brown within. The concave apex of the white lip is filled with straight, smooth, radiating ridges.

Dracula robledorum (P. Ortiz) Luer & Escobar

The handsome flowers of this large-flowered species, known from only one small area in the Western Cordillera of Colombia, are borne in succession by an erect stem. The widely spread, pubescent flowers are yellow or orange with prominent purple spots that coalesce toward the base. Above the column the pigment is arranged in radiating stripes. The tails of the sepals are not longer than the blades.

Dracula simia (Luer) Luer

This species is a native of southeastern Ecuador, where it is not uncommon. The large, reddish brown, long-tailed flowers are widely expanded to expose a broad, white halo around the petals and column and above the white, multi-ridged lip. The resemblance to the face of a capuchin monkey cannot be denied.

Dracula sodiroi (Schltr.) Luer

Unique in the genus, this species from northwestern Ecuador produces an erect raceme of several, simultaneous, orange, bell-like flowers. The drooping flowers,

each with three parallel, sepaline tails about as long as the flower, all point downward.

Dracula tubeana (Reichb.f.) Luer

Although a native of the forested slopes of northwestern Ecuador, this striking species was originally reported to be found in the hot, lowland, coastal plains. The narrowly ovate, long-tailed sepals, red-purple peripherally and white centrally, are widely expanded. The large, white, kidney-shaped lip is concave with many radiating ridges.

Dracula vampira (Luer) Luer

First known as the "black chimaera," this fabulous species is native to the forested slopes of northwestern Ecuador. The huge, hairless, widely expanded flowers are basically green, but usually the green is obscured by an intense purplish black suffusion and by streaking. A striped corona appears over the column and petals. The large lip is inflated and lined by many radiating ridges.

Dracula velutina (Reichb.f.) Luer

The concept treated as *Dracula velutina* is a variable complex widely distributed in all three cordilleras of Colombia. It is characterized by narrow leaves, and successive, small, white flowers variously suffused and dotted with purple. The flowers are pubescent within, and they vary from more or less cup-shaped to widely expanded. The petals and lips of all the forms are similar. The small, inflated apex of the lip contains only a few radiating ridges.

Dracula vespertilio (Reichb.f.) Luer

This species, locally but widely distributed from Central America to southern Ecuador, is very similar to *D. nycterina* and the much larger *D. bella*. The most distinguishing feature is the large, white, transverse lip with incurved sides which are completely smooth on the upper surface.

Dracula wallisii (Reichb.f.) Luer

Widely distributed in the Western and the Central Cordillera of Colombia, this large-flowered species is extremely variable in size, shape, and color. The sepals are densely long-pubescent and usually spotted with dark purple. Some forms are difficult to distinguish from *D. chimaera*. The lip of *D. chimaera* is oblong and immobile, while that of *Dracula wallisii* is more or less round and flexibly hinged.

DRAKAEA Lindley
DRAKE-ee-ah
Tribe: Diurideae
Subtribe: Caladeniinae
Etymology: After Miss Drake, nineteenth century English botanical illustrator

About eleven species are currently known, including five which are undescribed. All are endemic to Western Australia and are deciduous terrestrials with subterranean tuberoids. The broad leaves are somewhat thick and spongy, and the wiry flower stem bears a single terminal flower. This is dominated by an insect-like labellum which is hinged at the base. All species have four

Dracula tubeana

Dracula vampira

Drakaea glyptodon

pollinia and are pollinated by male wasps which attempt to mate with the labellum. These can be difficult to maintain in cultivation. Pot in a well-drained soil mixture containing wood shavings and eucalypt leaf litter. Keep moist when in active growth (autumn to spring), dry out as plants die down, and keep dry over summer. Repot carefully every one or two years. Use fertilizers sparingly.

Drakaea glyptodon Fitzg.

Named for the supposed resemblance of the labellum to *Glyptodon*, the genus of an extinct South American animal related to an armadillo, this orchid can only be described as bizarre. With the labellum being the most conspicuous feature, this very slender orchid is often difficult to discern in the heathy habitat where it grows in Western Australia. The labellum is the color of raw meat, and the flower releases a faint but distinct foetid smell.

DRESSLERELLA Luer
dres-ler-EL-lah
Tribe: Epidendreae
Subtribe: Pleurothallidinae
Etymology: Named for orchidologist-taxonomist Dr. Robert L. Dressler

The eight species of this genus apparently form isolated populations in the moist, tropical forests of Central America and the South American Andes as far as Peru. Most of the species are relatively uncommon. They are characterized by minutely ciliate to densely pubescent, thick, fleshy leaves that often lie prostrate in a rosette. The pubescent, fleshy flowers are borne singly

from the base of the leaf. Four pollinia are present: a large pair and a small pair. These plants may be cultivated in intermediate conditions in pots or on vertical slabs. They must be kept damp, but too much moisture causes rot.

Dresslerella pilosissima (Schltr.) Luer

This Costa Rican species and the Andean *D. hirsutissima* are the only two species of the genus with densely long-pubescent leaves and long-pubescent, widely spread flowers. The tips of their dorsal sepal and petals are minutely clavate, and their synsepals are

Dresslerella pilosissima

purple-spotted. The two species differ only in details of the lip.

Dresslerella stellaris Luer & Escobar

This large, coarse species, the largest of the genus, occurs rarely in Costa Rica and Colombia. Unfortunately, the huge, fleshy flower only barely opens at the tip. The dark, red-purple sepals are covered by a dense pubescence composed of thick, multiple-branching hairs.

DRESSLERIA Dodson
dres-LER-ee-ah
Tribe: Cymbidieae
Subtribe: Catasetinae
Etymology: In honor of Robert Dressler, contemporary orchid systematist

Dressleria is a genus of five species distributed from Nicaragua to Peru. The genus is characterized by the fleshy pseudobulbs of several internodes with thick, heavily veined, deciduous leaves; the inflorescence produced from the basal nodes; the bisexual, erect, green flowers; the short column embedded in the lip; the sensitive rostellum; and the two hard, clavate pollinia, attached to an elongate stipe connected to a rectangular viscidium. These are epiphytic plants in very wet forest at elevations from 500 to 1,300 meters. The plants can be cultivated under intermediate conditions but should not be allowed to dry out as with their related genus *Catasetum*.

Dressleria eburnea (Rolfe) Dodson

This species occurs on both sides of the Andes of South America. It is distinguished by the large flowers, with a diameter reaching five centimeters, evenly spaced on the inflorescence rather than in a subcapitate raceme. The flowers are extremely fragrant, and the leaves stink of dirty socks when crushed.

DRYADELLA Luer
dry-a-DEL-lah
Tribe: Epidendreae
Subtribe: Pleurothallidinae
Etymology: Named for the mythological Dryads

Prior to 1978 all the species of this genus had been included in *Masdevallia*. At present about 40 species range from southern Mexico into southern Brazil and northern Argentina. The densely tufted, thick-leaved plants are relatively small to very small, most bearing their small, successive flowers down deep within the foliage. The flowers, very similar in all the species, are characterized by a transverse

Dressleria eburnea

Dyakia hendersoniana

Dryadella simula

callus across the bases of the lateral sepals; short, multi-angled petals; and a long-unguiculate lip. The variously winged column bears two pollinia.

This genus has never been popular because of the small size and small, hidden flowers. Plants are easy to cultivate in moist, intermediate to cool-growing conditions.

Dryadella aviceps (Reichb.f.) Luer

This relatively common species from southern Brazil has been known as *D.* (or *Masdevallia*) *obrieniana*. It is one of the larger species with broad leaves usually suffused with purple. The yellow-green, purple-spotted flowers are of average size

with short, sepaline tails.

Dryadella edwallii (Cogn.) Luer

This Brazilian species is also common in collections. The yellow, purple-dotted flowers are larger than most — perhaps the largest in the genus — with long tails.

Dryadella guatemalensis (Schltr.) Luer

This species is frequent in Central America and adjacent Colombia. The leaves are long and very narrow. The purple-spotted flowers are above average in size. The sepals end in a point without forming true tails.

Dryadella simula (Reichb.f.) Luer

This species is frequent in the Andes. It does not occur in Central America where its name is usually applied to other species. The heavily spotted, tailless flowers are of average size.

DYAKIA E. A. Christ.
di-ACK-ee-a
Tribe: Vandeae
Subtribe: Sarcanthinae
Etymology: Malay *Dyak*, Borneo aborigines

A monotypic genus endemic to Borneo, *Dyakia* was previously included in a broadly defined *Saccolabium* and is also encountered under the name *Ascocentrum hendersonianum*. Although the bright rose-pink flowers borne on upright racemes superficially resemble *Ascocentrum*, *Dyakia* differs by its broader leaves, fleshy inflorescence and various floral characters. *Dyakia* should be grown in small pots under medium bright light levels. Without pseudobulbs or a pronounced dormant season, *Dyakia* plants should be kept evenly moist throughout the growing season.

Dyakia hendersoniana (Reichb.f.) E. A. Christ.

Endemic to Borneo, this is a choice miniature species. Fully mature plants rarely get more than ten centimeters tall and in the late spring bear rose-pink flowers with a white lip and spur on densely flowered erect racemes. The plants are unusual for their pale green leaves.

Embreea rodigasiana

Elleanthus aurantiacus

ELLEANTHUS Presl
ell-ee-ANTH-us
Tribe: Arethuseae
Subtribe: Sobraliinae
Etymology: Gr. *elle*, Helen; *anthos*, flower

Nearly 75 species range widely in the American tropics but are most diverse in the Andean countries. The stems are cane-like and distichously covered with plicate leaves. The inflorescences are terminal, usually racemes of brightly colored, small flowers. All species have eight pollinia.
Provide bright light and intermediate temperatures (15°C at night). Plants should be potted in relatively large containers to accommodate the thick roots and should be kept moist all year round.

Elleanthus aurantiacus (Lindley) Reichb.f.

A common species occurring from Costa Rica to Venezuela and Peru usually on roadbanks or open, rocky outcrops in areas of montane cloud forests at elevations of 1,200–2,500 meters. The scentless flowers are bright yellow or lemon yellow and are produced during July-October. *Elleanthus aurantiacus* will tolerate brighter light than most other species of the genus.

Elleanthus capitatus (Poeppig & Endl.) Reichb.f.

An interesting species from Ecuador and Peru at elevations of 500–1,200 meters with a capitate inflorescence of purple-red flowers, paler petals, and a white column. Several other species with capitate inflorescences are cultivated and confused with *Elleanthus capitatus* such as *E. sphaerocephalus* and *E. casapensis*.

ELYTHRANTHERA (Endl.)
A. S. George
ee-lee-thran-THER-ah
Tribe: Diurideae
Subtribe: Caladeniinae
Etymology: Gr. *elytron*, cover; *anthera*, the anther

Only two species and a natural hybrid are known in this very distinctive genus which is characterized by its glossy flowers which almost have an enamelled appearance. All species were previously placed in the genus *Glossodia*. They are deciduous terrestrials which have a subterranean tuberoid completely enclosed in a fibrous tunic. All species have four pollinia and are pollinated by small bees.
Grown mainly by specialist terrestrial growers. Pot in a well-drained soil mix containing wood shavings and eucalypt leaf litter. Keep moist when in active growth (winter to spring), dry out as plants die down, and repot carefully over summer. Use fertilizer sparingly.

Elythranthera emarginata (Lindley) A. S. George

The glossy, bright pink flowers of this Western Australian terrestrial have an arresting appearance. It often grows in colonies and produces an impressive floral display.

EMBREEA Dodson
em-BREE-ah
Tribe: Cymbidieae
Subtribe: Stanhopeinae
Etymology: In honor of Alvin Embree, contemporary patron of orchidology

Embreea is a monotypic genus known from western Colombia and southeastern Ecuador. The genus is characterized by the four-angled pseudobulbs with a single, grey-green leaf which is heavily veined on the underside; the pendent, single-flowered inflorescences; the dorsal sepal and petals not united to the column; the lateral sepals free or united only at the base; the lip excavate at the base and divided into hypochile, mesochile, and epichile, with the mesochile wings T-shaped; the claw of the lip without a callus; the bifid rostellum; and the two hard pollinia attached to an elongate stipe connected to a round viscidium.
These are epiphytic plants that grow in extremely wet cloud forest at elevations from 800 to 1,000 meters. They should be cultivated under intermediate conditions with abundant water throughout the year. Baskets provide the ideal container so that the pendent inflorescences can emerge. Continuous light fertilization is also beneficial.

Embreea rodigasiana (Claes ex Cogn.) Dodson

This species is found in northwestern Colombia and southeastern Ecuador. The very large, single flower on each inflorescence and the axe-shaped horns on the middle portion of the lip immediately distinguish the species.

ENCYCLIA Hook.
en-SIK-lee-ah
Tribe: Epidendreae
Subtribe: Laeliinae
Etymology: Gr. *enkyklein*, to surround; in reference to the lip enclosing the column

This is a genus of 242 species distributed throughout tropical America. The genus is characterized by the presence of pseudobulbs; the apical inflorescence; the flowers not exceeding four centimeters in diameter; the lip free from the column for most of its length; the column without a foot; and the four hard pollinia attached to caudicles.
These are mostly epiphytic plants with members of the subgenus *Encyclia*

Elythranthera emarginata

Encyclia alata

Encyclia cordigera

principally found in seasonally dry forest at elevations from sea level to 1,000 meters. Members of the subgenus *Osmophytum* are found in wet forest from sea level to 3,000 meters.

Most of the species can be accommodated under intermediate conditions with a few (mentioned in the text below) preferring cool conditions. They are usually cultivated similarly to members of *Cattleya* and do well on plaques.

Encyclia alata (Batem.) Schltr.

This species occurs from Mexico to Costa Rica and has been terribly confused with species occurring farther south. It is recognized by the large flowers with narrow, obtuse sepals and petals, the winged column, the broad lateral lobes of the lip that are constricted at the base, and the warty base of the lip. The flowers are yellow with brown apices of the sepals and petals, and the lip has red-brown lines on the apical lobe.

Encyclia brassavolae (Reichb.f.) Dressler

This species occurs from Mexico to western Panama at elevations from 1,200 to 2,500 meters. The flowers have long narrow sepals and petals and the lip has no side-lobes. The apical portion of the lip is red while the basal portion of the lip and the column are white. This spectacular species grows at higher elevations and requires cultivation in intermediate to cool conditions.

Encyclia citrina (La Llave & Lex.) Dressler

This species occurs in Mexico primarily on the western side. The gray-green plants hang pendently, and the flowers are pendent. The flowers do not open fully and are yellow with a white margin on the lip. *Encyclia citrina* was previously placed in the genus *Cattleya*. It is one of the cooler-growing species of the group and should have dry conditions during the winter.

Encyclia cordigera (H. B. K.) Dressler

Encyclia cordigera is one of the finest species in the genus. It occurs from Mexico to Colombia and Venezuela. The sepals and petals are red-brown and curled inward toward the apices. The lip varies in color from white with a red blotch at the disc to dark rose-red. It has been known as *Epidendrum atropurpureum* or *Encyclia atropurpurea*, but the name *Encyclia cordigera* predates *E. atropurpurea*.

Encyclia brassavolae

Encyclia fragrans

Encyclia pygmaea

Encyclia vespa

Encyclia fragrans (Sw.) Lemeé

This species occurs from Mexico, through Central America, the Greater Antilles and South America to Peru. The white to pale yellow flowers are sometimes spotted with red at the base of the petals, and the lip has red vein-lines that do not reach the apex. The flowers are held erect.

Encyclia mariae (Ames) Hoehne

This species is only known from northeastern Mexico at elevations from 1,000 to 1,200 meters. The plants have a grey-green color, and the erect inflorescence produces two to four flowers with a diameter up to seven centimeters. The sepals and petals are green, and the huge, white lip enfolds the column. The plants enjoy cooler conditions than most of the members of the genus.

Encyclia pygmaea (Hook.) Dressler

This is one of the smallest-flowered species in the genus. It has a creeping rhizome with widely spaced bifoliate pseudobulbs, and the flowers are produced singly in succession. The sepals and petals are yellow-brown and the lip is white.

Encyclia vespa (Vell.) Dressler

Encyclia vespa occurs from Nicaragua to Panama, Colombia, and Venezuela, and south through Ecuador to Bolivia. It also occurs in the Guianas and northern Brazil. The flowers are somewhat variable, though many of the supposed variants have proven to be valid species. The flowers are held on a stiffly erect inflorescence. The sepals and petals are green spotted with red-brown, and the lip is white with red-brown spots.

The flowers seldom exceed two centimeters in diameter.

Encyclia vitellina (Lindley) Dressler

This species is the coolest-growing member of the genus. The plants occur in the high mountains of Mexico and Guatemala from 1,500 to 2,600 meters. The flowers are held on an erect inflorescence, and the sepals and petals are orange-red. The lip is yellow with an orange-red apex.

EPIDENDRUM L.
eh-pee-DEN-drum
Tribe: Epidendreae
Subtribe: Laeliinae
Etymology: Gr. *epi*, upon; *dendron*, tree

With more than 1,000 species known, this genus is distributed throughout tropical America from Florida to northern Argentina. Recognized by the slit rostellum and the semiliquid viscidium produced thereof, most species have the lip united to the column, forming a nectary tube that

Encyclia vitellina

penetrates the pedicel. Most species have canelike stems (but many are thickened into pseudobulbs) and usually have four pollinia. In the past the genera *Dimerandra*, *Encyclia*, and *Oerstedella* have been included but are now recognized separately because of their very different rostella. The genus can be divided into more than 50 natural groups of species, and efforts have been made to recognize a number of artificial segregate genera which include, among others, *Diothonea*, *Epidanthus*, *Epidendropsis*, *Neolehmannia*, and *Neowilliamsia*.

Cultural conditions are widely varied, from lowland tropical to high alpine, but most species will grow well under intermediate temperatures (5°–15°C at night), with light shade and moisture throughout the year. In general they do not require a resting period. Many grow naturally in moss or on humus-covered rocks, so they may be grown in very light humus with high leaf content but always with very good drainage.

Epidendrum altissimum Lehmann & Kränzlin

This species is found in Colombia and Ecuador, along the western Andes at middle elevations, and produces rather lax scapes of white-and-purple flowers with no fragrance. It grows in cloud forests and requires watering throughout the year. It is rarely found in cultivation.

Epidendrum amethystinum Reichb.f.

Endemic to Ecuador, this species, though known for over a century, has hardly been seen in cultivation in spite of its being most attractive and relatively easy to grow. It was

Epidendrum altissimum

Epidendrum amethystinum

Epidendrum avicula

Epidendrum ciliare

Epidendrum cilindraceum

Epidendrum calanthum

Epidendrum cinnabarinum

referred to by Reichenbach as a "veritable little gem." It grows at high elevations and does well in the same conditions as *Masdevallia*.

Epidendrum avicula Lindley

An Amazonian species with short stems thickened into pseudobulbs and a hairy inflorescence including the outer surface of the sepals. It has been known under the name of *Lanium avicula*, but the separation of this and a few other species from the rest of *Epidendrum* is artificial. The species grows in warm, humid country, and requires these conditions throughout the year.

Epidendrum calanthum Reichb.f. & Warsc.

Closely related to *E. ibaguense*, this species has flowers that are smaller and usually pink. Pure white forms can frequently be found among the normal pink-colored form. Widespread along the Amazonian foothills of the Andes, at elevations between 600 and 1,600 meters, this terrestrial species grows frequently on roadbanks, in fully

exposed positions where rainfall is abundant. It should be grown in warm, humid conditions.

Epidendrum ciliare L.

A rather common species in Mexico and Central America, but also widespread in the West Indies and uncommon in South America, it is often sold as a white-flowered *Cattleya* as the plant is easily confused when not in flower. It does not, however, produce a sheath, and flowers appear on a scape with several to many imbricating bracts and between three and eight spider-like flowers. Plants usually grow on rocks, often in full sun at lower elevations. They should be grown with cattleyas.

Epidendrum cilindraceum Lindley

A species from southern Colombia and Ecuador, found at higher elevations, it produces an elegant raceme of cream-colored flowers, the scape enveloped by a prominent spathe at the base. Grow in an intermediate to cool condition, water year round, and place in a well-ventilated spot with abundant light.

Epidendrum cinnabarinum Salzmann

Endemic to coastal northeastern Brazil, the species has been in cultivation since the first half of the nineteenth century, when it was described. It produces tall caespitose plants, with non-resupinate flowers in orange-yellow-pinkish hues with a deeply lacerated lip. It flowers for a long time with many flowers in succession and should be grown in warm conditions in full sun, in light humus or any other medium which

Epidendrum coriifolium

Epidendrum coronatum

Epidendrum difforme

ensures very good drainage but humid roots.

Epidendrum conopseum R. Br.

This is the northernmost species of the genus, found from North Carolina in the United States, along the Gulf of Mexico coast to Louisiana, and then in northeastern Mexico. It grows epiphytically and should be kept in a cool house, with minimum night temperatures of 2°–15°C. Plants may be watered throughout the year, but roots prefer to grow exposed so they can dry out between waterings. Good ventilation and medium shade are important.

Epidendrum coriifolium Lindley

The name of this species, apparently endemic to Guatemala, has been used for a little-understood group of species that ranges from Mexico to Peru. The group can be recognized by the simple, compressed inflorescence with large, conduplicate bracts. The very fleshy flowers are usually all presented on one side of the scape and are green with various tones of reddish purple.

Plants are usually epiphytic but also grow on old lava flows and require intermediate- to cool-growing conditions, light shade, water throughout the year, and good drainage. The plant shown corresponds to the true *Epidendrum coriifolium* and can be recognized by the straight, acuminate, wide-open floral bracts.

Epidendrum coronatum Ruíz & Pavón

This widespread species, found from Mexico to Peru, has somewhat thickened canelike stems and fleshy leaves and an apical drooping raceme of between fifteen and 30 ivory-colored flowers. The stems may be up to 70 centimeters tall. The species grows at lower elevations and requires warm growing conditions, such as in a *Cattleya* house. Watering should be given throughout the year but in a well-drained compost.

Epidendrum difforme Jacq.

This species has been described as highly variable and widespread throughout the Neotropics, but in reality it is a complex group of some 100 species distributed from Florida to Brazil and Peru. Flowers of the group are usually green, sometimes white, successive or simultaneous, subcorymbose on a light green, succulent-leaved stem. They all grow well in a warm house with some shade, and usually high humidity throughout the year, though some species like to dry out their roots from one day to the next. The true *Epidendrum difforme* from Martinique, the island in the West Indies, can be recognized by the very compressed, ancipitous stems, the ovate

leaves keeled on the underside, and the two to four simultaneous flowers that appear from within the apical leaf without showing the scape.

Epidendrum falcatum Lindley

This lithophyte is endemic to Mexico on the high sierras of the Pacific mountain range at elevations of 1,400–1,600 meters. These very brittle plants with swollen stems always grow on rocks. They usually produce two to four white flowers, the sepals pinkish on the backside, and the middle lobe of the lip only slightly surpassing the lateral lobes. It has been said to be a variety of *E. parkinsonianum*, to which it is closely related, and at least one natural hybrid has been collected where the two forms grow sympatrically in the state of Guerrero. Cultivate in light shade and intermediate conditions. Water heavily after flowering, and once the growth has reached maturity water only sparsely.

Epidendrum gastropodium Reichb.f.

This very attractive Andean species grows near the treeline at higher elevations, in cloud forests. Its bunch of deep purple flowers, with black column and orange callus, makes it very attractive. It should be cultivated in cool conditions, with high humidity and good air movement, as with *Masdevallia* species.

Epidendrum geminiflorum H. B. K.

This Andean species with straggling plants grows at higher elevations on moss-covered rocky embankments and trees in well-

Epidendrum conopseum

Epidendrum falcatum

Epidendrum gastropodium

Epidendrum ibaguense

Epidendrum ilense

Epidendrum imatophyllum

Epidendrum geminiflorum

ventilated forest edges, often in full sun but usually in cloudy conditions. The species belongs to a group with flowers produced from a spathe that appears within the apical, fleshy leaves. The flowers are green to brownish, and are non-resupinate. It needs to be grown in cool conditions as for masdevallias — well ventilated, well drained, and with water throughout the year.

Epidendrum ibaguense H. B. K.

This caespitose species has upright stems, and erect, elongate scapes with a bunch of reddish yellow resupinate flowers. The column is about a centimeter long and is straight. It is restricted to Colombia. Some

plants from Venezuela, with purple flowers with a white blotch on the disk of the lip, have been considered as the same species. Cultivate in full sunlight, in light, well-drained humus and warm conditions. It has been very often confused with *E. radicans*, a repent species with similar flowers but which produces roots throughout the stems and has an arched column twelve millimeters long.

Epidendrum ilense Dodson

Endemic to Ecuador, this very showy species produces flowers from apical and lateral inflorescences. As a result of the felling of the tropical forests on the coastal plains of central Ecuador, where it grows as

an epiphyte, the species has been considered as endangered since it was first described. It has been successfully reproduced and introduced into horticulture by the Eric Young Micropropagation Centre at the Selby Botanical Gardens in Florida. Grow in warm conditions, with high humidity, throughout the year, but ensure that it is well drained.

Epidendrum imatophyllum Lindley

This lowland, widespread species, ranging from Mexico to tropical South America, grows as an epiphyte, always associated with ants, sometimes with *Coryanthes*. Its cultivation is problematic because of the high nitrogen requirements provided in nature by the ant nest. The species must be cultivated in a warm house with plenty of high nitrogen fertilizer, or ant manure — unless you allow for an ant nest in your greenhouse!

Epidendrum incomptum Reichb.f.

Native to Central America where it grows on trees at higher elevations, often in cloud forests, this species has a peculiar growth

Epidendrum laucheanum

Epidendrum incomptum

Epidendrum longipetalum

mode, whereby each new growth appears from a middle internode of the previous growth, sometimes with one or two roots at the base, thus forming a sort of ladder. Flowers are very fleshy, variously dotted or suffused with purple-brown. Cultivate under cool conditions with slight shade, on a piece of tree-fern slab or soft wood. The roots like to be well ventilated but often watered, as with cool-growing encyclias.

Epidendrum laucheanum Rolfe ex Bonhof

The long drooping flower-scapes of this species, up to 50 centimeters long, make it quite distinct. The fleshy flowers are long-lasting. This species grows in cloud forests in Costa Rica, and should be cultivated in cool, humid conditions, with good air movement, and with ample space below the plant for the inflorescence to develop to its full length, preferably by suspending the plant.

Epidendrum longipetalum A. Rich. & Galeotti [1]

Endemic to the Eastern Sierra Madre of Mexico, the mountain range that runs parallel to the Gulf of Mexico, this species inhabits cloud and oak forests at higher elevations, where the plants are constantly swept by the wet easterly winds. The long, hanging petals of flowers which are produced in long succession from the elongate spike keep this species in bloom over long periods. Some plants produce

Epidendrum macroclinium

Epidendrum marmoratum

Epidendrum oerstedii

light green-colored flowers. A similar species with a somewhat larger lip, and from the Southern Sierra Madre, is *E. tortipetalum* Scheeren.

Epidendrum macroclinium
Hágsater

This species from the lowlands of the Gulf of Mexico and Central America has a curious habit of maintaining the growths horizontal, the fleshy leaves elegantly striped, and the long scape producing a long succession of flowers over several years. It should be grown in warm conditions, with humidity throughout the year. The very long clinandrium, which is much longer than the column body, and the swollen vesicle behind the sepals have led to its separation, together with a few other species in the genus *Physinga*. However, these features are also found in other species of *Epidendrum*.

Epidendrum marmoratum
Reichb.f.

Endemic to the southern sierras of Mexico, at intermediate elevations, this species has the unusual feature of having the stems thickened into cigar-shaped pseudobulbs. It should be grown in intermediate conditions with cool nights (10°C), and kept well ventilated and under slight shade. Water well when the first roots and new growth appear, then sparsely once it has reached maturity. It grows under conditions similar to *Encyclia citrina*.

Epidendrum nocturnum Jacq.

This widespread species, ranging throughout the Neotropics, is apparently highly variable and often has self-pollinating flowers which produce distinct populations. It grows at lower elevations on rocky embankments, trees, and palms, sometimes in the hills where afternoon clouds provide high humidity during the better part of the year. Flowers are produced singly in succession over several years from the same stem, and, as the name suggests, have a sweet nocturnal fragrance. Cultivate in warm conditions on tree-fern slab or soft wood. Keep very well drained and watered throughout the year.

Epidendrum oerstedii Reichb.f.

A close relative of *E. ciliare*, ranging from Honduras to Panama, it also has a *Cattleya*-like habit, and produces its two-to-five-flowered inflorescence from the young growth, at the beginning of the rainy season, from May to July. It is also easily distinguished by the entire, non-fimbriate lateral lobes of the lip. Cultivate with cattleyas.

Epidendrum nocturnum

Epidendrum paranthicum

Epidendrum parkinsonianum

when in flower, with many stems flowering simultaneously. The plants are relatively easy to grow in warm to intermediate conditions. Water throughout the year and ensure good drainage.

Epidendrum pfavii Rolfe

This very attractive endemic species from Costa Rica produces large racemes of pink-purple flowers, which are rather long-lasting. The habit, with many-leaved stems up to a meter high, makes it an attractive garden plant for tropical and subtropical climates. It grows in rain forests at

Epidendrum peperomia

Epidendrum pfavii

Epidendrum paranthicum Reichb.f.

Known also as *Epidanthus paranthicus*, this species, like most of its close relatives, forms mats on branches and trunks in cloud forests at higher elevations. The plants frequently grow in association with moss. Grow in cool conditions, maintaining humidity throughout the year. Flowers are very small, some only three millimeters high. The closely related species *E. sancti-ramoni* has a red blotch on the lip.

Epidendrum parkinsonianum Hooker

This epiphytic species is common and

widespread from Mexico to Panama. It produces two-meter-long hanging plants with one to three large flowers with greenish sepals and petals (brown on the outside) and a white column and lip, the midlobe of the lip greatly surpassing the lateral lobes. It grows, in shade, in mixed forests where ventilation is good. Water when flowering begins to develop, and diminish once the growth has reached maturity.

Epidendrum peperomia Reichb.f.

This very popular small plant has large flowers which are glossy, especially on the prominent lip. It forms large mats on branches and in pots and can be spectacular elevations of 800–1,800 meters. The species is rare in nature as well as in horticulture, and its propagation should be encouraged.

Epidendrum porphyreum Lindley

This very attractive plant flowers for about four months, and can be a real spectacle. It grows in Ecuador, especially at intermediate elevations on the eastern side of the Andes, on rocks, embankments, and trees in wet forests. It makes a very good garden plant in wet climates with warm to intermediate temperatures. The long-lasting flowers develop their purple color with time, eventually fading into yellowish purple. Cultivate in rich humus with good drainage.

Epidendrum pseudepidendrum Reichb.f.

Possibly one of the most spectacular flowers in *Epidendrum* due to the color combination and the plastic aspect of the flowers, this species is endemic to Costa Rica and western Panama, where it grows at lower elevations. It produces one or more scapes of between one and three flowers at or near the apex of the stems. The species is rare if not endangered in nature, but fortunately nearly all of the plants available in commerce are from propagated sources, and this should be encouraged as an alternative source to wild-collected plants. It flowers from January to March. Grow in warm conditions.

Epidendrum pugioniforme Regel

Endemic to the southern sierras in Mexico, this plant grows hanging from oak trees at higher elevations in well-ventilated forests, often covered in clouds in the afternoon. It

Epidendrum porphyreum

Epidendrum pseudepidendrum

Epidendrum pugioniforme

is closely related to *E. lacertinum* Lindley from the Mexican-Guatemalan border areas overlooking the Pacific Ocean. Grow in intermediate conditions with minimum night temperature of 10°C. Water throughout the year but reduce the watering once the growth has reached maturity.

Epidendrum purum Lindley

This species from northern South America grows on trees at middle elevations in warm valleys. Its stems are somewhat thickened toward the middle, without forming pseudobulbs. It produces a panicle of creamy white, sweet-scented flowers. Grow in a well-drained pot or on a piece of wood, in warm conditions. Water throughout the

year but reduce the watering somewhat after growth has matured.

Epidendrum radicans Pavón ex Lindley

This is a common and widespread species ranging from Veracruz in Mexico to the Valle del Cauca in Colombia. It is terrestrial on road embankments and mixed woods at middle elevations. It grows in profusion in full sun, but its straggling habit makes it unsuitable for small spaces. It has been confused with *E. ibaguense* because of its very similar flowers, but the arched column and straggling habit with roots produced throughout the stems distinguish this species from all of its relatives in the same

Epidendrum purum

Epidendrum ramosum

Epidendrum raniferum

Epidendrum radicans

group. Cultivate in warm or intermediate conditions, with full sun. Keep wet but well drained.

Epidendrum ramosum Jacq.

This species, which is common and widespread at lower elevations, ranges from Mexico to Brazil and Peru and occurs also in the West Indies. The main stem produces shorter lateral stems which flower apically. The leaves of the main stem are typically larger than those of the branches, but are often lacking when a large plant is in flower. It grows epiphytically in tropical woods and should be grown in warm conditions. It needs plenty of watering throughout the year but should have good drainage; the roots like to be kept moist.

Epidendrum raniferum Lindley

A typical plant of this species will be about 60 to 100 centimeters tall, but some grow easily to 1.5 meters. At least one has been seen to reach five meters. The drooping raceme of green-and-white flowers speckled with reddish purple make it a very attractive garden plant. The species grows as a lithophyte or in humus and will grow well in a large pot with a light humus and good drainage in partial shade, with temperatures ranging between 10° and 30°C (daily minimum and maximum). It flowers from April to June. The species has been known as *E. cristatum* Ruíz & Pavón, which was originally described from Peru. The group is widespread throughout tropical America from Mexico to Brazil and Bolivia.

Epidendrum rigidum Jacq.

This, the most common *Epidendrum*, is

abundant in lowland, wet jungles, straggling on branches of trees with its inconspicuous flowers. It ranges from Florida to Brazil and Peru. It is also probably one of the more primitive species of the genus. Grow on tree-fern slabs or soft-wood branches in warm, humid conditions, in slight shade.

Epidendrum rigidum

Epidendrum sophronitoides

Epidendrum stamfordianum

Epidendrum secundum

Epidendrum veroscriptum

Epidendrum secundum Jacq.

This is a common lowland species, found from Florida, through Central America, to the West Indies and the coast of tropical South America. It produces short racemes of small yellowish green to purple flowers from an elongate scape, flowering from the same scape over many years. It requires warm and wet conditions but good drainage. The species has long been known as *E. anceps.*

Epidendrum sophronitoides
Lehmann & Kränzlin

This curious small plant has *Vanda*-like growths that flower from an inflorescence produced from the bottom part of the stem.

The scape itself produces one flower at a time, but in succession, and new flowering stems from the old ones. The plants inhabit high elevation cloud forests in the Andes in Colombia and Ecuador, usually in well-ventilated areas on moss-covered trees. Grow in cold conditions, as for *Masdevallia* species, but with plenty of air movement and high humidity throughout the year.

Epidendrum stamfordianum
Bateman

This attractive species usually produces white-and-yellow flowers, but plants from the eastern lowlands of Colombia produce pink flowers. The inflorescence usually appears from an abortive stem from the rhizome, rarely from the apex of a normal stem, which is thickened into a fusiform pseudobulb. It is found wild in dry lowlands, where there is a strict difference between the rainy and dry seasons. It is grown in warm conditions with cattleyas.

Epidendrum veroscriptum
Hágsater

One of the many species that have gone under the name *E. paniculatum*, it grows in Mexico at middle elevations. Stems, usually 50–90 centimeters high, produce a panicle of many flowers in the spring. Typical of this species is the ring of burgundy-red dots around the disc of the lip, although the same plant can vary the pattern every year. Other species have different markings: in some the disc is entirely pale lavender; in others the disc is covered with dark burgundy-red markings. This group of species is still little understood, but some studies show pollinator specificity.

Epidendrum vesicatum Lindley

A native of Brazil, this pendent plant, with glaucous, imbricating leaves, is quite unusual and attractive. The inconspicuous, whitish flowers are hidden within the apical leaf which forms an inflated envelope around them. Grow the plant hanging from a tree-fern slab or piece of wood in a humid, warm greenhouse. It also likes to have its roots covered with moss.

Epidendrum vesicatum

EPIPACTIS Sw.
ep-ee-PAC-tis
Tribe: Neottieae
Subtribe: Limodorinae
Etymology: Gr. *epipaktis*, name for a medicinal plant used by ancient Greeks

The genus comprises some 35 species distributed from Europe southward to Ethiopia then eastward through temperate Asia to Japan. Only one species, *E. gigantea*, is native to North America, but *E. helleborine* has thrived and spread as an introduction.

Epipactis gigantea

Epipactis palustris

The genus is ancient in origin, as is indicated by its wide distribution. All *Epipactis* have rhizomes, not tubers. Perianth segments are spreading, and the lip is in two parts: a cup-shaped hypochile near the base, and a heart-shaped to triangular epichile at the apex.

Epipactis gigantea Douglas ex Hook.

Although the stems are long (often 50 centimeters or more) they hardly merit the description "gigantic." A terminal inflorescence of between five and fifteen flowers is carried on a stem with from four to fifteen pleated, pubescent leaves. Each flower is subtended and overtopped with a leafy bract, which detracts from the attractive flowers. Coloring is a blend of yellowish or greenish flushed with purple on the sepals. Petals are broad with brownish purple veining. The lip has a white midlobe with a brown and yellow callus at its base. As a wild plant it thrives in moist places — whether in full sun along stream banks, in river gravels and even in shallow streams, or in shaded hillside seepages. In cultivation it can be readily established in a rock garden in a loam, peat, and leaf mold compost in shade or in sunnier spots. It is particularly attractive growing beside a small stream.

Epipactis palustris (L.) Crantz

This species is locally common and very widely distributed throughout Europe, the Middle East, and into Japan wherever conditions are alkaline: fens, marshes, dune slacks and gravel pits up to 1,600 meters in alpine regions. Plants from exposed sites in dune slacks tend to range from ten to 25 centimeters tall, yet in less rigorous conditions stems can reach a stately 60 centimeters or more with fifteen flowers in the raceme. Leaves are densely pubescent, from four to eight in number, rather narrow and arranged spirally up the stem. Sepals are greenish gray tinged with purple on their exterior surfaces and reddish inside. Petals are shorter, colored off-white with reddish brown tinge and red veining. The lip is a complicated structure: the hypochile is slightly concave with triangular red-striped side-lobes and an orange platelike structure in its upper portion which produces nectar; the white epichile is joined to it by a "hinge" which has a wavy margin and yellow ridges at its base. Flowering occurs from June through September. This species can be established as a garden plant in loamy soil to which leaf litter and limestone chips have been added. The soil must be kept moist throughout the growing season.

ERIA Lindley
EAR-ee-a
Tribe: Epidendreae
Subtribe: Eriinae
Etymology: Gr. *erion*, wool, in reference to the woolly flowers and stalks of some species

This very large genus, of an estimated 500 species, is distributed from the Indian subcontinent through China, southeast Asia, to the Pacific islands, but very few are presently in cultivation. Closely related to *Dendrobium*, they are readily distinguished by the eight pollinia. Great diversity exists in the floral and vegetative characters. The stems may be pseudobulbous, like those of *Bulbophyllum*, or may be elongated and reedlike with few to many leaves. The few-to many-flowered dense racemes are often ornamented with colorful bracts and arise from near the apex of the pseudobulbs. Those *Eria* species with creeping rhizomes should be mounted on tree-fern plaques, and those with reedlike stems do best in hanging baskets. A well-drained compost of osmunda fiber or tree-fern is suitable. Water should be applied freely in the growing season with a short rest period after growth is completed. Fertilizing with a balanced fertilizer at half-strength during growth is recommended. Avoid frequent repotting; allow plants to grow to specimen size.

Eria coronaria

Eria coronaria (Lindley)
Reichb. f.

Distributed throughout the Himalayas, northeast India, Burma and Thailand, this species produces a short, very attractive raceme of three to seven fairly large, waxy white, fragrant flowers with a golden yellow lip marked with purple veins. The reedlike pseudobulbs bear two or three leaves at the apex. Flowers are produced after formation of the new growth. *Eria coronaria* is a cool-growing species that prefers moisture around the roots throughout the year. The compost should contain equal parts of osmunda and chopped sphagnum and polystyrene granules for drainage. It can tolerate winter night temperatures down to 5°C.

Eria floribunda Lindley

Found in Burma, Thailand, Vietnam, Malaya, Sumatra, Java, Borneo, Sarawak, and the Philippines, this attractive species carries several horizontal, densely flowered racemes on elongated stems. The flowers are white tinged with pink, with purple on the apex of the column. The reedlike stems are often 45 centimeters long. It flowers April–June and should be grown under intermediate to warm conditions.

Eria javanica (Sw.) Blume

Widely distributed from India, southeast Asia to Indonesia and the Philippines, this species is perhaps one of the most beautiful, producing 60-centimeter-long racemes of several starlike well-spaced flowers more than once a year. The flowers are four centimeters in diameter and white to cream-colored, often with purple stripes. Pseudobulbs are ovoid with a pair of leaves at the apex. Cultivate in a warm house.

Eria ornata (Blume) Lindley

This very ornamental and rare species comes from the Malay Peninsula and produces arching racemes up to 45 centimeters long with large, orange-red to cinnabar-brown bracts enclosing the greenish yellow flowers. It should be cultivated under intermediate to warm conditions.

Eria vittata Lindley

Found in northeast India, Burma, and Thailand, this species produces arching racemes of highly fragrant, pale green flowers striped with brownish purple. The pseudobulbs are cylindric and tapered upward with two leaves at the apex. It requires intermediate conditions and can tolerate winter temperatures of 5°C. It flowers during March–April.

ERIOPSIS Lindley
ee-ree-OP-sis
Tribe: Cymbidieae
Subtribe: Cyrtopodiinae
Etymology: The orchid genus *Eria*; Gr. *opsis*, appearance

Four or five species are currently known in tropical America ranging from Honduras to Brazil and Peru. The plants have pear-shaped pseudobulbs bearing two to four leaves. The racemose inflorescence, arising from the base of the pseudobulbs, bears brownish yellow flowers.

All species should be potted in well-drained clay containers. Terrestrial species (e.g. *E. biloba*) thrive in the mixture recommended for *Cyrtopodium* species; epiphytic species (e.g. *E. sceptrum*) grow better in sphagnum moss. Fertilize during active growth and provide intermediate temperatures (20°–25°C during the day, 15°–18°C at night), shade, and humidity. Reduce water once new pseudobulb is fully developed.

Eriopsis biloba

Eriopsis biloba Lindley

This robust species, found in Colombia, Venezuela, the Guianas, and northern Brazil, produces erect, many-flowered racemes from December to August. Sepals and petals vary from orangish yellow to brownish yellow variously flushed with maroon; the lip is white spotted with maroon, dark maroon toward the base, with two basal parallel raised plates.

ESMERALDA Reichb.f.
es-mer-AL-da
Tribe: Vandeae
Subtribe: Sarcanthinae
Etymology: Gr. *smaragdus*, emerald

There are two species in this genus: *E. cathcartii* and *E. clarkei*. A third species that has been described, *E. bella*, is a form of *E. clarkei*. These are high-elevation plants, growing in the shaded, moist valleys of the eastern Himalayas, Burma, China, and Thailand. The plants produce stout stems about a meter high, with deep green leathery leaves. Three to five beautifully barred flowers are produced on short racemes. Both species have four pollinia. Provide intermediate temperatures, medium light and high humidity. The leathery leaves indicate a degree of drought-tolerance.

Esmeralda cathcartii (Lindley) Reichb.f.

This species excited the highest admiration from Lindley, Reichenbach and J. D. Hooker who stated that "No more remarkable orchid has been found in Northern India." The broad, pale yellow petals and sepals streaked with transverse brown stripes are set off beautifully by the yellow pendulous lip. This species is rare in collections.

Esmeralda clarkei Reichb.f.

Esmeralda clarkeii is very similar vegetatively to *E. cathcartii*, but differs in the narrowness of its sepals and petals and in its wider distribution. As well as the eastern Himalayas, *E. clarkei* also occurs in Burma, Thailand, and even Hainan, China.

EUANTHE Schltr.
yoo-AN-thee
Tribe: Vandeae
Subtribe: Sarcanthinae
Etymology: Gr. *euanthes*, blooming

Euanthe is a monotypic genus from Mindanao, in the Philippines. *Euanthe* is closely related to *Vanda* and is still treated as *Vanda sanderiana* by many authors. It differs from other vandas by having an

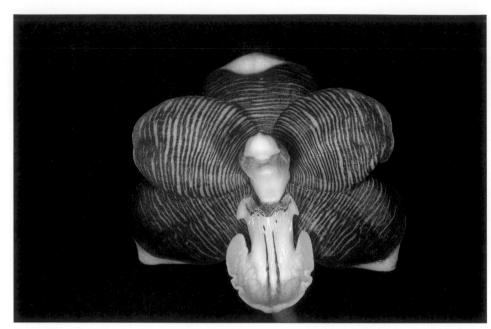

Esmeralda cathcartii

Esmeralda clarkei

essentially two-parted lip with the base (hypochile) inflated into a balloon-like structure. *Euanthe sanderiana* also differs from other vandas in having a very full-shaped flower with flat floral segments. Horticulturally, *Euanthe* is still treated as a *Vanda* and is the dominant parent in most *Vanda* hybrids and related genera (e.g. X *Ascocenda* [*Ascocentrum* x *Vanda*]). *Euanthe* should be given very bright light but not direct sunlight. Grown in a pot in an open epiphyte compost or in a basket, plants should be given frequent watering, heavy fertilizing, and constantly warm conditions.

Euanthe sanderiana (Reichb.f.) Schltr.

This Philippine species is one of the showiest of Asian orchids because of the large flowers with broad, overlapping floral segments. The pinkish green flowers are stained with greenish brown on their lower halves. An *alba* strain has been selected that bears white flowers stained with green. Unlike its ever-flowering hybrids, *Euanthe sanderiana* flowers seasonally in the fall. Rare because of wild-collection for horticulture, *Euanthe sanderiana* has been line-bred in cultivation, and much improved strains are readily available.

Euanthe sanderiana

Eulophia guineensis

Eulophia alta

Eulophia speciosa

EULOPHIA R. Br. ex Lindley
yoo-LOW-fee-ah
Tribe: Cymbidieae
Subtribe: Cyrtopodiinae
Etymology: Gr. *eu*, well or true; *lophos*, plume

This is a large genus of at least 250 species. It is widespread throughout the tropics but most of the species occur in Africa. A few are saprophytes, but most are terrestrial plants with upright pseudobulbs at ground level or chains of subterranean tubers. They grow in a wide variety of habitats, from swamps to forest and sandy beaches to montane grassland or semi-desert. The leaves are usually greatly elongated, folded or plicate, sometimes short-lived. The inflorescences are upright, often tall, bearing a succession of flowers in a wide variety of colors.

Species with pseudobulbs above the ground are easily maintained in cultivation in a well-drained compost. Those with subterranean tubers have also been maintained for a few seasons but are easily lost unless great care is paid to the watering regime.

Eulophia alta (L.) Fawcett and Rendle

This species was first described from Jamaica but is now known to be widespread throughout tropical America and Africa. It grows in swamps and wet grassland, the large inflorescence rising to one to two meters above the subterranean rhizome. The leaves are large and plicate. The flowers are olive green and reddish purple and do not open widely.

Eulophia guineensis Lindley

This is a handsome terrestrial species with the elegant inflorescence arising at the same time as fresh new leaves enveloping a new pseudobulb. It is widespread in tropical Africa, from Nigeria to Ethiopia and south to Angola and Zambia. It has also been found in N. Yemen and Oman. It grows in shade or partial shade among rocks, scrub or woodland. The showy flowers have purplish brown sepals and petals and a large pink lip which is white at the base.

Eulophia speciosa (Lindley) Bolus

This species is widespread throughout the continent of Africa and extends eastward into Arabia. The irregular tubers are underground, connected to each other by a stout rhizome. The fleshy leaves appear in a fan at the same time as the new inflorescence in the spring. The flowers are variable in size, showy, with greenish sepals and bright yellow petals and lip.

GALEANDRA Lindley
gal-ee-AN-dra
Tribe: Cymbidieae
Subtribe: Cyrtopodiinae
Etymology: L. *galea*, helmet; Gr. *andr-*, man; in reference to the helmet-like anther cap

Galeandra is a genus of 26 species distributed from Mexico to Bolivia but with strongest representation in the Amazon region. The genus is characterized by the elongate, cylindrical pseudobulbs (small and terrestrial in the *G. beyrichii* group), with thin, narrow, heavily veined, articulated, distichous leaves at the nodes; apical inflorescences; bisexual flowers with a spur at the base of the lip; the anther beaked at the apex; and the four pollinia superimposed to appear as one pair and attached directly to the viscidium.
Most species are epiphytes at lower elevations from sea level to 500 meters. A few are terrestrials on steep embankments at higher elevations. The species can be grown in intermediate to warm conditions along with members of *Cattleya.*

Galeandra batemanii Rolfe

This species grows as an epiphyte from Mexico to Costa Rica in seasonally dry regions. The pseudobulbs are top-shaped, and the leaves are deciduous during the dry season. The flowers have yellow-brown sepals and petals with the lip purple toward the apex and white at the base. The lip extends at the rear to form a curving spur.

Galeandra batemanii

Galeandra beyrichii Reichb.f.

Galeandra beyrichii occurs as a terrestrial in south Florida and from Mexico, through Central America, to Argentina. The pseudobulbs are cormlike and occur under the surface of the soil. The leaves are deciduous during flowering. The sepals and petals are green, and the lip is greenish white with red stripes in the throat.

GALEOTTIA A. Rich.
gal-ee-OT-ee-ah
Tribe: Maxillarieae
Subtribe: Zygopetalinae
Etymology: In honor of H. Galeotti, Italian botanist during the nineteenth century

Galeottia is a genus of eleven species distributed from Mexico to Venezuela, Peru, and Brazil. The genus is characterized by the approximate pseudobulbs; plicate leaves more than fifteen centimeters long; the inflorescence from the base of the pseudobulb, multiflorous; the fan-shaped callus; the three-lobed lip; the margin of the lip often fimbriate; and the four hard pollinia attached to a quadrate stipe. The plants are epiphytes in moist forest at elevations from 300 to 2,000 meters; some species occur as terrestrials. These plants can be cultivated under warm to intermediate conditions.

Galeottia burkei (Reichb.f.) Dressler & Christensen

This species occurs as a terrestrial in Venezuela and has been reported from Peru. The sepals and petals are pale brown with spots and lines of dark, shiny brown, and the lip is white with pink lines on the teeth of the callus. The lip is glabrous.

Galeottia fimbriata

Galeottia fimbriata (Linden & Reichb.f.) Dressler & Christensen

This species occurs as an epiphyte in Colombia and Venezuela. The sepals and petals are brown with darker brown stripes and vein-lines, and the lip is light brown with dark purple vein-lines and is covered with hairs. The pubescence is obvious on the margin of the lip.

GASTROCHILUS D. Don
gas-troe-KYE-lus
Tribe: Vandeae
Subtribe: Sarcanthinae
Etymology: Gr. *gaster*, belly; *cheilos*, lip

Gastrochilus is a genus of about 45 epiphytic species distributed from southern India to the Philippines, with a concentration of species in Indochina and China. Species of *Gastrochilus* were formerly included in a broadly defined *Saccolabium.* The genus is characterized by its distinctive stomach-shaped saccate lip, porate pollinia and umbellate inflorescences. Most species are short-growing, fan-shaped plants with a few trailing and pendent species. Flower color is variable but usually in shades of white to yellow with dark spotting and barring. The midlobe of the lip is fused to the outside edge of the sac and is often ornamented with fleshy hairs.
Of monopodial growth and lacking pseudobulbs, *Gastrochilus* should be kept evenly moist throughout the year. Even those species adapted to a monsoonal cycle do not require pronounced drying out in cultivation. Most species prefer intermediate temperatures and medium bright light levels. Some of the small-growing species from China, the Himalayas, and Taiwan prefer cool conditions and uniformly plentiful water.

Gastrochilus calceolaris D. Don

This species is native from the northwest Himalayas to Indochina and north to China. The fall flowers are translucent cream marked with dark brownish red spots. The lip is white with a bright yellow central patch and is raggedly fringed. The easiest species of *Gastrochilus* to grow, it freely produces lateral branches and readily forms specimen plants.

Gastrochilus obliquus (Lindley) O. Kuntze

Gastrochilus obliquus is native from northeast India to Vietnam. The species is widely cultivated from Thai material but usually under the misapplied name *G. dasypogon.* Several other species are grown as "dasypogon," including *G. bigibbus, G. intermedius,* and *G. suavis.* The rich yellow flowers of *Gastrochilus obliquus* have white sacs with purple edges

Gastrochilus calceolaris

Gastrochilus obliquus

Genoplesium rufum

and internal purple spots. The broad, white, fringed midlobe has a central yellow patch covered with fine red spots. Flowering occurs in the fall.

GENOPLESIUM R. Br.
gee-no-PLEASE-ee-um
Tribe: Diurideae
Subtribe: Prasophyllinae
Etymology: Gr. *genos*, race or kind; *plesios*, affinity

About 35, generally inconspicuous species are currently known, with most occurring in Australia, two in New Zealand and one in New Caledonia. All are very slender, deciduous terrestrials with subterranean tuberoids and a hollow, terete leaf through which the inflorescence emerges. Flowers are generally small and dull-colored; the segments of some species are fringed with delicate hairs. All species have four pollinia. Many species are self-pollinating; others release fruity perfumes and are pollinated by small vinegar flies.

Genoplesium fimbriatum (R. Br.)
D. Jones & M. Clements

The flowers of this Australian species, which are relatively large for the genus, are yellowish with prominent red stripes and a pale red labellum which is fringed with long fine hairs. This organ is delicately hinged and trembles in the slightest breeze. The flowers produce a strong lemon fragrance which is very noticeable in warm weather.

Genoplesium fimbriatum

Genoplesium rufum (R. Br.)
D. Jones & M. Clements

Although this Australian species has light red flowers, it is inconspicuous in the dull light of its natural habitat. The short, dense spikes are produced from midsummer to early spring. The individual flowers are very attractive when magnified under a lens.

GOMESA R. Br.
goe-MEZ-ah
Tribe: Cymbidieae
Subtribe: Oncidiinae
Etymology: In honor of Bernardino Antonio Gomes, Portuguese physician and botanist during the nineteenth century

This is a genus of thirteen species found in central and southern Brazil. The genus is characterized by the flattened, oblong pseudobulbs with two apical, rather soft leaves; the arching, multiflowered inflorescence produced from the base of the pseudobulb; the yellow-green flowers with wavy margins to the segments; and the two hard pollinia on a stipe attached to a viscidium.
The plants grow as epiphytes in forests of southern Brazil. They can be cultivated in intermediate conditions with members of *Cattleya*.

Gomesa barkeri (Hook.) Regel

This species occurs in southern Brazil. The sepals and petals are light green-yellow, spreading with crisped margins, and the apex is curved inward. The lip is abruptly bent downward at the midpoint. The lateral sepals are free nearly to the base.

Gomesa crispa (Lindley) Klotzsch & Reichb.f.

This species occurs in southern Brazil. The sepals and petals are green-yellow, spreading with crisped margins, and with the apex curved inward. The lip is abruptly bent downward at the midpoint. The lateral sepals are united nearly to the apex.

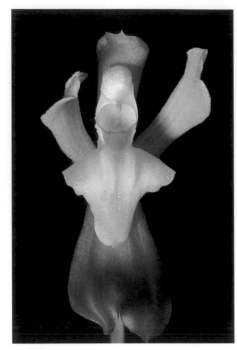

Gomesa crispa

Gongora armeniaca

Gongora cassidea

GONGORA Ruíz & Pavón
GON-goe-ra
Tribe: Cymbidieae
Subtribe: Stanhopeinae
Etymology: Dedicated to Don Antonio Caballero y Góngora, viceroy of New Granada (Colombia), during the eighteenth century

Gongora is a genus of 52 species distributed from Mexico to Bolivia. It is characterized by the prominent, ribbed, ovoid pseudobulbs; the two or three apical, thin, heavily-veined leaves and the elongate, pendent, many-flowered inflorescence produced from the base of the pseudobulb; the medium-sized upside-down flowers, non-resupinate by curving of the ovary; the dorsal sepal and petals small, adnate to the middle of the column; the lateral sepals large, reflexed, inserted on the column-foot; the lip divided into a hypochile and epichile; the column wingless; and the two, clavate, hard pollinia, attached to a stipe which is united to a round viscidium.

The plants grow as epiphytes in ant nests in wet forest from sea level to 1,000 meters. Many species in the *Gongora quinquenervis* group remain to be elucidated. All species are pollinated by male euglossine bees and usually very specifically. Morphological characters that distinguish species tend to be illusive, and only pollination observation clarifies them.

The species should be cultivated under intermediate to warm conditions in baskets that permit the inflorescences to hang. The plants should not be allowed to dry excessively. They benefit from copious fertilizer.

Gongora armeniaca (Lindley) Reichb.f.

This species which occurs in Nicaragua, Costa Rica, and Panama, is similar to the other members of the genus in plant habit but with the pseudobulbs more top-shaped. The inflorescence has five to fifteen flowers that are yellow or yellow-orange often spotted with red-brown. The dorsal sepal is smaller than the laterals and is united to the column at the base. The lip is fleshy and nearly square from a lateral view with a long, slender epichile projecting from the apex.

Gongora cassidea Reichb.f.

Gongora cassidea occurs from Mexico to Costa Rica. The inflorescence has five to nine cream-colored to yellow-brown flowers. The sepals are about equal in size with the dorsal sepal free from the column and deeply concave and with the column seated inside. The lip has a hypochile formed by the oblong lateral lobes of the lip. The epichile is elongate, concave, and bilobed at the apex.

Gongora galeata (Lindley) Reichb.f.

Gongora galeata is limited to Mexico in distribution. The plant and flowers are similar in habit to *Gongora cassidea*. The flowers are brownish yellow. The ovary is strongly arcuate-incurved. The sepals are free from the column and the dorsal sepal is helmet-shaped, covering the column. The lip has a nearly solid, somewhat rectangular hypochile and the epichile is subtriangular with a hook at the apex.

Gongora quinquenervis Ruíz & Pavón

Gongora quinquenervis occurs from Mexico to Bolivia, but many similar and poorly distinguished species are included within the broad sense of the species. Some of the more obviously distinct species have been recognized. The original collection was made in central Peru. The inflorescence produces nine to 35 flowers of extremely variable coloration. The dorsal sepal is much smaller than the laterals and mounted near the apex of the curving column along with the petals. The lip is fleshy with a quadrate hypochile that has a pair of fleshy lobules on each side at the base and a pair of downward-projecting, spine-like processes projecting from the apex. The hypochile is fleshy and subtriangular in shape.

Gongora tricolor (Lindley) Reichb.f.

This species is restricted to Panama in its distribution. It is similar to *G. quinquenervis* in most characters, but the flowers are larger, more robust, and the base of the hypochile is very broad across the fleshy lobules giving it a triangular shape from a dorsal view.

Gongora truncata Lindley

Gongora truncata occurs from Mexico to Honduras. This species belongs to a group that is distinct. The flowers are numerous and white with red-brown spots on the sepals. The lip is yellow sometimes marked with red-brown at the base or apex. The lip is rectangular from a lateral view, but the hypochile is formed by the broad lateral

Gongora tricolor

Gongora galeata

lobes held erect and parallel forming a deeply saccate structure. The epichile is an erect, tongue-like, concave structure.

GOODYERA R. Br.
good-YER-a
Tribe: Erythrodeae
Subtribe: Goodyerinae
Etymology: After John Goodyer, a seventeenth-century English botanist

As one of the larger genera of terrestrial orchids, *Goodyera* is also one of the most widespread with species (more than 30) occurring in both temperate and tropical regions of the Old and New Worlds. Although flowers are often small, it is the reticulated leaf venation which is obviously attractive in many species. Leaves are basal or clustered on the lower part of the stem. Inflorescences are erect, racemose, and often many-flowered. Flowers are usually small and often pubescent or glandular on their outer surfaces. The dorsal sepal forms a hood with the petals. The lateral sepals spread, and the lip has an acute, sometimes reflexed apex and is hollow or saccate with bristly hairs.

Goodyera species generally creep via stolons and so must be grown in shallow pans using a compost made from equal parts by volume of loam, sharp sand, and medium peat to which sieved leaf mold is added. Keep the compost evenly moist throughout the year and the pans in good shade. Plants can be readily propagated from side-shoots. Note that for the tropical species a winter minimum temperature of 12°–15°C is needed but temperate species are much hardier.

Gongora truncata

Gongora quinquenervis

Goodyera hispida Lindley

Goodyera hispida is a species from the Indian subcontinent — the Khasia Hills, Sikkim, and Bhutan — in woods above 1,000 meters. It is a small terrestrial species up to 15 centimeters tall with six to eight ovate, pointed basal leaves. Inflorescences are erect, glandular, and twisted. Flowers are small, white, and glandular.

Goodyera pubescens (Willd.) R. Br.

This North American species is closely related to *G. repens*. It differs mainly in its slightly larger white flowers in a denser inflorescence, in its downy stem, and in its more heavily silver-netted leaves. Its distribution is in the North American woodlands: southward from Minnesota, Ontario, and Maine.

Goodyera repens (L.) R. Br.

Goodyera repens is an almost prostrate species with a creeping rhizome from which leaves arise on a short stem. The evergreen, green- to silver-veined leaves are an attractive feature of the plant. Plants range from ten to 20 centimeters tall. The inflorescence is 3–7 centimeters long with up to 20 small, white, glandular flowers arranged in an open spiral. Sepals and petals are 3–4 millimeters long, the margins covered with glandular hairs. The lip has a strongly concave hypochile at the basal end with a triangular, downward-pointing epichile at the apex. It is widespread from northern Europe through mountain woods of central Europe into Asia, Japan and northern America.

Goodyera repens

Govenia liliacea

Grammangis ellisii

GOVENIA Lindley ex Loddiges
go-VEN-ee-ah
Tribe: Maxillarieae
Subtribe: Corallorhizinae
Etymology: For J. R. Gowen, an English gardener and plant collector

Thirty or more attractive terrestrial species are currently known in tropical and subtropical America, ranging from Florida to Argentina including the West Indies and the Galapagos Islands. The plant consists of an underground, cormlike pseudobulb and one to three thin deciduous leaves. The bases of the leaves are enclosed in two to four tubular sheaths. The racemes originate from the base of the pseudobulb and emerge between the leaves and the tubular sheaths, bearing brownish, greenish, orangish, pinkish, or whitish flowers; the yellowish white to white lip usually has reddish brown spots toward the apex. The dorsal sepal and the petals typically form a hood over the column and the lip. All species have four pollinia.
In nature plants of this genus grow in rich organic soils or organic-rich mineral soils in forests from 0–3,000 meters. Cultivate in large pots in rich, very porous compost with perfect drainage in light shade. Water freely when growing or in leaf, with added diluted fertilizers; after leaves fall keep almost totally dry. Repot annually when the new growth appears.

Govenia liliacea (Llave & Lex.) Lindley
This large, showy species, found from

northern Mexico to Costa Rica, produces dense, many-flowered inflorescences from June to August. Flowers are large, white, with petals barred magenta internally; the lip is usually flushed dull brown basally and spotted toward the apex on the lower surface only.
Other species in cultivation are *Govenia superba* and *G. purpusii*.

GRAMMANGIS Reichb.f.
gra-MAN-gis
Tribe: Cymbidieae
Subtribe: Cyrtopodiinae
Etymology: Gr. *gramma*, letter or mark; *angos*, vessel

Only two species of large epiphytes are known in this genus, both from central Madagascar. The plants have conspicuous pseudobulbs which develop within the base of five or six large, grayish green leaves. In the wild, they develop an extensive root system and the thick, succulent roots grow for many meters on and within the bark of forest trees. The large inflorescence arises from the base of the new pseudobulb at the same time as the new fan of leaves.
Plants introduced as adults seem to resent disturbance and, once established, are best left in the same container, pot or basket, for several years. They need bright light and intermediate temperatures in high humidity. The plants are heavy feeders while in active growth but need a rest after flowering.

Grammangis ellisii (Lindley) Reichb.f.

This species grows high on the trunks and lower branches of forest trees where there is good light filtering through the canopy. The inflorescence carries many showy flowers. The large sepals are the most conspicuous part, gold with heavy chestnut brown markings and very glossy. The petals and lip are small and paler.

GRAMMATOPHYLLUM Blume
gra-mat-oh-FIL-um
Tribe: Cymbidieae
Subtribe: Cyrtopodiinae
Etymology: Gr. *gramma*, letter; *phyllon*, leaf

There are about twelve species of these very large epiphytes distributed throughout southeast Asia to New Guinea, the Philippines, and Polynesia. Several species have very long leafy stems, somewhat resembling sugar cane, while others have more distinct pseudobulbs, with fewer leaves, and resemble some species of *Cymbidium*. The inflorescences are large and robust, usually carrying many flowers in various shades of green, brown and yellow. Plants of the largest species of this genus are difficult to accommodate in a glass-house but make a striking feature in a tropical garden where they are often grown as terrestrials. High light intensity and plenty of water and fertilizer during the

Graphorkis lurida

growing period are important for all the species to attain flowering size.

Grammatophyllum speciosum
Blume

This species from Malaysia, Sumatra, and the Philippines is reputed to be the largest of all orchids with its immense leafy stems, each several meters long in a mature specimen. The flowers are borne on upright, robust inflorescences, each about ten centimeters across. They are bright golden yellow with chestnut markings. Some of the lowest flowers on the inflorescence may be imperfect.

GRAPHORKIS Thouars
graf-OR-kis
Tribe: Cymbidieae
Subtribe: Cyrtopodiinae
Etymology: Gr. *graphe*, writing; *orchis*, orchid

There are five species of these pseudobulbous epiphytes in Madagascar and the Mascarene Islands and one in tropical Africa. They all have ovoid, upright pseudobulbs which grow close together and are surrounded by numerous slender upright roots which are in addition to the normal feeding roots attached to the substratum. The leaves are deciduous, and the spiky remains of the midrib are a conspicuous feature at the apex of each pseudobulb. The flowers are borne in paniculate inflorescences, yellowish with

Grammatophyllum speciosum

brown or purple markings. The three-lobed lip is spurred at the base.

Plants are easily maintained in a warm and humid greenhouse and need bright light to grow and flower well. A dry period once the pseudobulbs are mature is beneficial and hastens leaf abscission.

Graphorkis lurida (Sw.) O. Kuntze

This is the only species which occurs in Africa where it is often epiphytic on palms. It is widespread in countries across the equator, from Senegal in the west to Tanzania in the east and south as far as Gabon at elevations of about 1,000 meters above sea level. The flowers have purplish

green sepals which are pale green on the inside, petals greenish purple, and the lip bright yellow.

GROBYA Lindley
GRO-bee-ah
Tribe: Cymbidieae
Subtribe: Cyrtopodiinae
Etymology: For Lord Grey of Groby

Three species are currently known, all endemic to Brazil. Each roundish, fleshy pseudobulb bears eight to twelve long, narrow leaves. Racemes of few to many colorful flowers arise from the base of the

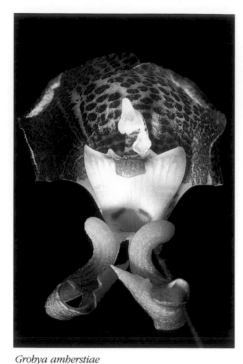

Grobya amherstiae

Gymnadenia conopsea

Habenaria rhodocheila

pseudobulbs. The long, flexuose lateral sepals are most characteristic. All species have two pollinia.

Culture as for *Catasetum* under moderate shade.

Grobya amherstiae Lindley

This showy species, found in eastern Brazil, produces many-flowered racemes from July to December. Flowers are pale green or pale yellow, tinged or spotted with maroon; the lip is yellow with a purple callus. As in other *Grobya* species, the lateral sepals are long and flexuose.

GYMNADENIA R. Br.

jim-na-DEN-ee-a

Tribe: Orchideae
Subtribe: Orchidinae
Etymology: Gr. *gymnos*, exposed; *aden*, gland

There are ten species in this Northern Temperate genus. Tubers are palmately lobed for about half their length. The stem is leafy, with flowers arranged in a spike. Dorsal sepals and petals converge to form a galea. The spur is long and slender. Plants in the genus are all fragrant and attractive to butterflies and moths with probosces long enough to reach the nectar in the long spurs.

Gymnadenia conopsea (L.) R. Br.

A familiar species on calcareous soils throughout Europe, *Gymnadenia conopsea* varies in height from fifteen to 45 centimeters with numerous flowers in a

dense cylindrical spike. Flowers are usually pink or reddish lilac with a three-lobed lip (all lobes roughly equal in length with rounded tips) and a long, slender, downward-pointing spur. Plants can be readily established in gardens on chalk or limestone where there are well-drained grassy slopes free of fertilizers. For pot growth use the basic "*Ophrys*" mixture with added limestone chippings. Flowering in the wild is from May to August depending on elevation.

HABENARIA Willd.

hab-e-NARE-ee-a

Tribe: Orchideae
Subtribe: Habenariinae
Etymology: L. *habena*, reins (referring to the straplike lip divisions)

Habenaria is a very large genus of terrestrial orchids known to include more than 500 species distributed in temperate and tropical grassland areas. The greatest concentration of species occurs in Asia, Africa, and tropical South America. Plants are leafy and have simple-lobed tubers and fleshy roots. Leaves are smooth, sheathing at the stem base. Flowers are carried in a spike or raceme and vary from small to large. In color they are most commonly green or white, but some species are yellow, orange, pink, or red. The dorsal sepal is shorter than the laterals. Petals are simple or bifid. The lip is continuous with the column, entire or three-lobed with a spur at the base. The column is very short and complex in structure: viscidia are exposed, the

rostellum small with divergent lateral lobes lying erect between the anther cells. *Habenaria* species can be grown in a compost comprising equal parts by volume of medium peat, loam, and sharp sand with added sieved leaf mold. For tropical species the minimum temperature is 15°C while resting and 18°C during growth; other species tolerate lower temperatures. Fleshy tubers are left underground when leaves die down after flowering, and at this stage they should remain almost completely dry but without becoming desiccated. When new green shoots appear, repot and grow under moderate to heavy shade. Plants should be watered carefully at first. In full growth they must not be allowed to dry out at any time.

Habenaria rhodocheila Hance

This is one of the showiest species with bulbous or fleshy roots, a stem 10–30 centimeters long with one or two leaves below and three or four above. The inflorescence is dense with between two and fifteen flowers. These are scarlet or brick-red in coloration (rarely orange or yellow). The dorsal sepal is elliptic (one centimeter long), the laterals slightly shorter and more lanceolate. Petals, seven centimeters long, are linear-lanceolate. The lip is four-lobed with side-lobes broad and oblique. The spur is slender and 4–5 centimeters long. This species is found in Indo-China and Malaya, north to the southern provinces of China.

Habenaria splendens Rendle

Habenaria splendens has stout, leafy stems up to 75 centimeters tall and ellipsoid tubers three centimeters long. The lax inflorescence is between eight and 20 centimeters long with from four to seventeen fragrant flowers. Sepals are pale green; petals are white. This African species is found in open grasslands and forest margins from 1,000 to 2,400 meters in Ethiopia, east Africa, Malawi, and Zambia.

Hagsatera brachycolumna

HAGSATERA González Tamayo
hag-sa-TER-ah
Tribe: Epidendreae
Subtribe: Laeliinae
Etymology: Dedicated to Eric Hágsater, 1945- , Mexican orchidologist

Although originally described as an *Epidendrum*, this genus is clearly differentiated by the very short column, the eight pollinia and the concave rostellum with a well formed viscidium. The plants are very curious, as the young plant has a short rhizome firmly rooted to its support. Once the plants achieve maturity, they produce a long, erect stem with a pseudobulb formed in the apical half, a new stem forming from the base of that pseudobulb, with no aerial roots, so the plants may grow as much as a meter high, nodding in the wind, with no more support than the roots of the old pseudobulbs at the base of the plant. Two species have been recorded.

Hagsatera brachycolumna (L. O. Wms.) Gonzalez Tamayo

This species grows epiphytically in open oak forests, well ventilated and with clear dry and rainy seasons. Plants should be grown on a piece of fern or other material which permits them to secure their roots with good drainage, and then grow the long aerial stalks. As plants root well only from the base of the young plant, it is preferable to start from a young plant, and not by cutting old plants.

HARAELLA Kudô
ha-ra-EL-ah
Tribe: Vandeae
Subtribe: Sarcanthinae
Etymology: Honoring Mr. Yoshie Hara

Haraella is a monotypic genus endemic to Taiwan. The plants lack pseudobulbs and resemble smaller species of *Gastrochilus* or *Thrixspermum*. The flowers are produced more or less among the leaves and are shown to best advantage when the diminutive plants are mounted on a slab. *Haraella* should be given medium bright light conditions, intermediate temperatures, and uniform, year-round watering.

Haraella retrocalla

Haraella retrocalla (Hayata) Kudô

Endemic to Taiwan, *Haraella retrocalla* is frequently encountered under the synonym *H. odorata* Kudô. The flowers are waxy greenish yellow. The lip is marked with a central glossy patch of maroon and closely resembles an insect. Flowering is periodic throughout the year.

HEXISEA Lindley
hex-EE-zee-ah
Tribe: Epidendreae
Subtribe: Laeliinae
Etymology: Gr. *hex*, six; *isos*, equal; in reference to the equal size of the six perianth segments

Hexisea is a genus, as traditionally treated, of six species primarily of Central America with one species in Amazonia and an undescribed, white-flowered species in the Choco of Colombia. The genus is characterized by the flattened, superimposed, swollen pseudobulbs

Hexisea bidentata

usually produced from the apex of previous pseudobulbs; the two apical leaves; the glomerate inflorescences produced from the apex of each stem; the red, orange, or white flowers; the free sepals and petals, spreading; the lip united to the column for the basal two-thirds forming a nectar cavity; and the four hard pollinia.

Debate concerning the validity of this genus is presently raging. With the discovery of new species in the genus the characters that separated *Hexisea* from *Scaphyglottis* have disappeared.

Members of this genus occur as epiphytic plants in lowland moist forest from 200 to 500 meters elevation. These plants can be easily cultivated under intermediate conditions. If they are grown on plaques the naturally lax stems show the flowers to their best advantage.

Hexisea bidentata Lindley

This species occurs from Mexico, throughout Central America, and on to Brazil on the Amazon side of the Andes. The stems are inserted at the apex of the previous pseudobulb. The flowers are brilliant red to red-orange with a yellow spot at the base of the lip.

HIMANTOGLOSSUM Koch
hi-man-toe-GLOSS-um
Tribe: Orchideae
Subtribe: Orchidinae
Etymology: Gr. *himas*, strap or thong; *glossa*, tongue

Current opinion recognizes six species in the genus *Himantoglossum*. Of these *H. hircinum* enjoys by far the widest distribution throughout southern Europe and north Africa, although it is often rather local. All species are tall, reaching some 30–90 centimeters, and have two large, ellipsoidal tubers and loose flower-spikes with large numbers of blooms. The central lobe of the lip is greatly elongated, twisted and divided at the tip. There is a short stumpy spur.

Himantoglossum hircinum

Himantoglossum hircinum (L.) Sprengel

The English name "lizard orchid" refers to the bizarre straplike lip some 40–50 millimeters long. Plants are robust with thick stems reaching 70 centimeters or more and with six to eight oval to broadly lanceolate leaves (produced in the previous fall and often turning brown by the time flowers appear). As many as 80 flowers have been recorded on strong plants, and the whole inflorescence has a rather straggling appearance due to the prominent "tails." Each flower has a "hood" formed by convergent sepals and petals. Sepals are greyish green on the exterior but striped and spotted with red on the inside. Petals are narrow, one-veined and marked with red. The lip is three-lobed, side-lobes forming crinkled "arms," the midlobe greatly extended. In the wild *Himantoglossum hircinum* grows on dry calcareous soils in sunny open grassland, scrub, forest edges, roadsides, and established sand dunes, preferring on the whole an oceanic climate. Plants can be pot-grown in the "*Ophrys*" mixture with added limestone chips. They are best left outdoors at flowering time because of the "heady" odor, which is particularly obvious in the early evening.

HOULLETIA Brogniart
hoo-LET-ee-ah
Tribe: Cymbidieae
Subtribe: Stanhopeinae
Etymology: In honor of M. Houllet, French collector and horticulturist in Paris during the nineteenth century

This is a genus of ten species distributed from Guatemala to Bolivia. The genus is characterized by the one-leaved pseudobulbs with large, petiolate heavily-veined leaves; the erect or pendent inflorescences; the large, colorful flowers with free sepals and petals; the lip with a hypochile and a fixed epichile and a solid claw at the base; the slender, wingless column with a foot to which the lip is firmly attached; and the two hard pollinia attached to an elongate stipe united to a small viscidium.

These plants are epiphytic or terrestrial on embankments at elevations from 1,000 to 2,200 meters. They are not easily cultivated. Most of the species are best grown in baskets that permit the pendent inflorescences to exit downward. Some of the species require cultivation under cool conditions with abundant water and humidity throughout the year.

Houlletia odoratissima Linden ex Lindley & Paxton

This species occurs from Panama to Bolivia along the flanks of the Andes. The inflorescence is stiffly erect with five to nine nodding flowers that reach seven centimeters in diameter. The sepals and petals are chocolate-brown marked with white spots and lines. The lip is white with brown spots. The lateral lobes of the lip are

Houlletia odoratissima

Houlletia tigrina

Houlletia wallisii

Huntleya burtii

Huntleya citrina

slender and hornlike and bent backward, and the apical lobe is subrectangular.

Houlletia tigrina Linden ex Lindley

This species occurs from Guatemala to western Ecuador. In Central America the species has been known as *H. lansbergii* Linden & Reichb.f. The inflorescence is pendent with two to four flowers reaching six centimeters in diameter. The sepals and petals are reddish orange with round red-brown spots. The petals have a notch on the upper margin. The lip is white with blood-red bars on the hypochile. The column is golden yellow with red spots.

Houlletia wallisii Linden & Reichb.f.

Houlletia wallisii occurs in Colombia, Ecuador, and Peru, on the eastern slope of the Andes. The inflorescence is suberect at

first but becomes pendent with the flowers held outward. The flowers reach five centimeters in diameter. The sepals and petals are yellow with red-brown spots and blotches. The lip is yellow with broad lateral lobes.

HUNTLEYA Batem. ex Lindley
HUNT-lee-ya
Tribe: Maxillarieae
Subtribe: Zygopetalinae
Etymology: In honor of Rev. J. T. Huntley, English orchid fancier

Huntleya is a genus of ten species known from Costa Rica to Bolivia. The genus is characterized by the lack of pseudobulbs; the foliaceous, distichous sheaths forming a fanlike plant; the leaves narrow and lightly veined; the one-flowered inflorescences from the axils of the leaf-sheaths; a large, ribbed callus, fimbriate with hairlike spines at the apex of each rib; and the four flattened, superimposed pollinia, on a short stipe connected to a flattened viscidium. The plants grow as epiphytes on tree-trunks in extremely wet cloud forest at elevations from 500 to 1,200 meters. They can be cultivated under intermediate conditions but should never be allowed to dry out completely. Because of their creeping habit they are best grown on plaques or in large baskets.

Huntleya burtii Endres & Reichb.f.

This species occurs in Honduras, Nicaragua, and Costa Rica. The flowers reach six centimeters in diameter. The sepals and petals are dark brown, white at the base, and with a red blotch on the white portion. They are spreading and flat with a pebbly surface. The lip is cordiform without lateral lobes, brown for the apical two-thirds, and the base is white.

Huntleya citrina Rolfe

This species occurs in western Colombia and Ecuador in extremely wet forests of the lowlands. The flowers are small, reaching three centimeters in diameter and are bright yellow, sometimes with small red spots at the base of the lip.

Huntleya wallisii

Ionopsis utricularioides

without a spur and subtended by small bracts; the sepals united at the base to form a short tube; the lip not surrounding the column; the column with a foot; the anther at the apex of the column; and the two hard pollinia attached to a stipe connected to a viscidium. These are common epiphytes in guava and mate trees from sea level to 800 meters elevation on both sides of the Andes. They can be grown under intermediate conditions with ample water supplied throughout the year. They develop best when grown on plaques.

Ionopsis utricularioides (Sw.) Lindley

This species occurs in Florida in the United States, in the West Indies, from Mexico to Peru and Venezuela, and in the Guianas and Brazil. The leaves are flat and very thick, often without an apical leaf on the pseudobulb. The inflorescence is elongate and branched toward the apex. Sepals and petals are somewhat hooded around the lip and are white to light pink. The lip varies from white with purplish vein-lines to purple.

ISABELIA Barb. Rodr.
iz-a-BEL-ee-ah
Tribe: Epidendreae
Subtribe: Laeliinae
Etymology: In honor of Isabel, countess d'Eu, patron of science and horticulture in Brazil during the nineteenth century

This is a genus of two species restricted to Brazil. The genus is characterized by the mat-forming plant with tightly clustered pseudobulbs each surrounded by a fibrous network with a single apical, awl-shaped leaf; the short one-flowered inflorescences produced from the apex of the pseudobulb; the small white flowers; the sepals forming a small sac with the lip base; and the flattened pollinia with prominent caudicles. The plants are epiphytic in humid forest. Both species grow well on plaques or in pots under intermediate conditions.

Isabelia virginalis Barb. Rodr.

Isabelia virginalis occurs in damp forests of southern Brazil. The white flowers are small, reaching less than a centimeter in diameter and not opening fully.

Huntleya wallisii (Reichb.f.) Rolfe

This species occurs along the western slopes of the Andes in Colombia and Ecuador. The flowers are very large, usually more than twelve centimeters in diameter, and in some forms reach 20 centimeters in diameter. The sepals and petals are yellow or white at the base with the apical two-thirds dark reddish brown, and the petals usually have a red spot at the base. The apical two-thirds of the lip is red to red-brown and the base yellow or white.

IONOPSIS H. B. K.
eye-on-OP-sis
Tribe: Cymbidieae
Subtribe: Oncidiinae
Etymology: Gr. *ion*, violet; *opsis*, appearance; in reference to the similarity of the flowers to violets

Ionopsis is a genus of five species distributed throughout lowland tropical America. The genus is characterized by the presence of unifoliate pseudobulbs of a single internode subtended by distichous, thick, leaflike sheaths, the leaves flat or terete; the inflorescence produced from the axils of the sheaths; the medium-sized flowers (about one centimeter in diameter)

ISOCHILUS R. Br.
eye-so-KYE-lus
Tribe: Epidendreae
Subtribe: Laeliinae
Etymology: Gr. *isos*, equal; *cheilos*, lip; in reference to the similarity of the lip to the sepals and petals

Isochilus is a genus of seven species

Isochilus linearis

Isabelia virginalis

primarily of Mexico and Central America. One of the species is known from Mexico to Amazonian Bolivia. The genus is characterized by the slender, canelike stems with narrow, distichous flat leaves at the nodes; the terminal, sessile inflorescence; the small flowers (not exceeding two centimeters in diameter); the sepals united at the base to form a tube; the lip acute at the apex; the column with a short, erect foot; the apical anther; and the four hard pollinia attached to a broad viscidium. The plants are epiphytes in lowland moist forest at elevations from 100 to 400 meters in the Amazon basin of Ecuador. They can be cultivated under intermediate conditions in well-drained pots with equal water throughout the year.

Isochilus linearis (Jacq.) R. Br.

This species is widespread in the lowlands from Mexico to Panama and the West Indies, and from Venezuela to Argentina on the eastern side of South America. The flowers are dark rosy-pink and are tubular with the sepals united at the base.

JACQUINIELLA Schltr.
jac-in-ee-EL-ah
Tribe: Epidendreae
Subtribe: Lacliinac
Etymology: In honor of Nikolaus Joseph von Jacquin, Austrian botanist during the eighteenth century

This is a small genus of eleven species distributed through much of tropical America. The genus is characterized by the small plants with canelike stems and distichous, thick, terete or laterally flattened leaves; the apical, one-flowered or glomerate inflorescence; the tiny, usually autogamous flowers; the sepals united at the base to form a short tube, the apices not spreading; the lip united to the underside of the column for a short distance; the apical anther; and the four hard pollinia united to a viscidium.
The plants are epiphytic and are often found growing in orange or mate trees from sea level to 700 meters elevation. The species can be cultivated in warm to intermediate conditions on plaques.

Jacquiniella globosa (Jacq.) Schltr.

This species is found from Mexico to Bolivia and Brazil and in the West Indies. The yellow brown flowers are very small, reaching five millimeters in diameter, and do not open well.

Jacquiniella globosa

Jumellea filicornoides

Jumellea fragrans

JUMELLEA Schltr.
joo-MEL-ee-ah
Tribe: Vandeae
Subtribe: Angraecinae
Etymology: Named in honor of Dr. H. Jumelle, French botanist

This is a genus of about 45 monopodial epiphytes and lithophytes which is centered in Madagascar and adjacent islands of the western Indian Ocean. Two species are known from adjacent parts of the African continent. They are allied to the genus *Angraecum* but easily distinguished from it by the single-flowered inflorescences and by the white flowers in which the narrow base of the lip is inserted below the column, not enfolding it. The upright dorsal sepal gives a somewhat bilabiate appearance to the flower which is also characteristic.

Plants are easily maintained in cultivation either mounted on pieces of bark or logs, or planted in pots or baskets. They need plenty of water during the growing season and a dry period after flowering. Several do best if kept moderately moist throughout the year.

Jumellea filicornoides (De Wild.) Schltr.

This is one of the African species which is known from Kenya and Tanzania and southward as far as Natal. It grows on riverine trees and on rocks. The upright stems branch so that tufts of plants usually develop, each with narrow, shiny green leaves. The white flowers have a characteristic spur, two to three centimeters long, which is bent like a knee.

Jumellea fragrans Schltr.

Leaves of this species have long been used in Reunion to brew an herbal tea known as faham. The plants are epiphytic or lithophytic and form clusters of upright stems. The white flowers have a slender spur about three centimeters long.

Jumellea sagittata H. Perrier

This species grows in mossy forests in Madagascar and has a large fan of leaves arising from a short stem, sometimes branched so that several fans arise close together. The size of the plants and flowers is extremely varied, some being very spectacular. The large white flowers are borne singly on slender inflorescences arising from the old leaf bases at the base of the plant. When well-flowered they are extremely attractive plants.

KEFERSTEINIA Reichb.f.
kef-er-STINE-ee-ah
Tribe: Maxillarieae
Subtribe: Zygopetalinae
Etymology: In honor of Herr Keferstein, German orchid grower during the nineteenth century

This is a genus of 36 species known from Mexico to Bolivia, but most abundant in the Andes of Colombia and Ecuador. The genus is characterized by the lack of pseudobulbs; the foliaceous, distichous sheaths forming a fanlike plant; the leaves narrow and lightly veined; the one-flowered inflorescences from the axils of the leaf-sheaths; the sides of the lip usually surrounding the column at the base; the presence of a pedestal-like callus at the base of the lip; the column with a keel on the underside; and the four flattened, superimposed pollinia on a short stipe connected to a hooked, cordiform viscidium.

The plants grow as epiphytes, or are rarely found growing terrestrially in wet forest from 300 to 2,500 meters elevation. Members of this genus should be cultivated under intermediate conditions with an ample supply of water throughout the year. They should not be allowed to dry out completely.

Kefersteinia costaricensis Schltr.

This species occurs in Nicaragua, Costa Rica, and Panama. The flowers are yellow-white with red-violet spots on the lip and petals. The lip is shallowly concave and nearly round, lightly deflexed at the midpoint. It does not surround the column as in many other species. The callus is bifurcate and nearly rectangular.

Kefersteinia gemma (Reichb.f.) Schltr.

Kefersteinia gemma is found in Colombia and Ecuador. The flowers are cream-white marked with flecks of red. Sepals and petals are truncate at the apex, and the narrow lip is abruptly reflexed at the midpoint. The flowers measure three centimeters in diameter.

Kefersteinia graminea (Lindley) Reichb.f.

This large-flowered species occurs in Venezuela and Colombia. The flowers are green heavily flecked and marked with red-

Jumellea sagittata

Kefersteinia graminea

Kegeliella boutteana

Kefersteinia gemma

brown. The lip is ovate in outline but is reflexed abruptly at the midpoint. The callus consists of two spreading plates with an irregular front margin. The flowers reach five centimeters in diameter.

Kefersteinia lactea

Kefersteinia lactea (Reichb.f.) Schltr.

This species has been reported from Mexico, Costa Rica, and Panama. The flowers are about three centimeters in diameter and are pure white. The lip is reflexed abruptly at the midpoint.

Kefersteinia mysticina Reichb.f.

Kefersteinia mysticina occurs sparsely from Panama, through Colombia and Ecuador, to northern Peru. The flowers are yellow-white and reach four centimeters in diameter. The margin of the lip is deeply lacerate-fimbriate.

Kefersteinia mysticina

Kefersteinia tolimensis Schltr.

This species is found in Venezuela and Colombia. The flowers are whitish and heavily covered with red-brown speckles. The lip is abruptly deflexed at the midpoint, and the callus consists of a pair of flat plates that are retuse across the front.

Kefersteinia tolimensis

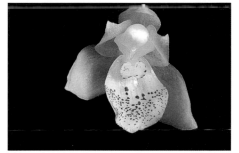

Kefersteinia costaricensis

KEGELIELLA Mansf.
keg-el-ee-EL-ah
Tribe: Cymbidieae
Subtribe: Stanhopeinae
Etymology: Diminutive of *Kegelia* (already applied to another genus), a name proposed by Reichb.f. in honor of Herr Kegel, German botanist of the nineteenth century

This is a genus of three species distributed from Nicaragua to Venezuela. The genus is characterized by the flattened, bifoliate pseudobulbs; the plicate, heavily veined leaves; the pendent, densely black-pilose rachis of the inflorescence; the claw of the lip without a callus; the dorsal sepal free of the column; the margin of the lip not papillose; and the two hard pollinia attached to an elongate, oblong stipe. The plants occur as epiphytes low on the trunks of trees in extremely wet cloud forest. They can be cultivated on plaques or in baskets so that the pendent inflorescence is free to creep out. They grow well under warm to intermediate conditions with abundant water throughout the year.

Kegeliella boutteana (Reichb.f.) L. O. Williams

This species occurs from Costa Rica to

Colombia, Venezuela, the Guianas, and the West Indies. The plants resemble small members of the genus *Gongora* with dark red backs of the leaves and flattened pseudobulbs. The flowers are cream-colored, heavily spotted, and flecked with red-brown and about 2.5 centimeters in diameter. The column is green.

KINGIDIUM P. Hunt
king-ID-ee-um
Tribe: Vandeae
Subtribe: Sarcanthinae
Etymology: Honoring Sir George King

Kingidium comprises five epiphytic species native throughout tropical Asia. Closely related to and resembling *Phalaenopsis*, kingidiums differ by having a saccate lip. Some species have broad leaves as in *Phalaenopsis* while others are essentially leafless.

Plants of *Kingidium* should be grown like *Phalaenopsis*. Lacking any storage organs, kingidiums should be kept evenly moist in a medium that retains moisture between waterings. Kept warm, the plants should be given intermediate light levels but can tolerate low light levels. Leafless species must be mounted on slabs to allow their photosynthetic roots to function.

Kingidium deliciosa (Reichb.f.) H. R. Sweet

This small *Phalaenopsis*-like species has a wide range from Sri Lanka to Nepal and east through southeast Asia, China, Borneo, Sulawesi, and the Philippines. The plant is frequently encountered under the

L

misapplied name *K. decumbens* (Griff.) P. Hunt. Two distinct color phases are known: a white-flowered phase found throughout the species range, and a yellow-flowered Himalayan phase sometimes segregated as *K. wightii*. The plants are distinctive, bearing deep green leaves with an undulate margin. Plants flower in the fall and periodically.

KOELLENSTEINIA Reichb.f.
kehl-en-STINE-ee-ah
Tribe: Maxillarieae
Subtribe: Zygopetalinae
Etymology: In honor of Kellner von Kollenstein, Austrian captain during the nineteenth century

This is a genus of sixteen species distributed from Panama to Bolivia and Brazil. The genus is characterized by the presence of small, inconspicuous pseudobulbs of several internodes surrounded by the bases of narrow leaves which are lightly veined; the lateral, multiflorous inflorescences often produced with the new growth; the free sepals and petals; the three-lobed lip with a bilobed, erect callus near the base, attached to an elongate column-foot, without a spur; the column thick, winged or terete; and the four hard pollinia superposed in two pairs, attached to a very short stipe united to a cordiform viscidium.

The plants grow as terrestrials in very wet cloud forests from elevations of 1,000 to 2,000 meters or as epiphytes on trunks of trees in lowland forest.

The plants of most species can be grown under intermediate conditions in pots with a well-drained medium. They should not be allowed to dry excessively.

Koellensteinia graminea (Lindley) Reichb.f.

This species occurs as an epiphyte through most of northern South America from Colombia to Brazil, Bolivia, and the Guianas. The leaves are narrow and are not heavily veined as in other members of the genus. The flowers are pink and are barred with red-brown on the segments and on the base of the lip. The flowers reach two centimeters in diameter.

Koellensteinia ionoptera

Koellensteinia ionoptera Linden & Reichb.f.

This species occurs in southeastern Ecuador and northeastern Peru. It is very similar to most of the other terrestrial members of the genus and has flowers to three centimeters in diameter. The flowers are pale pink to whitish with transverse bars of blue on the base of the lip.

LACAENA Lindley
la-KYE-na or la-SEE-na
Tribe: Cymbidieae
Subtribe: Stanhopeinae
Etymology: Gr. *Lakaina*; in reference to the beauty of Helen of Troy

Lacaena is a genus of two species distributed from Mexico to Panama. The genus is characterized by the large, ovoid, ribbed pseudobulbs with two or three thick, lightly veined leaves at the apex; the pendent, multiflowered inflorescences with large, white or yellow flowers; the lip articulated to the column-foot; the pubescent callus between the lateral lobes of the three-lobed lip; and the two hard pollinia on a short stipe and a round viscidium.

The genus is closely allied to *Acineta*, and the plants occur as epiphytes in lower montane forest. The plants should be cultivated under intermediate conditions in baskets so that the pendent inflorescences can emerge. They should not be allowed to dry excessively.

Lacaena spectabilis (Klotzch) Reichb.f.

This species occurs from Mexico to Panama.

Kingidium deliciosa

Koellensteinia graminea

The flowers are yellow-white with red-brown spots on the lip. The flowers reach four centimeters in diameter. The species differs from *L. bicolor* by the lack of a brown-violet spot on the lip and by the long, narrow claw of the midlobe with a single callus between the lateral lobes.

Lacaena spectabilis

LAELIA Lindley
LAY-lee-ah, LEE-lee-a, or LIE-lee-a
Tribe: Epidendreae
Subtribe: Laeliinae
Etymology: For *Laelia*, one of the vestal virgins or the Roman name *Laelius*

Some 60 species are currently known ranging from the West Indies to Mexico and Central America, and Brazil. Pseudobulbs bear one or two (rarely more) leaves. Erect to pendent racemes (rarely panicles) of few to many flowers arise from the apex of the pseudobulbs. In the past *Schomburgkia* species were included in *Laelia*, and thus the latter genus was thought to have a greater range than that reported here. All species have eight pollinia.
They grow well in well-drained hanging baskets, slabs, or clay pots. Provide cool temperatures with bright light and ventilation year round. Most species require little humidity, cool temperatures, and high light intensity during dormancy. In most Mexican species, in particular, a dry, cool dormancy period with bright light is highly recommended; watering during this period can be disastrous and often results in the decline and eventual death of the plant.

Laelia albida Bateman ex Lindley

This showy species, native to Mexico,

Laelia albida

produces racemes of five to ten flowers from September to February. The flowers can be white, rose, pink, or pale yellow with three yellow, raised keels on the labellum.

Laelia anceps Lindley

This showy species, native to Mexico, produces racemes of three to five flowers from October to March. Flowers are pale rose with the lip a dark reddish purple, the throat of the lip white with purple veining, and the three raised keels are yellow. However, many other color forms have been reported. This species is the most common *Laelia* from Mexico.

Laelia autumnalis (Llave & Lex.) Lindley

This species, native to Mexico, produces racemes of two to six flowers from October to February. The flowers are pink to purple, the lateral lobes of the lip white and the keels yellow. White forms are also known.

Laelia briegeri Blumenschein

This showy species, found in Brazil, produces racemes of three to five flowers from May to June. Flowers range in color from creamy white to dark yellow.

Laelia cinnabarina Bateman ex Lindley

This showy species, found in Brazil,

Laelia autumnalis

Laelia anceps

produces racemes of ten to twelve flowers from January to September. The large flowers are red-orange, with some purple veining on the side-lobes of the lip.

Laelia briegeri

Laelia cinnabarina

Laelia fidelensis

Laelia fidelensis Pabst

This miniature species, found in Brazil, produces racemes of one to three flowers from June to August. Flowers are lavender-pink or rose with some darker veining along the margins of lip and petals.

Laelia flava Lindley

This showy species, found in Brazil, produces racemes of five to ten flowers from January to October. Flowers are deep yellow with some faint red veining on the petals.

Laelia jongheana

Laelia flava

Laelia furfuracea Lindley

This species, found in Mexico, produces racemes of one to three flowers from September to March. Flowers are rose-purple with darker pigmentation on the midlobe of the lip.

Laelia harpophylla Reichb.f.

This species, found in Brazil, produces racemes of four to eight flowers from December to June, peaking in February to

Laelia lobata

Laelia harpophylla

March. Flowers are orange, the curled midlobe of the lip cream with orange veining. This species, one of the few epiphytic *Laelia* species from Brazil, requires no dormancy period and less light but more water than the rupicolous species.

Laelia jongheana Reichb.f.

This species, found in Brazil, produces racemes of one or two flowers from December to May. Flowers are bright amethyst-purple, the lip white with amethyst-purple margins and yellow keels.

Laelia lilliputana Pabst

This beautiful miniature species, found in Brazil, flowers from March to May. The

solitary flower is rose, and the lip has four yellow, raised keels. It is one of the smallest members of the genus *Laelia*.

Laelia lobata (Lindley) Veitch

This lovely species, found in Brazil, produces racemes of two to five flowers from March to July. Flowers are violet with purple veining, especially on the lip. This species does best in baskets. To obtain flowers, avoid repotting plants for several years.

Laelia lucasiana Rolfe

This species, found in Brazil, produces racemes of two or three flowers from May to December. Flowers are purple or magenta

Laelia lucasiana

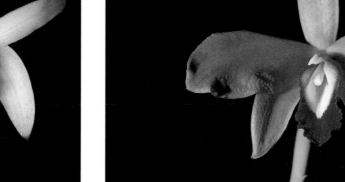

Laelia perrinii

with a yellow lip. White forms have also been reported.

Laelia lundii Reichb.f.

This species, found in Brazil, produces racemes of one to three flowers from December to March. Flowers are white with purple veining on the lip. The pseudobulbs of this species distinctly bear two leaves (one in all other Brazilian *Laelia* species).

Laelia milleri Blumenschein

This species, found in Brazil, produces two-to-six-flowered racemes from March to

Laelia lundii

October, peaking in May to July. Flowers are deep red or orange-red. The lip is yellow with red or orange margins and orange veining.

Laelia perrinii Lindley

This showy species, found in Brazil, produces one-to-four-flowered racemes from August to December, peaking in October to November. Flowers are light to dark purple, the margins of the lip dark purple. *Alba* and *coerulea* forms have also been reported.

Laelia pumila (Hook.) Reichb.f.

This miniature species, found in Brazil, produces racemes of one, and rarely two, flowers from September to November. Flowers are violet with white on the throat of the lip. Many color forms have been

reported. Unlike most other Brazilian laelias, this species grows best under some shade and high humidity.

Laelia purpurata Lindley

This lovely species, found in Brazil, produces three-to-five-flowered racemes from March to November. Many color forms have been reported varying from white with red veining on the lip to light pink with deep purple on the lip.

Laelia pumila

Laelia purpurata

Laelia milleri

Laelia rubescens

Laelia tenebrosa

Laelia rubescens Lindley

This showy species, found in Central America, produces racemes of four to seven flowers from October to June. Flowers vary from white to pink with a dark maroon patch at the base of the lip.

Laelia sincorana Schltr.

This charming species, found in Brazil, produces one-to-two-flowered racemes from March to September, peaking in May. Sepals and petals are purple, the lip darker purple with a white patch on the throat and five raised keels.

Laelia speciosa (HBK) Schltr.

This showy species, found in Mexico, produces one-to-three-flowered racemes from March to October. Sepals and petals are light purple, the lip white toward the base with purple veining and spotting and a yellow band extending beyond the two raised keels.

Laelia tenebrosa (Gower) Lindley

This large species, found in Brazil, produces two or three flowers from June to August. Sepals and petals are bronze, the lip purple

Laelia speciosa

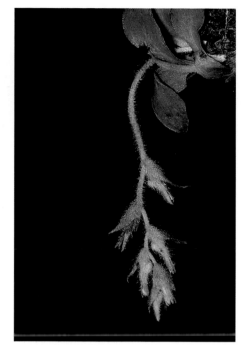

Lankesterella orotantha

Lemboglossum bictoniense

with a whitish margin and purple veining extending to the margins.

LANKESTERELLA Ames
lan-kes-ter-EL-ah
Tribe: Cranichideae
Subtribe: Spiranthinae
Etymology: In honor of Charles Lankester, English planter and horticulturist in Costa Rica during the twentieth century

This is a genus of ten species distributed from Costa Rica to Bolivia and Brazil. The genus is characterized by the tiny plants with a basal rosette of leaves and a terminal, pendent, few-flowered inflorescence with the flowers widely spaced; the resupinate flowers; and the soft but not sectile pollinia. This genus is closely allied to *Eurystylis*, which has the flowers arranged in a subcapitate rosette.
These plants grow epiphytically in wet forest at elevations from 1,000 to 2,000 meters. They can be cultivated under intermediate conditions on plaques or in pots where the pendent inflorescence is free to develop. They should never be allowed to dry out excessively.

Lankesterella orotantha
(Kränzlin) Garay

This species is found from Costa Rica to Peru. The flowers are arranged at the apex of a pendent inflorescence and do not open fully. They are green with white petals and lip. The whole inflorescence and the backs of the sepals are densely pubescent.

LEMBOGLOSSUM Halbinger
lem-bo-GLOSS-um
Tribe: Cymbidieae
Subtribe: Oncidiinae
Etymology: Gr. *leios*, smooth; *cheilos*, lip; in reference to the smooth lip

Most of the species are Mexican and Central American in distribution, but *L. cordatum* (Lindley) Halbinger does occur in Venezuela and was treated as *Odontoglossum cordatum* Lindley by Dunsterville & Garay. All species of this genus were previously accommodated in *Odontoglossum*.
The genus is characterized by the presence of pseudobulbs; the lateral inflorescences; the column and lip parallel to the apex of the column; the cordiform blade of the lip; the concave calli of the lip and the two hard pollinia, attached to a stipe and a viscidium. The plants grow as epiphytes at intermediate elevations in moist cloud forest. They should be cultivated under cool conditions similar to those for the genus *Odontoglossum*.

Lemboglossum bictoniense
(Bateman. ex Lindley) Halbinger

This species occurs from Mexico to Panama. The inflorescence is rigidly erect, to a meter tall, and branched with numerous flowers. The flowers reach five centimeters in diameter. The sepals and petals are spreading and brown with yellow bars. The lip is heart-shaped and pink to white.

Lemboglossum cervantesii

Lemboglossum cervantesii
(La Llave & Lex.) Halbinger

This species is native to central Mexico and Guatemala where it is often found on the trunks of pine trees in high-elevation cloud forest. The inflorescence is nodding to pendulous with from one to six flowers produced. The flowers reach six centimeters in diameter. The sepals and petals are white to pink with red-brown marks toward the base. The heart-shaped lip is somewhat concave and marked on the lower third with red-brown, concentric, transverse lines.

Lemboglossum cordatum

Lemboglossum rossii

Lemboglossum cordatum
(Lindley) Halbinger

This species occurs from Mexico to Costa Rica and in Venezuela. The inflorescence is stiffly erect at the base but becomes nodding toward the apex and is surrounded by large, papery bracts. Up to nine flowers are produced, each reaching eight centimeters in diameter. The sepals and petals are green-white blotched with red-brown and are long-acuminate at the apex. The heart-shaped lip is white or yellowish with red-brown blotches at the apex and base.

Lemboglossum rossii (Lindley) Halbinger

Lemboglossum rossii occurs from Mexico to Nicaragua. The inflorescence is erect and produces two to four flowers that reach seven centimeters in diameter. The sepals and petals are pale yellow to white blotched with red-brown toward the base. The heart-shaped lip is deep yellow spotted with red-brown.

LEOCHILUS Knowles & Westcott
lee-o-KYE-lus
Tribe: Cymbidieae
Subtribe: Oncidiinae
Etymology: Gr. *leios,* smooth; *cheilos,* lip; in reference to the smooth lip

Leochilus is a genus of ten species distributed throughout lowland tropical America. The genus is characterized by the presence of unifoliate pseudobulbs of a single internode subtended by distichous leaflike sheaths; the inflorescence produced from the axils of the sheaths; the flowers

without a spur; the lip usually unlobed; the column with a short foot and with a narrow arm on each side near the middle; and the two hard pollinia attached to a stipe connected to a viscidium.

These grow as epiphytic plants and are often common in guava and orange trees at elevations from 100 to 700 meters in very humid conditions. The species can be cultivated under intermediate conditions, preferably on plaques. Watering should be even throughout the year.

Leochilus labiatus (Sw.) Kuntze

This species is widely distributed in tropical America from Florida, through the West

Leochilus labiatus

Indies to Mexico and to Brazil. The leaves are often red on the backs, and the inflorescence reaches 25 centimeters long. Up to ten flowers are produced, and they reach two centimeters in diameter. The sepals and petals are yellow striped and barred with red-brown. The lip is yellow with a red-brown spot at the base.

LEPANTHES Sw.
le-PAN-theez
Tribe: Epidendreae
Subtribe: Pleurothallidinae
Etymology: Gr. *lepanthos,* a scale-like flower

This genus, widely distributed in moist tropical forests from Mexico to Brazil, contains over 800 species. All the species are characterized by a well-developed aerial stem (the ramicaul) enclosed by a series of ribbed sheaths with dilated openings. The margins and ribs of the sheaths are usually ciliate or scabrous (minutely warty). The flowers are produced simultaneously or successively in congested or loose racemes shorter to much longer than the elliptical leaf. A short, congested raceme is commonly held behind the leaf, but it often rests on top of the leaf. The small, wildly colorful flowers are very fragile. The sepals are sometimes fringed, and sometimes with tails. The petals are usually transverse with a pair of opposite lobes. The lip is usually developed into a pair of lobes closely associated with the column. A middle or third lobe is modified into a myriad of shapes and sizes that can be appreciated only with a magnifying glass. There are two pollinia.

These plants are often difficult to cultivate. Most require cool, moist growing conditions.

Lepanthes escobariana

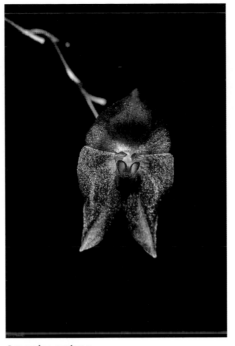

Lepanthes exaltata

Lepanthes felis

Lepanthes calodictyon J. D. Hook.

This species is uncommon in Ecuador and southern Colombia. It is easily recognized by the broad, thin, reticulated leaves with ruffled borders. The colorful, ornate flowers are borne on top of the leaf. They have reflexed sepals, long-tailed petals and a ciliate lip which is exceptional in being single-lobed.

Lepanthes calodictyon

Lepanthes escobariana Garay

This species is locally abundant in central Colombia. Although not vegetatively distinct, it is easily recognized by the long, loose, successively many-flowered raceme of large, orange, bowl shaped, tailless flowers.

Lepanthes exaltata Luer & Escobar

This species is rare in the Eastern Cordillera of Colombia. Although not vegetatively distinct, it can be recognized by the large, flat, purplish yellow flower that is borne successively in a raceme longer than the

leaf. The dorsal sepal is shortly acuminate while the laterals are more or less obtuse.

Lepanthes felis Luer & Escobar

Affectionately known as "the cat," because of the green, eyelike petals that peep out of the interior of the flower, this species is uncommon in the Western Cordillera of Colombia. The large, cup-shaped, short-tailed flowers sit on top of the leaf.

Lepanthes gargantua Reichb.f.

This truly gargantuan species is relatively frequent in much of Colombia and Ecuador. Several large, yellow, tailless flowers are almost always present in one or more congested racemes held behind the huge leaf atop a sturdy, aerial stem, approximately 30 centimeters high.

LEPANTHOPSIS (Cogn.) Ames
le-pan-THOP-sis
Tribe: Epidendreae
Subtribe: Pleurothallidinae
Etymology: Gr. *lepanthopsis*, like a *Lepanthes*

Like *Lepanthes*, this genus is characterized by a series of ribbed, tubular sheaths with dilated, more or less ciliate openings that enclose the aerial stems (ramicauls). The most distinguishing character is the short, broad column with a transverse, bilobed, apical stigma as seen in most of the species of *Stelis*. Two pollinia are produced in the apical anther. The flowers are usually produced simultaneously in congested racemes, often in two opposite-facing ranks,

longer or shorter than the elliptical leaf. These plants are relatively easy to cultivate in moist, intermediate to cool-growing greenhouse conditions.

Lepanthopsis astrophora
(Reichb.f. ex Kränzlin) Garay

This species is endemic in coastal Venezuela, but it is not rare. The tiny, brilliant purple, star-like flowers are produced several at a time in a loose, flexuous raceme much longer than the leaf.

Lepanthes gargantua

Lepanthopsis floripectin

Leptotes unicolor

Leptotes bicolor Lindley

This lovely species, found in eastern Brazil, blooms in cultivation from December to August. Sepals and petals are white or greenish white, the lip light to deep purple with whitish side-lobes and apical margin.

Leptotes unicolor Barb. Rodr.

This small species, found in Brazil, blooms in cultivation from October to March. Sepals and petals are white to rose-lilac, the lip magenta.

Lepanthopsis floripectin
(Reichb.f.) Ames

This species, which is common and widely distributed from Mexico into Brazil, is perhaps the most widely distributed species of all the pleurothallids. The greenish flowers are borne in a congested, double-ranked raceme that looks like a toothbrush.

Leptotes bicolor

The lateral sepals are deeply connate to near their obtuse apices. A similar species with the lateral sepals essentially free is *L. acuminata.*

LEPTOTES Lindley
lep-TOE-teez
Tribe: Epidendreae
Subtribe: Laeliinae
Etymology: Gr. *leptotes,* delicateness

Three species are currently known in Brazil, Paraguay, and Argentina. All species have short pseudobulbs bearing a single cylindrical leaf. Racemes of few flowers arise from the base of the leaves. All species have six pollinia.
Grow on slabs of tree-fern, cork bark, or in shallow clay pots. Provide moderate shade and humidity.

LIPARIS Rich.
LIP-per-is
Tribe: Malaxideae
Etymology: Gr. *liparos,* greasy or shiny, referring to the leaves

There are some 250 species in this cosmopolitan genus of terrestrial, lithophytic and, more rarely, epiphytic orchids. Most species occur in the tropics, but in the temperate zones there is a single species in Europe with others in China, Japan, and North America.
Plants are small with stems arising from pseudobulbs or corms and one or more leaves sheathing at the base. The inflorescence is racemose, varying from lax to many-flowered. The small flowers are green, yellow-green, dull orange, or purple. Sepals are free and spreading. Petals are filiform. Lips vary from entire to three-lobed and lack the basal auricles on either side at the base. The column is elongated and

Liparis loeselii

Liparis viridiflora

Listera cordata

narrowly winged above.
Generally, the tropical and subtropical species need a minimum winter temperature of 12°–15°C and can be grown in pans using a compost made from equal parts by volume of loam, sharp sand, and medium peat to which extra sieved leaf mold is added. They can also be grown in a general mix for tropical terrestrials (pine or fir bark, peat, chopped sphagnum, perlite, and charcoal). Plants need moist, shady conditions but should be kept rather drier when growth is complete.

Liparis lilifolia (L.) Lindley

This is a delicate North American species, rarely more than 20 centimeters tall, producing two shiny, elliptic leaves from a two-centimeter long, ovoid pseudobulb. The inflorescence can bear up to 25 flowers. Sepals and petals are slender and spreading. The lip is obovate, decurved, and colored pale purple with darker veins, making it a rather pretty species. It is found in the northeastern United States growing along streams, in gulleys, and in secondary woodland where it forms large colonies in suitable habitats. It can be established outdoors in a raised peat bed in a frost-free area with plenty of added leaf mold.

Liparis loeselii (L.) Rich.

This species is difficult to find because of its small stature (6–20 centimeters) and green coloring. It is becoming increasingly rare as suitable fenland sites are drained. A pair of oblong or ovate, bright green, shiny leaves lie on opposite sides of a stem with a more or less triangular section. The inflorescence is lax with between three and eight

yellowish green flowers. All perianth segments spread with petals shorter and narrower than sepals. The lip is as long as the sepals but has crinkled edges. Flowers are efficiently self fertilized in the main and can persist long after the ovary starts swelling. *Liparis loeselii* has a wide but scattered distribution throughout Europe (but not to the Mediterranean or farther north than southern Sweden and Norway), the eastern United States and Canada, growing in fens, bogs and dune slacks in live sphagnum. It flowers from June through July and in cultivation can be grown successfully in pans of live sphagnum moss.

Liparis viridiflora (Blume) Lindley

This is a variable terrestrial or epiphytic species with pseudobulbs that can range from short and ovoid to long cylinders, some 15 centimeters in length. There are two oblong-ovate leaves. The dense, cylindrical inflorescence is 15–25 centimeters long and many-flowered. Flowers are very small (sepals and petals only 2.5 millimeters long) and whitish with a yellow lip which is rather fleshy, recurved, and broadly ovate, no more than about 2.5 millimeters long. It is distributed from the tropical Himalayas eastward to the Khasia hills and Manipur, Malaya, Sri Lanka, the Pacific islands and China.

LISTERA R. Br.
LIS-ter-a
Tribe: Neottieae
Subtribe: Listerinae

Etymology: After M. Lister, an English scientist

There are about 30 species in this terrestrial genus which is restricted to the cold and temperate parts of Asia and North America. Only two species are found in Europe. The first of these, *L. ovata*, is almost certainly the most common European orchid species, while *L. cordata* has a circumboreal distribution.
Plants have short rhizomes with slender roots. Stems carry two broad leaves arranged more or less opposite one another just below the middle of the stem. The inflorescence is a lax, spikelike raceme. Sepals and petals are approximately equal in length and held patent or slightly convergent. The lip is two to three times the length of the other perianth segments, deeply bifid from the apex with nectar secreted from a basal "furrow."

Listera cordata (L.) R. Br.

This is a tiny species, 5–20 centimeters tall and, because of its dwarf stature together with a predilection for growing beneath sphagnum cushions, it is often overlooked. There are two cordate leaves halfway up the stem with one or two brownish sheaths at the base. The inflorescence is lax with few flowers. Sepals and petals are small (2–2.5 millimeters long) and spreading. In close-up the lip looks straplike and is three-lobed with tiny laterals and midlobe deeply forked to form two lobules. Flowers vary from reddish green to a deep purple-brown and persist long after fertilization even when the ovary is visibly swollen. In the wild it favors coniferous woodlands or moorlands among heather and under sphagnum, always on acid soils. This rather dainty species is seldom found in cultivation but could probably be grown in a "woodland" compost to which plenty of extra leaf mold had been added.

LOCKHARTIA Hook.

lock-HART-ee-ah
Tribe: Cymbidieae
Subtribe: Oncidiinae
Etymology: In honor of David Lockhart, Superintendent of the Royal Botanical Gardens in Trinidad during the eighteenth century

Lockhartia is a genus of 25 species distributed throughout tropical America. The genus is characterized by the slender stems completely surrounded by distichous, flattened sheaths, branching at the base; the racemose or paniculate inflorescence from the axils of the apical sheaths; the sepals and petals free, spreading; the lip free, variously lobed with a callus at the base; the column short, footless, winged; the anther apical; and the two hard pollinia attached to a stipe united to a viscidium.
The plants grow as epiphytes in dry or wet forest at elevations from sea level to 2,000 meters. Members of this genus can be cultivated in the intermediate house, preferably on plaques where the sometimes pendent stems are free to develop. They should receive water throughout the year.

Lockhartia elegans Hook.

This species occurs from the West Indies, through eastern Colombia and Venezuela, to Brazil. The stems are erect and seldom exceed ten centimeters in length. The inflorescence is one- or two-flowered and is produced from the upper leaf-axils. The sepals and petals are yellow-green, and the lip is bright yellow spotted toward the base with red-brown. The lip has short, oblong lateral lobes and an obtuse midlobe.

Lockhartia longifolia (Lindley) Schltr.

This species occurs from Venezuela to Bolivia along the flanks of the Andes. The plant tends to have pendent stems with broader leaves than in most other species. The flowers are produced singly in succession, reach one centimeter in diameter, and are yellow with small red-brown spots at the base of the lip. The lip is entire with a raised callus at the base.

Lockhartia serra Reichb.f.

This species is restricted to coastal Ecuador. It is characteristic of most species in the genus with several flowers produced at a time in inflorescences that develop from the apical leaf-axils. The flowers reach two

Lockhartia longifolia

centimeters in diameter and are yellow with red-brown markings on the callus of the lip. The lip has oblong lateral lobes that are curved toward each other at the apices, a low claw between the lobes with a callus on its surface, and a broad apical lobe.

LUDISIA A. Rich.

loo-DIS-ee-ah
Tribe: Erythrodeae
Subtribe: Goodyerinae
Etymology: Origin unknown

Ludisia is a monotypic terrestrial genus distributed from northeast India throughout southeast Asia and into Indonesia. *Ludisia* is most notable for its velvety, deep red leaves with golden veins. Together with other patterned-leaved genera, such as *Anoectochilus* and *Macodes*, *Ludisia* species are known as "jewel orchids."
Ludisia is one of the easiest orchids to grow and thrives on standard houseplant care — medium light levels, intermediate to warm temperatures, and even moisture throughout the year. The plants will thrive in any terrestrial compost including commercial potting soil. Easily propagated from stem cuttings, *Ludisia* is readily available from nurseries that do not otherwise specialize in orchids.

Ludisia discolor (Ker.-Gawl.) A. Rich.

Stiffly erect fleshy inflorescences terminate each rosette of leaves. The stark white flowers with a yellow center are highly unusual in the orchid family because they are contorted and asymmetric. *Ludisia discolor* is frequently encountered under the name *Haemaria discolor*.

Ludisia discolor

LUEDDEMANNIA Linden & Reichb.f.

loo-ed-e-MAN-ee-ah
Tribe: Cymbidieae
Subtribe: Stanhopeinae
Etymology: Dedicated to Herr Lueddemann, a friend of Linden and Reichenbach
Lueddemannia is a monotypic genus distributed from Venezuela to Peru. It is characterized by the large, prominently ribbed ovoid pseudobulbs; the two or three apical, thick, heavily veined leaves and the elongate, pendent, many-flowered inflorescences produced from the base of the pseudobulbs; the three-lobed lip that is not divided into a hypochile and an epichile; the claw of the lip with a toothlike, laterally flattened callus; the apical lobe entire; the column slender and swollen on each side of the stigma; the anther apical; and the two, hard pollinia attached to a stipe united to a viscidium. Epiphytic in wet forest on each side of the Andes at elevations from 400 to 1,000 meters. The plants are rare in nature and in cultivation. They should be planted in baskets so that the pendent inflorescences can emerge properly, and they should be watered liberally throughout the year. They enjoy intermediate conditions.

Lueddemannia pescatorei (Lindley) Linden & Reichb.f.

The species is notable for the two-meter-long inflorescences and the multitude of flowers produced. The pendent inflorescences and the ovaries have scurfy black hairs. The individual flowers measure up to three centimeters in diameter. The free sepals are orange, almost solidly spotted with red-brown inside. The petals and lip are yellow-orange. The column is yellow with a green cast, and the anther is yellow.

Lueddemannia pescatorei

Luisia megasepala

LUISIA Gaudich.
loo-EES-ee-ah
Tribe: Vandeae
Subtribe: Sarcanthinae
Etymology: Honoring Don Luis de Torres

The genus *Luisia* comprises about 40 epiphytic species distributed from India to the islands of the Pacific. All species produce terete leaves that are adapted to seasonally dry habitats. *Luisia* is frequently confused with *Papilionanthe* and other terete-leaved monopodial orchids but differs by its habit of producing roots only at the base of the growth. Flowers, ranging from white to green, all have darkly colored, velvety lips. Related to *Vanda, Luisia* species are distinctive for their short, fleshy inflorescences that amount to little more than a club-like knob.

Luisia species can be grown in pots or mounted on a slab. All species prefer very bright light, warm temperatures, and frequent water without excessive moisture retention at the roots. Most species flower sporadically throughout the year.

Luisia megasepala Hayata

Endemic to Taiwan, *Luisia megasepala* is among the largest-flowered species in the genus. It has been erroneously included in a broadly defined *L. teres,* a smaller-flowered species with narrower floral segments. The green flowers have a nearly black lip. The distinctive fragrance is not pleasant.

Luisia teretifolia Gaudich.

Luisia teretifolia is native to Guam, the Philippines, New Guinea, and the Solomon Islands. The first species described in the genus, the name has been generally applied to a suite of species that are horticulturally interchangeable. The small green flowers have a uniformly dark purple lip.

LYCASTE Lindley
lie-CAST-ee
Tribe: Maxillarieae
Subtribe: Lycastinae
Etymology: The beautiful sister of Helen of Troy

There are 45 species of *Lycaste,* as well as a dozen recognized subspecies, and half a dozen recorded natural hybrids. They are found in Latin America from Mexico to Peru, with one species from the Caribbean islands and one from the Perlas Archipelago off the Pacific coast of Panama. The majority grow between 500 and 2,500 meters.

The plants are epiphytic and lithophytic with two to four large, thin, plicate leaves from usually ovate, sometimes spined, pseudobulbs. The yellow Mexican species are deciduous during the dry winter season. One, and sometimes two, showy flowers are

Luisia teretifolia

produced per scape from the base of the pseudobulb; they last about four weeks in perfection but are easily bruised and so are not suitable as cut flowers. Flower colors are principally yellow, pink, green, orange, white, and brown with spotting and bicolors.

Lycastes were first introduced into cultivation in the 1790s. In the wild some may experience frost at night, but in general cultivation less harsh conditions are recommended. Aim for a minimum winter night temperature of 10°–15°C, a winter day temperature of 18°–21°C when resting, and a maximum summer day temperature below 30°C when growing. Vary appropriately according to elevation of species. Shade is required in those seasons and latitudes where day temperatures are over 15°C. Composts recommended vary from a free-draining acid compost (pH 4–6) of, for example, one to two parts perlite, one part chopped sphagnum moss and one part peat or, at the other extreme, simple lava pebbles. Plants should not be allowed to remain wet for long and should be kept on the dry side when the bulb is made up. Humidity should be 100 percent at night and between 45 and 55 percent in the day. Any water that lodges in the new growth may damage it.

Lycaste aromatica

Lycaste aromatica (Graham ex Hook.) Lindley

This is native to Mexico, Guatemala, and Nicaragua where it may be found epiphytically at between 900 and 1,500 meters in oak woodlands or lithophytically on limestone cliffs. Up to fifteen bright yellow/yellow-orange flowers per pseudobulb, scented of cinnamon, appear in May/June. The flowers occur with the new growth from the base of the spined, deciduous pseudobulbs.

Lycaste bradeorum Schltr.

This comes from Honduras, Costa Rica, and Nicaragua. It is rather variable and easily confused with *L. cochleata.* Up to fifteen small yellow-orange flowers per spined pseudobulb appear with the onset of the new growth.

Lycaste bradeorum

Lycaste ciliata

Lycaste brevispatha Klotzsch

Native to Costa Rica and Nicaragua, this plant grows epiphytically at between 1,200 and 1,800 meters near streams and waterfalls which give high humidity. Up to six small, pink flowers per pseudobulb, unscented, appear in February (later in cultivation in Europe) before new growths appear. Plants must be kept dry at the roots and maintained in a humid atmosphere from November to April, when there is no rain in its native habitat. It is distinguished from *Lycaste candida* in having a short flat callus and much broader lip which is only slightly concave.

Lycaste campbellii C. Schweinf.

This plant was discovered in 1946 in the Perlas Archipelago off the Pacific coast of Panama, where it grows in the moss on the trunks of big trees, in densely shaded marshy areas at sea level. The very small yellow, unscented flowers arise from long-spined, deciduous pseudobulbs before the appearance of the new growth. It is the only *Lycaste* to be found off the Pacific coast of Latin America.

Lycaste candida Lindley

This species is found in central Costa Rica and perhaps neighboring areas, but details of its habitat are unknown. It has up to ten unscented flowers per bulb, and flowers in February (later in cultivation) with the onset of the new growth. Distinguished from *Lycaste brevispatha* Klotzsch by its highly grooved linear callus and narrower, concave lip.

Lycaste brevispatha

Lycaste campbellii

Lycaste candida

Lycaste ciliata Ruíz & Pavón

This is found in Bolivia, Colombia, Ecuador, and Peru growing between 1,000 and 2,400 meters. It occurs lithophytically in river canyons or epiphytically, often on decaying tree stumps, with roots deep in humus. It was initially discovered in the 1790s by Ruíz and Pavón's expedition to Peru. Up to eight light green, scented flowers with a five-keeled callus arise from plump, spineless pseudobulbs.

Lycaste cochleata Lindley ex Paxt.

This grows epiphytically and lithophytically in Mexico and Guatemala. Small, slightly scented, orange-yellow flowers appear when the new growth is half made up. Pseudobulbs are elongated and spined.

Lycaste consobrina Reichb.f.

This is an extremely variable yellow species from Mexico and Guatemala. The Mexican lowland form from the central east coast is smaller and less attractive than the higher-elevation form from the southwest mountain ranges. Up to seven flowers appear from spined pseudobulbs as the new growth commences. The species is identifiable by the hooded appearance of the flower with its horizontal dorsal sepal, the large callus, and the reflexed spade-shaped lip.

Lycaste crinita Lindley

This distinct small-flowered yellow species, growing between 900 and 2,000 meters in western Mexico, is characterized by its very hairy lip. A dozen unscented yellow flowers appear in the spring from spined, resting pseudobulbs.

Lycaste cochleata

Lycaste consobrina

Lycaste denningiana

Lycaste deppei

Lycaste dowiana

Lycaste crinita

Lycaste cruenta Lindley

This is a rather variable species from Mexico, Guatemala, and El Salvador. There are several distinct forms, but all are characterized by yellow flowers with a dark red blotch and dimple at the base of the lip. The length of the floral bract, the lip characteristics, and the flowering season are the main distinguishing features of the different forms. The type plant has ten or more strongly cinnamon-scented, large golden yellow flowers on short stems. They appear from heavily spined pseudobulbs before the new growth commences. This popular plant needs heavy feeding, perfect drainage with good light and air in the summer, and no water in the winter.

Lycaste denningiana Reichb.f.

This is a tough, high-elevation lithophytic species which grows in huge colonies at 1,800 meters in the mountains of Peru and Ecuador. It produces about six pendulous, pale green flowers with an orange lip on erect scapes as the new growth commences in the summer. It is a large, robust plant which has unspined pseudobulbs, and thick, light green, shiny leaves that stay on the plant for eighteen months or more. It must be grown very dry and cooler than other lycastes.

Lycaste deppei (Lodd.) Lindley

This easy-to-identify *Lycaste* from Mexico, Nicaragua, and Guatemala is not always deciduous, and never yellow. Up to eight flowers (occasionally strongly scented) appear from unspined pseudobulbs when the new growth is about ten centimeters high. The flowers have green, spotted red sepals; white petals and a yellow, spotted red lip. *Lycaste deppei* is a popular and easy-to-grow species which flowers better following a long period of drought in the resting season.

Lycaste dowiana Endres & Reichb.f.

The distribution of this species is uncertain — possibly Panama to Guatemala and elsewhere in South America. It is a delightful small *Lycaste* that blooms sequentially throughout the summer and fall. Flowers are produced singly, sometimes up to five at once, during the growing season from the base of faintly spined pseudobulbs. It likes perfect drainage but does not need a prolonged drought over the winter.

Lycaste cruenta

Lycaste lanipes

Lycaste lasioglossa

Lycaste leucantha

1,200 to 1,800 meters in Costa Rica and northern Panama. It enjoys cool moist conditions (maximum temperature 25°C) throughout the year. Seven or more pale green-and-white flowers, often followed by a few more later, arise from leafy pseudobulbs, which when older have vestigial spines. Flowering is variable, occurring at the beginning or middle of the growing season (January/February or July/August).

Lycaste locusta Reichb.f.

This striking and easily distinguished lithophytic species occurs between 1,800 and 3,000 meters in the Peruvian Andes. It has up to eight pendulous, dark green, apple-scented flowers with a white bearded edge to the lip on tall, erect stems from leafy, unspined pseudobulbs at the start of the growing season. It enjoys cooler winter temperatures and greater sunlight in the summer than many other species.

Lycaste locusta

Lycaste longiscapa Rolfe ex E. Cooper

This *Lycaste* from Ecuador is made elegant by its tall stems which bear medium-sized, pendulous flowers. Three tall-stemmed,

Lycaste lanipes Lindley

A beautiful rarity from southwestern Ecuador, this species is easily distinguished from *L. ciliata* by its narrower segments, its only slightly serrate lip, and its seven-keeled callus. About seven pendulous, pale green, heavily scented flowers appear in early summer on short, erect stems from unspined pseudobulbs as the new growth commences.

Lycaste lasioglossa Reichb.f.

This easily identifiable large-flowered species from Guatemala is probably now extinct in Mexico. It is not deciduous. It has up to twelve unscented flowers per unspined bulb at the end of the growing season, with leaves still present. Sepals are orange to dark brown, the petals and lip yellow. Red spots and bars appear on the densely hairy lip.

Lycaste leucantha Klotzsch

This charming little *Lycaste* occurs from

Lycaste longipetala

Lycaste longipetala (Ruíz & Pavón) Garay

This large-flowered epiphytic and lithophytic *Lycaste* occurs between 1,000 and 3,000 meters throughout much of South America. At these elevations the tough leathery leaves cope with a considerable amount of sun. Up to eight flowers per pseudobulb appear on long stems. They flower throughout much of the year, but more commonly when the new growth is commencing between January and March.

Lycaste longiscapa

scented, pendulous, green-and-brown flowers arise from leathery, slightly spined pseudobulbs, bearing narrow, thickened leaves with the new growth partly made up.

Lycaste macrophylla (Poeppig and Endl.) Lindley

This is a large group of lycastes, found throughout Central and South America, with numerous subspecies and forms. Some are slightly scented. *Lycaste macrophylla* subsp. *desboisiana* is perhaps the best-known of the subspecies. Its flowers — up to ten per unspined, leafy pseudobulb — grow on tall stems.

Lycaste macrophylla

Lycaste suaveolens

Lycaste skinneri

Lycaste skinneri (Bateman ex Lindley) Lindley

This, the queen of lycastes, is found epiphytically at between 1,500 and 2,100 meters in Guatemala, Honduras, and El Salvador, but is probably extinct in Mexico except in cultivation. It has numerous forms and varieties. It has up to eight showy, unscented, pink flowers, usually at the end of the growing season (November to January). They arise from leafy, unspined or slightly spined pseudobulbs. All the clones of *Lycaste skinneri* make attractive pot-plants and are of easy cultivation if kept in cool, humid shade with good air movement and perfect drainage. Greenhouse-raised seedlings are recommended.

Lycaste suaveolens Summerh.

This is a large-flowered, yellow, epiphytic *Lycaste* from El Salvador. It has half a dozen cinnamon-scented, bright golden yellow flowers on erect stems. They arise in midsummer, when the new growth is half made up, from heavily spined, dark pseudobulbs.

Lycaste tricolor Klotzsch

A delightful, tiny *Lycaste* from Costa Rica, this plant grows epiphytically in lower levels of cloud forest. It produces from three to five small pink to white, unscented flowers on short stems from unspined, heavily ribbed leafy pseudobulbs at the beginning of the growing season.

Lycaste trifoliata Hort. ex Ross

This is a beautiful miniature fimbriate *Lycaste* from South America. It produces up

Lycaste tricolor

Lycaste xytriophora

Lycaste trifoliata

to four unscented, small, white, hooded, heavily bearded flowers. These arise from the base of thin, tapering, spineless pseudobulbs bearing long, thin, petiolated leaves.

Lycaste xytriophora Linden & Reichb.f.

A small-flowered lithophytic *Lycaste* from Panama and Ecuador, this plant produces half a dozen faintly scented brown-and-cream flowers in quick succession when the new growth is about 50 centimeters high.

Lyperanthus serratus

Lyperanthus suaveolens

LYPERANTHUS R. Br.
lie-per-AN-thus
Tribe: Diurideae
Subtribe: Caladeniinae
Etymology: Gr. *lyperos*, sad, mournful; *anthos*, flower

Four interesting species are currently known, all endemic to Australia. Others from New Zealand and New Caledonia have been recently placed in different genera. They are deciduous terrestrial orchids with subterranean tuberoids and grow in loose colonies. Two species have broad, ground-hugging leaves and flower only after fires;

the other two have erect, narrow leaves and do not require the stimulus of fire to flower. The flowers are generally dull-colored. All species have four pollinia.
Pot in a well-drained soil mix containing wood shavings. Keep moist when in active growth (autumn to spring), dry out as plants die down, keep completely dry, and repot over summer. Use fertilizers sparingly.

Lyperanthus serratus Lindley

A distinctive orchid from Western Australia, where it often grows among low shrubs. Stiff wiry racemes, for two months in early spring, carry leathery, brownish flowers which have a conspicuous, white, brush-like apex on the labellum. Grows in loose, scattered groups.

Lyperanthus suaveolens R. Br.

This vigorous species, which is widespread in eastern Australia, grows in loose colonies in sparse forests. Racemes are produced from late winter to late spring, and the stiff-textured flowers are long-lasting. Flower color ranges from yellowish brown to dark brown or blackish brown, with a yellow apex on the labellum. Fragrance is strong and musky. An easy, rewarding species to grow.

MACODES Blume
ma-KO-deez
Tribe: Erythrodeae
Subtribe: Goodyerinae
Etymology: Gr. *makros*, long

About 10 terrestrial species comprise this genus of "jewel orchids" which extends from Malaysia to the Pacific islands, with

most in New Guinea. Species are cultivated more for their beautifully reticulate-veined leaves than for their flowers. The inflorescences of small, non-resupinate flowers with twisted column and labellum arise from the stem apex. There are two pollinia.
Most species are from low- to medium-elevation rain forests and so require warm to intermediate temperatures, high humidity, and relatively shady conditions. They may be grown and displayed to some advantage along with other "jewel orchids" such as *Ludisia* and *Anoectochilus*.

Macodes sanderiana (Kränzlin) Rolfe

Known in European glasshouses since the late nineteenth century, *M. sanderiana* is the most common member of this pretty-leaved genus in the New Guinea lowland rain forests. It has also been recorded from the Sunda Islands, the Bismarck Archipelago, and Vanuatu. In nature it grows on humus-covered rocks or rock-crevices along the banks of creeks, from near sea level up to about 900 meters (temperature range 20°–35°C). It requires warm conditions, good air movement, and full shade. The large leaves up to 16 × 8.5 centimeters in size are variable in color, usually olive to bronze-green, perhaps purple or brown, with golden yellow to green or orange reticulation (quite wide veining). The scapes are many-flowered, up to 40 centimeters long or more, with the small flowers yellowish to yellow-green or brown-green.

Macodes sanderiana

MACRADENIA R. Br.
mak-ra-DEN-ee-ah
Tribe: Cymbidieae
Subtribe: Oncidiinae
Etymology: Gr. *makros*, long; *aden*, gland; in reference to the elongate stipe

Macradenia is a genus of thirteen species distributed from Guatemala to Brazil. The genus is characterized by the elongate, cylindrical pseudobulbs with a single apical, flat leaf; the pendent inflorescence produced from the base of the pseudobulb, the free, spreading sepals and petals, the lip not surrounding the column, spurless; the apical lobe of the lip elongate, slender, concave; the lateral lobes large forming a cavity under the column; the column twisted away from the axis of the inflorescence, shorter than the sepals; and the two hard pollinia attached to an elongate stipe united to a small viscidium. They are epiphytic plants in lowland wet forests at elevations from 200 to 800 meters. The species can be cultivated under intermediate conditions with abundant water throughout the year. They do best on plaques, thus providing room for the development of the pendent inflorescences.

Macradenia brassavolae Reichb.f.

This species occurs from Mexico, through Central America, and south to Ecuador. The flowers reach two centimeters in diameter. The sepals and petals are dark red-brown with a yellow, translucent margin. The three-lobed lip is white marked with red-brown toward the base. The lateral lobes of the lip are incurved around the column which is twisted slightly outward.

MALAXIS Sw.
ma-LAX-is
Tribe: Malaxideae
Etymology: Gr. *malaxis*, soft, tender

There are about 300 known species in this largely terrestrial genus of small orchids distributed worldwide with the greatest density of species in southeast Asia. The genus is closely related to *Liparis* but is distinguished by non-resupinate flowers. The stem is fleshy, extended basally into a small, jointed pseudobulb. Flowers are rather tiny and dull with perianth segments no more than a few millimeters long. The lip is auriculate at its base, almost encircling, but free from the short column. *Malaxis* species can be grown in a compost of equal parts by volume of medium peat, loam, and sharp sand with added sieved leaf mold. While growing, most require well-watered, humid, shady conditions with a minimum temperature of 15°C. Pseudobulbous species lose their leaves after flowering when growth is completed and should be kept much drier; other species should not be allowed to become very dry.

Malaxis monophyllos (L.) Sw.

As a consequence of the drainage of its wetland habitats this slender species is becoming increasingly rare. It largely escapes notice because its green color blends with surrounding vegetation. There is usually, but not exclusively as the name

Macradenia brassavolae

implies, a single oval or lanceolate leaf and a basal pseudobulb surrounded by leaf sheaths. Plants reach 10–25 centimeters with small, pale green flowers in a narrow, elongated, spikelike raceme. The species has a scattered distribution in Europe and is then circumpolar through Russia and Japan into North America (where the typical variety is replaced by var. *brachystachys*, sometimes called *M. brachystachys*). In North America the genus is commonly called "adder's mouth." Flowers appear in June through July.

MASDEVALLIA Ruíz & Pavón
mas-de-VAL-i-a
Tribe: Epidendreae
Subtribe: Pleurothallidinae
Etymology: Named for José Masdeval, physician in the court of Spain

This genus, one of the most spectacular of the subtribe, contains about 350 species that are found from Mexico into Brazil. Most grow epiphytically at relatively high elevations in the Andes of Colombia, Ecuador and Peru. The fleshy leaves are variable in size but always longer than their ramicaul. The inflorescence is either single-flowered or racemose. The flower-stem (the peduncle) is round or triangular (triquetrous) in cross-section. The variously colored sepals are more or less fleshy and commonly united (connate) toward their bases to form a sepaline cup or tube. The tips of the sepals are usually contracted into tails. The petals are small and thick with some form of a callus along their lower margin. The simple lip, also usually

Malaxis monophyllos

inconspicuous, is often verrucose. The column is stout with a pair of pollinia. Many species of *Masdevallia* can be cultivated with a great deal of success in cool greenhouse conditions. Many will also tolerate intermediate greenhouse conditions. However, a large number, especially those from high elevations, defy cultivation.

Masdevallia amabilis Reichb.f.

This pretty species commonly grows among rocks in full sun at high elevations in northern Peru. The solitary flowers vary in

Masdevallia angulata

Masdevallia angulifera

Masdevallia ayabacana

Masdevallia bicolor

size and range in color from purple to white. They are borne by slender stems which are much longer than the thick, leathery leaves. The blades and tails of the sepals spread beyond the narrow sepaline tube.

Masdevallia angulata Reichb.f.

This large, coarse species is frequent in northwestern Ecuador and adjacent Colombia. Numerous thick and leathery leaves often accumulate into huge plants. The fleshy, dark red flowers, produced singly but sometimes in profusion, are borne by short, reclining stems.

Masdevallia angulifera Reichb.f. ex Kränzlin

This species from the Western and the Central Cordillera of Colombia is characterized by the medium-sized, fleshy leaves and single flowers that are borne about as high as the leaves. The sepals are deeply connate into a purplish, more or less "S-shaped" tube that is dilated on the front surface. The tips of the tailless sepals spread into a triangular shape around the entrance into the flower.

Masdevallia ayabacana Luer

This large, coarse species occurs locally in northern Peru and southeastern Ecuador. The leaves are thick and rigid. The long-tailed, yellowish flowers, borne successively on a tall, stout stem, are also thick, fleshy, and rigid. The lip is verrucose. The flowers from the two localities differ only in a few details.

Masdevallia bicolor Reichb.f.

The common concept treated as *Masdevallia bicolor* probably includes several "look-alikes." Using crude, morphological features, it is not simple to decide where to draw lines between minor taxa. Nevertheless, *Masdevallia bicolor* is recognized by its medium stature and by a peduncle triangular in cross-section that produces two, or sometimes three, flowers simultaneously. The dark purple lateral sepals and the yellow dorsal sepal are connate about halfway into a sepaline tube. The petals have a rounded callus at the base. The apex of the lip is verrucose distal to a pair of marginal folds in common with all species with triquetrous peduncles.

Masdevallia caesia Roezl

This spectacular species from southwestern Colombia is the only one known to grow pendently. Large, bluish green, strap-shaped leaves hang in clusters and a single, large, long-tailed flower is produced on a pendent stem. The lip is large and warty.

Masdevallia campyloglossa Reichb.f.

This species is variable in its wide distribution through all the mountains of Colombia and Ecuador into Peru. Greenish white, tailless flowers dotted with purple along the veins are produced singly by a slender, suberect to reclining stem. The proportionately large lip is simple and verrucose at the apex.

Masdevallia caudata Lindley

This handsome species occurs in easternmost Colombia and adjacent

Venezuela. A showy, long-tailed flower is borne by an erect stem to the height of the leaves. The concave, red-striped dorsal sepal and tail are held erect while the purple lateral sepals spread or recurve from a very short sepaline tube. Exposed in the center of the flower stand the erect petals, lip and column.

Masdevallia caudivolvula Kränzlin

This unusual species is immediately identifiable by the pale green, rigid sepaline cup with thick, corkscrew-like sepaline tails.

Masdevallia caesia

It occurs locally in the Central Cordillera of Colombia. It does not thrive in cultivation.

Masdevallia chontalensis Reichb.f.

This small species is common in Central America with a disjunct station in southwestern Ecuador. A pair of white flowers with short, yellow tails is produced atop a slender stem about as tall as the leaves. A tiny, pointed tooth is present near the lower border of the petals.

Masdevallia coccinea Linden ex Lindley

This spectacular species grows terrestrially. It occurs abundantly but locally at high elevations in the Eastern Cordillera of Colombia. Large, solitary flowers of all colors from red, purple, yellow or white are borne by stems much exceeding the thick, leathery leaves. From a narrow sepaline tube the tail of the dorsal sepal reflexes acutely while the lateral sepals are connate below into a large, broad lamina with merely acute apices. Many cultivated forms have been given names, especially during the *Masdevallia* craze of the last century.

Masdevallia caudivolvula

Masdevallia chontalensis

Masdevallia coriacea Lindley

The large, long-stemmed, pale-flowered, typical form of this terrestrial species is found in the mountains of the Eastern Cordillera of Colombia. Smaller, short-stemmed, more colorful variations (e.g. *M. bonplandii*) occur through the Andes from the Eastern Cordillera into Peru. The leaves are thick and rigid, and the flowers are fleshy, cup-shaped, and short-tailed.

Masdevallia decumana Königer

This small but showy, large-flowered species has been recently discovered in northern Peru and southern Ecuador. The single flowers are borne near the tops of broad, petiolate leaves. The dorsal sepal is concave and erect with an erect tail while the proportionately large, diffusely purple-spotted lateral sepals spread widely below.

Masdevallia elephanticeps Reichb.f.

This, the giant of them all, occurs locally at high elevations in the Eastern Cordillera of Colombia. A huge, fleshy flower is produced by a short, thick stem from the base of a large, leathery leaf. The broad synsepal beyond the sepaline tube is yellow, suffused with purple centrally. The lip is large and warty.

Masdevallia encephala Luer & Escobar

Known affectionately as "the brain" because of the cephalic-shaped sepaline tube, this species is native to one valley in the Eastern Cordillera of Colombia. The sepals are deeply connate into a globose tube with only a small aperture into the interior. The three, slender sepaline tails diverge from the rim of this tiny opening. The flowers are borne singly to about the height of the leaves.

Masdevallia caudata

Masdevallia coccinea

Masdevallia coriacea

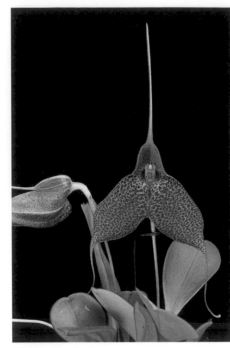

Masdevallia decumana

Masdevallia elephanticeps

Masdevallia floribunda

Masdevallia floribunda Lindley

The flowers of this species, which is frequent and widely distributed from southern Mexico into Honduras, are variable in size and color. Small, pale forms occur in Honduras while larger, red-purple forms (subsp. *tuerckheimii*) occur in Guatemala. The flowers, sometimes followed by a second on the same stem, are borne about as high as the leaves. The variously colored lamina of the connate lateral sepals spreads beyond the sepaline tube.

Masdevallia foetens

Masdevallia herradurae

Masdevallia foetens Luer & Escobar

This small, thick-leaved species produces one of the most foul-smelling flowers of the genus. From a short, thick, purple-striped sepaline tube, the three long, fleshy tails are spread.

Masdevallia herradurae Lehmann & Kränzlin

This floriferous little species occurs in the Western and the Central Cordillera of Colombia. Numerous, short-stemmed, dark purple flowers with slender sepals and tails are produced among the narrow leaves.

Masdevallia ignea Reichb.f.

This colorful species grows terrestrially in forests at high elevations in the Eastern Cordillera of Colombia. The flowers are similar to those of *M. coccinea*, but they are smaller with the tail of the dorsal sepal pointing forward and downward instead of backward. The color is usually fiery orange, hence the name. It has sometimes been called *M. militaris*, which is an intense red form of *M. coccinea*.

Masdevallia ignea

Masdevallia infracta

Masdevallia infracta Lindley

This species is widely distributed in southern Brazil, where numerous forms are to be found. Several have been given subspecific epithets. The species is easily recognized by the triquetrous flower-stem that bears a succession of flowers. The slender-tailed sepals are deeply connate into a gaping, suborbicular sepaline cup. The colors vary from purple or red-purple to yellow, brown, or white.

Masdevallia limax Luer

This floriferous little species occurs abundantly in the mountains of southeastern Ecuador. Bright orange or bright yellow, arcuate, tubular flowers are borne horizontally by suberect stems among the leaves. The orifice of the tube faces downward with three short tails.

Masdevallia livingstoneana Reichb.f. & Roezl

This species is one of the very few warm-growing species of the genus. It is known only from hot, lowland forests of central Panama. Fleshy, thickly short-tailed flowers are borne on stems to nearly the length of the leaves. A second flower usually follows the first. The flowers are cream-colored, suffused with red-brown basally and apically.

Masdevallia nidifica Reichb.f.

This little species is morphologically variable in its wide distribution from Central America to Ecuador, where it reaches its maximum development. The thin-tailed, more or less membranous, suborbicular flowers, colorless to prominently blotched

Masdevallia limax

Masdevallia livingstoneana

Masdevallia nidifica

or striped in purple, are borne amid small clusters of leaves. Within the flower the lip is hinged to a long, curved extension from the base of the column.

Masdevallia pachyura Reichb.f.

This species from the western slopes of the Andes of Ecuador is the most colorful of the simultaneously multiflowered species. Four to seven fleshy, short-tailed flowers are arranged loosely in a raceme that reaches above the leaves. The cup-shaped sepaline tubes are white and prominently spotted with purple, while the thick, clubbed tails are bright orange. A similar species, with minutely purple-dotted flowers and slender tails, is *M. leptoura.*

Masdevallia pelecaniceps Luer

This species, differing in a combination of features from all the other species, is segregated as a monotypic subgenus. It is known only from a forest in central Panama. The solitary, reddish flower is borne by the stem to nearly as high as the leaf-tips. The concave, connate lateral sepals are tailless and roughly rugose within.

Masdevallia pachyura

Masdevallia pinocchio

Masdevallia reichenbachiana

Masdevallia pelecaniceps

Masdevallia peristeria Reichb.f.

This species is relatively frequent, both epiphytically and terrestrially, through western Colombia into Ecuador. The leaves are thick and rigid. The fleshy, short-stemmed flowers are yellowish green and diffusely dotted with purple-brown. The simple lip is comparatively large and warty.

Masdevallia pinocchio Luer & Andreetta

This most unusual species is rarely found

on the eastern slopes of the Andes of central Ecuador. Tall, triquetrous stems bear the successive flowers in a long-lasting, congested raceme far above the thick leaves. From a shallow sepaline cup the narrowly triangular dorsal sepal stands erect. The broad, connate lamina of the lateral sepals extends below, the apices ending in short tails. The little protruding lip wobbles in the center of the flower.

Masdevallia polysticta Reichb.f.

This species from the western slopes of the Andes of Ecuador and northern Peru is the largest and most frequent of the simultaneously multiflowered species.

Three to seven or more white, slender-tailed flowers are formed loosely in a raceme that reaches well above the leaves. The cup-shaped sepaline tubes, occasionally with a few purple spots, are sparsely long-pubescent inside.

Masdevallia prodigiosa Königer

Discovered recently, this spectacular species is presently known only from northern Peru. Proportionately large, orange flowers are produced on short, horizontal stems. The dorsal sepal is deeply concave with a long, slender, reflexed tail. From the short sepaline cup the lateral sepals curve backward.

Masdevallia racemosa

Masdevallia racemosa Lindley

This unique species grows terrestrially at high elevations in the mountains of southern Colombia. The creeping rhizome produces individual leaves. The inflorescence bears a succession of single, scarlet flowers. Old published drawings showing numerous, simultaneous flowers are the result of wishful imagination. The broad, tailless lamina of the connate lateral sepals spreads from the narrow sepaline tube. Plants are difficult to maintain in cultivation for more than a few years.

Masdevallia reichenbachiana Endres ex Reichb.f.

This attractive species occurs locally in central Costa Rica. The large, membranous, long-tailed flowers are produced successively by stems round in cross-section to carry the flowers just above the leaves. The broad sepaline tubes are pale yellowish green and variously suffused with pale purple, especially on the dorsal sepal.

Masdevallia rosea Lindley

This spectacular species is found relatively frequently on the eastern slopes of the Andes of Ecuador and southern Colombia. Solitary, bright crimson flowers are borne by weak, suberect stems among long-stemmed leaves. The sepaline tube is orange at the base, and from the opening of the tube the broad lateral sepals spread. The attenuated dorsal sepal arches over them.

Masdevallia rubiginosa Königer

This variable species occurs frequently in southern Ecuador and northern Peru. Widely expanded, rusty red-brown flowers

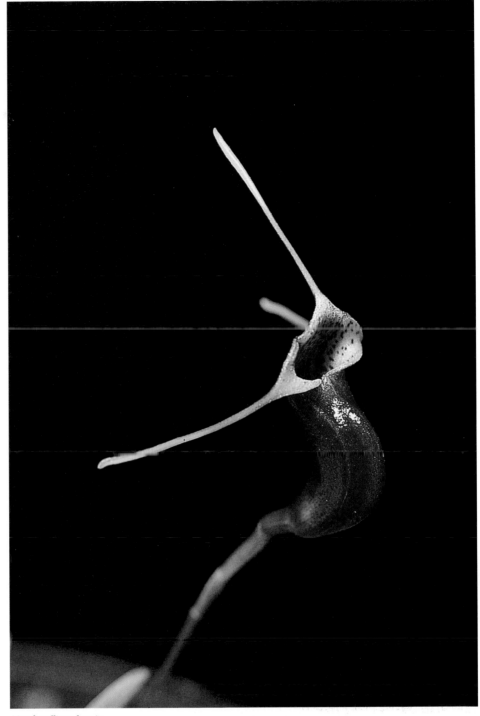

Masdevallia saltatrix

Masdevallia rosea

Masdevallia rubiginosa

are borne horizontally to suberect by short stems among broad, petiolate leaves. The tiny lip, elevated and rounded at the base, is loosely hinged in the center of the flower.

Masdevallia saltatrix Reichb.f.

This species, found in the Western Cordillera of Colombia, is characterized by the medium-sized, fleshy leaves and single flowers that are borne about half as high as the leaves. The sepals are deeply connate into a purplish and orange "S-shaped" tube that is dilated anteriorly. From the opening of the tube the long-tailed apices reflex. The tips of the slender tails are slightly thickened.

Masdevallia schmidt-mummii Luer & Escobar

This handsome species is uncommon in the Eastern Cordillera of Colombia. It is distinguished by solitary, white, purple-flecked flowers held by slender stems about as high as the leaves. The sepaline cup is shallow with the concave dorsal sepal arching above with a long, decurved tail. The lateral sepals diverge and recurve with their slender tails crossing behind.

Masdevallia schmidt-mummii

Masdevallia setacea

Masdevallia strobelii

Masdevallia setacea Luer & Malo

This species occurs in southeastern Ecuador and northern Peru as well as in the distant Eastern Cordillera of Colombia — unless they are just two exceedingly similar species. From among the petiolate leaves the erect stems bear a solitary, erect, white to rose-colored, very long-tailed flower. The three oblong sepals spread from a very shallow sepaline cup, leaving the erect lip, petals, and column exposed in the center.

Masdevallia stenorhynchos Kränzlin

This unusual species is infrequently encountered in the Western Cordillera of Colombia. Triquetrous peduncles carry the congested, successively flowered racemes near the tips of the leaves. From the very shallow sepaline cup the yellow dorsal sepal lies forward with the equally long tail bent upward. The lateral sepals, diffusely marked with brown, are connate about half their length with short, forwardly directed tails. The apex of the lip is bristly.

Masdevallia strobelii Sweet and Garay

Endemic in southeastern Ecuador along with numerous other species of orchids, this species is recognized by the long-tailed, orange sepaline tube that is densely long-pubescent inside. The single flowers, often produced in profusion, are borne on stems shorter than the petiolate leaves.

Masdevallia tovarensis Reichb.f.

Known locally as the Christmas flower because of its flowering season, this beautiful, snow-white-flowered species is

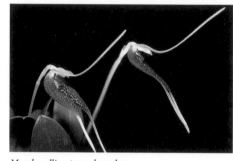

Masdevallia stenorhynchos

endemic to the coastal mountains of Venezuela. The triquetrous flower-stem bears two to five large flowers simultaneously. The broad lamina of the connate lateral sepals spreads beyond the sepaline tube.

Masdevallia triangularis Lindley

This species is frequent in the mountains of coastal Venezuela but rare in easternmost

Masdevallia tovarensis

Masdevallia triangularis

Masdevallia veitchiana

Colombia. A disjunct station in southeastern Ecuador has recently been discovered. The yellow sepals, minutely flecked with purple and with slender, purple tails, are widely spread beyond a shallow sepaline cup to form a flat, triangular flower. The erect lip, petals and column stand exposed in the center of the flower.

Masdevallia uniflora Ruíz & Pavón

This species from central Peru was the first of the genus to be found and described in 1794. Tall stems bear the solitary, bright pink flowers high above the thick leaves. The broad sepals spread from a gaping sepaline cup. The short tails are yellow.

Masdevallia veitchiana Reichb.f.

Endemic to the high mountains of southeastern Peru in the vicinity of Machu Picchu, this species grows terrestrially among rocks. Large, solitary, bright vermilion flowers are borne by long stems above the leaves. The broad, short-tailed sepals expand from a short sepaline tube. The inner surfaces of the sepals are covered with numerous, tiny, bright purple, clubbed hairs that impart a fluorescent sheen in the sunlight.

Masdevallia xanthina Reichb.f.

No doubt a number of look-alike species are treated within a species-complex under the name of *Masdevallia xanthina*. Although every population seems to differ from the next, they all are characterized by single flowers held erect among petiolate leaves. The three oblong sepals spread from a shallow sepaline cup, leaving the erect lip, petals and column exposed in the center.

Masdevallia uniflora

All the petals are provided with a prominent basal tooth. The colors of the sepals range from orange or yellow to pure white. A patch of dark purple at the base of the sepals occurs in flowers of all the color forms, suggesting an assortment of different pollinators.

Masdevallia xanthina

MAXILLARIA Ruíz & Pavón
max-ill-AIR-ee-a
Tribe: Maxillarieae
Subtribe: Maxillariinae
Etymology: L. *maxilla*, jawbone

There are close to 700 species in this genus, ranging from Florida through the West Indies and Central America to southern Brazil and northern Argentina. Most species are epiphytic. There are several groups within the genus, sometimes having been recognized as distinct genera: *Ornithidium, Camaridium, Dicrypta, Pseudomaxillaria,* etc. There are several growth forms in *Maxillaria*: pseudobulbless plants with short or elongate stems or pseudobulbous plants with stems or rhizomes of variable lengths. The pseudobulbs, when present, are one-to-four-leaved apically, but most of the species have only one leaf on top of the pseudobulb. The inflorescences are one-flowered, produced singly or in groups from the base of the pseudobulbs or from the axils of the sheaths of the rhizome or young stems. The flowers are variable in color and size. All species have four pollinia.

Cultural requirements vary with the habitats of the particular species, but most of them enjoy bright light (but not direct sun) and could be grown successfully in an intermediate greenhouse. As most of the species come from humid or cloud forests, they need to be watered year round. Many species are intolerant of being disturbed.

Maxillaria brunnea Linden & Reichb.f.

A common species occurring from Costa Rica southward to southeastern Brazil at elevations of 900–1,800 meters. The caespitose plants produce one to several inflorescences from the base of the pseudobulbs. The flowers are dull to bright yellow often with some dull maroon or purplish flush without, cream labellum, sometimes with dull purple streaks and a band or spot of very dark red-purple on the underside of the midlobe and apex of the lateral lobes. *Maxillaria brunnea* is frequently confused with *M. ringens* and allies that are more common in Central America, but it is easy to recognize by its broader sepals with obtuse or rounded apex and the dull yellow-brown coloration.

Maxillaria cucullata Lindley

This beautiful species ranges from Mexico southward to Panama. The one-leaved pseudobulbs are closely set on a shortly repent rhizome. Flowers are orange to pink with small red maculations, and the smell is somewhat fetid. The species occurs at elevations of 1,500–2,000 meters and can be grown in a cool greenhouse.

Maxillaria cucullata

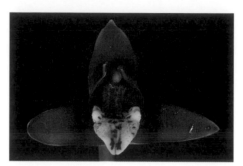
Maxillaria curtipes

Maxillaria densa

Maxillaria curtipes Hook.

This species ranges from Mexico to Honduras and El Salvador at elevations of 1,000–2,500 meters. Flowers are produced throughout the year from the axils of the new growth cataphylls and are purple-red or, less frequently, greenish with purple-red spots. The labellum is white or pale yellow with dark red spotting. *Maxillaria curtipes* can be cultivated in an intermediate or cool greenhouse.

Maxillaria densa Lindley

This interesting species ranges from Mexico to Honduras at elevations of 1,500–2,500 meters. The shoots are elongated and rooting only at the base. The one-leaved pseudobulbs are closely set on the rhizome. Dense clusters of up to 30 flowers are produced from the axils of the sheaths of the youngest pseudobulb. The flowers are variable in color, ranging from almost pure white to reddish purple or deep maroon. *Maxillaria densa* will grow in an intermediate or cool greenhouse and will flower several times a year as the new pseudobulbs mature.

Maxillaria elatior Reichb.f.

This vegetatively large species ranges from Mexico to Costa Rica at elevations of 400–1,500 meters. The elongate shoots root only at the base and feature large one- or two-leaved pseudobulbs. The flowers are produced singly from the axils of the cataphylls of the new growth and are greenish yellow with dark red or purplish flushing. The labellum displays a large

Maxillaria elatior

Maxillaria luteo-alba

orange or reddish callus. *Maxillaria elatior* is tolerant of a wide range of temperatures in nature and in cultivation and will flower intermittently from September to April.

Maxillaria friedrichsthallii
Reichb.f.

This common species ranges from Mexico to Panama at elevations of 50–1,500 meters. The two-leaved pseudobulbs are produced on elongate shoots that root only at the base. The inflorescences are produced singly from the cataphylls of the pseudobulbs from November to March. The flowers do not open fully and are whitish or yellowish, turning greenish with age. The fragrance is somewhat disagreeable, like rancid urine. *Maxillaria friedrichsthallii* is easy to grow in the warm or intermediate greenhouse.

Maxillaria lepidota Lindley

This showy species is known from the Andes in Colombia, Ecuador, and Venezuela at elevations of 1,500–2,000 meters. The plants are caespitose with elongate inflorescences arising from the base of the one-leaved pseudobulbs. Flowers are spidery, yellow with brown apices to the sepals, the labellum yellow with red spots. It requires an intermediate or cool greenhouse, high humidity, and good air movement for successful cultivation.

Maxillaria luteo-alba Lindley

One of the showiest species of the genus, *Maxillaria luteo-alba* is known from Costa Rica, Panama, Colombia, Ecuador, and Venezuela at elevations of 500–1,500 meters. Plants are caespitose with one-leaved pseudobulbs. The inflorescences are shorter than the leaf. The flowers are sweetly fragrant, white or pale yellow externally, pale yellow to orange internally, the labellum yellow with purple nerves. It requires an intermediate greenhouse with bright but not direct light. Similar species are *M. angustisegmenta, M. callichroma, M. endresii, M. setigera,* and *M. triloris.*

Maxillaria nigrescens Lindley

This spectacular Andean species occurs in Venezuela, Colombia, and Ecuador at

Maxillaria lepidota

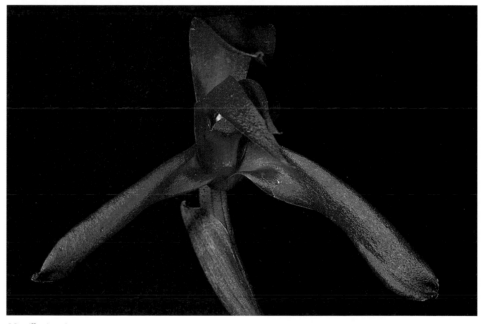

Maxillaria nigrescens

elevations of 1,500–2,500 meters. Plants are caespitose, and the pseudobulbs are apically one-leaved. The large, spidery flowers are brilliant or dull dark purple-red or dark red, and the labellum is much darker, almost black. Flowering is mostly in November–February. Cultivation requires cool temperatures, bright light (but not direct sun), high humidity and good ventilation. A similar Peruvian species, *M. calantha,* has not yet been introduced to horticulture, and displays a somewhat narrower, more lobed labellum.

Maxillaria picta Hook.

This species occurs in the states of southeastern Brazil where it is often found on trees or rocks at intermediate elevations.

Pseudobulbs are one-leaved and set along a shortly creeping rhizome. The inflorescences are produced in profusion from the base of the pseudobulbs during the last months of the year. The flowers are sweetly fragrant, pale bright or dull yellow with red spots and faint brown barring, the labellum white or pale yellow with a yellow midlobe, the anther a bright dark red-purple. *Maxillaria picta* can be successfully grown in a relatively large pot or a slab with bright light in the intermediate greenhouse. Similar but less frequently cultivated species are *M. porphyrostele, M. rupestris,* and *M. ubatubana.*

Maxillaria reichenheimiana
Endr. & Reichb.f.

A small but colorful species found from

Costa Rica southward to Amazonian Brazil at elevations of 800–1,500 meters. The plants are densely caespitose with dull gray-green leaves variably maculated or tessellated with white on the upper surface and often dark, dull maroon on the underside. The flowers are dull yellow or orange with a pale yellow or white labellum with red or orange midlobe. *Maxillaria reichenheimiana* requires a shady spot in a well-ventilated, humid, warm or intermediate greenhouse. The similar *Maxillaria pachyacron* lacks the spots on the leaves.

Maxillaria ringens Reichb.f.

A showy species ranging from Mexico south to Panama at 500–1,500 meters. Plants are caespitose, and the relatively short, one-flowered inflorescences are produced in profusion from the base of the mature, one-leaved pseudobulbs. Flowers are sweetly fragrant and do not spread widely; colors are white or pale yellow, paler toward the apex, the labellum white with yellow central lobe. *Maxillaria ringens* will grow in the intermediate greenhouse with bright but not direct light.

Maxillaria reichenheimiana, showing plant only

Maxillaria rufescens

Maxillaria sanderiana

Maxillaria sophronitis

Maxillaria rufescens Lindley

This species is known from Trinidad and the Amazon Basin in Colombia, Ecuador, Peru, Bolivia, Venezuela, the Guianas, and Brazil at elevations of 200–1,200 meters. The caespitose plants produce inflorescences from the base of the apically one-leaved pseudobulbs. The flowers have a strong vanilla-like fragrance and are dull yellow or yellow-brown with purple or reddish blotches or spots on the labellum, especially on the large apical lobe. Cultivation is easy in the warm or intermediate greenhouse with bright light and good ventilation. Flowers are produced several times a year. Several closely related species are frequently cultivated under this name (*M. hedwigae, M. acutifolia, M. richei* and a few others), but *Maxillaria rufescens* is easily distinguished by the vanilla fragrance.

Maxillaria sanderiana Reichb.f.

This spectacular species is known from Peru and Ecuador where it grows at elevations of 1,200–2,400 meters. The large plants are caespitose, and the pendent inflorescences are produced from the base of the one-leaved pseudobulbs. The flowers are very large and resemble a *Lycaste* with pure white perianth segments with blood-red spots or blotches, especially at the base. The fragrance is sweet. Cultivation requires high humidity, good ventilation, and a cool or intermediate greenhouse.

Maxillaria sophronitis (Reichb.f.) Garay

This interesting little species comes from Venezuela and northeast Colombia at elevations of 750–1,600 meters. The plant is creeping and mat-forming with distant, small pseudobulbs topped by a single leaf. The flowers, produced from the base of the newest mature pseudobulbs, are proportionally large, scentless, and bright scarlet. Flowering occurs from October to January. *Maxillaria sophronitis* is reputedly

difficult to grow, and it requires an intermediate, well-ventilated greenhouse.

Maxillaria striata Rolfe

A spectacular species from Ecuador and Peru at elevations of 700–1,550 meters. The showy flowers resemble those of *M. sanderiana* but are somewhat smaller, yellowish or pale red-brown, densely striated with dark red-brown and with yellow, non-striated petal apices. Cultivation is similar to that for *M. sanderiana*.

Maxillaria tenuifolia Lindley

A commonly cultivated species found from Mexico to Nicaragua and doubtfully from Costa Rica at elevations of 100–1,200 meters. Elongate shoots that root only at the base comprise apically one-leaved pseudobulbs distantly set on the rhizome. The inflorescences are produced singly from the cataphylls of the most recently matured pseudobulb. The flowers are somewhat variable in color, ranging from blood-red (commonly) to yellowish spotted with red with a white or yellow labellum spotted with deep red. The strong fragrance of coconut aromatized with vanilla distinguishes this species that usually flowers from March to May. Cultivation requires a warm or intermediate greenhouse with bright light and good ventilation.

Maxillaria uncata Lindley

This widespread species occurs from sea level to 1,500 meters and ranges from southern Mexico to southern Brazil, although there might be several species with narrower geographic and ecologic

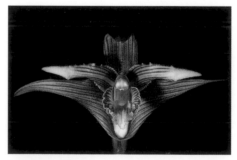

Maxillaria striata

Maxillaria tenuifolia

Maxillaria valenzuelana

Maxillaria uncata

ranges included in this concept. The shoots are elongated and root only at the base. The closely or distantly set, small pseudobulbs are apically one-leaved with very fleshy leaves. The small flowers are produced throughout the year and are cream, yellowish, pale lavender, or white often with maroon, purple, or reddish nerves, but some forms have entirely maroon flowers. Cultivation is easy in a warm or intermediate greenhouse.

Maxillaria valenzuelana
(A. Richard) Nash

This unusual species, known from Cuba, Nicaragua to Panama, Colombia, Venezuela, and Brazil, produces pendent, fan-like, fleshy-leaved plants. The leaves are laterally compressed and usually glaucous. The inflorescences are produced year round from the axils of the leaves and are much shorter than the leaves. The flowers are fleshy, yellow or greenish yellow, with a deeper yellow or orange labellum spotted in red, purple, or dark orange. The fragrance is spice-like. It should be grown on a tree-fern or cork slab but could grow in a pot. *Maxillaria valenzuelana* can be grown in the intermediate or warm greenhouse. This species can be grown into a magnificent specimen plant.

Maxillaria variabilis Batem. ex Lindley

This commonly cultivated species ranges from Mexico to Panama and probably in Guyana at elevations of 0–1,900 meters. The plants produce more or less elongate shoots that root mostly at the base, with closely set, apically one-leaved pseudobulbs. The flowers are produced from the cataphylls of the newly growing shoots and are variable in color, ranging from pure yellow, yellow

Maxillaria variabilis

with a dark purple labellum, or entirely dark purple. The callus is dark, "wet" purple-black or reddish. Flowering occurs throughout the year but most commonly during November-January. Cultivation is easy in a warm or intermediate greenhouse.

MEIRACYLLIUM Reichb.f.
my-ra-SIL-ee-um
Tribe: Epidendreae
Subtribe: Meiracylliinae
Etymology: Gr. *meirakyllion*, stripling; in reference to the reduced, creeping habit

A genus of two species distributed from Mexico to Costa Rica. The genus is

characterized by the creeping stems with minute pseudobulbs and a single, leathery leaf at their apices; the flowers produced in short, subcapitate inflorescences from the minute pseudobulbs at the base of the leaf; the red-purple flowers with the lip free from the column; and the eight hard pollinia. The plants are epiphytic or lithophytic in moist cloud forests on the slopes of the mountains. They grow well on plaques under intermediate conditions.

Meiracyllium wendlandii
Reichb.f.

This species occurs from Mexico to El Salvador. The attractive purplish flowers reach 2.5 centimeters in diameter. The

Meiracyllium wendlandii

Mexicoa ghiesbrechtiana

Micropera obtusa

species is recognized by the petals being broader toward the apex, the scoop-shaped lip, and the slender base of the column.

MEXICOA Garay
mex-ee-CO-ah
Tribe: Cymbidieae
Subtribe: Oncidiinae
Etymology: In reference to the origin of the plant from Mexico

This is a monotypic genus from Mexico. The genus is characterized by the presence of bifoliate pseudobulbs of a single internode; the inflorescence produced from the axils of the sheaths; the flowers without a spur; the sepals spreading, the petals parallel and hooded over the column; the lip articulate with the short column-foot; the column arcuately bent, wingless; and the two hard pollinia attached to a stipe connected to a viscidium.
The plants are epiphytic in humid forests at elevations from 800 to 1,500 meters. They can be cultivated under cool conditions as with members of the genus *Odontoglossum*.

Mexicoa ghiesbrechtiana
(A. Richard & Gal.) Garay

This species is restricted to Mexico. The leaves are broad, and the pseudobulbs are conspicuous and flattened. The inflorescence is erect, and the flowers are yellow. The petals are hooded over the column, and the lip is three-lobed with the apical lobe broader than the distance between the lateral lobes. The column is wingless.

MICROPERA Lindley
my-KROE-pe-ra
Tribe: Vandeae
Subtribe: Sarcanthinae
Etymology: Gr. *mikros*, small; *pera*, sac

Micropera is a genus of about fifteen epiphytic species found from northeast India to Australia, New Guinea, and the Philippines. Until recently the species were known under the synonym *Camarotis*. *Micropera* is unusual among the epiphytic orchids in having a long, twisted column so that the flowers are not symmetric. All *Micropera* species have prominent, saccate lips.
Micropera species should be given standard monopodial culture with intermediate to warm temperatures, medium bright light levels, and uniform watering throughout the year. Most species are readily grown in pots using a medium-grade epiphyte compost. Rambling species can be grown in baskets or mounted on slabs.

Micropera obtusa (Lindley) Tang & Wang

Micropera obtusa is native from northeast India to Thailand. The pink flowers are produced on racemes over a long period in the spring. This species is given to producing lateral branches and plants quickly form large, interlocking masses of vegetation.

Micropera philippinensis
(Lindley) Garay

Endemic to the Philippines, this is one of the showier species in the genus. Large

Micropera rostrata

green and white, non-resupinate flowers are produced in the fall on branched inflorescences above the upright growing plants. The flowers are set off by their glossy sheen.

Micropera rostrata (Roxb.) Balakr.

Native from northeast India to Thailand. This is the most dramatic species in *Micropera* because of its rich purple flowers produced in the spring. Appropriately, the plant is frequently encountered under the synonym *Camarotis purpurea*. A large plant

Micropera philippinensis

for *Micropera*, *Micropera rostrata* is similar to an *Aerides* or *Vanda*.

MILTONIA Lindley
mil-TONE-ee-ah
Tribe: Cymbidieae
Subtribe: Oncidiinae
Etymology: In honor of Earl Fitzwilliam, Viscount Milton, patron of horticulture during the nineteenth century

Miltonia is a genus of ten species primarily distributed from central to southern Brazil, but one species also is found in Peru. The genus is characterized by the presence of unifoliate or bifoliate pseudobulbs of a single internode subtended by distichous leaflike sheaths; the inflorescence produced from the axils of the sheaths; the flowers without a spur; the sepals and petals free; the lip large and flat; the callus essentially lacking; the column without a foot; and the two hard pollinia attached to a stipe connected to a viscidium.
Like many botanists — including Lindley when he described *Miltonia spectabilis* (1837) in the first place — we find that the features which served to distinguish this genus are untenable in separating it from *Oncidium*. However, in keeping with the classical approach we here retain the genus but remove the so-called "Andean miltonias" to the genus *Miltoniopsis*. The species formerly known as *Miltonia warscewiczii* Reichb.f. does not belong with *Miltonia* but rather is an *Oncidium*. When placed in that genus it is called *O. fuscatum* Reichb.f.

Miltonia cuneata

The members of *Miltonia*, as now recognized, all occur in eastern South America with most species occurring in central and southern Brazil. The species can be cultivated in pots under intermediate conditions with members of *Cattleya*.

Miltonia candida Lindley

This species occurs in southeastern Brazil. It is distinguished by the inflorescence having a round stem and the floral bracts much shorter than the ovary. The flowers reach seven centimeters in diameter. The sepals

and petals are brown with yellow apices and are blotched with yellow spots. The lip is white, funnel-shaped at the base, and surrounds the column; it has a pair of red blotches in the throat.

Miltonia clowesii Lindley

This species occurs in southeastern Brazil. The inflorescence has a round stem, and the floral bracts are much shorter than the ovary. The flowers reach seven centimeters in diameter. The sepals and petals are yellow-orange, barred, and blotched with red-brown. The lip is white with a large blotch of purple at the midpoint. The lateral lobes are spreading and are narrower than the apical lobe.

Miltonia cuneata Lindley

This species occurs in southeastern Brazil. The inflorescence is provided with a round stem, and the floral bracts are much shorter than the ovary. The flowers reach seven centimeters in diameter. The sepals and petals are dark brown tipped with yellow at the apices. The lip is white, sometimes spotted with red at the base. The lateral lobes of the lip are nearly nonexistent.

Miltonia flavescens Lindley

This species occurs in southern Brazil and Paraguay and has been reported from eastern Peru. The inflorescence has a flattened stem, and the floral bracts are as long as the ovary. The flowers reach seven centimeters in diameter and have narrow sepals and petals, giving the flower a star shape. The flowers are pale yellow with a white lip that is spotted with red at the base. The lateral lobes of the lip are about equal to the apical lobe.

Miltonia spectabilis Lindley

This species occurs in extreme eastern Brazil and has been erroneously reported as occurring naturally in Venezuela. The inflorescence produces a single flower, has a flattened stem, and the floral bracts are as long as the ovary. The flowers reach a diameter of eight centimeters. The normal form has yellowish white sepals and petals tinged with red toward the base. The lip is wine-red with darker vein-lines. Var.

moreliana is more frequently cultivated than the typical form and has larger, much darker-colored flowers.

MILTONIOPSIS Godf.-Leb.

mil-tone-ee-OP-sis
Tribe: Cymbidieae
Subtribe: Oncidiinae
Etymology: Gr. *opsis*, appearance; in reference to a similarity to the genus *Miltonia*

This is a genus of six species distributed from Costa Rica to Peru. The genus is characterized by the presence of unifoliate or bifoliate pseubobulbs of a single internode subtended by distichous leaflike sheaths; the grey-green leaves; the inflorescences produced from the axils of the sheaths; the flowers without a spur; the sepals and petals free; the lip large and flat; the callus essentially lacking; the column without a foot; and the two hard pollinia attached to a stipe connected to a viscidium. The plants are epiphytes from extremely wet cloud forest at elevations from 500 to 2,000 meters. They can be cultivated in pots under intermediate to cool conditions with abundant water supplied throughout the year.

Miltoniopsis phalaenopsis

(Nichols.) Garay & Dunsterv.

This species is known only from Colombia. The inflorescence is shorter than the leaves and produces three to five flowers that reach six centimeters in diameter. The flowers are white and the disc of the lip has

bright purple vein-lines. The lip is four-lobed, and the basal lobes are short and roundish while the apical lobes are larger and subquadrate.

Miltoniopsis roezlii (Reichb.f.) Garay & Dunsterv.

This species occurs in Panama and western Colombia. The inflorescence is about as long as the leaves with two to five flowers, each reaching ten centimeters in diameter. The flowers are white with a purple blotch at the base of each petal and an orange blotch on the disc of the lip. The lip is four-lobed with the lateral lobes small and hornlike on each side of the column.

Miltoniopsis vexillaria (Reichb.f.) Garay & Dunsterv.

This species occurs from Colombia to Peru. In nature the flower color varies from light pink to dark red. The inflorescences are usually longer than the leaves and have four to seven flowers, each reaching ten centimeters in diameter. The lip is four-lobed with tiny, hornlike lobes at the base, and the pair of apical lobes are very broad. Many spectacular hybrids have been produced by crossing this species with others of the genus and with distinctive clones.

Miltoniopsis warscewiczii

(Reichb.f.) Garay & Dunsterv.

This species occurs in Costa Rica. The inflorescence is about equal to the leaves and produces three to five flowers that reach seven centimeters in diameter. The flowers are pale pink or white with a pale

Miltonia spectabilis

Miltoniopsis phalaenopsis

Miltoniopsis roezlii

Miltoniopsis vexillaria

slender and twisted so that the dorsal side rests on the lip and with an apparatus for throwing the pollinarium onto the pollinator in the male phase; the column straight and erect in the female phase; and the two hard, round pollinia attached to an elongate stipe united to a round viscidium. These are epiphytic plants of moist or wet forests at elevations from sea level to 800 meters, and often occur on dead limbs of trees. The species are pollinated by specific male euglossine bees, tend to have population distributions of small size, and have relatively few good distinguishing characters. Many more species can be expected as inaccessible regions of South America are opened and critical study of the species is accomplished. Unfortunately, many of the species have been confused by authors who tended to apply names indiscriminately, often basing them on color and not on structure.

The species can be cultivated under warm to intermediate conditions with abundant water and fertilizer during the growing season, but with a pronounced drier period when resting.

Mormodes aromaticum Lindley

This species occurs from Mexico to Honduras. The flowers have a lip that is entire on the margin and is unguiculate at the base with a broadly cordate blade. The flowers vary in color from yellow to red-brown.

Mormodes atropurpureum Lindley

This species occurs from Costa Rica to Colombia but has also been reported from Mexico and Brazil. The latter reports may be associated with dark red-brown color forms of other species. The lip is distinctly three-lobed with the apical lobe projecting beyond the laterals and abruptly apiculate. The flowers are glabrous. The sepals and petals are red-brown with small spots and the lip is pink spotted with red-brown.

purple blotch at the base of each segment. The species is not very different from *M. vexillaria* and may represent only a geographically distinct form.

MORMODES Lindley
mor-MOE-deez
Tribe: Cymbidieae
Subtribe: Catasetinae
Etymology: Gr. *mormo*, phantom, bugbear, frightful object; *oides*, resembling; in reference to the weird appearance of the flower

Mormodes is a genus of 67 species distributed from Mexico to Bolivia and Brazil. The genus is characterized by the fleshy pseudobulbs of several internodes with thin, heavily veined, deciduous leaves and the inflorescence produced from the median nodes; the bisexual flowers; the lip usually trullate or three-lobed; the column

Mormodes aromaticum

Mormodes atropurpureum

Mormodes igneum

Mormodes rolfeanum

Mormodes buccinator

Mormodes buccinator Lindley

This species was described from northeastern South America and definitely occurs in Venezuela and the Guianas but may also occur in eastern Colombia and northern Brazil. Reports of its occurrence in Mexico, Central America, and Ecuador are probably based on similar species. The lip is broadly obovate with a sharp apicule at the apex and with the sides strongly recurved. The surface is glabrous. The flowers are yellow-brown, and the sepals and petals have parallel lines of small dots.

Mormodes igneum Lindley & Paxt.

This species has been reported from Mexico, Costa Rica, Panama and Colombia. The lip is entire, suborbicular when spread, with the sides strongly reflexed, shortly apiculate at the apex, and glabrous. The flowers are very variable in color, from nearly white to dark reddish brown or yellow.

Mormodes rolfeanum Linden

This species occurs in southeastern Ecuador

and northeastern Peru. The lip is broadly obovate when spread with the sides strongly reflexed, entire, shortly apiculate at the apex, and glabrous. The flowers are very large, reaching ten centimeters in diameter. The sepals and petals are yellow-brown, and the lip is often dark wine-red.

Mormodes sinuatum Reichb.f. & Warsc.

This species has been reported from Guatemala, Costa Rica, Venezuela, and Brazil. Some of the reports from Central America may represent erroneous identifications. The lip is three-lobed when spread with the side-lobes strongly reflexed and thrust forward, with a tiny apicule at the apex of the midlobe. The surface is glabrous. The flowers vary in color from yellow to wine-red.

Mormodes vernixium Reichb.f.

This species occurs in Venezuela and the Guianas. The lip is three-lobed with the lateral lobes very broad and obovate and the apical lobe small and apiculate at the apex. The lateral lobes are strongly reflexed and thrust forward. The surface is glabrous. The flowers are dark wine-red in color.

MORMOLYCA Fenzl
mor-mo-LYE-kah
Tribe: Maxillarieae
Subtribe: Maxillariinae
Etymology: Gr. *mormolyca*, hobgoblin

Seven interesting species are currently

Mormodes sinuatum

recognized in this genus that is closely related to *Maxillaria* and *Trigonidium*. Some species were previously placed in the genus *Cyrtoglottis*. The species range from Mexico to southeastern Brazil, but most of the species occur in the Andes from Venezuela to Bolivia at elevations of 750–1,800 meters. The rhizome is shortly creeping and the pseudobulbs usually one-leaved apically, but in one species there are up to four leaves on top of the pseudobulb. The one-flowered inflorescences arise from the base of the mature pseudobulb and are subequal to longer than the leaves. The flowers are medium-sized, usually yellow or yellow-brown. Four pollinia are present in all the species.
Most species require bright light and intermediate temperatures (15°C at night). Keep plants moist but well-drained all the time. Plants can be grown in pots or on tree-fern or cork slabs with some protection for the roots.

Mormolyca gracilipes (Schltr.) Garay & Wirth

This unusual species ranges along the

Mormolyca gracilipes

Mormolyca ringens

Mystacidium capense

Andes from Venezuela to Bolivia at elevations of 1,000–2,700 meters. The interesting flowers are large for the plant and occur on elongate, thin-stemmed inflorescences during April-June, often two inflorescences per pseudobulb. The perianth segments are clear maroon-yellow, orange-yellow, to pink salmon with yellow margins, the labellum usually darker and with maroon or purple dots. Plants of this species coming from higher elevations in the Andes can be cultivated in the cool greenhouse (10°C at night).

Mormolyca ringens (Lindley) Schltr.

A commonly cultivated species found in nature from Mexico to Costa Rica at elevations of 0–1,000 meters. The elongate inflorescences are produced throughout the year. The flowers are widely open and are yellow or greenish (rarely light lavender) with dark maroon or reddish veins. The labellum is dark maroon or reddish with a paler margin. *Mormolyca ringens* will tolerate warmer temperatures than the other members of the genus, up to 25°C at night.

MYSTACIDIUM Lindley
mis-tah-SID-ee-um
Tribe: Vandeae
Subtribe: Aerangidinae
Etymology: Gr. *mystax*, moustache

There are about ten species of dwarf epiphytic orchids in this monopodial genus from Africa. One species is found in Tanzania and Malawi, but the rest are South African endemics. All the plants have short

Nageliella purpurea

stems with few leaves and copious roots, perhaps because they have to survive a dry season of several months' duration. The leaves are dark green, leathery, and may be deciduous. One species (*M. gracile*) is leafless. The flowers are white or a translucent pale green, borne on long inflorescences.
Plants are easily maintained in cultivation if they are mounted on bark or logs so that their roots have plenty of space. They need high humidity and can withstand long periods of little extra moisture. Most of the species flower best if the plants are kept in strong light.

Mystacidium capense (L.f.) Schltr.

This is the largest species in the genus and is known from the drier forests in eastern South Africa and Swaziland. The white flowers are produced in great abundance in spring and early summer. The flowers are

star-shaped with the lateral sepals somewhat larger than the other parts and a long spur at the base of the narrow lip.

NAGELIELLA L. O. Williams
nag-el-ee-EL-ah
Tribe: Epidendreae
Subtribe: Laeliinae
Etymology: In honor of Otto Nagel, collector of Mexican orchids during the early part of the twentieth century

This is a genus of three species distributed from Mexico to Costa Rica. The genus is characterized by the slender, jointed, stemlike pseudobulbs with a single thick, fleshy, red-spotted leaf at the apex; the inflorescence produced from the apex of the stem at the junction with the leaf; the elongate, wiry inflorescence with several bell-shaped, bright pink flowers produced successively; and the saccate lip fused to the base of the column.
The plants occur as epiphytes in cloud-forest associations. They can be easily grown under intermediate conditions on plaques or in pots with ample water throughout the growing season.

Nageliella purpurea (Lindley)
L. O. Williams

The species occurs from Mexico to Costa Rica. It is distinguished from the other species by the slightly wider and thinner leaves, the larger flowers, and the lip with a protruding saclike spur. The flowers are purplish red.

Neobathiea filicornu

Neocogniauxia hexaptera

NEOBATHIEA Schltr.
nee-oh-BAH-tee-ah
Tribe: Vandeae
Subtribe: Angraecinae
Etymology: Named in honour of H. Perrier de la Bâthie, French botanist

This small genus of monopodial epiphytes has about seven species in Madagascar and the Comoro Islands. The plants are rather small with short stems and two rows of narrow leaves. Roots are usually poorly developed. The flowers are large for the plants, white, green, or green-and-white, with a long spur from a broad mouth at the base of the lip. They grow in moist humid forests and are attached to small twigs and branches within the canopy.
Plants grow best in small pots or mounted on bark in intermediate or cool temperatures. They need to be kept in rather shady and very humid conditions and do well if kept moist.

Neobathiea filicornu Schltr.

This attractive species occurs in both central Madagascar and the Comoro Islands. The leaves are elliptic, and the large flowers are borne singly on a short inflorescence. They are pale green at first, becoming white and then turning yellow as they age.

NEOBENTHAMIA Rolfe
nee-oh-ben-THAM-ee-ah
Tribe: Polystachyeae
Etymology: Gr. *neos*, new — a second genus named in honor of George Bentham, English botanist

This is a curious African genus containing a single species of terrestrial or lithophytic orchid. The plants look like a tropical grass, with a long reedy stem and many narrow leaves, until they produce a terminal inflorescence at a height of a meter or more. The flowers are borne in a dense cluster, white or pale lilac with many small purplish dots on the lip.
Plants are easily maintained in a well-lit greenhouse with intermediate temperatures and plenty of moisture at the roots. They are easily propagated from the keikis which form at the nodes along the old inflorescences. Rather difficult to flower unless they are brought into strong light during the warmest season.

Neobenthamia gracilis Rolfe

The only species in the genus seems to be restricted to Tanzania where it grows on cliffs and sloping rock faces in warm and humid sites. The attractive inflorescences last well when cut, but the white flowers may become badly marked in a humid greenhouse.

Neobenthamia gracilis

NEOCOGNIAUXIA Schltr.
nee-oh-kon-YOE-ee-ah
Tribe: Epidendreae
Subtribe: Laeliinae
Etymology: Gr. *neos*, new; a second genus named in honor of the Belgian botanist Alfred Cogniaux, active during the nineteenth century

This is a genus of two species from Hispaniola and Jamaica. The genus is characterized by the slender, stemlike pseudobulbs with a single, linear leaf at the apex; the inflorescence produced from the apex of the pseudobulb at the junction with the leaf with a single, vividly orange-red flower at the apex of each inflorescence; and the eight hard pollinia with conspicuous caudicles.
The plants grow as epiphytes in moist cloud forests at upper elevations in the mountains of the islands. They are difficult to maintain unless kept with cool-growing orchids and provided with excellent drainage and daily watering.

Neocogniauxia hexaptera
(Cogn.) Schltr.

This species occurs on the island of Hispaniola in the West Indies. The inflorescences are one-flowered, and the flowers reach five centimeters in diameter. The segments are vivid orange-red, and the anther cap is purple. This species is difficult to maintain in cultivation.

NEOFINETIA Hu
nee-oh-fi-NET-ee-ah
Tribe: Vandeae
Subtribe: Sarcanthinae
Etymology: Gr. *neo*, new; honoring M. Achille Finet

Neofinetia is a monotypic genus native to Japan and Korea where it grows both as a lithophyte and an epiphyte. The miniature plants have tightly two-ranked leaves yielding a formal fan-shape appearance. Racemes of white flowers with long, thin nectar spurs are similar to African members of *Angraecum*. This plant can still be found under the name *Angraecum falcatum*. *Neofinetia falcata* has been hybridized with species of *Ascocentrum* to produce X *Ascofinetia*, an ideal pot-plant for hobbyists.
Neofinetia should be given intermediate temperatures, medium bright light, and even watering. Although closely related to *Ascocentrum* and *Vanda*, *Neofinetia* plants do not like to dry out fully between waterings, and a compost that retains some moisture should be used. Plants freely produce basal offshoots and rapidly form specimen plants.

Neofinetia falcata

Neomoorea irrorata

Neofinetia falcata (Thunb.) S. Y. Hu

In Japan this species is known as the "furan" plant and was considered sacred by the Samurai class. As part of Japanese classic horticulture, many clonal selections have been made, idealizing variation in leaf shape, spur length and types of variegation. The pure white flowers are unusual for their very long, arching pedicels and ovaries and their strong, sweet fragrance. Flowering is primarily during the summer. Extremely rare pink-flowered clones are known but rarely cultivated outside Japan.

NEOMOOREA Rolfe
nee-oh-MOOR-ee-ah
Tribe: Maxillarieae
Subtribe: Lycastinae
Etymology: Gr. *neos*, new; a second genus named in honor of F. W. Moore, British horticulturist during the nineteenth century

Neomoorea is a monotypic genus found in Panama and adjoining northern Colombia. The genus is characterized by the large, egg-shaped, laterally compressed pseudobulbs with two thick, heavily veined leaves at the apex; the erect inflorescence produced from the base of the pseudobulb with ten to 25 flowers; the sepals and petals orangeish toward the apex and white at the base; the three-lobed lip yellow, heavily banded and marked with red-purple; and the two hard pollinia.
These are epiphytic or terrestrial plants from moist cloud forests. They are highly prized in horticulture but grow to a large size and require two years to mature a pseudobulb;

thus only a very large plant will flower each year. A well-flowered specimen is one of the most spectacular of orchids. The species grows well under intermediate conditions with a rest after the bulbs are mature.

Neomoorea irrorata (Rolfe) Rolfe

Neomoorea irrorata occurs in eastern Panama and northern Colombia. The sepals and petals are reddish brown with white bases. The three-lobed lip has yellow lateral lobes marked with red-brown, and the midlobe is pale yellow spotted with red.

NEOTTIA L.
Tribe: Neottieae
Subtribe: Listerinae
Etymology: Gr. *neottia*, nest

The generic name derives from a distinctive creeping rhizome with thick fleshy roots in a tangled mass, a characteristic of this genus of yellowish brown saprophytes. There are nine species, most of which grow in temperate Asia with *N. nidus-avis* as the sole European representative. There are no green leaves, though some species have been shown to produce chlorophyll in small amounts; instead the stem is covered with brownish scales. Flowers are numerous, fragrant, and arranged in a spikelike raceme. Petals and sepals converge to form a loose hood. The lip is saccate at its base, two-lobed distally.

Neottia nidus-avis (L.) Rich.

The honey-brown spikes of this species are a familiar sight in the dark recesses of beech and pine woods over much of central and northern Europe, often in mountainous regions up to 2,000 meters. Perianth segments are 4–6 millimeters long and curve inward to form a hood. The lip is 8–12 millimeters and deeply divided to form two lobes. The species is an interesting and tricky subject for pot cultivation starting with a woodland compost to which plenty of leaf mold had been added, together with some limestone chips.

Neottia nidus-avis

Nephelaphyllum pulchrum

Nidema boothii

NEPHELAPHYLLUM Blume
neff-eh-la-FILL-um
Tribe: Arethuseae
Subtribe: Bletiinae
Etymology: Gr. *nephela*, cloud; *phyllon*, leaf

Rare in collections, this genus of twelve terrestrial species ranges throughout Malaysia, Indonesia, and the Philippines. Small, slender pseudobulbs bear attractively variegated, cordate leaves and racemes of non-resupinate flowers in brilliant colors. There are eight pollinia.
Mostly low-elevation plants from shady forest floors, they should receive dappled light, intermediate to warm temperatures, high humidity, and water and fertilizer throughout the year.

Nephelaphyllum pulchrum Blume

This is the most commonly cultivated species of the genus, ranging from Malaysia to Indonesia. The upper surface of leaves is yellowish green with gray markings, while the lower surface is entirely green. Pink to brown-green flowers up to three centimeters long appear from May to July.

NIDEMA Britton & Millsp.
ny-DEE-ma
Tribe: Epidendreae
Subtribe: Laeliinae
Etymology: Anagram of *Dinema*, a related genus

Nidema is a genus of two species distributed from Mexico to Peru. The genus is characterized by the unifoliate pseudobulbs; the racemose inflorescence produced from the apex of the pseudobulb; the sepals and petals free; the ligulate lip completely free from the column; the column footless; the anther apical; and the four hard, compressed pollinia with caudicles.
The plants grow as epiphytes in tree-tops in wet forest from sea level to 500 meters elevation. The species are easily cultivated under intermediate conditions in pots.

Nidema boothii (Lindley) Schltr.

This species occurs from Mexico to Panama and in the West Indies. The plant has short-stalked pseudobulbs on a creeping rhizome. The apical inflorescence is shorter than the leaves with three to seven flowers that reach 2.5 centimeters in diameter. The sepals and petals are reflexed, greenish white, and the lip is white with yellow calli at the base.

NIGRITELLA Rich.
ni-gri-TEL-la
Tribe: Orchideae
Subtribe: Orchidinae
Etymology: L. *nigritella*, black

Until recently, this genus was thought to comprise only two species and one of those, *N. rubra*, was often considered as a subspecies of the other, *N. nigra*. Statistical analysis of the lengths of flower parts has led to five species currently being recognized. The genus is mainly restricted to the subalpine zone of the European Alps

Nigritella nigra

from 1,000–2,800 meters. In Sweden some colonies occur at low elevations near the sea.
There are two oval tubers divided into fingers at their ends with numerous narrow leaves at the stem base. The inflorescence is dense.

Nigritella nigra (L.) Reichb.f.

Although growing no more than 8–25 centimeters tall, this species is easily noticed because of the deep blackish red inflorescence on top of a ridged stem. It is the best known of European mountain

Notylia barkeri

Octomeria gracilis

Octomeria grandiflora

orchids and often occurs in large numbers, provided grazing is not too heavy. The inflorescence is conical at first, becoming cylindrical as flowers open. Sepals are lanceolate and spread widely. The lip points upward since the ovary is not twisted and is entire or barely three-lobed. The flowers are strongly scented with vanilla, and the usual color is a deep red, almost black. In the Dolomite region of northern Italy, delightful color varieties occur in pure white, cream, pink, or even bicolored red and yellow, red, and white. Flowering is from June to August and in cultivation this species needs alpine house conditions with a well-drained compost such as suggested for *Orchis*.

NOTYLIA Lindley
no-TIL-ee-ah
Tribe: Cymbidieae
Subtribe: Oncidiinae
Etymology: Gr. *noton*, back; *tylon*, hump; probably in reference to the anther on top of the column.

Notylia is a genus of 54 species distributed from Mexico to Brazil and Bolivia. The genus is characterized by the pseudobulbs with a single, flat apical leaf and one or two foliaceous sheaths surrounding the base; the pendent, densely flowered inflorescence produced from the base of the pseudobulb; the ventral sepals often united nearly to the apex; the free petals; the spurless lip with a cordiform blade and an elongate claw; the slender column with a dorsal anther near the apex and the slitlike stigma at the apex; and the two hard

pollinia attached to a slender stipe connected to a small, round viscidium. The plants grow as epiphytes in wet forest from sea level to 800 meters elevation. The species are best cultivated on plaques because of the pendent inflorescences. They do well under warm to intermediate conditions with constant water throughout the year.

Notylia barkeri Lindley

This species occurs from Mexico to Panama and has also been dubiously reported from Brazil. Recent investigation reveals that this species has been a "dumping ground" for several valid species that are admittedly not very distinct in floral characters but are pollinated by separate male euglossine bees that keep the species distinct. This species has flowers that are loosely arranged and reach one centimeter in diameter. The sepals are green while the petals are white with a pair of orange bars near the midpoint. The lip is greenish white.

Notylia sagittifera (H. B. K.) Link & Klotzch

This species is known from Venezuela. Reports of its much wider distribution refer to other species. The flowers are yellow with orange bars on the petals, densely arranged and reach a diameter of 1.5 centimeters.

OCTOMERIA R. Br.
ok-toe-MER-ee-ah
Tribe: Epidendreae
Subtribe: Pleurothallidinae
Etymology: Gr. *octo*, eight; *meros*, part

Some 150 species are currently known in Central and South America and the West Indies, with the largest diversity in southern Brazil. Plants vary in size from miniatures barely five centimeters tall to large clusters over 25 centimeters tall. Flowers are produced sequentially or in fascicles from the axil of the leaves. *Octomeria* has many showy species, but few are currently in cultivation. As the name of the genus indicates, all species have eight pollinia. Grow on slabs of tree-fern or cork bark or in small clay pots filled with shredded tree-fern fiber.

Octomeria gracilis Lodd. ex Lindley

This Brazilian species produces loose fascicles of two to four small flowers only about 5 millimeters across. Sepals and petals are cream-colored, and the lip is yellow. Flowering may occur variously throughout the year under warm to intermediate conditions.

Octomeria grandiflora Lindley

This relatively large species, found in the Guianas and Brazil, produces fascicles of two to four flowers throughout the year. Sepals and petals are yellowish white to deep yellow, the lip pale to deep yellow marked with maroon on the base and the side-lobes.

Odontoglossum cirrhosum

ODONTOGLOSSUM H. B. K.
oh-dont-oh-GLOS-um
Tribe: Cymbidieae
Subtribe: Oncidiinae
Etymology: Gr. *odonto*, tooth; *glossa*, tongue; in reference to the toothlike callus on a tonguelike lip

Odontoglossum is a genus of about 175 species distributed in the mountains of South America. The genus is characterized by the presence of unifoliate or bifoliate pseudobulbs of a single internode subtended by distichous leaflike sheaths; the inflorescence produced from the axils of the sheaths; the flowers without a spur; the sepals and petals free; the lip usually large and parallel to the column at least at the base; the callus usually composed of fleshy lamellae with obvious teeth; the column without a foot and usually with lacerate wings; and the two hard pollinia attached to a stipe connected to a viscidium. We find that the characters used to distinguish this genus from *Oncidium* are untenable, as have many other botanists, including Lindley (1837). The continued use of the genus *Odontoglossum* to include many disparate concepts, some of which are probably sufficiently distinct to warrant generic recognition in their own right, does not serve to elucidate the status of the group. However, in the interest of clarity we choose to retain the genus in its customary sense, excluding the Mexican and Central American species that have been placed in *Lemboglossum, Ticoglossum*, etc.
The plants grow as terrestrials or epiphytes at elevations from 1,500 to 3,500 meters in wet cloud forests. Members of the genus *Odontoglossum* should be cultivated under

cool to cold conditions with abundant water throughout the year.

Odontoglossum cirrhosum
Lindley

This species is found in southwestern Colombia and western Ecuador at elevations of 1,600 to 2,200 meters. The plants have clustered, ovoid pseudobulbs that are bifoliate at the apex and are surrounded at the base by foliose sheaths. The inflorescence is branched and reaches 50 centimeters long with up to 50 flowers produced. The flowers reach ten centimeters in diameter. The sepals and petals are white, sometimes with small round red spots, and the apices are long-attenuate. The lip has a rounded, cup-shaped base that is yellow with a pair of long toothlike yellow calli, and the apical lobe is white and very narrow. The wings of the column are slender and hornlike.

Odontoglossum crinitum
Reichb.f.

This species is found at upper elevations in Colombia and Ecuador. The plants have clustered, ovate, pseudobulbs that are sharp on the margin and one-leaved at the apex and are surrounded at the base by foliose sheaths. The inflorescence is unbranched and reaches eight centimeters long with up to fifteen flowers produced. The flowers reach five centimeters in diameter. The sepals and petals are similar, narrow, attenuate at the apex and yellow blotched with red-brown. The three-lobed lip is white with a wine-red callus and lateral lobes. The lateral lobes are erect and surround the column at the base, and the midlobe is covered with elongate white hairs. The column wings are small, forward-projecting teeth.

Odontoglossum crispum

Odontoglossum crispum Lindley

This species occurs in Colombia from 2,200 to 3,000 meters. The plants have clustered, ovoid pseudobulbs that have sharp edges, bifoliate at the apex and surrounded at the base by foliose sheaths. The inflorescence is branched and reaches 30 centimeters long, producing up to 25 flowers. The flowers reach ten centimeters in diameter. The flowers are white often flushed with light purple, and the callus is yellow. The sepals and petals are similar with the petals broader, and the margins are undulate to lacerate. The lip is subrectangular with an elongate claw at the base which is attached to the underside of the column. The callus

Odontoglossum crinitum

has an undulate plate on each side and is terminated in a pair of elongate teeth. The column wings are narrow and serrate on the margin.

Odontoglossum cristatum Lindley

This species is found in Colombia, Ecuador, and Peru at elevations from 1,600 to 1,800 meters. The plants have clustered, ovoid pseudobulbs that have sharp edges, bifoliate at the apex and surrounded at the base by foliose sheaths. The inflorescence is unbranched and reaches 25 centimeters long with up to twelve flowers produced. The flowers reach nine centimeters in

Odontoglossum cristatum

diameter. The sepals and petals are narrow, attenuate at the apex, similar in form, and yellow spotted with red-brown. The lip is subrectangular with an acuminate apex, yellow for the basal half and red-brown for the apical half. The callus is composed of several radiating teeth with a pair of longer teeth at the apex. The column wings are bipartite and form a pair of elongate teeth.

Odontoglossum gloriosum
Reichb.f.

This species is found in Colombia at elevations of 2,000 to 3,000 meters. The plants have clustered, ovate, compressed pseudobulbs with sharp margins that are bifoliate at the apex and are surrounded at the base by foliose sheaths. The inflorescence is branched and reaches 50 centimeters long with up to 35 flowers produced. The flowers reach seven centimeters in diameter. The sepals and petals are narrow, attenuate at the apex, similar in form, and pale yellow with small red-brown spots. The lip is narrowly ovate with an acuminate apex, pale yellow with a white crest and spotted with red-brown below the crest. The crest consists of a pair of parallel lamellae that are slightly divergent and form teeth at the apex. The column wings are threadlike and bent backward.

Odontoglossum harryanum
Reichb.f.

This species occurs from Colombia to

Odontoglossum harryanum

Odontoglossum lehmannii

Ecuador at elevations of 1,800 to 2,300 meters. Another species that is very similar, differing only in minor details, is the Peruvian O. wyattianum Wilson. The plants have clustered, compressed, oblong-ovate pseudobulbs with sharp edges that are unifoliate or bifoliate at the apex and are surrounded at the base by foliose sheaths. The inflorescence is branched and reaches 25 centimeters long with up to nine flowers produced. The flowers reach ten centimeters in diameter. The sepals and petals are similar in size and shape with the petals held forward along the lip and column. Sepals are yellow heavily spotted with red-brown and are spreading. Petals are yellow with a large red-brown blotch toward the apex and with red stripes toward

the base. The lip is large, subrectangular in outline, with four lobes. The apical lobes are white; the basal lobes are white and heavily striped with red. The callus consists of five low, parallel lamellae that are toothed along the margin. The column wings are small and toothlike.

Odontoglossum lehmannii
Reichb.f.

This species is found in Ecuador at elevations of 2,400 to 3,000 meters. Some authors have reduced this species to a subspecies of O. cristatellum Reichb.f. The plants have clustered, ovoid, compressed pseudobulbs with sharp edges that are bifoliate at the apex and are surrounded at

Odontoglossum lindleyanum

the base by foliose sheaths. The inflorescence is often branched and reaches 30 centimeters long with up to 25 flowers produced. The flowers reach seven centimeters in diameter. The sepals and petals are narrow, acute at the apex, similar in form, and are yellow blotched with red-brown. The lip is subrectangular with a rounded apex, yellow for the basal half and red-brown for the apical half with a yellow margin. The callus consists of radiating teeth with the apical pair much larger and white. The column wings are broad and hatchet-shaped.

Odontoglossum lindenii Lindley

This species is distributed from Venezuela to Ecuador at elevations from 2,700 to 3,200 meters. The plants have clustered, ovoid pseudobulbs that are two- or three-foliate at the apex and are surrounded at the base by foliose sheaths. The inflorescence is densely branched and reaches one meter long with up to 50 flowers produced. The flowers reach four centimeters in diameter. Sepals and petals are bright yellow. Sepals are long-clawed at the base. Petals are obovate and slightly cupped. The lip is also yellow and ovate in shape. The callus consists of a pair of broad lamellae that surround the column at the base with a central keel

Odontoglossum luteo-purpureum

between them that expands into four diverging teeth. The column is wingless.

Odontoglossum lindleyanum Reichb.f.

This species is found in Colombia and

Ecuador at elevations of 1,800 to 2,400 meters. The plants have clustered, ovate, compressed pseudobulbs that are sharp on the edges, bifoliate at the apex and surrounded at the base by foliose sheaths. The inflorescence is unbranched and reaches 30 centimeters long with up to twelve flowers produced. The flowers reach six centimeters in diameter. Sepals and petals are similar, narrow, spreading, and yellow spotted with red-brown. The lip is trowel-shaped with a long slender claw that is closely confluent with the column for most of its length. The lip is white at the base with a brown blotch covering the base and with a yellow apex. The callus consists of a pair of diverging finger-like processes. The column wings are narrow and projecting to a point at the apex alongside the anther.

Odontoglossum luteo-purpureum Lindley

This species is found in Colombia and Ecuador at elevations of 2,300 to 3,000 meters. The plants have clustered, compressed, ovate pseudobulbs that are bifoliate at the apex and surrounded at the base by foliose sheaths. The inflorescence is unbranched and reaches 30 centimeters long with up to twelve flowers produced. The flowers reach ten centimeters in diameter. The sepals and petals are similar in size and shape, narrow and acute to acuminate at the apex, and white heavily blotched with red-brown. The lip is rectangular for the lower half and then flares to a bilobed apex. It is white with a bar of red-brown across the middle. The callus consists of a series of radiating, serrate teeth with the central pair much longer and extending to the middle of the lip. The column wings consist of a series of threads on each side of the stigma.

Odontoglossum naevium Lindley

This species is distributed from Venezuela to Ecuador at elevations from 1,600 to 2,000 meters. The plants have clustered, ovoid pseudobulbs that are bifoliate at the apex and are surrounded at the base by foliose sheaths. The inflorescence is unbranched and reaches 25 centimeters long with up to twelve flowers produced. The flowers reach eight centimeters in diameter. The sepals and petals are similar in size and shape, narrow and long-acuminate at the apices, and white with evenly spaced red-brown spots. The lip is white with red-brown spots on the lower half, narrowly ovate, long-acuminate at the apex. The callus consists of a pair of fleshy, toothed, parallel lamellae. The column wings are a pair of threads extending well beyond the anther.

Odontoglossum odoratum Lindley

This species is found in Venezuela and Colombia and has been reported from Bolivia at elevations from 1,600 to 2,500 meters. The plants have clustered, ovoid pseudobulbs that are bifoliate at the apex and surrounded at the base by foliose sheaths. The inflorescence is branched and

Odontoglossum pardinum

reaches 60 centimeters long with up to 40 flowers produced. The flowers reach six centimeters in diameter. The sepals and petals are similar in size and shape, narrow and long-acuminate at the apices, and yellow with brown spots and blotching. The lip is yellow with red-brown spots and has a large, pubescent spot in the middle of the blade. It is narrowly ovate with a long-acuminate apex, and the base surrounds the base of the column. The callus consists of a pair of fleshy, parallel lamellae. The column wings are a pair of threads extending well beyond the anther.

Odontoglossum pardinum Lindley

This species is found from Colombia to Peru at elevations from 2,500 to 3,500 meters, usually growing terrestrially. The plants have clustered, ovoid pseudobulbs that are one- or two-leaved at the apex and surrounded at the base by foliose sheaths. The inflorescence is branched and reaches 70 centimeters long with up to 50 flowers produced. The flowers reach seven centimeters in diameter. The sepals and petals are similar in size and shape, narrow and long-acuminate at the apices, and bright yellow with small red brown spots. The lip is yellow with red-brown spots on the lower half, narrowly ovate-pandurate, and is long-acuminate at the apex. The callus consists of a fleshy, raised plate that surrounds the base of the column at its base and has teeth along the margin and two pairs of elongate teeth toward the apex. The column is wingless.

Odontoglossum praestans Reichb.f. & Warsc.

This species is found from Colombia to

Peru. The plants have clustered, ovoid pseudobulbs that are bifoliate at the apex and are surrounded at the base by foliose sheaths. The inflorescence is branched and reaches 40 centimeters long with up to 50 flowers produced. The flowers reach six centimeters in diameter. Sepals and petals are similar in size and shape, narrow and long-acuminate at the apices, and bright yellow with numerous small, red-brown spots. The lip is yellow with red-brown spots on the lower half, narrowly ovate, and long-acuminate at the apex. The callus has three spreading, parallel, serrate lamellae with the central lamellae much shorter than the laterals. The column has long, slender threadlike wings.

Odontoglossum purum Reichb.f.

This species is found from Colombia to Peru at elevations from 1,800 to 2,000 meters. Some authors reduce this species to synonymy with *O. wallisii* Reichb.f. The plants have clustered, somewhat flattened, ovoid pseudobulbs that are bifoliate at the apex and surrounded at the base by foliose sheaths. The inflorescence is branched and reaches 25 centimeters long with up to twelve flowers produced. The flowers reach six centimeters in diameter. Sepals and petals are similar in size and shape, narrowly ovate, somewhat acuminate at the apices, and yellow with evenly spaced red-brown spots. The lip is yellow with red-brown spots on the lower half, narrowly pandurate, acute at the apex, the base shrouding the underside of the base of the column. The callus consists of a pair of toothed, parallel lamellae with a lateral threadlike projection from the midpoint. The column wings are a pair of teeth extending well beyond the anther.

Odontoglossum triumphans

Odontoglossum sanderianum
Reichb.f.

This species occurs in Venezuela and Colombia at elevations from 1,700 to 2,400 meters. Some authors reduce this species to synonymy with *O. constrictum* Lindley. The plants have clustered, ovoid pseudobulbs that are bifoliate at the apex and are surrounded at the base by foliose sheaths. The inflorescence is branched and reaches 25 centimeters long with up to 25 flowers produced. The flowers reach seven centimeters in diameter. The sepals and petals are similar in size and shape, narrow and acute at the apices, and yellow with red-brown spots. The petals have the spots in the form of parallel lines. The lip is white with red-brown spots on the lower half, three-lobed, with small, obovate lateral lobes and an ovate apical lobe, and the base surrounds the base of the column. The callus consists of a pair of fleshy, toothed, parallel lamellae. The column wings are a pair of threads extending well beyond the anther.

Odontoglossum sceptrum
Reichb.f. & Warsc.

This species is found in Colombia at elevations from 2,400 to 2,800 meters. The plants have clustered, flattened, ovate pseudobulbs with sharp margins that are bifoliate at the apex and are surrounded at the base by foliose sheaths. The inflorescence is unbranched and reaches 30 centimeters long with up to sixteen flowers produced. The flowers reach 7.5 centimeters in diameter. Sepals and petals are similar in size and shape, ovate, and yellow with heavy blotches of red-brown on the sepals and smaller spots on the petals which are lacerate on the margin. The lip is yellow with red-brown blotches on the lower half, broadly obovate, and lacerate on the apical margin. The callus consists of a series of radiating, lacerate teeth with the two apical teeth extended to the middle portion of the lip. The column wings are a series of threads on each side of the stigma.

Odontoglossum schillerianum
Reichb.f.

This species occurs in Venezuela and Colombia at elevations from 2,000 to 2,700 meters. The plants have clustered, ovoid pseudobulbs that are bifoliate at the apex and are surrounded at the base by foliose sheaths. The inflorescence is sparsely branched and reaches 25 centimeters long with up to fifteen flowers produced. The flowers reach five centimeters in diameter. Sepals and petals are similar in size and shape, ovate, acute at the apices, and yellow, heavily marked with evenly spaced red-brown spots. The lip is yellow with a large papillose red-brown blotch on the blade, narrowly ovate, acute-acuminate at the apex, and the base surrounds the base of the column. The callus consists of a pair of fleshy, finger-like, parallel lamellae. The column wings are a pair of threadlike, serrate projections extending well beyond the anther.

Odontoglossum triumphans
Reichb.f. & Warsc.

This species is found in Colombia at elevations from 2,300 to 2,700 meters. Some authors reduce this species to synonymy with *O. spectatissimum* Lindley. The plants have clustered, flattened, ovate pseudobulbs with sharp edges that are bifoliate at the apex and are surrounded at the base by foliose sheaths. The inflorescence is unbranched and reaches 25 centimeters long with up to fifteen flowers produced. The flowers reach seven centimeters in diameter. Sepals and petals are similar in size and shape, ovate and acute at the apices, and yellow with large blotches of red-brown. The lip is white with red-brown blotches on the lower half, elliptic, and acute at the apex. The callus consists of a pair of fleshy, toothed, diverging lamellae with a pair of diverging teeth at the midpoint. The column wings are broad and truncate across the front.

Odontoglossum wallisii

Odontoglossum wallisii Reichb.f.

This species is found in Venezuela and Colombia and has been reported from Bolivia at elevations from 2,000 to 2,500 meters. The plants have clustered, flattened, ovate pseudobulbs with sharp edges that are bifoliate at the apex and arc surrounded at the base by foliose sheaths. The inflorescence is unbranched and reaches fifteen centimeters long with up to six flowers produced. The flowers reach 4.5 centimeters in diameter. Sepals and petals are similar in size and shape, narrowly ovate and acute at the apices, and yellow with the sepals heavily blotched with red-brown and the petals less so with parallel red-brown lines toward the base. The lip is white with red spots on the lower half, narrowly pandurate-ovate, serrate on the margin, acute at the apex, and the long-clawed base surrounds the underside of the base of the column. The callus consists of a pair of fleshy, toothed, parallel lamellae that are elevated at the apex and with an elongate threadlike, spreading, projection on each side of the callus. The column wings are a pair of narrow, toothlike projections extending well beyond the anther.

OECEOCLADES Lindley
ee-see-o-CLA-deez
Tribe: Cymbidieae
Subtribe: Cyrtopodiinae
Etymology: Gr. *oikeios*, private; *klados*, branch

The genus has 31 species in tropical South America, the West Indies, Florida, tropical Africa, Madagascar, the Mascarene Isles, and the Seychelles.
Plants are terrestrial, rarely epiphytic. Leaves are rather leathery. The inflorescence can be racemose or paniculate with rather small, thin-textured flowers. Sepals and petals are free; the lip is three-lobed and spurred at its base.
Oeceoclades plants can be grown in a compost of equal parts by volume of medium peat, loam, and sharp sand and require a minimum winter temperature of 15°–18°C. For cultivation purposes, species fall into two groups: forest species from tropical Africa and South America, and

Oeceoclades maculata

species from Madagascar. Plants in the first group need quite heavy shade and require only a short rest; water carefully as only a few thick roots are produced. Plants in the second group are much hardier and require far less shade; again water carefully during active growth but keep nearly dry when growth is complete.

Oeceoclades maculata (Lindley) Lindley

Oeceoclades maculata is the best-known species in the genus with a wide distribution: Florida, the West Indies, tropical South America, and throughout tropical Africa from Senegal to Angola, Zimbabwe, and Tanzania. The distribution has led to a proliferation of names including *Angraecum maculatum, Eulophia maculata* and *Eulophidium ledienii.* Stems are dark greenish brown. Leaves are up to 22 centimeters long, coriaceous, green mottled with darker green. The lax inflorescence is up to 40 centimeters long, erect, and carries twelve or more flowers. Sepals and petals are pinkish green. The lip is white, lined dark red on the side-lobes. Plants flower in the fall though flowers can be short-lived if they self-pollinate and wither.

Oerstedella wallisii

Oerstedella centradenia

OERSTEDELLA Reichb.f.
er-ste-DEL-lah
Tribe: Epidendreae
Subtribe: Laeliinae
Etymology: Honoring Herr Anders Sandøe
Ørsted, the Danish collector of the type

Long considered a synonym of
Epidendrum, the flowers of this genus show
constant differences in the rostellum, and
the plants themselves can be easily
recognized by the purple-warted stems.
Though found from Mexico to Bolivia, their
main center for speciation is found in Costa
Rica and western Panama. Several species
are highly desirable because of their showy
flowers, but most species do not thrive
outside their natural environment.

Oerstedella centradenia
(Reichb.f.) Reichb.f.

This warm-growing species grows easily in a
warm greenhouse when placed on a twig
with the roots well ventilated. It can easily
grow into a thick bush with its bunches of
lilac flowers. Native to Costa Rica and
Panama, it grows at lower elevations on the
Pacific slopes of the cordilleras, where wet
and dry seasons succeed each other.

Oerstedella wallisii (Reichb.f.)
Hágsater

This species is found growing in citrus trees
in Costa Rica and then, both epiphytic and
terrestrial, at lower elevations in Colombia.
The plants from Costa Rica show spotted
lips; those from Colombia have striped
lips, which have given rise to another epithet —
O. pseudowallisii — though there is no clear
limit between these forms. The rich yellow
color and heavy substance of the flowers
make this species especially attractive.

ONCIDIUM Sw.
on-SID-ee-um
Tribe: Cymbidieae
Subtribe: Oncidiinae
Etymology: Gr. *onkos,* tumor, swelling; in
reference to the warty callus of the lip

Oncidium is a large genus distributed
throughout most of tropical America with
more than 600 species (as treated here).
The genus is characterized by the presence
of unifoliate or bifoliate pseudobulbs of a
single internode usually subtended by
distichous leaflike sheaths; the
inflorescence produced from the axils of
the sheaths; the flowers without a spur; the
basal part of the lip spreading from the
column; sometimes united for a short
distance at the base; the lip often with a
callus at the disc; the column without a
foot, often with elaborate wings on each
side of the stigma; and the two hard pollinia
attached to a stipe connected to a viscidium.
Most of the species are epiphytic but some
occur facultatively on embankments and
others are strictly terrestrial. Species occur
from sea level to 4,000 meters elevation.
Cultivation of the majority of the species of
Oncidium can be accomplished in the
intermediate house in pots of well-drained
media and with abundant water throughout
the year. Some species come from higher
elevations and require cooler conditions.
Those species are indicated in the text.

Oncidium altissimum (Jacq.) Sw.

This species is found in the West Indies,
Venezuela, and Colombia. The plants have
clustered pseudobulbs that are
conspicuous, compressed, with acute edges,
one- to two-leaved at the apex, and with
sheathing leaves around the base. The
inflorescence reaches one meter long, with
short branches from the nodes above the
middle, each branch with two to five
flowers. The flowers are about 2.5
centimeters in diameter. Sepals and petals
are similar in size and shape, yellow with
red-brown bars and blotches. The lip is
yellow with a brown blotch across the
sinus; it is three-lobed, with the lateral
lobes small and turned backward, and the
midlobe is broadly oblong. The crest has
ten teeth arranged in two parallel rows of
five with the central tooth largest. The
column wings are narrow and rounded.

Oncidium ampliatum Lindley

This species occurs from Guatemala to
Panama, in the West Indies, and in
Venezuela and Colombia. It has also been
dubiously reported from Ecuador and Peru.
The plants have large, ovoid to round,
flattened, clustered pseudobulbs that are

Oncidium ampliatum

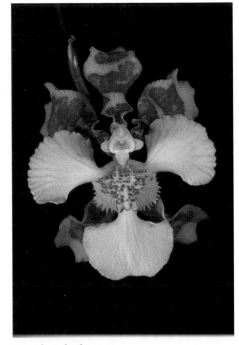

Oncidium barbatum

Oncidium baueri

Oncidium bicallosum

Oncidium bicallosum Lindley

This species occurs from Mexico to Honduras. The plants have very tiny, clustered pseudobulbs, with a large, fleshy, leathery, apical leaf and no leaflike sheaths around the base. The inflorescence is erect and unbranched. The flowers reach five centimeters in diameter. Sepals and petals are similar in size and shape, and are yellow sometimes flushed with brownish green. The lip is three-lobed with small basal lobes and with the midlobe much larger and kidney-shaped with a notch at the apex. The callus is two-parted with the rear part kidney-shaped and the anterior part with three rounded tubercles.

Oncidium bicolor Lindley

This species is found in Venezuela and Colombia and has been dubiously reported from Ecuador. The plants have conspicuous, clustered, oblong pseudobulbs with two leaves at the apex and no lateral sheathing leaves. The inflorescence is erect, to one meter tall, and branched toward the apex. The flowers reach three centimeters in diameter. The sepals and petals are small, yellow barred with red-brown, the petals larger. The large yellow lip is blotched with red-brown around the crest and is three-lobed with the lateral lobes small and angular and the midlobe very large, kidney-shaped, and with a conspicuous claw at the base. The crest has two pairs of diverging toothlike plates at the base and an elongate, keel-like lamella that is hollow at the apex.

Oncidium bifolium Sims

This species occurs in Bolivia, Brazil, and Paraguay. The plants have conspicuous, clustered, ovoid pseudobulbs with two leaves at the apex and no lateral sheathing leaves. The inflorescence is erect, to 40 centimeters tall, and unbranched. The flowers reach three centimeters in diameter. Sepals and petals are small, yellow barred with red-brown, the petals larger. The yellow lip is three-lobed with the lateral lobes small and triangular and the midlobe very large, kidney-shaped, and with a conspicuous claw at the base. The callus is on the claw of the lip and is tripartite with the midlobe larger and noselike. The column wings are subquadrate with dentate margins.

Oncidium bracteatum Reichb.f. & Warsc.

This species is found in Costa Rica and Panama. The plants have clustered pseudobulbs that are conspicuous, compressed, with acute edges, one- or two-leaved at the apex, and with sheathing leaves around the base.
The arching inflorescence is two meters long, with short branches from the nodes above the middle, each branch with two to

usually flattened against the tree-trunk and are wrinkled with a rib down the midline, and are spotted with red-brown, with two or three leathery leaves at the apex. The erect inflorescence reaches one meter long and is usually branched. The flowers reach 2.5 centimeters in diameter and are bright yellow with a white lip callus. Sepals and petals are small with the petals much broader. The lip is three-lobed with small lateral lobes and a large, bilobed, kidney-shaped apical lobe with a deep notch at the apex. The callus is three-toothed at the apex.

Oncidium barbatum Lindley

This species is found in Bolivia and Brazil. The plants have conspicuous, clustered pseudobulbs with a single leaf at the apex. The inflorescence is slender, erect to arching, about 40 centimeters long, and often branched near the apex. The flowers reach three centimeters in diameter. Sepals and petals are yellow, blotched with brown, and are clawed at the base with the petals broader than the sepals. The lip is three-lobed with the lateral lobes larger than the apical lobe and the area between the lateral

lobes and the apical lobe deeply lacerate. The crest is five-toothed with a fringed margin with the two posterior teeth spreading. The column wings are small and nearly square.

Oncidium baueri Lindley

This species is found from Costa Rica to Bolivia, including Venezuela, Brazil, and Guyana. The plants have clustered pseudobulbs that are conspicuous, compressed, with acute edges, one- or two-leaved at the apex, and with sheathing leaves around the base. The inflorescence reaches two meters long, with short branches from the nodes above the middle, each branch with two to five flowers. Flowers are about 2.5 centimeters in diameter. Sepals and petals are similar in size and shape, yellow with red-brown bars and blotches. The lip is yellow with a brown blotch across the claw; it is three-lobed, with the lateral lobes small, and the midlobe clawed, and broadly oblong. The crest has three series of teeth arranged in two lateral groups of four each and one tooth in front; the midtooth is larger. The column wings are short and truncate.

Oncidium carthagenense

Oncidium cheirophorum

five flowers, and the bracts of the inflorescence large and scarious. The flowers are about three centimeters in diameter. The sepals and petals are similar in size and shape and are yellow with red-brown bars and blotches. The lip is yellow with a brown blotch across the elongate claw. It is three-lobed, with the lateral lobes small, and the midlobe broadly oblong. The callus is erect and is more or less triangular with several teeth. The column wings are narrow.

Oncidium carthagenense (Jacq.) Sw.

This species is distributed from Mexico to Panama, the West Indies, and in Venezuela and Colombia. The plants have very tiny, clustered pseudobulbs, with a large, fleshy, leathery, apical leaf and no leaflike sheaths around the base. The inflorescence is erect, to 1.5 meters long, and with short branches from the nodes above the middle. Flowers reach two centimeters in diameter. Sepals and petals are similar in size and shape, and are white blotched with red-purple. The lip is three-lobed with small basal lobes; the midlobe is much larger and kidney-shaped

with a notch at the apex. The callus is composed of three warty lamellae with the middle lamella shorter. The column wings are large and triangular.

Oncidium cavendishianum Batem.

This species occurs from Mexico to Honduras. The plants have very tiny, clustered pseudobulbs, with a large, fleshy, leathery, apical leaf, and no leaflike sheaths around the base. The inflorescence is about a meter tall, erect, and with short branches at the nodes above the middle. The flowers reach four centimeters in diameter. Sepals and petals are similar in size and shape and are yellow blotched with red-brown. The lip is yellow, three-lobed with small basal lobes, and the midlobe much larger and kidney-shaped with a notch at the apex. The callus has four tubercles in the form of a cross. The wings of the column are finger-like and deflexed.

Oncidium cebolleta (Jacq.) Sw.

This species is distributed at lower elevations from Mexico to Colombia, the

West Indies and the Guianas, and dubiously in Brazil and Argentina. The plants have round, clustered pseudobulbs that are tiny and have a single, terete, grooved, and very fleshy leaf at the apex. The inflorescence is usually branched, and the flowers are densely produced. The flowers reach three centimeters in diameter. Sepals and petals are small, similar in size and shape, and are yellow spotted with red-brown. The lip is large for the flower, three-lobed with small lateral lobes, and with a broad, kidney-shaped apical lobe with a notch at the apex. The callus consists of an elevated, rounded plate with two large teeth behind it and with small teeth on each side.

Oncidium cheirophorum Reichb.f.

This species occurs from El Salvador to Panama and Colombia. The plants have ovoid, compressed, clustered pseudobulbs with a solitary leaf at the apex. The inflorescences are slender, arched, and densely branched, reaching 30 centimeters long. The yellow flowers are very numerous and reach two centimeters in diameter. The dorsal sepal is concave and the lateral sepals reflexed. Petals are spreading. The lip is three-lobed with the lateral lobes broad and similar to the apical lobe. The callus consists of a fleshy keel with two rectangular wings forming a hood on the upper margin.

Oncidium cimiciferum Reichb.f. ex Lindley

This species is found from Venezuela to Bolivia along the flanks of the Andes. The plants have clustered pseudobulbs that are conspicuous, compressed, with rounded

Oncidium bifolium

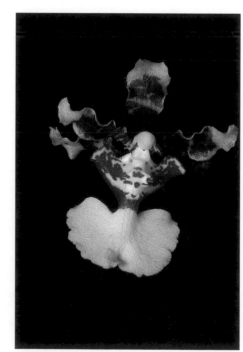

Oncidium bracteatum

Oncidium cavendishianum

edges, one- or two-leaved at the apex, and with sheathing leaves around the base. The arching inflorescence is two meters long, with short branches from the nodes above the middle, each branch with five to nine flowers. The flowers reach 1.5 centimeters in diameter. The yellow-brown sepals and petals are similar in size and shape and are clawed at the base. The lip is yellow spotted with red-brown and is trowel-shaped. The crest is yellow, large, fleshy, and consists of a central, broad lamella with lumps extending from the sides. The column is wingless. The plants should be grown under cool conditions.

Oncidium concolor Hook.

This species occurs in Brazil and Argentina. It has plants with clustered, oblong, ribbed pseudobulbs with two or three leaves at the apex. The inflorescences are about 20 centimeters long, hang with the weight of the flowers, and have six to twelve flowers. The flowers reach five centimeters in diameter and are bright yellow. The dorsal sepal and petals are ovate. The lateral sepals are longer and united for about half their length. The lip is obovate, long-clawed and roundish at the two apical lobes. The crest has two lamellae. The column wings are tooth-like and ascending.

Oncidium crispum Lodd.

This species is found in Brazil. The plants have oblong, clustered, flattened, dark brown pseudobulbs that are ribbed, with two or three leaves at the apex. The inflorescence is erect or hanging with the weight of the flowers and reaches 70 centimeters long with 40 to 80 flowers produced. The flowers reach eight centimeters in diameter. Sepals and petals

Oncidium crispum

are brown, crisped on the yellow margins, and spotted with yellow. The petals are very large. The lip is three-lobed with the lateral lobes small and the midlobe large with a broad claw and a bright yellow spot in front of the crest. The crest has three lamellae with the middle one the largest. The column wings are large and toothed. The plants should be grown under cool conditions.

Oncidium crista-galli Reichb.f.

This species occurs from Mexico to Colombia and has been dubiously reported from Ecuador and Peru. The plants have ovoid, clustered pseudobulbs with the apical leaf reduced, and with leafy sheaths

Oncidium concolor

Oncidium crista-galli

surrounding the base of the pseudobulb. The inflorescence is short with a single flower at the apex. Flowers reach three centimeters in diameter. The sepals are small, similar, and greenish yellow. The petals are larger and yellow with red-brown bars. The yellow lip is three-lobed and marked with red brown on the callus. The lateral lobes are small, and the large midlobe is divided into four lobules. The callus consists of three superimposed plates. The column is broadly winged.

Oncidium cucullatum Lindley

This species is known from the high Andes of Colombia and Ecuador. The plants have

Oncidium cebolleta

Oncidium cimiciferum

Oncidium cucullatum

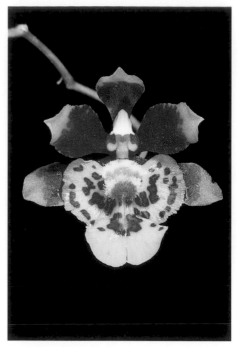

Oncidium divaricatum

clustered, somewhat compressed, ovoid pseudobulbs with one or two apical leaves and with sheathing leaves at the base. The inflorescence is stiffly erect, branched, and zigzagged between the flowers. The flowers reach four centimeters in diameter. Sepals and petals are similar in size and shape with the petals a little larger. They are usually reddish to chocolate-brown inside. The lip is large, rose-red, and spotted at the base with dark red. The crest is bright yellow with two pairs of tubercles and a fifth smaller one between the posterior pair. The column is thick and hooded over the anther. The plants should be grown under cool conditions.

Oncidium divaricatum Lindley

This species is found in Brazil. The plants have roundish, compressed, clustered pseudobulbs with a single apical leaf. The inflorescence reaches 1.5 meters long and is profusely branched. The flowers reach two centimeters in diameter. Sepals and petals are clawed and golden brown with a blotch of yellow near the apex. The lip is three-lobed with the lateral lobes larger than the midlobe, yellow spotted with red-brown, and the midlobe is yellow with a brown spot in front of the four-lobed, pubescent crest. The column wings are rounded.

Oncidium ensatum Lindley

This species is found from Mexico to Panama. The plants have clustered pseudobulbs that are conspicuous, compressed, with rounded edges, one- or two-leaved at the apex, and with sheathing, non-deciduous leaves around the base. The inflorescence is produced from the base of the pseudobulb, to two meters long, with

Oncidium ensatum

Oncidium falcipetalum

short branches from the nodes above the middle, each branch with two to five flowers, the flowers open singly in succession. The flowers are about 2.5 centimeters in diameter. The reflexed sepals and petals are similar in size and shape, and yellow-green. The lip is yellow, three-lobed, and fiddle-shaped with the lateral lobes small and the midlobe kidney-shaped. The callus is white and seven-toothed. The column is short with prominent wings.

Oncidium falcipetalum Lindley

This species occurs from Venezuela to Peru at upper elevations in the Andes. The plants have obvious, thick, clustered pseudobulbs with two leaves at the apex and the base surrounded by three or four leafy sheaths. The inflorescence is elongate and viny, reaching two meters long with five- to seven-flowered branches produced from the nodes above the middle. The flowers reach seven centimeters in diameter. Sepals and petals are dark brown with a yellow margin, and are long-clawed with the sepals broader than the petals. The lip is smaller, tongue-shaped with narrow lateral lobes, and is

purplish brown. The callus is composed of five lacerate lamellae. The column wings consist of a pair of projections that are split at the apex. The plants should be grown under cool conditions.

Oncidium fimbriatum Lindley

This species is found in Brazil and Paraguay. The plants have pseudobulbs that are oblong, thick and bifoliate at the apex. The inflorescence reaches 80 centimeters in length and is branched toward the apex. The flowers are densely arranged and reach 1.5 centimeters in diameter. The yellow sepals and petals are similar in size and shape, but the lateral sepals are united near the base and the petals are broader. The petals have transverse red bars, and the lip is yellow. The lip is three-lobed with narrow, oblong lateral lobes with the lower margin fimbriate and a larger, long-clawed, kidney-shaped midlobe. The callus is composed of an apical portion located on the claw of the lip that is many-tuberculate and a basal portion between the lateral lobes that is pubescent. The column wings are linear.

Oncidium flexuosum

Oncidium fimbriatum

Oncidium forbesii

arc brown and crisped on the yellow margins. The petals are very large. The lip is three-lobed with the lateral lobes yellow and the large midlobe brown with a yellow margin. The crest is five-lobed and warty. The column wings are roundish and purple spotted with red. The plants should be grown under cool conditions.

Oncidium fuscatum Reichb.f.

This species is found from Panama to Peru along the flanks of the Andes at lower elevations and has been known as *Miltonia warscezwiczii* Reichb.f. The plants have clustered pseudobulbs that are conspicuous, compressed, with sharp edges, one-leaved at the apex, and with sheathing leaves around the base. The inflorescence has large sheaths, reaches 50 centimeters long, and is usually branched. The flowers are about five centimeters in diameter and open simultaneously. Sepals and petals are similar in size and shape and brownish red with a yellow or white margin. The oblong lip is usually purplish with a yellow or white margin and has a shiny red-brown disc with two small teeth. The column wings are rounded and red-purple.

Oncidium gardneri Lindley

This species occurs in Brazil. The plants have ovoid, clustered, flattened, grooved pseudobulbs, with two leaves that are purple on the underside, at the apex. The inflorescence is erect, reaches one meter long, and is branched. The flowers reach five centimeters in diameter. Sepals and petals are brown, with the petals much larger and marked with yellow along the margin. The lip is fan-shaped; the lateral lobes are yellow with red-brown basal markings, and the midlobe is yellow with red-brown spots near the margin. The callus is triangular with the apex covered with red-brown warts on each side of the tip. The column wings are narrow and roundish. The plants should be grown under cool conditions.

Oncidium globuliferum H. B. K.

This species is found from Costa Rica to Peru. The plants have a very elongate, viny, slender inflorescence with one or more

Oncidium fuscatum

Oncidium flexuosum Sims

This species is known from Brazil, Paraguay, and Argentina. The plants have pseudobulbs that are separated on a conspicuous rhizome, are compressed, with acute edges, one- or two-leaved at the apex, and with sheathing leaves around the base. The inflorescence is produced from the base of the pseudobulb, to one meter long, with short branches from the nodes toward the apex, each branch with 10 to fifteen flowers. The flowers are about 2.5 centimeters in diameter. Sepals and petals are similar in size and shape, and are yellow with red-brown bars and blotches toward the base of the segments. The lip is large, yellow with

red-brown around the callus, and is four-lobed with the lateral lobes small. The callus is composed of two parts, the basal half a fuzzy cushion and the apical half three- to five-toothed. The column wings are quadrate and twisted forward at the apex.

Oncidium forbesii Hook.

This species occurs in Brazil. The plants have oblong, clustered, flattened, pseudobulbs with one or two leaves at the apex. The inflorescence is erect or arching, reaches to one meter long, and branches toward the apex. The flowers reach seven centimeters in diameter. Sepals and petals roundish, clustered pseudobulbs at nodes. Each pseudobulb has a single apical leaf and is surrounded at the base by leafy sheaths. The inflorescence consists of a short, one-flowered scape about as long as the leaf. The flowers reach three centimeters in diameter. Sepals and petals are small, yellow, and barred with red. The lip is yellow, large, and has three lobes with small lateral lobes and a large kidney-shaped midlobe. The callus is triangular and seven-toothed. The column wings are large and spreading.

Oncidium haematochilum Lindley

This species occurs in Colombia and Trinidad. It is considered to be a natural hybrid between *O. luridum* and *O. lanceanum*. The plants have very tiny, clustered pseudobulbs, with a large, fleshy, leathery, apical leaf and no leaflike sheaths around the base. The inflorescence is erect and reaches 60 centimeters tall. The flowers reach five centimeters in diameter. The sepals and petals are similar in size and shape and are yellow blotched with red-brown. The lip is three-lobed with small basal lobes, and with the midlobe much larger and kidney-shaped with a notch at the apex. The midlobe of the lip is blood-red with the yellow margin spotted with red. The crest is five-parted with the middle part a raised subtriangular plate; the other parts are warty. The column wings are kidney-shaped and rose-purple.

Oncidium hastatum (Batem.) Lindley

This species is found in Mexico but has been dubiously reported from Colombia.

Oncidium globuliferum

The plants have clustered pseudobulbs that are conspicuous, compressed, with acute edges, two-leaved at the apex, and with sheathing leaves around the base. The inflorescence is produced from the base of the pseudobulb, reaches 1.2 meters long, and has short branches from the nodes above the middle, each branch with two to five flowers. The flowers are about 2.5 centimeters in diameter. Sepals and petals are similar in size and shape and are yellow with red-brown bars and blotches. The yellow-white lip is hastate and three-lobed.

The lateral lobes are narrowly oblong and the pinkish apical lobes are broadly ovate. The callus consists of two purplish lamellae.

Oncidium hastilabium (Lindley) Garay & Dunsterv.

This species occurs from Venezuela to Peru at upper elevations in the Andes. This species has been treated as an *Odontoglossum* until recent times. The plants have obvious, thick, clustered pseudobulbs with one leaf at the apex, and with the base surrounded by three to four leafy sheaths. The inflorescence is elongate and branched, reaching one meter long. The flowers reach eight centimeters in diameter. Sepals and petals are yellow-green with thin bars of purple, are similar to each other, and are narrow and long-pointed at the apex. The lip is purple at the base, three-lobed, with hastate lateral lobes and a white, cordate midlobe. The callus has a raised central lamella that is three lobed at the apex with lateral, lamellar plates on each side. The column has very narrow lateral wings. The plants should be grown under cool conditions.

Oncidium jonesianum Reichb.f.

This species is found in Bolivia, Brazil and Argentina. The plants have round, clustered pseudobulbs that are tiny and have a single, terete, and very fleshy leaf at the apex. The inflorescence is erect and usually unbranched with ten to 15 flowers produced. The flowers reach seven centimeters in diameter. The sepals and petals are yellowish white, spotted with red-brown. The lip is large for the flower, three-lobed with small lateral lobes, and with a

Oncidium gardneri

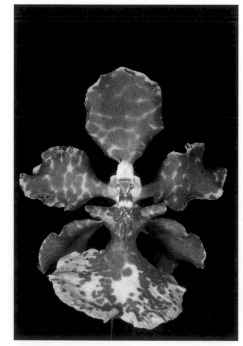

Oncidium haematochilum

Oncidium hastatum

broad, kidney shaped, white apical lobe with a notch at the apex and red spots near the callus. The callus consists of a broad central ridge with lateral processes at each end and with many tubercles. The column wings are oblong, white, and dotted with red.

Oncidium lanceanum Lindley

This species occurs in the West Indies, and from Venezuela to Peru and the Guianas at lower elevations. The plants have very tiny, clustered pseudobulbs, with a large, fleshy, leathery, purple-spotted, apical leaf and no leaflike sheaths around the base. The inflorescence is erect and often branched and reaches 40 centimeters long. The flowers reach six centimeters in diameter. The sepals and petals are yellow spotted with dark brown and the petals are somewhat broader than the sepals. The rose-purple lip is three-lobed with small basal lobes, and the midlobe is larger and kidney-shaped. The callus consists of a raised plate with a central lamella passing through it. The column wings are oblong and purple.

Oncidium luridum Lindley

This species is distributed from Florida to the West Indies, and from Mexico to Peru. The plants have very tiny, clustered pseudobulbs, with a large, fleshy, leathery, apical leaf and no leaflike sheaths around the base. The inflorescence is erect, to 2.5 meters tall, and branched at the nodes above the middle. The flowers reach 2.5 centimeters in diameter. The sepals and petals are similar in size and shape, and are yellow spotted with red-brown. The lip is three-lobed, with small basal lobes, and the midlobe is yellow spotted with red-brown, larger, and kidney-shaped with a notch at the apex. The crest is five-lobed with the middle lobe an erect lamella flanked on each side by a twisted smaller tubercle. The column wings are kidney-shaped.

Oncidium macranthum Lindley

This species occurs in southern Colombia, Ecuador, and northern Peru at high elevations in the Andes. The plants have obvious, thick, clustered pseudobulbs with two leaves at the apex, and the base is surrounded by three to four leafy sheaths.

The inflorescence is elongate and viny, reaching two meters long with three- to five-flowered branches produced from the nodes above the middle. The flowers reach ten centimeters in diameter. The sepals are yellow or brown, and the petals are yellow. Both are long-clawed with the petals broader than the sepals. The violet-purple lip is smaller and triangular with a tongue-shaped midlobe. The callus has three large teeth in front and three smaller, white teeth at the base. The column wings are hatchet-shaped. The plants should be grown under cool conditions.

Oncidium nubigenum Lindley

This species is found in Colombia, Ecuador, and Peru at high elevations in the Andes. The plants have clustered, somewhat compressed, ovoid pseudobulbs with one or two apical leaves and with sheathing leaves at the base. The inflorescence is arched and unbranched and is not zigzagged between the flowers. The flowers reach four centimeters in diameter. The sepals and petals are similar in size and shape with the petals a little larger. They are usually pink-brown inside. The lip is large,

Oncidium hastilabium

Oncidium jonesianum

Oncidium nubigenum

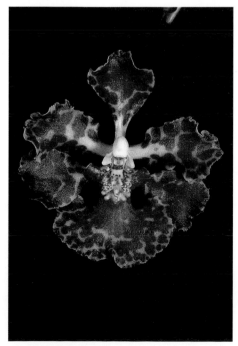

Oncidium luridum

Oncidium lanceanum

Oncidium macranthum

Oncidium obryzatum

Oncidium onustum

Oncidium ornithorhynchum

pink and spotted at the base with light red. The plants should be grown under cool conditions.

Oncidium obryzatum Reichb.f.

This species occurs from Costa Rica to Peru and Venezuela. The plants have clustered pseudobulbs that are conspicuous, compressed, with acute edges, one-leaved at the apex, speckled with red-brown, and with sheathing leaves around the base. The inflorescence is produced from the base of the pseudobulb, and reaches 1.5 meters long, with branches from the nodes above the middle, each branch with five to nine flowers. The flowers are about 2.5 centimetres in diameter. The truncate sepals and petals are similar, yellow with red-brown bars and blotches toward the base. The petals are broader than the sepals. The bright yellow lip is three-lobed; the lateral lobes are small, the claw is elongate with red-brown bars, and the midlobe is kidney-shaped with a deep notch at the apex. The crest is complex with a raised lamella down the middle that is flanked by longer projections toward the apex and with two pairs of lacerate shelves toward the base. The column wings are broad.

Oncidium onustum Lindley

This species is found in very dry regions of Ecuador and Peru, often growing in arborescent cacti. The plants have clustered, ovate pseudobulbs that are heavily marked with red-brown and shrivel during the dry season. There are two thick, leathery leaves at the apex, and the base is surrounded by leathery leaf-sheaths. The inflorescence is often branched and reaches 50 centimeters in length. The flowers reach three

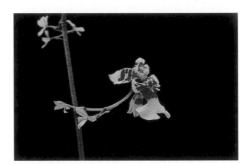

Oncidium pentadactylon

centimeters in diameter and are bright yellow. The sepals are small, and the petals are much larger. The lip is three-lobed with the lateral lobes broader than the midlobe which is kidney-shaped and notched at the apex. The callus consists of a raised, concave shelf with a pair of projecting teeth. The column wings are broad and form a hood over the anther.

Oncidium ornithorhynchum H. B. K.

This species occurs from Mexico to Colombia. The plants have clustered pseudobulbs that are conspicuous, compressed, two-leaved at the apex, and with sheathing leaves around the base. The inflorescence reaches 60 centimeters long, with elongate branches from the nodes above the middle. Each branch has five to fifteen flowers. The flowers are about two centimeters in diameter. Sepals and petals are pink with the petals broader. The lip is three-lobed with the smaller lateral lobes reflexed on the margins; the midlobe is narrower than the lateral lobes, kidney-shaped and notched at the apex. The callus

consists of five yellow, toothed lamellae in front of which are two hornlike teeth. The column wings are triangular and large. The anther is elongate and resembles a bird's head with an elongate beak. The plants should be grown under cool conditions.

Oncidium pentadactylon Lindley

This species occurs in upland western Ecuador and Peru. The plants have ovoid, clustered pseudobulbs with two leaves at the apex and the base surrounded by three or four leafy sheaths. The inflorescence is branched, exceeds the leaves, and has numerous flowers. The flowers reach two centimeters in diameter. Mixed among the fertile flowers are aborted flowers with five small, free, spreading segments. Sepals and petals are clawed with the petals broader than the sepals. The lip is three-lobed with the lateral lobes larger than the triangular midlobe. The callus is oblong and papillose. The column wings are large, hatchet-shaped, and the anther is shaped like a bird's head.

Oncidium phalaenopsis Linden & Reichb.f.

This species is found in Ecuador. The plants have clustered, somewhat compressed, ovoid pseudobulbs with one or two apical leaves and with sheathing leaves at the base. The inflorescence is arched-erect and unbranched. The flowers reach three centimeters in diameter. The white sepals and petals are marked with purple-red and are similar in size and shape with the petals a little larger. The lip is large, white, and spotted at the base with purple. The callus consists of a broad plate with five teeth at the apex. The column is wingless but the apex is hooded over the anther. The plants should be grown under cool conditions.

Oncidium planilabre Lindley

This species occurs from Nicaragua to Peru. The plants have clustered pseudobulbs that are conspicuous, compressed, with acute edges, two-leaved at the apex, and with sheathing leaves around the base. The inflorescence reaches one meter long, with short branches from the nodes above the middle, each branch with two to five flowers. The flowers are about two centimeters in diameter. Sepals and petals are similar in size and shape and are brown with a faint yellow margin. The yellow lip is marked with brown at the base. It is three-lobed with narrow lateral lobes and a broad, kidney-shaped midlobe with a notch and an apicule at the apex. The callus is complex with a large, shelflike, tuberculate base and noselike lamella at the apex flanked by a pair of tuberculate teeth. The column wings are very small and appressed, and the stigma is separated by a fleshy tubercle that projects upward from the underside of the column.

Oncidium pulchellum Hook.

This species is found in the West Indies in Jamaica and Hispaniola. The plants usually have elongate rhizomes between leaf clusters and the pseudobulbs are very reduced to absent. The three to five leaves are narrow, thick, and fleshy, overlapping at the base in one plane so as to be equitant. The inflorescence is erect, reaching 50 centimeters long and often branched. The flowers are about 2.5 centimeters in diameter. The sepals and petals are similar in size and shape and are usually dark pink.

Oncidium planilabre

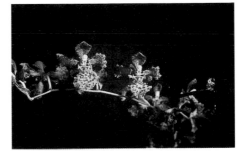

Oncidium sarcodes

The white to pink lip is much larger, nearly quadrate and four-lobed with the lobes rounded and nearly equal in size. The callus is three-lobed with a dark yellow-brown spot in front of it on the lip. The column wings are large and usually pink.

Oncidium pulvinatum Lindley

This species occurs in Brazil. The plants of this species have roundish, compressed, clustered pseudobulbs with a single apical leaf. The branched inflorescence reaches 1.5 meters long. The flowers reach 2.5 centimeters in diameter. The green-yellow sepals and petals with red bases are similar in size and shape with the petals broader. The lip is bright yellow with red dots around the margin. It is four-lobed with a cordate base, orbicular lateral lobes and a bilobed midlobe that is kidney-shaped with a notch at the apex. The callus is a large, pubescent disc. The column wings are small.

Oncidium sarcodes Lindley

This species is found in Brazil. The plants have clustered, subcylindrical pseudobulbs

with two or three leaves at the apex and small leaflike sheaths at the base. The inflorescence is multiflowered, erect to arched, and branched above the middle. The flowers reach three centimeters in diameter. The brown dorsal sepal has a yellow margin and is round and cupped with the lateral sepals narrow and hidden behind the lip. The petals are brown at the base with a yellow apex and are much larger than the sepals. The clear yellow lip has a few brown spots at the midportion and is four-lobed with the quadrate lateral lobes small and the pair of apical lobes subquadrate. The callus is short with a pubescent, bifid tip. The column has truncate wings.

Oncidium sphacelatum Lindley

This species occurs from Mexico to Costa Rica and Venezuela. The plants have clustered pseudobulbs that are conspicuous, compressed, with acute edges, one- or two-leaved at the apex, and with sheathing leaves around the base. The inflorescence reaches two meters long, with short branches from the nodes above the

Oncidium phalaenopsis

Oncidium pulchellum

Oncidium pulvinatum

middle, each branch with two to five flowers. The flowers are about 2.5 centimeters in diameter. The sepals and petals are similar in size and shape and are yellow with red-brown bars and blotches. The yellow lip has a brown blotch across the isthmus. It is three-lobed, with small, round lateral lobes and a kidney-shaped apical lobe. The callus is depressed and pubescent with a three-dentate apex and with the midtooth elongate. The column wings are narrow and acute at the apex.

Oncidium spilopterum Lindley

This species is found in Brazil and Paraguay. It is also known as *O. batemanianum* Parmentier ex Knowles and Westcott. The plants have ovate, compressed, bifoliate pseudobulbs with sharp edges and leaflike sheaths surrounding the base. The inflorescences reach one meter long and are branched above the midpoint. The flowers reach two centimeters in diameter. The small, brownish purple sepals and petals are similar in size and shape with the petals broader. The lip is three-lobed with a brownish purple base and yellow lobes; the lateral lobes are small, earlike, and obovate, and the apical lobe consists of two obovate lobules. The callus is prominent and consists of five short plates at the base and three irregularly lobed, diverging plates at the apex with several other processes surrounding the apical lobes. The column wings are suborbicular.

Oncidium splendidum A. Richard ex Ducharte

This species occurs from Guatemala to Nicaragua. The plants have quadrate, flattened pseudobulbs with a large, fleshy, oblong leaf at the apex. The inflorescence is

erect to one meter tall, branched, and produces 20 to 30 flowers. The flowers can be to six centimeters tall. The yellow sepals and petals are barred with red-brown and are similar in size and shape with recurved apices. The lip is three-lobed with small, round lateral lobes and a large, reniform, bright yellow midlobe with a red spot on each lateral lobe. The callus is white with long lamellae. The column has large suborbicular wings.

Oncidium stacyi Garay

This species is found in Bolivia. The plants have round, clustered pseudobulbs that are tiny and have a single, terete, and very fleshy leaf at the apex. The inflorescence is usually branched, and the flowers are densely produced. The flowers reach three centimeters in diameter. The sepals and petals are small, similar in size and shape, and are yellow spotted with red-brown. The lip is large for the flower, three-lobed with small lateral lobes, and with a broad, kidney-shaped apical lobe with a notch at the apex.

Oncidium stenotis Reichb.f.

This species occurs from Nicaragua to Ecuador. The plants have clustered pseudobulbs that are conspicuous, compressed, with acute edges, one- or two-leaved at the apex, and with sheathing leaves around the base. The inflorescence reaches two meters long, with short branches from the nodes above the middle, each branch with two to five flowers. The flowers are about 2.5 centimeters in diameter. The sepals and petals are similar in size and shape and are yellow with red-brown bars and blotches. The yellow lip is three-lobed with brown spots around the

Oncidium splendidum

callus. The lateral lobes are small and rounded. The apical lobe is narrower than the lateral lobes and is bilobed at the apex. The callus consists of several swollen lobes with the apical lobe projecting. The column wings are very small and slender.

Oncidium stipitatum Lindley

This species is found from Honduras to Colombia. The plants have round, clustered pseudobulbs that are tiny and have a single, terete, and very fleshy leaf at the apex. The inflorescence is usually branched, and the flowers are densely produced. The flowers reach three centimeters in diameter. The sepals and petals are small, similar in size and shape, and are yellow spotted with red-brown. The yellow lip is spotted at the base and is large for the flower. It is three-lobed, with small falcate lateral lobes and a broad, kidney-shaped apical lobe with a notch at the apex. The callus is composed of three fleshy lobes. The column wings are rotund.

Oncidium stramineum Batem. ex Lindley

This species occurs in Mexico and has been

Oncidium sphacelatum

Oncidium spilopterum

Oncidium stacyi

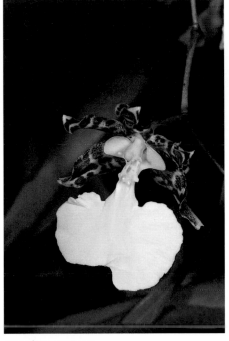

Oncidium tigrinum

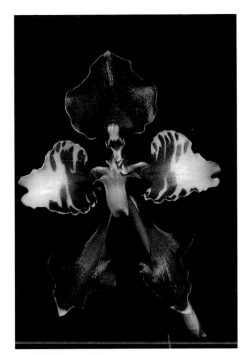

Oncidium superbiens

Oncidium stenotis

dubiously reported from Brazil. The plants have very tiny, clustered pseudobulbs, with a large, fleshy, leathery, apical leaf and no leaflike sheaths around the base. The inflorescence is erect and branched, reaching 30 centimeters tall. The flowers reach 2.5 centimeters in diameter. The sepals and petals are similar in size and shape, and are yellow sometimes flushed with brownish green. The greenish white lip is flecked with red and is three-lobed with small basal lobes, and the midlobe is much larger and kidney-shaped with a notch at the apex. The column wings are narrow, linear, and deflexed.

Oncidium superbiens Reichb.f.

This species is found in Colombia and has been erroneously reported from Ecuador, Peru, and Bolivia. The plants have obvious, thick, clustered pseudobulbs with two leaves at the apex and the base surrounded by three or four leafy sheaths. The inflorescence is elongate and viny, reaching two meters long with three- to five-flowered branches produced from the nodes above the middle. The flowers reach seven

Oncidium stipitatum

centimeters in diameter. The chocolate-brown sepals are tipped with yellow and are long-clawed. The yellow petals are smaller and barred with chocolate brown. The lip is dark purple and is trowel-shaped with tiny lateral lobes. The callus is yellow. The column wings are narrow. The plants should be grown under cool conditions.

Oncidium teres Ames & C. Schweinf.

This species occurs from Honduras to Panama. The plants have round, clustered pseudobulbs that are tiny and have a single, terete, and very fleshy leaf at the apex. The inflorescence is usually branched, and the flowers are densely produced. The flowers

reach three centimeters in diameter. The sepals and petals are small, similar in size and shape, and yellow spotted with red-brown. The lip is large for the flower, three-lobed with small lateral lobes and a broad, kidney-shaped apical lobe with a notch at the apex.

Oncidium tigrinum La Llave & Lex.

This species is known only from Mexico. The plants of this species have clustered pseudobulbs that are conspicuous, compressed, with acute edges, one- to two-leaved at the apex, and with sheathing leaves around the base. The unbranched inflorescence reaches 40 centimeters long.

Oncidium stramineum

Oncidium triquetrum

The flowers are about six centimeters in diameter. The sepals and petals are similar in size and shape and are yellow with red-brown bars and blotches. The yellow lip is three-lobed; the basal lobes are round, and the apical lobe is broad and kidney-shaped with a notch at the apex and is separated from the lateral lobes by a long claw. The callus consists of low lamellae. The column wings are roundish.

Oncidium triquetrum (Sw.) R. Br.

This species is found in the West Indies on the island of Jamaica. The plants have closely set leaf clusters. The three to five leaves are narrow, thick, and fleshy, and overlapping at the base in one plane so as to be equitant. The inflorescence is erect, produces ten to fifteen flowers, and reaches ten centimeters long. The flowers reach 2.5 centimeters in diameter. The sepals are narrow, and the lateral sepals are united. The pink petals are broadly ovate with a white margin. The pink lip has a white margin and is marked with red at the base. It is sessile and trowel-shaped. The crest is tridentate. The column wings are oblong.

Oncidium urophyllum Lodd.

This species occurs in the West Indies and Brazil. The plants lack pseudobulbs and have leaf clusters spaced on a short rhizome. The three to five leaves are narrow, thick, and fleshy, overlapping at the base, and arranged in one plane so as to be equitant. The inflorescence is erect and branched, and reaches 50 centimeters long. The flowers reach two centimeters in diameter. The yellow sepals and petals are similar in size and shape with the petals broader. The yellow lip is marked around

Oncidium varicosum

the crest with purple, is three-lobed with small, linear, reflexed lateral lobes, and has a reniform midlobe with a notch at the apex. The callus is in two parts with the rear part three-dentate and the middle tooth longest. The column wings are hatchet-shaped.

Oncidium varicosum Lindley ex Paxt.

This species is found in Bolivia, Brazil, and Paraguay. The plants have clustered pseudobulbs that are conspicuous, compressed, with acute edges, one- to two-leaved at the apex, and with sheathing leaves around the base. The inflorescence is produced from the base of the pseudobulb, reaches 80 centimeters long, has short branches from the nodes above the middle, and each branch has two to five flowers. The flowers are about five centimeters in diameter. Sepals and petals are similar in size and shape and are yellow with red-brown bars and blotches. The bright yellow lip is spotted and barred around the callus and is three-lobed. The lateral lobes are much smaller than the apical lobe and are

rounded. The apical lobe is four-lobulate with the apical pair of lobules much smaller than the lateral pair. The callus is tridactylate with the central finger larger and the whole crest surrounded by small projections. The column wings are roundish.

Oncidium variegatum Sw.

This species occurs in the West Indies on the islands of Cuba and Hispaniola. The plants have leaf clusters separated by a short rhizome. The three to five leaves are narrow, thick, and fleshy, and overlapping at the base in one plane so as to be equitant. The inflorescence is erect and is often branched. The flowers reach two centimeters in diameter. The sepals and petals are similar in shape and size with the petals broader. The white to pinkish lip is three-lobed with small, narrow, reflexed lateral lobes and a broadly kidney-shaped midlobe that is notched in front. The callus is three-lobed with the median lobe largest.

Oncidium vernixium Linden & Reichb.f.

This species is known from Ecuador. The plants have obvious, thick, flattened, clustered pseudobulbs that are sharp on the edges and have one leaf at the apex, with the base surrounded by three or four leafy sheaths. The inflorescence is branched and reaches 30 centimeters long. The flowers reach two centimeters in diameter. The yellow sepals and petals are marked with red-brown and are similar in size and shape. The cinnamon-brown lip is four-lobed, with the lobes yellow. The apical lobes are larger than the laterals. The callus is formed of two

Oncidium urophyllum

parallel lamellae. The column wings are lacking.

OPHRYS L.

OFF-riss
Tribe: Orchideae
Subtribe: Orchidinae
Etymology: Gr. *ophrys*, eyebrow (referring to hairy lip)

The genus is essentially circum-Mediterranean in its distribution with four species venturing north and west as far as Britain and into Scandinavia. Several species reach Iran, and a single species marks the eastern limits in Afghanistan. North Africa forms the southern boundary. *Ophrys* has received more attention than any other European genus, and employment of very fine criteria to separate populations has resulted in a confusing proliferation of "species." Currently, there are some 68 species and numerous subspecies, and the list increases annually.

Below ground there are two tubers: one being used to produce the current leaves and flowering stem, the other in the process of formation for the next year's growth. Flowers are comparatively few in number, but their dominant feature is a rather fleshy, spurless lip. This can be either three-lobed or entire, usually hairy, and often carries a shiny speculum with surrounding markings. Lip edges are curled under to give a rounded or inflated appearance. With the spreading sepals and antenna like petals, the overall effect is often insect-like, particularly so with species such as *O. vernixia* and *O. insectifera*.

In cultivation *Ophrys* had the reputation of being difficult until it was realised their "summer baking" could be replaced by a period of aestivation in alpine house conditions. A suitable compost for pot growth is given in the account for *Orchis* below. Each fall, tubers are carefully repotted and watered. Leaf-rosettes then appear which over-winter until the following spring (early species appear from January onward). Opinions differ about the use of a small quantity of the old compost with the new as a way of preventing viral and fungal diseases to which the genus is prone.

Ophrys apifera Hudson

Probably the best known of all *Ophrys* and the favorite early summer flower of many European flower lovers. Plants range from 20–50 centimeters, with two to four foliage leaves forming a rosette and between four and seven farther up the stem. Sepals range from white to reddish pink (11–17 millimeters). Petals are triangular, hairy, and greenish to pink (3–7 millimeters). The lip is deeply three-lobed, the midlobe chestnut-brown with a reflexed tip and creamy yellow markings near the base. Distribution is very wide in Europe, north Africa, and the Near East. It grows in limestone grassland, dune slacks and chalk pits. In cultivation it can be established in gardens on limestone or chalk. They also appear "spontaneously" in lawns, tennis courts, and on banks and will multiply if seed is set before grass is cut. In pots they need a well-drained compost with added limestone and a sunny position. Tubers are left to dry off in the pots and repotted in the fall.

Ophrys fusca Link

A variable species with small flowers rather unfairly known as the "dull Ophrys." It is common in the Mediterranean area and has a number of more spectacular relations such as *O. iricolor* with its vivid blue speculum. Stems range from ten to 40 centimeters tall with two to nine flowers. Sepals are green to yellowish. Petals are about two-thirds as long and yellowish to light brown. The lip is 10–15 millimeters long, dark brown at the apical end with a greyish blue to the bluish violet speculum. Although found in scrub on dry soils it flowers very well under pines in the open

Oncidium variegatum

Ophrys apifera

Ophrys fusca

plantations near the sea. *Ophrys fusca* is a reliable species on which to learn how to deal with *Ophrys* cultivation in pots. Use the basic compost given with added limestone chips in alpine house conditions. In the wild it flowers from early February (Cyprus) to April (France) depending on latitude.

Ophrys holoserica (Burm.f.) Greuter

In a good population of this species it sometimes seems as if no two lip patterns are the same. There are also yellow-lipped and narrow-lipped variants. The species is characterized by between two and six flowers on a raceme with sepals varying in color from white, through greenish, to pale and deep pink. Petals are pink, triangular in shape and a third to half the length of the sepals. The lip is squarish and entire, velvety dark brown with a bordered speculum near the base; white lines and bluish areas contribute to a variable pattern. Many flowers have well-developed protuberances at the lip base and a prominent forward-pointing apex. The species is one of four found in Britain (where it is very rare) through France and southern Germany to the Mediterranean region. It flowers from mid-May onward.

Ophrys insectifera L.

Small flowers and a very slender appearance (stems 20–50 centimeters with two to fourteen flowers) make this species difficult to see at first in the beechwoods and wood margins it often favors. Unlike other *Ophrys* species, its seven to nine broadly lanceolate leaves grow up the stem rather than forming a rosette. Sepals are small (six to eight millimeters) green, and more or less concave. Petals are very narrow and four to six millimeters long. Blackish violet in color, they form a remarkable pair of "antennae" to the insect body of the lip. The lip is velvety dark brown with a dark blue or violet speculum at its base. *Ophrys insectifera* extends farther north than any other *Ophrys* species but is absent from the southeast of Europe and rare in the extreme south as well as much of the north. It flowers from May onward. In cultivation it can be treated in the same way as *O. fusca*.

Ophrys lutea (Gouan) Cav.

Although there are several subspecies and variants occurring commonly in the wild, typical *Ophrys lutea* is the most handsome. Plants stand 10–30 centimeters tall with four or five leaves and between two and seven flowers. Sepals are green and about ten millimeters in length. Petals are yellowish green and about half this length. The lip is three-lobed and twelve to eighteen millimeters long. It has a two-lobed dark speculum on a central velvety brown area surrounded by a bright yellow border two to three millimeters wide. It grows in grassy areas, garigue, and light woodland, and flowers from March to May. In cultivation it can be treated in the same way as *O. fusca*.

Ophrys scolopax Cav.

Ophrys scolopax is the best known of a closely linked group of species (or subspecies depending on the view taken). It is a variable orchid not only in terms of sepal color (which ranges from green through white to reddish pink) but also lip patterning. The speculum is violet or dark blue but can be saucer-, ring-, X- or H-shaped with a complicated margin. Viewed

Ophrys insectifera

from the side, the extended column looks distinctly like a bird's head, and the complex markings on the lip suggest the plump body of a woodcock. The species is distributed throughout southern Spain and southern France into Italy and Greece. Flowers appear from March to May, depending on latitude, on scrub-covered hillsides, grassy verges, and open woods, and always on calcareous soils. In cultivation it can be treated in the same way as other *Ophrys* species with limestone chippings added to the basic mix.

Ophrys holoserica

Ophrys lutea

Ophrys scolopax

Ophrys tenthredinifera

Ophrys vernixia

Orchis mascula

Ophrys tenthredinifera Willd.

The common name "sawfly Ophrys" seems inelegant for what must be one of the most handsome members of the genus. Plants appear robust: 10–40 centimeters tall, with from three to eight flowers. Sepals are large (11–14 millimeters), broad, rounded, and colored bright pink. Petals are about one-third their length and broadly triangular. The lip is large and rectangular, usually entire, with the edges flared near the apex. The lip margin is very hairy and pale, varying from greenish through yellow to pale brown, and is deeply notched near the forward pointing apex. The central area is brown with a dark blue or purple speculum finely bordered in white or yellow, and there is a tuft of rather coarse hairs just above the apical protuberance. In the wild it grows in grassy and stony areas in hillside scrub or garigue. It begins flowering in March (through April to early May) and is widely distributed throughout the Mediterranean region. In cultivation it can be treated in the same way as *O. fusca* with limestone chippings added to the basic compost.

Ophrys vernixia Brot. (also *O. speculum* Link)

The old name, *O. speculum*, corresponded directly with the common name "mirror Ophrys," appropriate because of the shining, bright blue speculum that dominates the lip of this remarkable plant. Surprisingly easy to overlook, plants are 10–30 centimeters in height with five to seven oblong leaves and between two and ten flowers in a lax spike. In close-up, the appearance of the flowers is almost bizarre. Sepals are six to eight millimeters long,

colored green with fine reddish brown stripes. Petals are only a quarter to a third their length and purple-brown. The lip is three-lobed with margins covered in dense purple-brown hairs, often with a narrow yellow margin framing the blue speculum. Mediterranean in distribution, *Ophrys vernixia* prefers undisturbed grassy areas, garigue, and light pine woods, flowering from March to April. In cultivation it can be treated in the same way as *O. fusca* with additional limestone chippings.

ORCHIS L.
OR-kiss
Tribe: Orchideae
Subtribe: Orchidinae
Etymology: Gr. *orchis*, testicle

Both the generic name *Orchis* and the word "orchid" derive from the same ancient Greek word for testicle, a reference to the twin tubers possessed by the plants. The early interest taken in the plants was "medicinal" in that when the "doctrine of signatures" held sway anything with even a passing resemblance to a part of the body could be used to cure or aid it. Inevitably a potion made from *Orchis* tubers was used to increase fertility. In Turkey, a national drink, salep, is made from wild orchid tubers with disastrous consequences for the wild populations because of overcollecting. The genus comprises some 37 species in Europe, the Middle East and north Africa along with others in temperate Asia from the Himalayas to Japan. All species possess a pair of entire ovoid tubers (one for current growth, one for the following year's). Leaves vary in shape and can be spotted in some

species. Perianth segments are free but sometimes converge to form a galea. Lips are variable in shape, ranging from entire to three-lobed. The most fascinating are those in which the lip divisions produce remarkable tiny "figures" with common names such as monkey, lady, and military orchids.

Orchis can be cultivated in much the same way as *Ophrys*, using a similar compost and alpine house conditions:

> 3 parts heat-sterilized loam
> 3 parts coarse, gritty sand
> 2 parts beech/oak leaf mold (pass through 13 millimeter sieve)
> 1 part composted pine bark (6 millimeters size)
> Basic dressing of hoof-and-horn meal at 10 milliliters per 10 liters

Orchis mascula (L.) L.

Long known as a herald of spring in Europe's woodlands, the early purple orchid can grow abundantly in mountain woodlands on neutral or slightly acidic soils or in short turf above limestone sea cliffs. Plants grow from 20–50 centimeters with between three and five leaves in the lower part and sheaths above. Leaves are broadly lanceolate, shining green and spotted with dark purple. The flower spike is cylindrical, varying from lax to dense depending on the number of flowers carried, usually from between seven and twenty. These have spreading or slightly reflexed lateral sepals and a dorsal sepal which curves with the petals to form a helmet, all colored mauve or reddish purple. The lip is three-lobed; side-lobes are only slightly deflexed, if at all, and the midlobe is notched at its apex. The central part of the lip is whitish with

Orchis militaris

Orchis morio

Orchis purpurea

deep crimson spots. The flower scent is of cat's urine. *Orchis mascula* is a locally common orchid over much of west and central Europe, flowering in May and June on a variety of soils.

Orchis militaris L.

Robust plants can reach 65 centimeters in suitable locations with four to seven large, oblong leaves and a fairly dense cylindrical inflorescence. *Orchis militaris*, together with *O. simia* and *O. purpurea* mentioned below, is one of a number of *Orchis* species in which the sepals and petals converge to form a hood, and the three-lobed lip takes on the appearance of a tiny figure. In this case the hood is greyish pink or whitish outside with purple veins inside. The lateral lobes of the lip are more or less curved, widening slightly toward their rounded tips. The midlobe is narrow except at the apex where it spreads to give a deeply divided triangular shape, forming "legs" which widen noticeably towards their tips. A very small protuberance forms a "tail." Ground color varies from white to deep pink; the midlobe is lighter in shade toward its base where there are tufts of reddish hairs which produce a "speckling" effect.

Orchis morio L.

Less than a century ago this species was one of the most common of European plants, coloring whole meadows with its magenta spikes. Due to the widespread use of fertilizers and intensive agriculture it is now far from common. Plants are usually short in stature (20 centimeters) with a basal leaf-rosette and crowded sheaths above. The inflorescence is widely spaced and looks as if it has been cut off at the top. Sepals and

petals form a hood, and their rich green veining, particularly on the lateral sepals, gives rise to the common name of green-winged orchid. The lip is shallowly three-lobed and folded to form a saddle shape with a dark spotted centre. In any population there is a tremendous range of color forms, from almost white through pale pink to deep magenta. Flowers appear from April to June, usually, but not exclusively, on calcareous soils such as unspoiled limestone pastures or dune grasslands. Distribution is throughout Europe.

Orchis purpurea Hudson

This is another tall species, often more robust than *O. militaris* (up to 80 centimeters tall) and even from a distance distinguishable from it. The flowers have a galea which is a deep rich reddish purple, giving the spike a darker appearance. Leaves are large and glossy with sheaths higher up the stem. In this species the lip divisions provide for two arms and a triangular "skirt" or even wide-legged "harem pants" where the midlobe is slightly more divided. The lip ground color is light pink or white with clumps of tiny dark hairs forming purple spots. The lip with galea gives the impression of ladies in old-fashioned "poke" bonnets and provides the reason for the common name "lady orchid."

Orchis simia Lam.

Orchis simia is a less robust species than either *O. militaris* or *O. purpurea*, and has the distinction that the flowering sequence is from top to bottom of the spike. Stems are from 20–45 centimeters tall with a short, fairly dense inflorescence. Sepals and petals are roughly the same length (ten

millimeters) and converge to a helmet with a peak formed by their extended tips. The helmet can vary from pale greyish pink through pink to reddish. The three-lobed lip has lateral lobes drawn into narrow arms with reddish tips. The midlobe is deeply divided to produce two narrow, red-tipped legs and a noticeable "tail," the apical protuberance. The common name "monkey orchid" is appropriate, and the raceme looks like a troop of tiny animated creatures in a wild dance. This species occurs in Europe from Britain (very rare) in the north to the Mediterranean, Russia, Asia Minor, and Iran. It flowers from March to May in the south and from late May in the north.

ORNITHOPHORA Barb. Rodr.

or-nith-OF-oh-ra
Tribe: Cymbidieae
Subtribe: Oncidiinae
Etymology: Gr. *ornis*, bird; *phoros*, bearing; in reference to the lateral view of the column which resembles a bird

Ornithophora is a monotypic genus from Brazil. The genus is characterized by the narrowly ovoid, flattened pseudobulbs of a single internode subtended by distichous leaflike sheaths, separated by a creeping rhizome and two apical, thin leaves; the unbranched inflorescence produced from the axils of the sheaths; the flowers without a spur; the sepals and petals free; the lip entire with projections from the sides; the slender column without a foot; and the two hard pollinia attached to a stipe connected to a viscidium.
The species is epiphytic in moist forest. The creeping rhizome and unbranched inflorescence separate this genus from the closely allied genus *Sigmatostalix*, to which it is often referred.

Orchis simia

The species is easily cultivated under intermediate conditions with abundant water throughout the year.

Ornithophora radicans
(Reichb.f.) Garay & Pabst

The plants have bifoliate pseudobulbs with sheathing basal leaves and are arranged on an elongate, creeping rhizome. The inflorescence reaches ten centimeters long and has eight to eleven flowers. The flowers reach a diameter of one centimeter. The white sepals and petals are small and similar in size and shape. The lip is yellowish, quadrangular with erect lobes at

the basal margin, and with an elongate claw at the base. The purple column is slender and without wings.

Ornithophora radicans

Osmoglossum convallarioides

Osmoglossum pulchellum

OSMOGLOSSUM (Schltr.) Schltr.
oz-moe-GLOS-um
Tribe: Maxillarieae
Subtribe: Oncidiinae
Etymology: Gr. *osme*, odor; *glossa*, tongue, lip; in reference to the fragrant lip

Osmoglossum is a genus of seven species distributed from Mexico to Panama. The genus is characterized by the presence of unifoliate or bifoliate pseudobulbs of a single internode subtended by distichous leaflike sheaths; the inflorescence produced from the axils of the sheaths; the flowers white, without a spur; the lateral sepals united and concave at the base; the basal portion of the lip parallel to and adnate to the column to its apex; the column without a foot and with a clinandrium and short wings at the apex, not sulcate on the underside; and the two, hard pollinia attached to a stipe connected to a viscidium. The plants are epiphytes in seasonally dry pine–oak forest at elevations from 500 to 2,000 meters. Cultivation of the species should be under intermediate conditions in pots in well-drained media.

Otoglossum brevifolium

Osmoglossum convallarioides
Schltr.

This species occurs from Mexico to Panama. The species is distinguished from *O. pulchellum* by the much smaller flowers which reach only two centimeters in diameter, the flowers flushed with pink, the yellow callus of the lip, and the concave rather than the deflexed lip of most other species.

Osmoglossum pulchellum (Batem. ex Lindley) Schltr.

This species is found from Mexico to Costa Rica. The flowers are larger than in the other species, reaching 3.5 centimeters in diameter, and the lip is abruptly deflexed beyond the callus. The very fragrant flowers are usually flushed with pink outside. The callus is yellow spotted with red-brown.

OTOCHILUS Lindley
oh-toe-KYE-luss
Tribe: Coelogyneae
Subtribe: Coelogyninae
Etymology: Gr. *otus*, resemblance; *cheilos*, lip, in reference to the resemblance of the lip to the sepals and petals

Otochilus fuscus

This genus comprises four species of particularly straggly plants with jointed pseudobulbs occurring in the Himalayas through Burma, Thailand, and Vietnam. The fine chains of brownish white to pure white flowers in profusion from the nodes give this genus a charm of its own. The jointed pseudobulbs bear a pair of glossy leaves. Quite hardy and of easy culture, these plants can tolerate temperatures up to 25°C

in summer. They can be grown attached to tree-fern slabs or in hanging baskets in 30–50 percent shade.

Otochilus fuscus Lindley

This common species extends from Nepal through Sikkim Himalaya to Vietnam. Pendulous chains of white flowers and jointed, cylindric stems with shiny leaves make this an attractive species. It will tolerate night temperatures of 5°C, flowering in December.

OTOGLOSSUM Garay & Dunsterv.
oh-toe-GLOS-um
Tribe: Cymbidieae
Subtribe: Oncidiinae
Etymology: Gr. *otos*, ear; *glossa*, tongue, lip; in reference to the earlike lip

A group of eight species formerly placed in *Odontoglossum* but recently separated as the genus *Otoglossum*, distributed from Costa Rica to Peru. The genus is characterized by the scandent plants with ovoid pseudobulbs; the basal leaves reduced or with several as large as the apical leaf; the inflorescences erect and racemose with the flowers clustered apically; the flowers large (four to six centimeters in diameter); the sepals and petals subequal, undulate; the lip diverging sharply from the column, equal to or shorter than the lateral sepals, three-lobed with a weak isthmus and basal lobes equal to or smaller than the apical lobe; the lip callus confined to the center of the basal lobes and composed of an upper and lower lobulate-tuberculate mass with a series of accessory tubercles scattered over the basal lobes; the column elongate, incurved apically; and two ovoid pollinia, short caudicles, a short, flat stipe, and an oval viscidium.

The plants are epiphytic or terrestrial on embankments or cliffs in very moist montane forests, usually from 1,000 to 3,000 meters.

The species are difficult to cultivate because of their clambering habit but are well worth the effort when flowering is achieved. A large specimen is one of the most spectacular of orchids. They should be grown under cool conditions with *Odontoglossum*.

Otoglossum brevifolium (Lindley) Garay & Dunsterv.

This species occurs from Colombia to Bolivia at upper elevations in the Andes. The plants have thick, flattened, nearly round pseudobulbs with a pair of thick leaves at the apex. The inflorescence reaches 40 centimeters in length and carries five to nine flowers. The flowers are yellow, heavily blotched with dark brown, and reach a diameter of four centimeters.

Otoglossum coronarium (Lindley) Garay & Dunsterv.

This species occurs in Colombia and Ecuador on the slopes of the Andes. The plants have elongate, compressed pseudobulbs with two or three leaves at the apex and several sheathing leaves at the base. The leaves are thinner and longer than in other species. The inflorescence reaches one meter in length and has seven to eleven flowers. The flowers are yellow blotched with light brown and reach a diameter of six centimeters.

Pabstia jugosa

PABSTIA Garay
PAB-sti-ah
Tribe: Maxillarieae
Subtribe: Zygopetalinae
Etymology: For G. F. J. Pabst, a Brazilian orchidologist

Some five species are currently known, all endemic to Brazil. Species of *Pabstia* are sometimes listed under *Colax* (e.g. *C. jugosus*). *Colax*, however, was established twice for two different groups of orchids and only the one established first (a synonym of *Lycaste*) has nomenclatural priority. *Pabstia* was proposed to accommodate the species previously placed in the invalid genus. The pseudobulbs typically bear two leaves. Few-flowered racemes arise from the base of the pseudobulbs. All species have four pollinia. Follow growing instructions for *Zygopetalum*.

Pabstia jugosa (Lindley) Garay

This showy species, found in Brazil, blooms in cultivation from January to September. Sepals are white to greenish white, the petals and lip white to greenish white spotted dark wine-red.

Otoglossum coronarium

Palumbina candida

Panisea uniflora

centimeters, carry a pair of leaves at the apex. Short racemes from the base of the pseudobulb bear one to six flowers of translucent white to pale apricot.

Plants can be cultured in small, shallow pans or fern-blocks using the medium prescribed for *Pleione*. Provide 50 percent shade and intermediate temperatures for all species except *Panisea demissa*, which requires cool growing conditions. Constant moisture during the growing season is essential for optimum formation of pseudobulbs. In nature the pseudobulbs are often embedded in moss, which provides humidity even during the dry winter season.

Panisea uniflora (Lindley) Lindley

This easy-growing species is found from Nepal to Vietnam. It produces pale, translucent brownish yellow flowers on short racemes from the base of the pseudobulb. From elevations of 250–1,500 meters, it can be cultivated under intermediate conditions but will tolerate warmer conditions when grown well.

PALUMBINA Reichb.f.
pal-um-BEE-na
Tribe: Cymbidieae
Subtribe: Oncidiinae
Etymology: *palumbina*, pertaining to wood-pigeons; in reference to a similarity of the flower to a dove with spreading wings

Palumbina is a monotypic genus known from southern Mexico and Guatemala. The genus is characterized by the ellipsoid, flattened pseudobulbs of a single internode with a single apical leaf; the few-flowered inflorescence emerging from the basal sheaths of new growths; the white flowers with a few purple spots at the base of the petals and a yellow callus; the completely united lateral sepals; the lip spreading away from the column at the base; and the two hard pollinia on a stipe with a round viscidium.

The plants are epiphytic in moist cloud forest. They are cultivated under intermediate conditions with cool night temperatures.

Palumbina candida (Lindley) Reichb.f.

This species occurs in Mexico and Guatemala. The inflorescence is erect, reaching 30 centimeters tall and with five to seven flat flowers that reach 2.5 centimeters in diameter. The flowers are distinguished from *Oncidium*, to which this species is closely allied, by the completely united lateral sepals hidden behind the lip, the pure white flowers with small violet dots at the base of the petals and on the yellow callus, and the fleshy callus firmly connected to the short column.

PANISEA (Lindley) Steudel
pan-EE-see-ah
Tribe: Coelogyneae
Subtribe: Coelogyninae
Etymology: Gr. *pan*, all; *isos*, same

Currently seven species are known, ranging from Nepal and Sikkim Himalaya to Vietnam. All are miniature epiphytes or lithophytes quite rare in cultivation. They are closely related to *Coelogyne* but differ in the lip and column. The conical pseudobulbs, scarcely exceeding 2.5

Paphinia cristata

PAPHINIA Lindley
(pa-FIN-ee-ah)
Tribe: Cymbidieae
Subtribe: Stanhopeinae
Etymology: Gr. *Paphia*, the name of Aphrodite of Cyprus

Paphinia is a genus of about ten species distributed from Venezuela to Bolivia. The genus is characterized by the pseudobulbs of a single internode with two or three thin, heavily veined leaves at the apex and surrounded at the base by distichous, foliaceous sheaths. The inflorescence is pendent and produced from the base of the pseudobulb. The dorsal sepal and petals are free. The lateral sepals are united at the base, and the lip has an epichile and a hypochile united to the elongate column-foot. The epichile has fleshy, hairlike protuberances around the margin, and the callus has an erect lamella or hair-like protuberances. The column is elongate and winged, with two hard pollinia attached to an elongate stipe united to a small, round viscidium.

The plants are epiphytes in very wet forest at elevations from 500 to 1,000 meters. Cultivation of paphinias should be done on plaques so that the inflorescence can hang. The plants do well under intermediate conditions with abundant water applied throughout the year.

Paphinia cristata Lindley

This species occurs in Panama, the West Indies, Venezuela, Colombia, Brazil, Guyana, and Bolivia. The inflorescence is pendent and usually produces three to five flowers. The flowers reach ten centimeters

Paphiopedilum acmodontum

in diameter. The sepals and petals are white or yellow-white with red-brown streaks on the basal half and blotches of red-brown on the apical half. The lip is white marked with red-brown, and the fleshy hairs around the apex of the epichile are white. The distinguishing character of this species is the notched base of the column wings.

PAPHIOPEDILUM Pfitzer
paf-ee-oh-PED-i-lum
Subfamily: Cypripedioideae
Etymology: Gr. *Paphia*, of Paphos, epithet of Venus; *pedilon*, sandal

The genus *Paphiopedilum* comprises about 60 species in the Asian tropics from southern India to New Guinea and the Philippines. Like the temperate genus *Cypripedium*, *Paphiopedilum* species are known as "lady's slippers" because of their pouchlike lips. Unlike *Cypripedium*, *Paphiopedilum* plants readily adapt to cultivation and are the slipper orchids most commonly seen under cultivation. *Paphiopedilum* species are notoriously difficult to raise from seed, and collection of *Paphiopedilum* plants from the wild has placed undue strain on native populations. As a result, *Paphiopedilum* has been at the center of orchid conservation efforts and controversy.

All *Paphiopedilum* have flowers of a similar plan. The lateral sepals are fused into a "synsepal" that is usually small and more or less hidden behind the pouchlike lip. The dorsal sepal is large and showy. Petals may be round and similar to the dorsal sepal or linear and variously twisted, curved, and

undulate. A prominent feature and one critical to their classification is the shield-shaped "staminode" in the center of the flowers. Among the fascinating aspects of these plants are the warts and hairs borne on the petals of some species. All species bear fan-shaped growths that bear a central (terminal) scape. Most species are solitary-flowered, but several groups of species bear multiple flowers either concurrently or successively.

Lacking pseudobulbs, paphiopedilums prefer a moisture-retaining epiphytic compost and medium light levels. Horticulturally the plants can be divided into three groups: mottled-leaved species tend to be lowland plants requiring warm temperatures; plain-leaved species bearing one flower usually prefer intermediate or cool temperatures; plain-leaved species bearing multiple flowers prefer warm temperatures and brighter light conditions.

Paphiopedilum acmodontum Schoser ex M. Wood

This species is endemic to the Philippines. The green flowers produced in late spring are prized for their pink petals and pink-flushed dorsal sepal. The flowers are borne singly above richly green-mottled leaves.

Paphiopedilum adductum Asher

One of the more dramatic species from the Philippines, *Paphiopedilum adductum* bears flowers similar to *P. rothschildianum*. Unlike the latter's boldly marked flowers, however, the flowers of *Paphiopedilum adductum* are in muted brown with narrow, downcurved petals. The two- to three-

flowered inflorescences are produced in early winter above unmarked leaves.

Paphiopedilum appletonianum (Gower) Rolfe

Paphiopedilum appletonianum is native to Thailand, Laos, and Cambodia. It is very closely related to *P. bullenianum* and has been treated as one of its varieties. The flowers, produced in winter atop extremely long, erect scapes, are greenish with a muted pink pouch and bright pink petals. One unusual feature is the habit of the dorsal sepal to recurve so that the edges touch behind the flower. The green-mottled leaves have variable amounts of purple on their undersurface.

Paphiopedilum argus (Reichenbach) Stein

Endemic to the Philippines, this species flowers in the early spring. The red-pouched flowers are notable for their cleanly dark-green-striped white dorsal sepal and petals covered by warts and bordered by hairs. The flowers are borne singly on long scapes above green-mottled leaves.

Paphiopedilum armeniacum S. C. Chen & Liu

Native to China, this species is unique in *Paphiopedilum* for its clear apricot-colored flowers. The round flowers, produced in spring, are held above narrow leaves that are richly mottled with light and dark bluish green. *Paphiopedilum armeniacum*, with other species from mainland China, has

Paphiopedilum appletonianum

Paphiopedilum argus

Paphiopedilum adductum

Paphiopedilum armeniacum

Paphiopedilum barbatum

Paphiopedilum bellatulum

been at the center of conservation efforts to limit collection of plants from the wild for horticultural purposes.

Paphiopedilum barbatum
(Lindley) Pfitzer

This species is native to the Malay Peninsula and the inland of Penang. The flowers are deep purple with a green- and purple-striped white dorsal sepal. The species is sometimes considered to be an extreme form of *P. callosum* with intermediates known as *P. sublaeve* and *P. thailandense.* Horticulturally, *Paphiopedilum barbatum* comprises those plants with petals that project straight out from the flower, unlike the downswept petals of *P. callosum.* The flowers appear in late spring above richly green-mottled leaves.

Paphiopedilum barbigerum Tang
& Wang

Native to China, this is a small-growing species that has only recently been introduced to horticulture. The solitary, light brown flowers have a white dorsal sepal. The narrow leaves are unmarked, and the plants casually resemble narrow-leaved *P. exul.* Plants of *Paphiopedilum barbigerum* freely produce multiple growths and rapidly form clumps.

Paphiopedilum bellatulum
(Reichb.f.) Stein

Native to Burma and Thailand, this species is prized for its large round white flowers covered with large purple spots, flowering in late spring and early summer. A pure ivory-white form is in cultivation. The species is unique in the genus for its heavy, fleshy flowers borne on short scapes that

Paphiopedilum barbigerum

rest directly on the richly mottled, dark bluish-green leaves. *Paphiopedilum bellatulum* has been widely used in hybrids for its round, overlapping shape.

Paphiopedilum callosum
(Reichb.f.) Stein

This species is native to Thailand, Cambodia, Laos, and northern Malaya. The deep purple and green flowers have striking green- and purple-striped white dorsal sepals as well as hair-covered warts along the petals. Flowering is in early summer. A green and white form, lacking any purple pigment, is known. The characteristic downswept petals separate *Paphiopedilum callosum* from the closely related *P. barbatum.* An easy growing species, *Paphiopedilum callosum* is frequently used as a pot-plant, competing in vigor with most hybrids.

Paphiopedilum charlesworthii
(Rolfe) Pfitzer

This species, endemic to Burma, is singular for the oversized rose dorsal sepals above an otherwise greenish brown flower, the

dorsal sepals frequently equaling the span of the petals. It is easily recognized when not in bloom, as the undersurface of the plain green leaves are covered with purple marbling toward the base. Solitary flowers are produced in the fall.

Paphiopedilum ciliolare
(Reichb.f.) Stein

This species is native to the Philippines. Similar to the Sumatran *P. superbiens* (*P. curtisii*), *Paphiopedilum ciliolare* has been considered a subspecies of the latter by some authors. The purple-suffused flowers are large for *Paphiopedilum* and highlighted by the striped dorsal sepal and wart- and hair-covered petals. Appearing in late spring, the flowers are held on a strong scape above green-mottled leaves. The flower-stalk and ovary are covered with fine purple hairs.

Paphiopedilum concolor
(Lindley) Pfitzer

Paphiopedilum concolor is native from Burma and southwest China through Indochina. Flowering in late summer, this species is unusual in *Paphiopedilum* because of its pale yellow flowers covered with varying levels of fine purple spots. The richly patterned leaves are variable in length, width, and degree of purple suffusion. Like its close relative *P. godefroyae, Paphiopedilum concolor* has short flower-stalks that hold the flowers just above the leaves.

Paphiopedilum dayanum
(Lindley) Stein

Endemic to the fabled Mount Kinabalu of

Paphiopedilum callosum

Paphiopedilum concolor

Paphiopedilum ciliolare

Paphiopedilum charlesworthii

Paphiopedilum dayanum

Paphiopedilum druryi

Paphiopedilum emersonii

Sabah, northern Borneo, *Paphiopedilum dayanum* is notable for its strongly contrasting patterned leaves. The solitary flowers on long scapes above the foliage have a purple pouch, a green-striped white dorsal sepal, and rose-suffused petals edged with fine hairs. The flowers appear during the summer. Limited to a very small area in nature, this species is particularly vulnerable to habitat destruction and commercial orchid collecting.

Paphiopedilum delenatii
Guillaumin

This endemic of north Vietnam is known only from a few collections made at the beginning of the century. Artificial propagation has made it widely available in cultivation. The white flowers with a pink lip are reminiscent of temperate lady's-slippers and the South American *Phragmipedium schlimii*. Flowering is in early spring. The small plants bear narrow, richly mottled leaves.

Paphiopedilum druryi (Beddome) Stein

Endemic to southern India, this species is thought to be extinct in the wild because of overcollecting and habitat destruction. The yellowish green flowers have a bold, thin purple stripe down the center of the petals and dorsal sepal. Flowering is in late spring. Unlike other *Paphiopedilum* species, *Paphiopedilum druryi* is native to exposed grassland habitat and should be given very bright, though indirect, light conditions.

Paphiopedilum emersonii
Koopowitz & Cribb

Endemic to China, this is an unusual spring-flowering species with broad white petals. The creamy yellow pouch of *Paphiopedilum emersonii* is dotted on the inside with purple spots that show through to the outside — unlike any other species in the genus. The proportionately large flowers are produced in the spring above unmarked leaves.

Paphiopedilum fairrieanum

Paphiopedilum exul (Ridley) Rolfe

This species is endemic to Thailand where it grows near sea level. The flowers in late spring are light brown with a greenish, brown-spotted dorsal sepal with a white edge. *Paphiopedilum exul* is closely related to the Himalayan *P. insigne* and was originally described as a variety of the latter. A sturdy grower that freely produces offshoots, *Paphiopedilum exul* easily forms specimen plants.

Paphiopedilum fairrieanum (Lindley) Stein

The species is native to northeast India and Bhutan. Flowering in late fall, it is beloved for its downswept petals with upcurved tips that yield a shape unlike that of other paphiopedilums. The flowers are white with dark purple veins and have a tan pouch. An elegant green-and-white-flowered form is known. The pale green leaves are proportionately narrow for the genus.

Paphiopedilum glanduliferum (Blume) Stein

Paphiopedilum glanduliferum is native to western New Guinea and associated islands, where it grows near sea level. It is one of the plain-leaved multiflora species, and its flowers, in late spring and summer, are similar to those of *P. rothschildianum*, differing by their light brown color and twisted petals. It is frequently known as *P. praestans*, one of several synonyms in cultivation.

Paphiopedilum exul

Paphiopedilum haynaldianum

Paphiopedilum glanduliferum

Paphiopedilum godefroyae
(Godef.-Leb.) Stein

This native of peninsular Thailand is closely related to *P. bellatulum, P. concolor,* and *P. niveum.* In many ways resembling a mosaic of these species, *Paphiopedilum godefroyae* has the full round floral form of *P. bellatulum* and a creamy yellow color and flower-stalk length similar to *P. concolor.* The summer flowers are covered with purple spots smaller than those of *P. bellatulum*; plants with unspotted lips are often called *P. leucochilum.* Like its related species, *Paphiopedilum godefroyae* has richly patterned leaves with purple undersides.

Paphiopedilum haynaldianum
(Reichb.f.) Stein

This species is endemic to the Philippines. Very closely related to *P. lowii* from neighboring Borneo and Sulawesi, *Paphiopedilum haynaldianum* is readily separated by its longer, spotted dorsal sepal. A multiflora species with plain leaves, the flowers are widely separated on long flower stalks. Flowering is in the spring. The flowers are green with large red spots and broad red borders on the outer halves of the petals.

Paphiopedilum hirsutissimum
(Lindley ex J. D. Hook.) Stein

This species is native to northeast India and southwest China. The Chinese plants are often encountered as *P. esquirolei.* The flowers, produced in late spring and early summer, are deep green with a purple suffused dorsal sepal and rose petals. The most distinctive feature, and the basis for

Paphiopedilum hirsutissimum

the name, is the dense coating of hairs on the flower-stalk, ovary and back of the flowers. A vigorous grower with unmarked leaves, *Paphiopedilum hirsutissimum* rapidly produces specimen plants.

Paphiopedilum hookerae
(Reichb.f.) Stein

Endemic to Borneo, typical plants are native to Sarawak and western Kalimantan. Plants of *Paphiopedilum hookerae* from Sabah are often found under the name *P. volonteanum.* Flowering in midsummer, *Paphiopedilum hookerae* is prized for its richly colored flowers. The green dorsal sepal has a broad pale green border, and

the proportionately broad green petals are edged with and end in bright rose. In addition, the leaves are intensely tessellated and offset by an unmarked greenish white undersurface.

Paphiopedilum insigne (Wallich ex Lindley) Pfitzer

Native to Nepal and northeast India, this is a well-known species in the background of most modern hybrids. The glossy brownish yellow flowers have a green-and-white dorsal sepal heavily spotted with brown. Flowering in late fall and early winter, *Paphiopedilum insigne* is a vigorous grower and rapidly forms specimen plants. The

Paphiopedilum godefroyae

Paphiopedilum hookerae

Paphiopedilum insigne

Paphiopedilum malipoense

Paphiopedilum Maudiae

Paphiopedilum micranthum

leaves are unmarked. It is closely related to *P. exul* and the rarely seen *P. gratrixianum*.

Paphiopedilum lawrenceanum
(Reichb.f.) Pfitzer

Paphiopedilum lawrenceanum is endemic to Borneo. The purple and green flowers, similar to those of *P. callosum*, are notable for their very large purple-striped white dorsal sepals. Flowering in late spring and early summer, *Paphiopedilum lawrenceanum* is perhaps most famous as one of the parents of the hybrid *P.* Maudiae. The solitary flowers are borne on long flower-stalks above richly green-mottled leaves.

Paphiopedilum lowii (Lindley) Stein

Native to the Malay Peninsula, Sumatra, Java, Borneo, and Sulawesi (Celebes), *Paphiopedilum lowii* is similar to the Philippine *P. haynaldianum*, readily differentiated by its shorter, unspotted dorsal sepal. Appearing in late spring and early summer, the green flowers have large purple spots on the lower half of the petals and rose purple-flushed outer petal halves. Like *P. haynaldianum*, *Paphiopedilum lowii* has widely spaced flowers on a very long flower-stalk above unmarked leaves.

Paphiopedilum malipoense
Chen & Tsi

Endemic to China, this is one of the most unusual species in the genus, having large green flowers veined with purple. The flowers are carried on extremely long flower-stalks above very broad, richly green-mottled leaves, purple-marbled on their undersurfaces. *Paphiopedilum malipoense*

Paphiopedilum lawrenceanum var. *album*

Paphiopedilum lowii

flowers in the spring. Found among water seeps in protected locations behind cliffs, *Paphiopedilum malipoense* appears to like more water than other species in the genus.

Paphiopedilum mastersianum
(Reichb.f.) Stein

Endemic to the Moluccas, this is an infrequently grown species, notable for its stiffly erect, one- to two-flowered scapes in late spring. The greenish flowers have brown petal tips and a highly glossy brown pouch. The flat floral segments have led to this species' use in hybridization programs; hybrids can be recognized by their proportionately broad, flat dorsal sepals. The leaves are green-mottled.

Paphiopedilum Maudiae

Paphiopedilum Maudiae is a nineteenth-century hybrid made by crossing *P. callosum* and *P. lawrenceanum*. Easy to grow and tending to flower twice a year, it is commonly designated as a "beginner's orchid." *Paphiopedilum* Maudiae was originally created using the *alba* forms of its parent species, resulting in a pleasing

flower with an apple green pouch and a large, white dorsal sepal striped with green. Subsequently, *Paphiopedilum* Maudiae was remade using normally colored representatives of *P. callosum* and *P. lawrenceanum*. This resulted in a flower with a purple pouch and purple-striped white dorsal sepal.

Paphiopedilum micranthum
Tang and Wang

Paphiopedilum micranthum is endemic to Yunnan, China. Initially described from a flower bud, the name *micranthum* means "little flower," an inappropriate appellation for one of the largest-flowered species in the genus. The green floral segments, striped and suffused with purple, are overshadowed by the enormous pink pouch. Flowers are produced in the spring. The narrow leaves are richly mottled with shades of dark green and marbled with purple on their undersides.

Paphiopedilum niveum (Reichb.f.) Stein

This species is native to southern Thailand

Paphiopedilum randsii

Paphiopedilum mastersianum

Paphiopedilum niveum

Paphiopedilum primulinum

Paphiopedilum rothschildianum

and northern Malaya. The round, white flowers are produced in the late spring and summer. The flowers typically have fine purple spotting on the petals, although pure white forms are known. The solitary flowers are borne above richly dark green-mottled narrow leaves that have solid purple undersurfaces. *Paphiopedilum niveum* is closely related to *P. bellatulum, P. concolor,* and *P. godefroyae.*

Paphiopedilum parishii (Reichb.f.) Stein

This is a plain-leaved multiflora species native to Burma, southwest China, and Thailand. Plants from China are often seen under the name *P. dianthum.* Flowering in late summer, *P. parishii* is notable for its strongly twisted petals. The green flowers have contrasting purple petals. *Paphiopedilum parishii* likes brighter light levels than other species.

Paphiopedilum primulinum M. Wood & Taylor

This species is endemic to northern Sumatra. Closely related to *P. glaucophyllum* and *P. liemianum,* it shares the habit of producing one flower after the other in slow sequential progression. As a result, inflorescences may stay in flower for years. The flowers of *Paphiopedilum primulinum* are a delicate pale yellow-green and smaller than those of related species.

Paphiopedilum randsii Fowlie

Paphiopedilum randsii is endemic to Mindanao in the Philippines. One of the

plain-leaved multiflora species, it is notable for its pale green to nearly white flowers, cleanly marked with dark brown stripes. The petals are strongly downcurved and give the flowers a "bow-legged" appearance. The flowers are produced in late spring.

Paphiopedilum rothschildianum (Reichb.f.) Stein

Paphiopedilum rothschildianum is endemic to Mount Kinabalu in Sabah, northern Borneo. It is among the finest species of

Paphiopedilum, and both the species and its hybrids are in great demand in horticulture. Because of its limited habitat, the species is significantly threatened by horticultural collection. Flowering in spring, it produces multiple flowers above large, unmarked leaves. Unlike those of other multiflora species, the petals of *Paphiopedilum rothschildianum* are held strongly perpendicular to the flower, yielding a larger-appearing flower. The pouch is brownish purple, and the dorsal sepal and petals are greenish white boldly striped with brown. Like other large multiflora species, *Paphiopedilum rothschildianum*

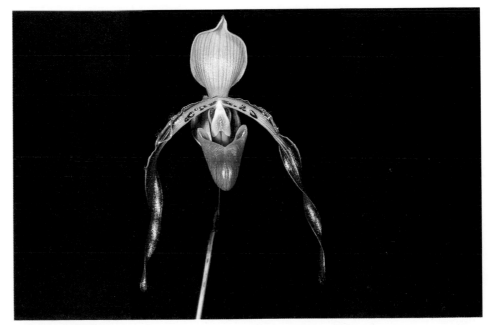

Paphiopedilum parishii

Paphiopedilum spicerianum

Paphiopedilum stonei

should be given brighter light levels than most paphiopedilums.

Paphiopedilum sanderianum (Reichb.f.) Stein

Endemic to a small area of Sarawak, Borneo, this is one of the most sought-after plants in horticulture. A close relative of *P. rothschildianum*, the dark brown flowers are similar except for their incredibly long petals which may reach 90 centimeters in length. The petals, covered with warts and hairs, are spiraled toward the base before hanging limply. The flowers appear in early winter. The species is threatened by horticultural collecting because of its very limited habitat in nature.

Paphiopedilum spicerianum (Reichb.f. ex Masters & T. Moore) Pfitzer

This species is native to northeast India and northwest Burma. The winter flowers are green with a brown pouch and undulate petals. The large dorsal sepal is white with a green base and a narrow central purple stripe. Characteristic of the species is the curving of the dorsal sepal's edges so that the whole structure resembles a funnel. The

flowers are solitary above unmarked leaves.

Paphiopedilum stonei (Hook.) Stein

Endemic to Sarawak, Borneo, *Paphiopedilum stonei* is a coveted multiflora plain-leaved species that flowers in the summer. The large flowers are white with a brownish purple-veined pouch and yellow petals spotted with dark purple. The dorsal sepal ranges from pure white to variously striped. In cultivation a form with wide petals is known as var. *platytaenium*, and a large-leaved form is known as var. *latifolium*.

Paphiopedilum sukhakulii Schoser & Senghas

Native to northeast Thailand, *Paphiopedilum sukhakulii* is related to *P. wardii*. The green flowers have a brownish pouch, a darkly striped dorsal sepal, and petals covered with glossy purple spots and edged with prominent dark hairs. The fall flowers are solitary above richly green-mottled leaves. A vigorous species similar in growth to *P. callosum, Paphiopedilum sukhakulii* has proven most amenable in cultivation.

Paphiopedilum tonsum (Reichb.f.) Stein

This species is endemic to Sumatra, flowering in late fall and early winter. *Paphiopedilum tonsum* bears greenish brown, glossy flowers with a white dorsal sepal lightly striped and infused with purple. The solitary flowers are held above richly marked leaves, usually with a purple undersurface.

Paphiopedilum urbanianum Fowlie

This species is endemic to the Philippines and is similar to *P. acmodontum*. The flowers have a brownish pouch, a boldly purple-striped white dorsal sepal and rose petals with black warts. Unlike the plain green staminode found in *P. acmodontum*, the staminode of *Paphiopedilum urbanianum* is pale green with dark green stripes.

Paphiopedilum venustum (Wallich) Pfitzer ex Stein

Native to Nepal, northeast India, and Bhutan, *Paphiopedilum venustum* is sometimes called the "snakeskin orchid" because of its incredible foliage. The upper surfaces are marbled with deep bluish green, and the undersurfaces are mottled with purple. The winter flowers are solitary and have a brownish gold pouch intricately veined with dark green. The dorsal sepal is

Paphiopedilum sukhakulii

Paphiopedilum tonsum

Paphiopedilum urbanianum

Paphiopedilum victoria-mariae

Paphiopedilum villosum

Paphiopedilum victoria-regina

Paphiopedilum wardii

Paphiopedilum venustum

white or pale green striped with dark green, and the petals are green with rose tips.

Paphiopedilum victoria-mariae
(Sanders ex Masters) Rolfe

Endemic to Sumatra, this is one of the multiflora species that produces flowers sequentially over a long period. It is closely related to and has been confused with *P. glaucophyllum* and *P. victoria-regina*, from which it can be separated by its mottled leaves. The green flowers have a rose pouch and a reddish border to the petals. Unlike *P. victoria-regina*, *Paphiopedilum victoria-mariae* lacks spots on the petals.

Paphiopedilum victoria-regina
(Sander) M. Wood

This species is endemic to Sumatra. It is often seen in cultivation under the synonym *P. chamberlainianum*. One of the sequentially flowering multiflora species, *Paphiopedilum victoria-regina* is closely related to *P. glaucophyllum*, *P. primulinum*, and *P. victoria-mariae*. The flowers of *Paphiopedilum victoria-regina* are similar to those of *P. victoria-mariae*, differing by

their boldly striped dorsal sepal and spotted petals.

Paphiopedilum villosum (Lindley) Stein

Paphiopedilum villosum is native to northeast India, Burma, and Thailand. One of the plain-leaved species, it has solitary, glossy greenish yellow flowers overlaid with reddish brown. In addition to the lacquered sheen, the flowers are unusual in having petals with the upper halves more darkly pigmented than the lower halves. The species flowers from midwinter to early spring.

Paphiopedilum wardii
Summerh.

Native to northern Burma and Yunnan, China, *Paphiopedilum wardii* is a choice horticultural plant, both for its unusual flowers and its richly marked foliage. Flowering in midwinter, the erect dorsal sepal is white with dark, clearly delineated green stripes, and the pouch and petals are green overlaid with red, the petals covered by hairs and warts. The leaves, like those of the closely related *P. venustum*, are richly patterned like snakeskin.

PAPILIONANTHE Schltr.
pa-pil-ee-oh-NAN-thee
Tribe: Vandeae
Subtribe: Sarcanthinae
Etymology: L. *papilio*, butterfly; *anthe*, flower

A genus of ten species native to the Asian

tropics from Sri Lanka to Sulawesi, species of *Papilionanthe* were previously divided between *Aerides* and *Vanda*. All species produce showy flowers in shades of white and pink in few-flowered racemes toward the apex of vinelike plants. *Papilionanthe* species are usually known as "terete vandas" in cultivation because of their terete leaves, unlike the flat leaves of true vandas. A spontaneous garden hybrid between *P. hookeriana* and *P. teres* resulted in "Vanda" Miss Agnes Joaquim, a widely grown plant that was adopted as the national flower of the Republic of Singapore.

Adapted to exposed conditions, *Papilionanthe* species prefer full sunlight, warm temperatures, and abundant water and fertilizer. Roots are produced at nodes along the stem. Plants readily propagate by tip cuttings. The species tend to flower periodically throughout the year.

Papilionanthe hookeriana
(Reichb.f.) Schltr.

This species is native to the lowlands of Thailand, Vietnam, Sumatra, Malaya, and Borneo. *Papilionanthe hookeriana* has a white to pale pink flower with a velvet-textured, three-lobed lip that is sumptuously marked with cerise spotting and suffusion. Unlike related species, it often scrambles over herbaceous plants in swampy habitats, and the species prefers plentiful water in cultivation.

Papilionanthe teres (Roxb.) Schltr.

Native to Nepal and northeast India through Indochina and China, *Papilionanthe teres* is an epiphytic species that scrambles over woody plants. The flowers are variable in

Papperitzia leiboldii

Papilionanthe bookeriana

Papilionanthe teres

color, most frequently pale pink with a darker pink lip bearing a yellow center. A pure white form is known and widely cultivated. Unlike *P. bookeriana*, *Papilionanthe teres* has a two-lobed lip.

PAPPERITZIA Reichb.f.
pah-per-ITS-ee-a
Tribe: Cymbidieae
Subtribe: Oncidiinae
Etymology: Dedicated to William Papperitz, a friend of Reichenbach

This one-species genus is endemic to Oaxaca and Veracruz in southern Mexico. It is quite peculiar because of the complicated lip which forms a deep hair-covered vessel under the column. Plants are small and were originally placed in *Leochilus.*

Papperitzia leiboldii Reichb.f.

The species grows at intermediate elevations in mixed forests, and should be cultivated with good drainage, air movement and light, but without letting the plants dry out. The species is rare and no specimens are known to have survived in cultivation for more than half a dozen years.

PERISTERIA Hook.
per-is-TER-ee-ah
Tribe: Cymbidieae
Subtribe: Stanhopeinae
Etymology: Gr. *peristerion*, little dove; in reference to the similarity of the column, anther, and lateral lobes of the lip to a dove with spread wings

Peristeria is a genus of eleven species

distributed from southern Central America to Brazil. The genus is characterized by the large, ovoid pseudobulbs of several internodes with two or three apical, thin, heavily veined leaves and foliaceous lateral sheaths; the erect or pendent inflorescence produced from the base of the pseudobulb, usually with the new growth; the fleshy flowers; the lateral sepals united to the column-foot; the sepals and petals hooded around the lip and column; the lip with a rigid hypochile united to the column-foot at the base and an epichile flexible at the union with the hypochile; the column thick, wingless or winged; and the two, hard pollinia attached to a viscidium.

The plants are epiphytes or terrestrials in open grassy areas in wet forest at elevations from 600 to 1,200 meters. Most species are best cultivated in baskets so that the pendent inflorescences can emerge from the side. All species do well under intermediate conditions with abundant water applied throughout the year.

Pescatorea cerina

Phaius flavus

Peristeria elata

Pescatorea lehmannii

Peristeria elata Hook.

This species occurs from Costa Rica to Colombia and Venezuela. The plants produce very large pseudobulbs and an erect inflorescence to two meters tall. All other species in the genus produce pendent inflorescences. The cup-shaped flowers are waxy and reach five centimeters in diameter. The flowers are white with small flecks of red on the petals and lip. The lip has broad wings on the hypochile, and the epichile is hinged to the hypochile.

PESCATOREA Reichb.f.
pes-ka-TORE-ee-ah
Tribe: Cymbidieae
Subtribe: Stanhopeinae
Etymology: In honor of M. Pescatore, French patron of the orchids

Pescatorea is a genus of sixteen species distributed from Costa Rica to Ecuador. The genus is characterized by the lack of pseudobulbs, the foliaceous, distichous sheaths forming a fanlike plant; the leaves narrow and lightly veined; the one-flowered

inflorescences from the axils of the leaf-sheaths; the sides of the lip not surrounding the column and with a large, fleshy, ribbed callus not fitting under the terete column; and the four flattened, superimposed pollinia, on a short stipe connected to a flattened, cordiform viscidium.
The plants are epiphytes in very wet forest at elevations from 100 to 1,000 meters. Cultivation of members of this genus should be under intermediate conditions with abundant application of water throughout the year.

Pescatorea cerina (Lindley & Paxt.) Reichb.f.

This species occurs from Costa Rica to Colombia. The flowers reach four centimeters in diameter and have white sepals and petals. The lip is yellow and smooth with a large, grooved callus at the base. The column is club-shaped, white, and has a reddish anther.

Pescatorea lehmannii Reichb.f.

This species is found in southwestern Colombia and northwestern Ecuador. The

flowers reach five centimeters in diameter. The cupped sepals and petals have a base color of white or yellow heavily marked with red stripes for the basal half and a red blotch toward the apex. The lip is purple to bluish, and the apical lobe has a covering of fleshy, bristle-like hairs.

PHAIUS Lour.
FAY-us
Tribe: Arethuseae
Subtribe: Bletiinae
Etymology: Gr. *phaios*, dark, referring to the dark flower color of the first species described

A genus of about 50, usually terrestrial species distributed from Africa through India, southeast Asia and China to the Pacific islands. The popularity of this genus is attributable to the often large and handsome flowers as well as to ease of cultivation. Closely allied to *Calanthe*, it differs in having a lip that is attached to the base of the column. Pseudobulbs are usually large, thick, and clustered with large and distinctly veined leaves. Tall racemes of showy flowers are erect and arise from the base of the pseudobulbs. All species have eight pollinia.
Grow these plants in humus-rich compost supplemented with well-decomposed cow manure, chopped tree-fern fiber, and polystyrene granules for good drainage. They require heavy feeding during the growing season from April through August but a rest after October for two months for best flowering. They make excellent garden subjects for semishaded areas in places where the winter temperature does not fall

Phaius tankervilleae

below 5°C. Shading of about 25–30 percent prevents leaves from burning and promotes sturdy flower-spikes.

Phaius flavus (Blume) Lindley

One of the loveliest in the genus, this species from Nepal, through southeast Asia and New Guinea, is readily identified by the large leaves with yellow spots and blotches. The stout, angular pseudobulbs carry tall spikes of fragrant, long-lived flowers of deep sulfur-yellow with a warm brown to reddish brown band on the lip margins. It requires an intermediate climate and flowers during April–May.

Phaius tankervilleae (Banks ex L'Hér) Blume

This attractive and easy-to-grow species is cultivated all over the world, loved for its tall, upright racemes of fragrant, brown to red, heavy-textured flowers with white on the outer surfaces. The trumpet-like lip is white with a purple-brown to wine-red throat. The large, ornamental plicate leaves provide greenery throughout the year. It can be grown fully exposed to the sun, but better foliage results when grown in 25–30 percent shade. It flowers in April–May.

PHALAENOPSIS Blume
fail-eh-NOP-sis
Tribe: Vandeae
Subtribe: Sarcanthinae
Etymology: Gr. *phalaina*, moth; *opsis*, appearance

The genus *Phalaenopsis* comprises about 50 epiphytic and occasionally lithophytic species distributed throughout tropical Asia from southern India and Nepal east to Papua New Guinea, north to China and Taiwan, and south to tropical Australia. The Philippines are particularly rich in *Phalaenopsis* species. *Phalaenopsis* species have very short stems that bear succulent leaves and copious fleshy roots. Inflorescences produced among the leaves may bear a few to more than 100 flowers in various colors and a diversity of patterns. All *Phalaenopsis* species have a three-lobed clawed lip.

Phalaenopsis is closely related to *Kingidium*, and some authors consider them congeneric. *Phalaenopsis* is also closely related to *Doritis*, and many intergeneric hybrids have been made under the name X *Doritaenopsis*. In the past a terete-leaved group of species from Borneo were called *Phalaenopsis*, but these have been separated as *Paraphalaenopsis*. *Phalaenopsis* species are among the most frequently cultivated orchids because of their rapid growth and early flowering. As well as having long-lasting flowers, *Phalaenopsis* plants have the tendency to reflower from old nodes along a previously flowered inflorescence. This tendency extends the characteristic spring flowering season. A favorite group for orchid breeders, modern *Phalaenopsis* hybrids come in a wide range of size, shape, color, and pattern.

Phalaenopsis species are monopodial and lack pseudobulbs or similar storage organs. For this reason they should be kept always lightly moist and do best in a compost that retains some moisture between waterings. Adapted to low light levels in nature, in cultivation they should be grown in medium light levels to increase flower production and disease resistance. Abundant air circulation also reduces disease problems.

Phalaenopsis amabilis (L.) Blume

Phalaenopsis amabilis is the most wide-ranging species and is native from Java to Papua New Guinea, north to the Philippines, and south to Queensland, Australia. Smaller-flowered plants from the eastern portion of the range are sometimes distinguished as *P. rosenstromii*. The largest-flowered species in the genus, *Phalaenopsis amabilis* is the parent of most modern hybrids. Branched sprays of large, stark white flowers are offset by variable yellow-and-red lip markings.

Tolerant of higher light levels than most species, *Phalaenopsis amabilis* should be grown under medium bright light levels. Most strains of the species have a degree of red leaf pigment, and a slight reddish cast to the leaves indicates that the plants are receiving proper light levels.

Phalaenopsis cornu-cervi

Phalaenopsis amboinensis

Phalaenopsis amboinensis
J. J. Smith

Native to Sulawesi and the Molucca Archipelago, the species is named for the island of Amboina. Star-shaped flowers with concentric brown markings come in two distinct color forms: one with a creamy white background color, and one with a golden yellow background color. The flowers are otherwise notable for their fleshy substance which makes for very long-lasting flowers. *Phalaenopsis amboinensis* has become a mainstay in producing yellow hybrids.

Phalaenopsis aphrodite Reichb.f.

Phalaenopsis aphrodite is native to the Philippines and Taiwan. The large white flowers are similar to those of *P. amabilis* and the two species differ primarily by their lip callus: the callus of *P. amabilis* is two-horned, while that of *Phalaenopsis aphrodite* is four-horned. Taiwanese plants, sometimes under the name of *P. formosana*, have recently been used to impart limited cold-tolerance to hybrids.

Phalaenopsis equestris

Phalaenopsis gigantea

Phalaenopsis fasciata

Phalaenopsis hieroglyphica

Phalaenopsis corningiana
Reichb.f.

This species is endemic to Borneo. The flowers are greenish and covered with variable amounts of reddish brown barring that runs parallel to the length of the segments. Closely related to *P. sumatrana*, *P. corningiana* has flowers with a greenish white center and barring that runs perpendicular to the length of the segments. *Phalaenopsis corningiana* has proven difficult to maintain in cultivation, although it is the parent of many red hybrids.

Phalaenopsis cornu-cervi (Breda)
Blume & Reichb.f.

Native from Burma and the Nicobar Islands east to Borneo, *Phalaenopsis cornu-cervi* is distinctive because of its fleshy, flattened inflorescence that sequentially produces flowers. In addition, the leaves are proportionately narrow for the genus. Similar species include *P. lamelligera* and *P. pantherina* from Borneo, and *P. thalebanii*

from Thailand. *Phalaenopsis cornu-cervi* is adapted to drier conditions than most *Phalaenopsis* species and should be grown under bright light. The large fleshy roots prefer a coarser epiphyte compost than other species. As the inflorescences produce periodic flushes of flowers, they should not be removed from the plant as long as they remain green.

Phalaenopsis equestris (Schauer)
Reichb.f.

Native to the Philippines and Taiwan, *Phalaenopsis equestris* is frequently encountered under the synonym *P. rosea*. The small pink flowers are produced in abundance on branched sprays above compact plants. This floriferous habit has led to the hybridization of "multiflora" *Phalaenopsis*, ideal pot-plants for hobbyists with limited growing space. Normally pink with a darker pink center, the flowers are variable, and selections have been made that range from pure white to deep rose. This miniature species is most readily accommodated in a small pot.

Inflorescences should be left on the plant after flowering because the species tends to produce plantlets ("keikis") at the tips of old inflorescences.

Phalaenopsis fasciata Reichb.f.

This endemic Philippine species is prized for its deep yellow flowers with brown barring. It is frequently included in a broadly defined *P. lueddemanniana*, confused as that species' var. *ochracea*. *Phalaenopsis fasciata* has been widely used in breeding programs to produce dark yellow hybrids.

Phalaenopsis gigantea J. J. Smith

This species from Borneo is named for its gigantic leaves which make it the largest species in the genus. Very round, waxy cream, or yellow flowers spotted with brown are produced on fleshy, long pendulous racemes. Very slow-growing compared to other species, *Phalaenopsis gigantea* should be given brighter light levels. Water and fertilize as for other species. Although it may be accommodated in a large pot, this species is best grown in a basket that allows for the large, drooping leaves.

Phalaenopsis hieroglyphica
(Reichb.f.) H. R. Sweet

Endemic to the Philippines, *Phalaenopsis hieroglyphica* is the largest-flowered species formerly included in the "catch-all" *P. lueddemanniana*. The creamy white flowers are covered with ornate markings or "hieroglyphics." Unlike most of the other species confused with *P. lueddemanniana*, *Phalaenopsis hieroglyphica* is a prolific bloomer and makes a substantial floral display.

Phalaenopsis lindenii Loher

Phalaenopsis lindenii is endemic to the Philippines and one of the smallest species in the genus. It is prized for its richly patterned leaves, a trait shared with the closely related *P. celebensis*. The flowers, borne on an arching upright inflorescence, are pale pinkish-white striped with darker pink. *Phalaenopsis lindenii* has been used to produce candy-striped multiflora hybrids. Native to the mountains of Luzon, it should be grown under intermediate temperatures rather than the warm temperatures usually given *Phalaenopsis*. The small plants are easily accommodated in pots or mounted on slabs.

Phalaenopsis lobbii (Reichb.f.)
H. R. Sweet

Phalaenopsis lobbii is native to northeast India, Bhutan, and Burma. It is very similar to *P. parishii* and was previously considered to be a variety of that species. Few-flowered inflorescences of stark white flowers with

Phalaenopsis lobbii

Phalaenopsis mariae

Phalaenopsis pulchra

Phalaenopsis lindenii

Phalaenopsis lueddemanniana

Phalaenopsis maculata

yellow-and-brown banded lips are borne close to the miniature plants. The flowers are remarkable for their mobile, hinged lip, and the leaves are remarkable for their prismatic surface, unlike those of other species in the genus. In nature *Phalaenopsis lobbii* is semideciduous, shedding its leaves during the dry season. Such extremes are unnecessary in cultivation, and the plants should be kept evenly moist throughout the year. Plants of *Phalaenopsis lobbii* can be grown in small pots. Because of their small stature, however, they are best when mounted on small slabs.

Phalaenopsis lueddemanniana Reichb.f.

Native to the Philippines, this species has included a large number of entities now considered as separate species, such as *P. fasciata, P. hieroglyphica, P. pallens,* and *P. pulchra. Phalaenopsis lueddemanniana* bears flowers that have a greenish white background covered with concentric purple barring. Unlike the related species, *Phalaenopsis lueddemanniana* has fragrant flowers.

Phalaenopsis maculata Reichb.f.

Native to Borneo and the Malay Peninsula, this is one of the smallest species in the genus. The small, cream-colored flowers covered with reddish brown barring are remarkable for their scarlet-red lips. Considered extremely difficult to maintain in cultivation, *P. maculata* has given rise to a number of miniature hybrids. Like *P. gigantea, Phalaenopsis maculata* should be given brighter light conditions than other *Phalaenopsis* species.

Phalaenopsis mannii Reichb.f.

Phalaenopsis mannii is native to Nepal, northeast India, and Vietnam. The yellow flowers have narrow segments and are heavily marked with brown barring. Immaculate forms, bearing clear yellow-green flowers, are known. The flowers are produced in great numbers on much-

branched inflorescences. The leaves are unusual in the genus as they may have fine spotting along the midrib and toward the base of the blade.

Phalaenopsis mariae Burb.

This species is native to the Philippines and Borneo. The white flowers are boldly marked with large, rose and brownish red spots and tend to have strongly recurved segments. The branched inflorescences are laxly pendent and somewhat obscured by the leaves. The distinctive leaves are glossy dark blue-green.

Phalaenopsis parishii Reichb.f.

This species is native to the eastern Himalayas and Burma. Closely related to and confused with *P. lobbii, Phalaenopsis parishii* differs by its bright reddish lip, which is unlike the brown-and-yellow

Phalaenopsis mannii

Phalaenopsis stuartiana

Phalaenopsis violacea

philippinensis (often called *P. leucorrhoda*) which differs by its pallid flowers and yellow side-lobes.

Phalaenopsis stuartiana Reichb.f.

Native to the Philippines, this is a white-flowered species closely allied to the pink-flowered *P. schilleriana*. Massive, branched sprays of white flowers are produced above richly silver-and-green-mottled leaves. The flowers bear characteristic brown spots on the lip and lower halves of the lateral sepals, enhanced in selected strains to include all floral segments.

Phalaenopsis violacea Witte

Native to Malaya and Borneo, *Phalaenopsis violacea* occurs in two distinct forms. Plants from peninsular Malaysia bear starry flowers with even pink coloration and produce more or less typical *Phalaenopsis* leaves. Plants from Borneo bear round flowers with broad petals that are greenish white with purple confined to the lateral sepals and lip and very broad, nearly round leaves. Both forms are strongly fragrant. While most *Phalaenopsis* species are strongly spring-flowering, *Phalaenopsis violacea* flowers in late summer with *P. sanderiana*.

striped lip of *P. lobbii*. The species is deciduous in nature although it does not normally shed its leaves in cultivation. A miniature species, *Phalaenopsis parishii* is best accommodated in a small pot or mounted on a slab.

Phalaenopsis pulchra (Reichb.f.) H. R. Sweet

Endemic to the Philippines, this is one of a number of species frequently included in a broadly defined *P. lueddemanniana*. *Phalaenopsis pulchra* has solid purple flowers with a varnish-like glossy sheen. The only species with similar coloration is the rare *P. speciosa* from the Andaman Islands. *Phalaenopsis pulchra* produces relatively few flowers, often on the ends of long, wiry inflorescences. The species is highly prone to producing "keikis," frequently in lieu of flowers.

Phalaenopsis reichenbachiana Reichb.f. & Sander

Phalaenopsis reichenbachiana is endemic to Mindanao in the Philippines. It is rare in cultivation and may be confused with other yellow-flowered species in cultivation, such as *P. fasciata*. *Phalaenopsis reichenbachiana* has creamy yellow flowers barred with brown.

Phalaenopsis sanderiana Reichb.f.

Endemic to the Philippines, this is a large-flowered species similar to *P. amabilis* and *P. aphrodite*. Unlike those species, the flowers of *Phalaenopsis sanderiana* are flushed with variable amounts of pink, and

the leaves are variably mottled with a silver sheen. While most species of *Phalaenopsis* are strongly spring-flowering, *Phalaenopsis sanderiana* flowers in late summer.

Phalaenopsis schilleriana Reichb.f.

Phalaenopsis schilleriana is native to the Philippines. Similar to the white-flowered *P. stuartiana*, it bears rose-pink flowers on massive, branched inflorescences above richly silver-and-green-mottled leaves. Unlike other large-flowered species, some clones of *Phalaenopsis schilleriana* have a light fragrance. It is similar to *P.*

Phalaenopsis parishii

Phalaenopsis sanderiana

Phalaenopsis schilleriana

Pholidota imbricata

Phragmipedium besseae

PHOLIDOTA Lindley ex Hook.
fol-i-DOE-ta
Tribe: Coelogyneae
Subtribe: Coelogyninae
Etymology: Gr. *pholidotos*, scaly

Pholidota is a genus of about 30 species, widely distributed from Sri Lanka to New Guinea. The long, chainlike inflorescences produced from the top of the pseudobulbs are similar to those of *Dendrochilum* but differ by their large, usually imbricating bracts. The white to pale brown flowers have a broad saccate lip. The plants fall into two groups by their growth habit. One group has clustered pseudobulbs similar to *Dendrochilum*. The other bears its new growths from the apex of the previous pseudobulb and thus forms chainlike plants. Depending on the species, the plants have one to three leaves per pseudobulb. *Pholidota* species prefer intermediate to warm temperatures and medium bright light levels. They should be given copious water when in active growth with water withheld to an extent after maturation of the pseudobulbs. Species flower best when slightly potbound.

Pholidota imbricata Hook.

One of the most widely distributed species, *Pholidota imbricata* is known from Sri Lanka to Nepal and east to New Guinea. It is frequently confused with *P. bracteata* (*P. pallida*). The pinkish flowers in late spring have a white lip and are borne in a pendent two-ranked pseudospiral. *Pholidota imbricata* has one very leathery leaf per pseudobulb.

Phragmipedium lindleyanum

PHRAGMIPEDIUM Rolfe
frag-mi-PEE-dee-um
Subfamily: Cypripedioideae
Etymology: Gr. *phragma*, division; *pedilon*, slipper; in reference to the trilocular ovary and the slipper-like lip

This is a genus of 21 species distributed from Mexico to Brazil and Bolivia. The genus is characterized by the lack of pseudobulbs; the short stems; the distichous, flat leaves without obvious veins; the terminal inflorescence; the lateral sepals united to their apices to form a synsepal; the petals often elongate; the lip forming a hollow slipper; the column short with two fertile anthers and a staminode at the apex; and the soft pollinia.
The plants are epiphytes or, more commonly, lithophytes or terrestrials at elevations from 400 to 2,200 meters. Most species can be cultivated under intermediate conditions in pots with abundant water throughout the year.

Phragmipedium besseae Dodson & J. Kuhn

This species occurs along the eastern slope of the Andes from southeastern Colombia to northeastern Peru. It is the only species in the genus with dark red flowers, marked with yellow in the lip. The inflorescence reaches 60 centimeters in length and is frequently branched. The flowers reach a diameter of six centimeters. The petals are broad and about the same length as the sepals. The plants grow on cliff faces over which a constant supply of water flows at elevations of about 1,500 meters. Consequently, the plants should be cultivated under cooler conditions and with more water than most species of the genus.

Phragmipedium caudatum (Lindley) Rolfe

This species is known from Colombia to Bolivia but does not occur in Ecuador where it is replaced by *P. wallisii*. The inflorescence reaches 40 centimeters in length and has three to six flowers that open simultaneously. The flowers are yellow-brown, striped and marked with red-brown. The petals are slender and extremely elongate, reaching 50 centimeters long in some cases.

Phragmipedium lindleyanum (Schomburgk) Rolfe

This species occurs in Venezuela, Brazil, and the Guianas. The inflorescence reaches one meter in length and is branched. The flowers are produced singly in succession at the apex of each branch. The flowers reach 4.5 centimeters in diameter and are pale green with red-brown stripes. The petals are blunt at the apex and have a ciliate margin.

Phragmipedium longifolium
(Reichb.f. & Warsc.) Rolfe

This species is known from Costa Rica and Panama, and from western Colombia and western Ecuador. It also has been dubiously reported from Peru and Brazil. The inflorescence reaches 1.5 meters in length and is usually unbranched. The flowers are produced singly in succession for a long period and reach a diameter of seven centimeters. Sepals and petals are green marked with green or red-brown vein-lines; the lip is yellow-green tinged with red-brown in front and with red-brown spots on the infolded side-lobes. The species is distinguished by the angular auricle projecting from each side of the lip along the margins of the entrance to the sac.

Phragmipedium pearcei
(Reichb.f.) Rauh & Senghas

This species occurs as a lithophyte on large boulders in small rivers in Ecuador and Peru. The inflorescence reaches 30 centimeters long and is rarely branched. The flowers are produced singly in succession and reach a diameter of seven centimeters. Sepals and petals are green with red-brown vein-lines. The petals are subpendent and twisted. The lip is yellow-green with red-brown markings but completely lacks the angular auricles projecting from the sides of the lip above the entrance to the sac.

Phragmipedium caudatum

Platystele stenostachya

Phragmipedium longifolium

Phragmipedium pearcei

PLATYSTELE Schltr.
plat-e-STEE-le
Tribe: Epidendreae
Subtribe: Pleurothallidinae
Etymology: Gr. *platystele*, a broad column

Platystele is a genus of about 75 species scattered through the American tropics from Mexico to southern Brazil. Some are frequent and widely distributed while others are local and rare. All the species are small, many growing in tufts similar to those of some other genera, while some species are creeping and form dense, entangled mats. The inflorescence is a weak, simultaneously or successively flowered raceme of very small flowers that can be appreciated only with a strong hand lens. The sepals and petals are membranous and one-veined. The lip is simple and connate to the base of a tiny but broad column with an apical anther and bilobed stigma. Two pollinia are present.

Although not showy, most of these plants are relatively easy to cultivate in moist, intermediate to cool-growing greenhouse conditions.

Platystele compacta (Ames) Ames

This species is frequently encountered in Central America. The erect inflorescence produces several tiny flowers simultaneously in a congestion at the apex of the raceme. The raceme continues to elongate far above the little rosette of leaves for a very long period, so that almost every plant is continuously in flower.

Platystele jungermannioides
(Schltr.) Garay

This species, found locally in Central America, is reported to be the smallest known orchid. Tiny leaves, about two millimeters long, are produced along a minute, creeping rhizome. Two to three tiny flowers, with sepals about one millimeter long, are produced successively in racemes about five millimeters long. The lip is similar to and as large as the sepals.

Platystele oxyglossa (Schltr.) Garay

This species is the most frequent of the genus in its wide distribution from Mexico into Brazil. The tiny, tufted plants produce hairlike, usually zigzag racemes of successive flowers. The flower parts are ovate and acute, the small, pointed lip varying in color from red to green or yellow. Similar plants, limited to Costa Rica with simultaneous flowers in a loose, straight raceme, are *P. lancilabris*.

Platystele stenostachya (Reichb.f.)
Garay

This species is frequent and variable in its wide distribution through Central America and northern South America. Dense clusters of nearly microscopic flowers are produced simultaneously in one or more racemes that are much shorter than the petiolate leaves. The lip is proportionately large and studded with capitate cells that are easily visible with a strong lens.

PLECTRELMINTHUS Raf.
plek-trel-MIN-thus
Tribe: Vandeae
Subtribe: Aerangidinae
Etymology: Gr. *plektron*, spur; *helminthion*, worm

This African genus contains a single species which is a monopodial epiphyte. It was originally classified in the genus *Angraecum*, as were many African epiphytes, but is actually closer to *Aerangis* with its long and prominent rostellum which bears the viscidium and stipe. The species is widespread in west Africa, from Sierra Leone to Cameroun, where it grows on the trunks and lower branches of large trees usually in full sun.
Easily cultivated like other vandaceous epiphytes from warm regions. This species does well mounted or in a pot and needs warm, humid conditions throughout the year in strong light. It takes time to get established and does not easily produce new roots after disturbance.

Plectrelminthus caudatus
(Lindley) Summerh.

This is a large epiphyte with rather short stems and a fan of tough leathery leaves. The conspicuous inflorescences are much longer than the leaves and bear three to 20 large flowers. The white lip is on the upper side of the flower, and the other parts are greenish or yellowish. The thick spur is spirally twisted like a corkscrew and extends to 20–25 centimeters long.

PLEIONE D. Don
PLEE-o-nee
Tribe: Coelogyneae
Subtribe: Coelogyninae
Etymology: Gr. *Pleione*, Mother of Pleiades

A very attractive group of about fifteen

Pleione praecox

species distributed from the Himalayas through south China and Formosa. Closely allied to *Coelogyne*, it was once considered a section of that genus. The pseudobulbs are characteristically ovoid, flask-shaped or turbinate (shaped like a top) with one or two deciduous leaves at the apex.
Compared to the rest of the plant, the flowers are very large, showy and borne either before or along with the new growth from the base of the pseudobulbs. On each spike are one or two flowers, ranging in color from white to rose-purple or, rarely, yellow.
About 30 hybrids have been registered to date, beginning with *P.* Versailles. Some of the best ones include *P.* Shantung, *P.* Alishan, *P.* Stromboli, *P.* Vesuvius, and *P.* Eiger.
Plants are best cultivated in shallow, well-drained pans with a mixture of chopped sphagnum, perlite or polystyrene granules and fibrous loam in equal parts with a little bone meal and fine-grade charcoal added. Repot every year before new growth begins. Space the plants one to two centimeters apart and cover with compost to about half the depth of the bulb. Water sparingly until new growth commences. Once the roots are well formed and the plant is growing vigorously, feed regularly with 30–15–15

Pleione bulbocodioides

Plectrelminthus caudatus

Pleurothallis allenii

Pleurothallis amparoana

fertilizer at half-strength from April through June. In July and August switch to a balanced fertilizer. From October to December do not water, and keep the plants in a cold frame at a night temperature of 0–2°C until flower buds emerge.

Pleione bulbocodioides (Franchet) Rolfe

This dark purple-flowered *Pleione* comes from central China and is widely cultivated. Though considered difficult to flower, it is certainly one of the finest in the genus. Flowers on erect 10–15 centimeter spikes are pink to purple to magenta with dark markings on the lip. It flowers during February–March.

Pleione forrestii Schltr.

This is the only yellow-flowered species of the genus, found in north Burma and southwest China. It has been very important in the breeding of yellow hybrids. Plants can withstand temperatures of 0–15°C. There are brownish red spots on the lip.

Pleione praecox (Smith) D. Don

The top-shaped pseudobulb and the fall-flowering habit of this species readily distinguishes it from all other species except *P. maculata*, from which it differs in the purple-mottled pseudobulbs, the warty sheaths that cover the flower stalk, and the rose-purple to lilac-purple flowers. Two large flowers are borne, two per spike, in October, when the foliage is just turning yellow. Pseudobulbs should not be covered more than one-fourth their depth with compost.

PLEUROTHALLIS R. Br.
plu-ro-THAL-lis
Tribe: Epidendreae
Subtribe: Pleurothallidinae
Etymology: Gr. *pleurothallos*, riblike branches

The numerous subgeneric taxa and species included in this huge conglomerate genus cannot be simply described. At the present time 27 subgenera with 25 sections include over 1,000 species. Over 1,800 epithets have been attributed to *Pleurothallis*, but many of the epithets are synonyms. Members of the genus are found throughout the American tropics.
Plants vary in size from minute to huge, epiphytic to terrestrial, short to tall, erect to pendent, clumped to creeping, with long or short leaf-stems, thick or thin leaves, and single-flowered to many-flowered racemes. The flowers vary from coarse to delicate. The sepals are free to variably connate, with or without tails. The petals, lip, and column exhibit all sizes and shapes. There are always two pollinia.

Plants of this genus are found in all collections, although usually unidentified or misidentified. There are species that thrive in warm, intermediate, or cool greenhouse conditions; some can be grown dry, while others must be grown wet.

Pleurothallis acuminata Humboldt, Bonpland & Kunth

This species is widely distributed in the Andes where it has several close relatives. It is distinguished by simultaneously several-flowered racemes, longer than the elliptical leaf, of yellow flowers. The leaf-bearing stem is about as long as the leaf. The free sepals and petals are acute, and the lip is simple and oblong.

Pleurothallis allenii L. O. Williams

This species is native to central Panama where it is not uncommon. A single, attractive, purple flower with the floral parts edged in yellow is produced from the apex of a slender stem at the base of the narrow leaf. The completely connate lateral sepals are free from the dorsal sepal. The pointed petals are nearly as large. The cordate, spiculate lip bears a prominent, peculiar, horseshoe-shaped callus.

Pleurothallis amparoana Schltr.

This species occurs occasionally in Costa Rica. Racemes of several, simultaneous, snow-white, membranous flowers are produced from the apex of a slender stem at the base of a slender leaf. The lateral sepals are adherent into a bowl-shaped blade, while the dorsal sepal is free above. All the sepals are densely long-pubescent inside.

Pleurothallis brighamii S. Watson

This species is frequent in Central America. Tufts of small leaves produce a hairlike flower-stem from low on the short leaf-stem. The delicate flowers are produced successively in a congested raceme beyond the leaves. Sepals are yellowish and variously suffused or marked with brown. The laterals are only loosely adherent toward the base.

Pleurothallis cordata

Pleurothallis dressleri

is stiff and leathery. From the base of the leaf a long-stemmed flower hangs. The color varies from white to yellow, and variously marked with purple. The flower with connate lateral sepals gapes widely. The tiny, dark purple lip deep within the flower can hardly be seen. It has a pair of narrowly acute, basal lobes that fold over the pubescent, middle lobe.

Pleurothallis dressleri Luer

Endemic to the mountains of central Panama, this unique, tiny, creeping species forms large, loose mats of overlapping, reclining leaves and rhizomes. The minute, round leaves are striped like a watermelon. A single, monstrous flower, several times larger than the leaf, is borne barely above the leaves. The flower is mottled in red. A warty callus stands at the base of the denticulate lip.

Pleurothallis endotrachys Reichb.f.

This robust species is variable in its range through Central America. The leathery leaf is much longer than its short, stout stem from which a long, flattened peduncle arises. From the apex the raceme produces a rigid flower successively over a long period of time. The pointed sepals, which vary in color from yellow to purple, are warty inside. The petals and lip are simple and arcuate.

Pleurothallis erinacea Reichb.f.

This robust species, superficially similar to *P. endotrachys*, is also variable in its range through Central America. The leathery leaf is much longer than its short, stout stem from which a long peduncle, round in cross-section, arises. From the apex a zigzag, two-ranked raceme produces a flower successively over a long period of time. The pointed sepals vary in color from yellow to purple. The petals are lobed at the base, and the lip is acutely lobed below the middle. The ovary is densely prickly.

Pleurothallis flexuosa (Poeppig & Endl.) Lindley

This species occurs rather frequently in the Andes of South America. Long flexuous, flexible, successively several-flowered racemes are borne from the junction between the rigid, elliptical leaf and the considerably shorter stem. The purple-spotted flowers are densely long-pubescent inside. The lateral sepals are connate. The petals are fan-shaped, and the lip is arcuate with longitudinal lateral lobes.

Pleurothallis floribunda Poeppig & Endl.

This robust species is frequently encountered throughout the Andes where

Pleurothallis cordata (Ruíz & Pavón) Lindley

This species is the most common of all in the "frog" group, in which single flowers are produced on top of the base of a cordate (heart-shaped) leaf. It is found commonly throughout the Andes. The broad, pointed leaf is borne by a much longer stem. The relatively small, variously colored, short-stemmed flowers are characterized by obtuse sepals, and the laterals are connate into a bowl-shaped lamina. The petals are minutely toothed. The small, obtuse lip is usually shiny.

Pleurothallis crocodiliceps Reichb.f.

This species is variable in its wide distribution through Central America and the Andes. The leaf-bearing stems are compressed (flattened), and the shorter leaf

Pleurothallis endotrachys

Pleurothallis grobyi

Pleurothallis hemirhoda

there are a number of related species. Stout, clustered stems, longer than the oblong, leathery leaf, are enclosed in a series of large, loose, papery sheaths. Several simultaneous, many-flowered racemes — shorter than the leaf — of small yellow flowers are produced from a conspicuous spathe at the base of the leaf.

Pleurothallis gelida Lindley

This large species is found from Florida through Central America and the Andes of South America. Stout, long-sheathed stems bear an oblong, leathery leaf. From a spathe at the base of the leaf several long, many-flowered racemes of small, yellowish white, hairy, sweet-smelling flowers are produced simultaneously.

Pleurothallis grobyi Bateman ex Lindley

Frequent throughout the American tropics and frequent in collections, this species is probably a complex of many look-alikes. Some populations grow at sea level while others grow at 3,000 meters above sea level. Small, white, membranous flowers are produced in a loose raceme held beyond the small, clumped plant of variously shaped leaves. The floral parts are obtuse. Those plants with striped, acute floral parts are *P. picta.*

Pleurothallis hemirhoda Lindley

This handsome species is found fairly frequently in most of the Andes of South America. Tall, stout, purple stems bear a shorter, elliptical, leathery leaf, and from a small spathe at the base of the leaf a colorful flower is produced on an arching

stem. The acute dorsal sepal, the connate lateral sepals, and the long-pointed petals spread gracefully around a large, striped, denticulate lip.

Pleurothallis hirsuta Ames

A native of southern Mexico, this species is frequent in collections. A few hairy, purple-spotted flowers are borne simultaneously in a loose raceme longer than the rigid, elliptical leaf. The raceme emerges from the base of the leaf, which is about as long as the stem that bears it.

Pleurothallis immersa Linden & Reichb.f.

This large species is variable in its wide range through Central America. The leaf-stems are stout and shorter than the thick leaf. The stem of the inflorescence is grasped in the center fold of the leaf, only to emerge higher on the blade where it bears, in a loose raceme, several fleshy flowers which vary from yellow or brown to purple.

Pleurothallis imperialis Luer

Basically similar to all the other members of the "frog" group, this Ecuadorian species is easily recognized by the huge, heart-shaped leaf with a long, sturdy stem and the large flower that sits upon the leaf. The yellow dorsal sepal is concave, and the purple united sepals stretch below, while the broad, purple lip, erect in the middle, is flanked by wide, curved petals.

Pleurothallis imraei Lindley

This peculiar species is variable in its wide distribution through Central America, the

West Indies and the Andes. The more or less concave, broadly elliptical, shortly petiolate leaf is borne by a longer leaf-bearing stem. The petiole is twisted to permit the short, several-flowered raceme to be borne along the back surface of the leaf. The flowers, furnished within by a dense, long pubescence, are usually dark purple.

Pleurothallis loranthophylla Reichb.f.

This species is widely distributed in the Andes of South America. It has a few close relatives. The leaf and its slender stem are about equal in length. From a large, conspicuous spathe at the base of the leaf a weak raceme of several very delicate, short-lasting flowers emerges. The thin, membranous dorsal sepal, the united lateral sepals, and the ovate lip are variously spotted with purple.

Pleurothallis mystax Luer

This unusual species is known from only one area in central Panama. The leaves of the small, clumped plant are broad and petiolate and borne by stems with loose sheaths. From the base of the leaf emerges a loose raceme of two to three successive, dark red flowers, broadly striped in white. The lateral sepals bend abruptly outward from the middle. The white lip is spathulate with a long, grooved handle.

Pleurothallis niveoglobula Luer

This novelty, known as "snow ball," is frequent in southeastern Ecuador and adjacent Peru. From the base of small, rigid, cordate leaves borne by slender, flattened stems, several tiny, single, snow-white, long-

Pleurothallis pubescens

Pleurothallis racemiflora

Pleurothallis schiedei

stemmed flowers are produced. The spherical flowers, about the size of BB shots, do not spread.

Pleurothallis pectinata Lindley

This fabulous Brazilian species is readily recognized by the huge, funnel-shaped leaf which hangs down from a long, slender, flexible, flattened (laterally compressed) stem. Within the cavity of the leaf short, congested, several-flowered racemes are produced from the base. The sepals and petals are acute and spotted with purple. The sides of the lip are fringed, resembling a comb.

Pleurothallis pubescens Lindley

Although not frequent, this variable species is known in many forms and by many names in its wide distribution from Mexico to Brazil. It is probably another complex composed of many look-alikes. A raceme of several, simultaneous, fleshy, shortly pubescent flowers lies on top of an elliptical, leathery leaf. The flowers are white and variously suffused and spotted with purple. The lateral sepals are connate, and the fan-shaped petals are minutely denticulate.

Pleurothallis racemiflora Lindley ex Loddiges

Relatively common from Mexico through Central America and the West Indies into northern South America, this species is known by several other names (e.g. *P. quadrifida* and *P. ghiesbreghtiana*). Many yellow to yellow-green, membranous flowers are produced simultaneously in a raceme about as long as the oblong leaf.

The lateral sepals are connate, and the lip is shaped more or less like a violin.

Pleurothallis ruscifolia (Jacq.) R. Br.

This species is frequently encountered throughout most of the American tropical forests. It is the "type" species of the genus, having been described in 1760 as an *Epidendrum.* Slender stems bear elliptical leaves that are roughly equal in length. From near the base of the leaf a cluster of single, pale yellow flowers appears. The lateral sepals are connate, and the little, ovate lip is bent upon itself.

Pleurothallis schiedei Reichb.f.

This unique Mexican species is immediately recognized by the conspicuous white appendages that dangle from the margins of the reflexed, purple-spotted sepals. The flowers are produced successively in a loose, several-flowered raceme held beyond the thick, short-stemmed leaves.

Pleurothallis secunda Poeppig & Endl.

This robust species is found relatively frequently in most of the Andes of South America. It has several very similar relatives.

Pleurothallis mystax

Pleurothallis tuerckheimii

Podangis dactyloceras

Large, strong stems bear large, leathery, elliptical leaves. From the base of the leaf one to several drooping, few-flowered racemes hang loosely. The membranous flowers are yellowish and variously spotted with purple.

Pleurothallis segoviensis Reichb.f.

This variable species, widely distributed in Central America, is closely related to several others. The leaf-bearing stem is shorter than the narrow leaf, and the leaf is shorter than the erect, simultaneously several-flowered raceme. The gaping flowers, pubescent inside, vary in size and in color from yellow to purple. The lip has a pair of hooklike basal lobes.

Pleurothallis sicaria Lindley

This species, rather frequent in the Andes of South America, has several similar relatives. The leaf-bearing stem of the plant is sharply three-edged and grooved in front, and more or less triangular in cross-section. Two edges are continuous with margins of the leaf. A short, several-flowered raceme is borne from the apex of the stem at the base of the leaf. The yellowish sepals are striped in red, and the lip has a pair of pointed lateral lobes.

Pleurothallis sonderana Reichb.f.

This little species is rather frequent in southern Brazil. It is characterized by clumped, short-stemmed leaves with the short, few-flowered, congested racemes of orange flowers held as high as the leaves by slender, erect stems. The lateral sepals are connate about midway. The petals are acute, and the lip is obscurely three-lobed.

Pleurothallis tribuloides (Sw.) Lindley

This distinctive species is relatively frequent in Central America and the Greater Antilles. Cinnabar-red flowers are produced low among the clumped, short-stemmed leaves. The rigid sepals meet at their tips to create lateral openings into the flower.

Pleurothallis tuerckheimii Schltr.

This rather frequent, coarse, Central American species is easily recognized by the conspicuous spathe at the base of a large, leathery leaf from which the inflorescences emerge. Large, dark purple, gaping flowers are produced simultaneously. The petals are three-striped, and the thick, ligulate lip bears a pair of white lobes at the base.

PODANGIS Schltr.
poe-DAN-gis
Tribe: Vandeae
Subtribe: Aerangidinae
Etymology: Gr. *podos*, foot; *angos*, vessel

This genus contains a single dwarf epiphytic species that is confined to the rain forest of equatorial Africa. It extends from Guinea and Sierra Leone in the west to Uganda and Tanzania in the east. The plants consist of a short fan of succulent leaves which are iris-like, laterally compressed with the upper surfaces united. The inflorescences arise below the fan of leaves and bear up to 20 translucent flowers close together near the apex of the short peduncle.
Plants are easily maintained in a warm greenhouse with high humidity. The root system is not extensive, and they do best in

Pleurothallis secunda

small pots with fine compost which is kept evenly moist throughout the year.

Podangis dactyloceras (Reichb.f.) Schltr.

This species has become quite rare but is easily raised from seeds. The glistening white flowers have a dark green ovary and anther cap. The long spur at the base of the funnel-shaped lip is bifid at its tip.

Polycycnis barbata

POLYCYCNIS Reichb.f.
pol-ee-SIK-nis
Tribe: Cymbidieae
Subtribe: Stanhopeinae
Etymology: Gr. *polys*, many; *kyknos*, swan; in allusion to the many flowers, which resemble small swans

Polycycnis is a genus of fourteen species distributed from Costa Rica to Bolivia. The genus is characterized by the ovoid pseudobulbs with one or two apical, thin, heavily veined leaves; the arching or pendent, many-flowered inflorescence; the sepals and petals free; the lip with a lobed hypochile united to the base of the column and an epichile connected under the hypochile, usually covered by sparse, stiff hairs; the elongate, slender column; and the two hard pollinia attached to an elongate stipe united to a very small viscidium. The plants are epiphytes or terrestrials on embankments in wet forest at elevations from 500 to 1,000 meters.
The plants should be cultivated on plaques so that the pendent inflorescences have room to develop. Water should be applied generously throughout the year, and regular spraying is necessary as the species are susceptible to rot.

Polycycnis barbata (Lindley) Reichb.f.

This species is known from Costa Rica and Panama. It has also been dubiously reported from Colombia and Ecuador. It is distinguished by the single leaf at the apex of the pseudobulb with a petiole for the basal one-third, the arching inflorescence, and the large colorful flowers. The flowers reach a diameter of five centimeters. The sepals and petals are yellow-pink, and the lip is pink with scattered red spots.

Polycycnis muscifera (Lindley & Paxt.) Reichb.f.

This species has been reported from Venezuela to Bolivia. It is distinguished by the single leaf at the apex of the pseudobulb with a petiole for the basal one-third, and the nearly erect inflorescence. The flowers are very similar to those of *P. barbata* but are much smaller, reaching a diameter of three centimeters.

Polycycnis ornata

Polystachya campyloglossa

Polycycnis muscifera

The sepals and petals are yellow-pink, and the lip is yellow with large red spots.

Polycycnis ornata Garay

This species has been reported from Panama and from Venezuela to Ecuador. It is distinguished by the two or three leaves at the apex of the pseudobulb that are not reduced to distinct petioles at the base, the pendent inflorescence, and the small flowers with an extremely narrow lip. The flowers reach a diameter of 2.5 centimeters. The flowers are gray-pink with a pinkish lip.

POLYSTACHYA Hook.
pol-ee-STAK-ee-ah
Tribe: Polystachyeae
Etymology: Gr. *polys*, many; *stachys*, ear of grain or spike

This is a large genus of about 150 species. They are mostly confined to tropical Africa, but a few species are pantropical or found in Madagascar, Asia, or America. The plants are mostly rather small with pseudobulbs of various shapes standing close together on a basal rhizome. They are somewhat similar to some of the species of *Bulbophyllum* but

can be distinguished from that genus by the terminal inflorescence. The flowers are mostly rather small, in a wide variety of colors, and non-resupinate — the paired lateral sepals form a prominent mentum on the upper side of the flower.
Plants are easily maintained in small or medium-sized pots in a moisture-retentive compost. They need warm or cool conditions depending on their origin. Some species are easier to maintain if mounted on bark.

Polystachya adansoniae Reichb.f.

This small species is widespread in the tropical parts of Africa, usually occurring in high rainfall areas. It is an epiphyte of forest trees with short cane-like pseudobulbs close together. The greenish white flowers have a purple column and anther cap. They are small and subtended by bristle-shaped bracts which are longer than the flowers and give a characteristic appearance to the inflorescence.

Polystachya bella Summerh.

This erect epiphyte is known only from the

Polystachya adansoniae

Polystachya bella

Polystachya concreta

Polystachya paniculata

Pomatocalpa spicata

rain forests of western Kenya. The compressed pseudobulbs bear one or two dark green leaves. The inflorescence bears many golden yellow flowers which darken as they age. It is one of the prettiest species, as its name implies.

Polystachya campyloglossa Rolfe

A dwarf epiphyte in Kenya, Uganda, Tanzania, and Malawi which produces relatively large but rather few flowers. The sepals and petals are yellowish green or brownish green, and the lip is white with some purple lines on the side lobes.

Polystachya concreta (Jacq.) Garay and Sweet

This species is widely distributed throughout the tropical parts of the world, from Brazil to Florida and the Caribbean, in Africa and parts of Asia. The inflorescence has several branches and bears many small flowers which are yellow, green or pinkish.

Polystachya odorata Lindley

An epiphytic or lithophytic species from west Africa and Uganda which has many small pale flowers, larger than those of *P. concreta*. They are white or pale green, flushed with pink or purple, and the white lip has a yellow callus.

Polystachya paniculata (Sw.) Rolfe

This species is widespread in tropical Africa from Sierra Leone across to Uganda. The upright, compressed pseudobulbs and rather wide leaves are usually flushed with purple. The inflorescence has several branches and many small orange flowers, each part of which has a median red stripe. One of the prettiest of the species.

Polystachya pubescens (Lindley) Reichb.f.

This species may be epiphytic or lithophytic and is rather short. The inflorescence arises between the leaves on the young developing pseudobulb. The flowers are a bright golden yellow, lined with red streaks on the inner surface of the basal half of the lateral sepals. The lip has a few long white hairs on the upper surface.

Polystachya villosa Rolfe

This yellowish green species is closely related to *P. campyloglossa* but has rather hairy flowers on somewhat larger plants. It is found in Tanzania, Malawi, and Zambia, usually as an epiphyte in riverine forest.

POMATOCALPA Breda
poe-mat-oh-KAL-pa
Tribe: Vandeae
Subtribe: Sarcanthinae
Etymology: Gr. *poma*[*atos*], drinking cup; *kalpe*, pitcher

Pomatocalpa comprises about 40 epiphytic species distributed throughout tropical Asia from Sri Lanka and India to the Philippines, New Guinea, and Samoa. Once included in a broadly defined *Sarcanthus* (= *Cleisostoma*), *Pomatocalpa* has a tonguelike projection at the back of the saccate lip, a midlobe fused to the front surface of the side-lobes, and four pollinia in two pairs. Numerous yellow to green flowers are typically produced on large, branched inflorescences above medium-sized monopodial plants. *Pomatocalpa* should be grown like other *Vanda* relatives with warm temperatures, even copious watering throughout the year, and bright light levels. Most can be

Polystachya pubescens

Polystachya villosa

accommodated in large pots or baskets. The few miniature species, such as *P. brachybotryum*, should be mounted on slabs.

Pomatocalpa bicolor Lindley

Pomatocalpa bicolor is endemic to the Philippines. One of the largest-flowered species in the genus, it has green flowers with dark red markings at the base of the segments. It is closely related to the smaller, yellow-flowered *P. latifolia*. The flowers are produced over several months from a slowly elongating inflorescence.

Pomatocalpa spicata Breda

Widespread in tropical Asia, *Pomatocalpa spicata* has been recorded from northeast India through southeast Asia and Hainan to Java, Borneo, and the Philippines. Multiple densely flowered, pendent racemes of yellow flowers are produced in the spring

from the lower leaf-axils. The inflorescences are shorter than the leaves. Because of the manner in which the flowers are presented, *Pomatocalpa spicata* is best mounted on a slab.

PONERORCHIS Reichb.f.
poe-ner-OR-kis
Tribe: Orchideae
Subtribe: Orchidinae
Etymology: Gr. *poneros*, miserable; *orchis*, orchid

Ponerorchis is a small genus of diminutive terrestrials native to cooler regions of east Asia. They are closely related to *Amitostigma* and *Orchis* and differ by technical characters of the flowers.
Native to areas similar to those of the commonly grown *Pecteilis radiata*, *Ponerorchis* species should be grown in a

Pomatocalpa bicolor

light terrestrial compost. The plants should be given intermediate to cool temperatures and plentiful water when in growth and cool temperatures and minimal water when dormant.

Ponerorchis graminifolia
Reichb.f.

Ponerorchis graminifolia is endemic to Japan. Two or three flowers are produced on a wiry stem above several long, grasslike leaves. The flowers are light pink with a darker pink, three-lobed lip.

PORROGLOSSUM Schltr.
por-ro-GLOS-sum
Tribe: Epidendreae
Subtribe: Pleurothallidinae
Etymology: Gr. *porroglossa*, a distantly held tongue

At present 30 species constitute this genus, which is limited to the Andes of Colombia, Ecuador and Peru, with a single species in Bolivia. There are no close allies. All the species are characterized by successively flowered racemes which exceed the leaf in length. The leaves are often verrucose. The dorsal sepal is concave while the laterals are broader than they are long. All three are variously tailed. The spoon-shaped lip and the column-foot actively interrelate to create an extremely specialized mechanism. The strap-like base of the lip is bent with tension around the tip of the column-foot, so that minute changes in turgidity, precipitated by some stimulation, cause the lip either to snap quickly upward or to return gradually to the original position. The sudden lifting of the lip lifts the pollinator to the column. Two pollinia are present.
Most of these plants are relatively easy to cultivate in moist, intermediate to cool-growing greenhouse conditions.

Porroglossum amethystinum
(Reichb.f.) Garay

This bright pink-flowered species from the western slopes of the Andes of Ecuador is

Ponerorchis graminifolia

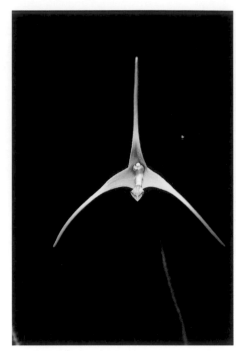

Porroglossum muscosum

Porroglossum olivaceum

distinguished by the short, reflexed tail of the dorsal sepal and the long, slender, diverging tails of the lateral sepals. The base of the lip is barely thickened above the strap.

Porroglossum echidna (Reichb.f.) Garay

This coarse species is from high elevations of the Eastern Cordillera of Colombia. The peduncle is densely and stiffly long-pubescent like a pipe cleaner. The greenish flowers suffused with brown along the veins are verrucose, and the ovaries are densely spiculate. All three tails are long and swollen toward the tips. A longitudinal callus runs along the base of the lip.

Porroglossum muscosum (Reichb.f.) Schltr.

This species, very similar to the last but less robust, is from lower elevations and is relatively frequent in Ecuador and all three cordilleras of Colombia. The peduncle is similarly pubescent. The sepals are not verrucose, and the tails of the sepals are slender without thickening.

Porroglossum olivaceum Sweet

This species with brown flowers occurs in the mountains of northwestern Ecuador and adjacent Colombia. The sepaline tails are slender, the dorsal no longer than the blade. The callus of the base of the lip is longitudinal and tall.

Porroglossum portillae Luer & Andreetta

This species is endemic in southeastern

Ecuador. The ovary is twisted with the pink, purple-spotted flowers non-resupinate. The thick sepaline tails are no longer than the blades.

PRASOPHYLLUM R. Br.
pray-so-FIL-um
Tribe: Diurideae
Subtribe: Prasophyllinae
Etymology: Gr. *prason*, leek; *phyllon*, leaf

About 60 species make up this essentially Australian genus which also has a few representatives in New Zealand. All are deciduous terrestrials with subterranean tuberoids and a terete, hollow leaf through which the inflorescence emerges. The flowers, which are produced in showy spikes, are mainly green, white or pinkish and frequently have sweet floral odors. Many species only flower in the year following summer fires. All species have four pollinia. Pollination is by a range of insects including beetles, bees and wasps.

Prasophyllum australe R. Br.

A widespread species from eastern Australia which grows in colonies in moist to wet areas. Multiflowered spikes are produced from early spring to midsummer. Flowers are reddish brown with a crystalline white labellum which has strongly crisped margins. The fragrance is sweet and pervading.

Prasophyllum elatum R. Br.

Vigorous plants of this species may grow to 1.5 meters tall and commonly in the years

following summer fires produce an impressive floral display. Flower color ranges from yellowish green to purplish black, and the labellum is frequently mauve or purplish. A sweet perfume is noticeable on warm days.

PROMENAEA Lindley
pro-men-EYE-ah
Tribe: Cymbidieae
Subtribe: Stanhopeinae
Etymology: Gr. *Promeneia*, a priestess at Dodona

Promenaea is a genus of fourteen species from central and southern Brazil. The genus is characterized by the prominent pseudobulbs surrounded at the base by foliaceous sheaths; the leaves lightly veined; the one-flowered inflorescences from the axils of the leaf-sheaths; the lateral lobes of the three-lobed lip erect on each side of the column; the prominent subsaccate callus; and the four flattened, superimposed pollinia on a short stipe connected to a flattened, broad viscidium.
The plants grow as epiphytes in moist forest. Cultivation of members of this genus is relatively easy in pots under intermediate conditions.

Promenaea stapelioides (Link & Otto) Lindley

This species occurs in southern Brazil. The flowers reach five centimeters in diameter. The sepals and petals are greenish yellow densely barred and blotched with purple-red. The lip is dark purple-red spotted with darker black-purple, and is nearly round.

Porroglossum portillae

Prasophyllum australe

Psychopsis krameriana

Promenaea stapelioides

Promenaea xanthina

Prasophyllum elatum

Psychopsis papilio

Promenaea xanthina Lindley

This species is known from southern Brazil. The flowers reach five centimeters in diameter. They are bright yellow with red spots on the lip and petals. The apical lobe of the lip is oblong and broader toward the apex.

PSYCHOPSIS Raf.
sye-KOP-sis
Tribe: Cymbidieae
Subtribe: Oncidiinae

Etymology: Gr. *psyche*, butterfly; *opsis*, like; in reference to the resemblance of the flower to a tropical butterfly

Psychopsis is a genus of four species distributed from Costa Rica to Peru. The genus is characterized by the presence of unifoliate pseudobulbs of a single internode subtended by distichous non-leaf-bearing sheaths; the leaves red-brown with irregular spots and blotches of green; the inflorescence produced from the axils of the sheaths, erect; the flowers produced singly in succession at the apex; the dorsal sepal and petals similar, narrow; the lateral sepals expanded, petaloid; the lip without a spur; the column without a foot; and the two hard pollinia attached to a stipe connected to a viscidium.

The plants occur as epiphytes in the canopy of wet or moist forest at elevations from sea level to 800 meters. Cultivation of the species is relatively easy under intermediate to warm conditions on plaques or in pots. The medium should not be allowed to become sour. Without fresh medium the plants die suddenly.

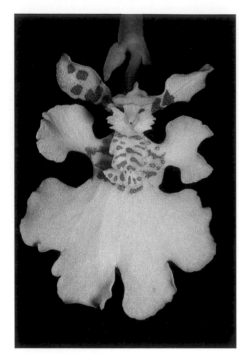

Psygmorchis pusilla

Pterostylis alobula

Pterostylis baptistii

Psychopsis krameriana
(Reichb.f.) H. G. Jones

This species occurs from Costa Rica to Ecuador. In the Andes it occurs on the western slope. The flowers are brown, barred and striped with red-brown. The lip has a large yellow spot in the center with yellow spots around the margin. The species is distinguished by the round internodes at the apical portion of the inflorescence.

Psychopsis papilio (Lindley)
H. G. Jones

This species is known from the West Indies and from Colombia to the Guianas and Brazil. The flowers are brown with a large yellow spot in the center of the lip. The species is distinguished by the flat internodes toward the apical portion of the inflorescence.

PSYGMORCHIS Dodson & Dressler
sig-MOR-kis
Tribe: Cymbidieae
Subtribe: Oncidiinae
Etymology: Gr. *sigma*, C-shaped; *orchis*, orchid; in reference to the fan-shaped growth habit

Psygmorchis is a genus of four species distributed from Mexico to Brazil and Bolivia. The genus is characterized by the fan-shaped plants with the leaves dorsiventrally flattened, imbricating at the base; the lateral inflorescences with flowers produced singly in succession at the apex,

Psygmorchis glossomystax

spurless; the dorsal sepal and petals free; the lateral sepals partially connate; the large four-lobed lip at right angles to the column, with a callus at the base; the column winged; and the two hard pollinia attached to a stipe united to a viscidium.

The plants grow as epiphytes in guava or coffee trees or in trees overhanging rivers at elevations from sea level to 1,400 meters. The plants are very short-lived with some species producing flowers in less than one year from generation of the seed. Cultivation under intermediate conditions on plaques or twigs is possible for relatively short periods.

Psygmorchis glossomystax
(Reichb.f.) Dodson & Dressler

This species is known from Guatemala to Costa Rica and from Venezuela to Bolivia and the Guianas. The species is distinguished by the brushlike margins of the callus and the brown spots at the base of the lip. The other species of this group with a similar callus produce flowers that are completely yellow. The plants are short-

lived, seldom lasting more than three years in their natural habitat.

Psygmorchis pusilla (L.) Dodson & Dressler

This species occurs from Mexico to Bolivia, the West Indies, Brazil and the Guianas. The species is distinguished by the entire, smooth margins of the callus. The petals have a single dark red-brown spot near the base, and the callus area of the lip is spotted with red-brown. The plants live longer than the other species in the genus, reaching five to eight years in their natural habitat.

PTEROSTYLIS R. Br.
terr-oh-STY-lus
Tribe: Diurideae
Subtribe: Pterostylidinae
Etymology: Gr. *pteron*, wing; *stylis*, column or style

More than 150 species mostly found in southern Australia but with a well-developed group in New Zealand and a few species in New Guinea and New Caledonia. Several very distinct groups based on growth habit and floral features can be discerned within the genus. The flowers of these orchids are characteristically hooded, and the labellum is hinged and sensitive to touch. All species are deciduous terrestrials which have small, subterranean tuberoids. Some species reproduce vegetatively and grow in colonies; others occur in loose, scattered groups or as solitary individuals. All species have four separate pollinia. Pollination is by mosquitoes and gnats.

Pterostylis alobula (Hatch) L. B. Moore

An attractive, small, New Zealand species which adapts well to cultivation. Non-flowering plants consist of a rosette of dark green, rounded leaves. Flowers, which are produced from midwinter to early spring, are green-and-white with a red-brown labellum, the tip of which protrudes from below the hood.

Pterostylis banksii Cunn.

A highly attractive species which is representative of a group restricted to New Zealand. It is most distinctive with its channeled, grass-like leaves and large, basically green flowers with distinctive long, brown tails on the sepals. As flowering takes place over summer, plants should be kept moist for longer than Australian members of the genus.

Pterostylis baptistii Fitzg

This vigorous, colony-forming species, found in eastern Australia, produces the largest flowers of any *Pterostylis*. These may

Pterostylis banksii

arise from early autumn to late spring, and a well-grown potful is a most impressive sight. Colors are mainly green-and-white with brown suffusions (which intensify with age) toward the apex of the flower.

Pterostylis boormanii Rupp

Commonly known as "sikh's whiskers" because of the broad, hairy lateral sepals, this distinctive species occurs naturally in southeastern Australia where it grows in relatively dry habitats. Flowers are dark red to reddish brown and are produced on a short, sturdy inflorescence from late spring

Pterostylis cucullata

to midwinter. Plants usually occur as solitary individuals.

Pterostylis concinna R. Br.

Widely distributed in eastern Australia, this vigorous species is popular with growers because of its ease of culture and flowering. The neat, green, white-and-brown flowers appear from May to October. The easily seen labellum has a prominent broad apical notch. An interesting mutant with yellow to orange flowers is grown by enthusiasts.

Pterostylis cucullata R. Br.

The dark reddish brown, velvety flowers of this distinctive species always attract attention when displayed. A native of the southern areas of Australia, this species grows in small colonies under shrubs. Plants are relatively easy to grow but have a longer dormant period than most other species in the genus.

Pterostylis curta R. Br.

A robust, colony-forming species, widely distributed in eastern Australia, which produces its relatively large flowers from July to October. These are mostly green-and-white with brown suffusions. The prominent labellum has a characteristic sideways twist near the apex. An extremely easy and rewarding species to grow.

Pterostylis grandiflora R. Br.

The large, handsome flowers of this Australian species, produced from late autumn to late winter, are translucent white-

Pterostylis boormanii

Pterostylis concinna

Pterostylis curta

Pterostylis grandiflora

Pterostylis longifolia

Rangaeris rhipsalisocia

and-green with rich, red-brown suffusions toward the apex. The broad, flared petals are suggestive of the hood of a cobra. The labellum tapers rapidly and expands again just before the apex. Non-flowering plants of this colony-forming species consist of a rosette of dark green, arrowhead-shaped leaves. A desirable and rewarding species to grow.

Pterostylis longifolia R. Br.

Representative of a distinctive Australian group within the genus, these plants are characterized by grass-like leaves and a raceme of relatively small, green flowers which have a very sensitive, insect-like labellum. Non-flowering plants consist of a rosette of narrow leaves. Although relatively easy to grow, the species is slow to increase in numbers.

Pterostylis plumosa Cady

The yellow hairs which adorn the labellum are one of many distinctive features found on this remarkable Australian orchid. Flowers are translucent green with darker reticulate markings and have a bird-like appearance. Plants usually grow as scattered individuals and are more difficult to grow than other species in the genus.

Pterostylis rufa R. Br.

A native of New South Wales, this distinctive species usually grows in drier forests and flowers from September to December. Flowers, which are produced on sturdy racemes, are usually reddish and are often shiny. Plants usually occur as solitary individuals and must be kept completely dry when dormant.

RANGAERIS (Schltr.) Summerh.
ran-gah-ER-is
Tribe: Vandeae
Subtribe: Aerangidinae
Etymology: A near-anagram of the name *Aerangis* to which the species are allied

This is a genus of five epiphytic or lithophytic plants, all with a monopodial growth habit. Some of the species are widespread in tropical Africa, but others are more localized. The plants are mostly rather small, but *R. amaniensis* may form large clumps of many branching stems. They are related to *Aerangis* but the narrow leaves are folded and the rostellum is two-lobed. The flowers are white with long spurs in short inflorescences.
Plants are easily maintained in cultivation and do best if mounted on a log or bark so that the long spurs on the flowers are well displayed. Intermediate temperatures and high humidity are beneficial, but the plants can be kept quite dry once growth of the new leaf is complete.

R

Pterostylis plumosa

Pterostylis rufa

Rangaeris muscicola (Reichb.f.) Summerh.

This species is widespread throughout Africa, usually epiphytic but sometimes lithophytic at high elevations. The stems are short with a fan of dark green leaves. The inflorescences are axillary and bear six to sixteen flowers with long spurs.

Rangaeris rhipsalisocia (Reichb.f.) Summerh.

This dwarf species has a fan of compressed leaves rather like those of *Podangis*, but plants are easily distinguished from that genus by the much longer inflorescences. The flowers are white with short spurs and do not open fully. The species is widespread but nowhere common in tropical Africa, from Senegal eastward to Uganda.

RENANTHERA Lour.
ren-AN-the-ra
Tribe: Vandeae
Subtribe: Sarcanthinae
Etymology: L. *renes*, kidney; *anthera*, anther

Renanthera comprises about fifteen species distributed from northeast India and China to the Philippines and New Guinea. Generally large vining species, plants of *Renanthera* are reminiscent of *Arachnis* and other scrambling monopodial orchids. The orange to red flowers are usually borne on massive, branched inflorescences and typically have lateral sepals much larger than the other floral segments. The saccate lip has three lobes with the midlobe frequently strongly deflexed. All species have four kidney-shaped pollinia. The genus is closely related to *Renantherella*, which differs by its longer column, and *Ascoglossum*, which differs by its cerise color and long bulbous sac.
Renanthera species should be grown like *Vanda* with bright light, warm temperatures, and copious, even watering. Smaller-growing species can be accommodated in a pot, but larger species are more readily managed in a basket, with

Renanthera bella

Rangaeris muscicola

or without additional support for their vining stems.

Renanthera bella J. J. Wood

This species is endemic to Mount Kinabalu in Sabah, Borneo. It is one of the smaller-growing species and is vegetatively similar to *R. monachica*. The flowers are deep red with darker markings. It is the slowest-growing species in the genus, producing only a few leaves per year.

Renanthera imschootiana Rolfe

Renanthera imschootiana is native to

northeast India and Burma. It is an unusual species of *Renanthera* because of its short, rigid leaves which resemble those of *Trichoglottis brachiata*. The dorsal sepal and petals are pale orange overlaid with fine red spots, and the large lateral sepals are brick-orange. *Renanthera imschootiana* flowers during the summer. The species has been endangered by habitat destruction and collecting for the horticultural trade.

Renanthera monachica Ames

This species is endemic to the Philippines. The small plants produce branched inflorescences in early spring. The yellow

Restrepia antennifera

Restrepia aristulifera

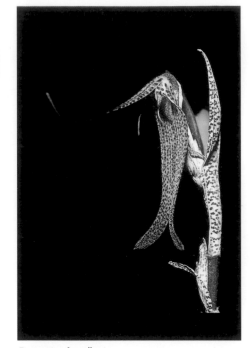

Restrepia chocoënsis

Renanthera monachica

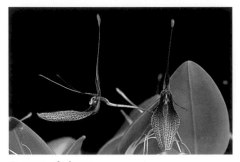

Restrepia dodsonii

flowers are completely covered with red spots, and the floral segments are almost equal to each other so that the flowers lack the exaggerated shape of other *Renanthera* species.

Renanthera storiei Reichb.f.

This species is endemic to the Philippines. One of the larger species, *Renanthera storiei* is considered the finest species in the genus because of its large, deep red flowers produced during the summer in large masses on branched inflorescences. It has been widely used in hybridization with other *Renanthera* species as well as with other genera.

Renanthera storiei

RESTREPIA Humboldt, Bonpland & Kunth
re-STREP-i-a
Tribe: Epidendreae
Subtribe: Pleurothallidinae
Etymology: Named for José Restrepo, an early Colombian botanist

This is a well-defined genus of about 25 ill-defined species found in Central America and the Andes of South America. No close relatives are known. The leaf-stems, covered by a series of compressed, dilated sheaths,

bear oblong or ovate leaves. The inflorescence is single-flowered, the flowers commonly rising up the back surface of the leaf. The dorsal sepal is erect, thinly striped, slender, and clavate. The lateral sepals are connate into a colorful lamina (the synsepal). The petals are membranous at the base, where they usually bear a few, slender appendages, and with the apex caudate and also clavate. The lip is violin-shaped with a pair of hairlike processes above the base. The column is slender and arcuate with four pollinia.

Most of the species are easy to cultivate in moist, intermediate to cool-growing greenhouse conditions. Many can be propagated from cuttings.

Restrepia antennifera Humboldt, Bonpland & Kunth

This large species is widely distributed, extremely variable in color and color pattern, and relatively frequent in the Andes of South America. Many of the color forms have been described as different species, but when the flowers of all these forms become colorless in preserving solutions they are indistinguishable. The flower-stems are long and flexible, bearing the flower near the tips of the leaves. The elliptical synsepal varies in color from yellow to rose and has either stripes or spots of brown to purple. The lip is usually yellow, intensely dotted with purple, and minutely denticulate.

Restrepia aristulifera Garay & Dunsterv.

This species is endemic to westernmost Venezuela and adjacent Colombia. It is very

Restrepia muscifera

Restrepia pelyx

Restrepiella ophiocephala

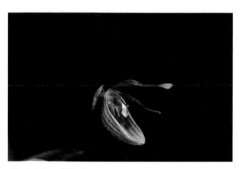

Restrepia schlimii

similar to *R. antennifera*, and best distinguished by much shorter flower-stems that bear the flowers against the back surface of the leaves.

Restrepia chocoënsis Garay

This most distinctive species is rare in the Chocó of Colombia. The leaves are thick, long, and narrow, and the flower is borne on a short stem just above the base. The yellow-orange synsepal, diffusely dotted with dark purple, is split from the apex into two diverging portions.

Restrepia dodsonii Luer

This pretty species is endemic to the western slope of the Andes of central Ecuador. It is distinguished by a small habit, a dark red-spotted synsepal, and a lip with the blade narrowly elliptical and coarsely denticulate and spiculate.

Restrepia muscifera Lindley

Probably a group of indistinguishable look-alikes with several names (e.g. *R. xanthophthalma*) is included in the species-

Restrepia teaguei

complex called *Restrepia muscifera*. Each population seems to vary somewhat in its wide distribution through Central America and adjacent Colombia. The habit is slender with narrow leaves. Small, variously colored flowers are borne by short stems behind the base of the leaf.

Restrepia pelyx Luer & Escobar

This large species is endemic to the Central Cordillera of Colombia. It is distinguished by flowers borne by stems about half as long as the purplish leaf. The purple-spotted synsepal is deeply concave at the

base, where it is suffused with dark purple except for a pair of white patches.

Restrepia schlimii Reichb.f.

This species is endemic to the Eastern Cordillera of Colombia. The habit is rather large with small flowers borne by long stems. The synsepal is broadly concave and yellow, sparsely dotted with red, and the small lip is proportionately broad.

Restrepia subserrata Schltr.

This species, known by several names (e.g. *R. filamentosa*), is frequently encountered in its wide Central American distribution that extends into coastal Colombia and Ecuador. It is distinguished by its small flower with a yellow synsepal, usually with fine, longitudinal, brown stripes. The blade of the dotted lip is denticulate.

Restrepia teaguei Luer

This colorful species is endemic to the eastern slope of the Andes of southern Ecuador. It is distinguished by a small habit and an orange, purple-dotted, elliptical synsepal with an acute apex suffused with red.

RESTREPIELLA Garay & Dunsterv.
re-strep-i-EL-la
Tribe: Epidendreae
Subtribe: Pleurothallidinae
Etymology: Named for the genus *Restrepia*

Only one species, distributed from Mexico to Costa Rica, constitutes this genus.

Restrepiella ophiocephala (Lindley) Garay

This species, most commonly found in Mexico, is characterized by an oblong, leathery leaf borne by a stout leaf-stem. Solitary, fleshy, minutely pubescent, short-stemmed, variously colored flowers are produced from a spathe at the base of the leaf. The lateral sepals are connate into a synsepal similar to the dorsal sepal. The petals are ciliate, and the lip is thick with erect, basal angles. The column is stout and denticulate with four pollinia.

RHYNCHOLAELIA Schltr.
rink-oh-LYE-lee-ah
or rink-oh-LEE-lee-ah
Tribe: Epidendreae
Subtribe: Laeliinae
Etymology: Gr. *rhynchos*, snout; *Laelia*, orchid genus; referring to the rostrate apex of the fruit

This is a genus of two species distributed from Mexico to Honduras. The genus is characterized by the presence of stemlike, jointed pseudobulbs with a single, thick, apical, gray-green leaf; the inflorescence of one flower produced from a spathelike sheath at the apex of the pseudobulb; the pale green sepals and petals with a white lip; the lip surrounding the column and united to its base; and the eight hard, flattened pollinia with prominent caudicles. The plants grow as epiphytes in seasonally dry, lower montane forests. They are easily cultivated under intermediate conditions along with members of the genus *Cattleya*.

Rhyncholaelia digbyana (Lindley) Schltr.

This species is known from Mexico to Honduras. The flowers are very large, reaching 15 centimeters in diameter. The sepals and petals are green and the lip is lighter green with a dark green, lumplike callus on the disc. The margin of the lip is deeply lacerate-fimbriate.

Rhyncholaelia glauca (Lindley) Schltr.

This species occurs from Mexico to

Rhyncholaelia digbyana

Honduras. The flowers reach ten centimeters in diameter. The sepals and petals are green, and the lip is greenish white with red spots in the throat. The margin of the lip is entire.

RHYNCHOPHREATIA Schltr.
rink-o-FREET-ee-ah
Tribe: Epidendreae
Subtribe: Thelasiinae
Etymology: Gr. *rhynchos*, a beak or snout; *Phreatia*, another genus

A small genus comprising about eight species of epiphytes which are distributed in Australia, New Guinea, Solomon Islands, Indonesia, and New Caledonia. Plants grow monopodially with the leaves arising in opposite rows and overlapping at the base. The small, white flowers are not showy. All species have eight pollinia arranged in two groups of four.
Plants are easily grown if given warm to hot, humid conditions, free air movement and bright light. They are best mounted on a slab; if grown in a pot they require excellent drainage.

Rhynchophreatia micrantha (A. Richard) Hallé

An unusual epiphyte from Australia and New Guinea which can be recognized by its distinctive, fan-like growths, in which the base is thickened and fleshy, the leaves arising alternately in a single plane. Each plant consists of a single growth which

Rhyncholaelia glauca

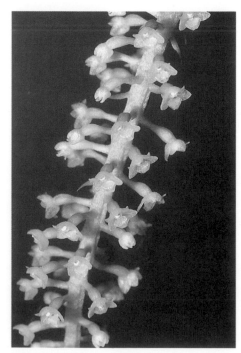

Rhynchophreatia micrantha

Rhynchostylis coelestis

Rhynchostylis gigantea

enlarges each year and is supported by the basal mat of fine, wiry roots. Small, white, cupped flowers are crowded on a slender, foxtail-like raceme which emerges from the upper leaf axils. Plants are very easy to grow but are extremely sensitive to periods of cold.

RHYNCHOSTYLIS Blume
rink-oh-STY-lis
Tribe: Vandeae
Subtribe: Sarcanthinae
Etymology: *rhynchos*, beak; *stylis*, column

Rhynchostylis comprises three species distributed from India to Borneo and the Philippines. The genus is closely related to *Vanda* and differs by its one-lobed lip. The name refers to the very broad, fleshy column. The flowers are borne in dense racemes and are noted for their strong, spicy fragrance. Although the plants lack pseudobulbs, the leathery leaves are drought-resistant.
Rhynchostylis will thrive if given consistently warm temperatures, uniform moisture, and bright but indirect light. The plants can be grown in pots but are better when grown in baskets because of their extremely fleshy roots.

Rhynchostylis coelestis Reichb.f.

Native to Indochina, *Rhynchostylis coelestis* is prized for its white flowers marked with rich violet. It differs from other species by

Robiquetia wassellii

its upright inflorescences. The flowers are unusual in having an abruptly upturned lip and a downwardly bent spur. The summer flowers are sweetly fragrant.

Rhynchostylis gigantea (Lindley) Ridley

Rhynchostylis gigantea is native to Burma, Indochina, China, Malaya, Borneo, and the Philippines. The flowers are normally white with purple-spotted segments and a purple lip. A pure white-flowered form is known as var. *petotiana*. At the other extreme, orchid breeders have selected a richly colored strain with completely purple flowers. The species is easily recognized even when not in bloom by its broad leathery leaves striped by lighter green veins.

ROBIQUETIA Gaudich.
roe-bi-KET-ee-ah
Tribe: Vandeae
Subtribe: Sarcanthinae
Etymology: Honoring M. Pierre Robiquet

Robiquetia is a genus of about 40 epiphytic species distributed throughout the Asian tropics from Sri Lanka and India to the islands of the Pacific. Species of *Robiquetia* have previously been included in a broadly

Rodriguezia bracheata

Rodriguezia decora

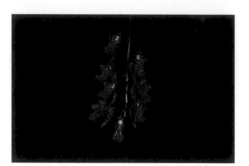

Rodriguezia lanceolata

Robiquetia wassellii Dockr.

This species is endemic to tropical Australia. It is remarkable in the genus for its deep green flowers with petals that appear black. The long nectar spurs are contrastingly bright yellow. Rarely cultivated, *Robiquetia wassellii* is more a curiosity for its dark color.

RODRIGUEZIA Ruíz & Pavón
rod-ri-GEEZ-ee-ah
Tribe: Cymbidieae
Subtribe: Oncidiinae
Etymology: In honor of Don Manuelo Rodríguez, Spanish botanist

Rodriguezia is a genus of 40 species distributed throughout tropical America. The genus is characterized by the presence of unifoliate or bifoliate pseudobulbs of a single internode usually subtended by distichous leaflike sheaths; the inflorescence produced from the axils of the sheaths; the lateral sepals connate, sometimes appearing as a spur; the spur of the lip solid, extending downward from the base of the lip; the lip not saccate; the slender column with a subdorsal anther and forward-projecting arms on each side of the terminal stigma; and the two hard pollinia attached to a stipe united to a stigma. All the species are epiphytes and occur in wet cloud forest regions from sea level to 1,500 meters, often growing in guava trees. The plants are easily cultivated under intermediate conditions. They are best managed on plaques with abundant water throughout the year.

Rodriguezia batemannii (left)

defined *Saccolabium*. A taxonomically difficult genus, *Robiquetia* is most closely related to *Malleola*, but the plants differ by their linear stipes which are broadened in *Malleola*. *Robiquetia* is variable in all features, and flowers range from stark white to deep red, as well as yellow variously marked with brown. Plant size varies from miniature vinelike plants to very large epiphytes. All species have long nectar spurs, and many species produce densely flowered racemes that appear clublike. *Robiquetia* plants should be grown like other *Vanda* relatives, provided with warm temperatures, even watering, and bright but not direct light. Unlike many other large Asian monopodials, *Robiquetia* plants do

not like to dry out at the roots for extended periods. They may be grown in pots or baskets but should be provided with some moisture-retaining compost.

Robiquetia spathulata (Blume) J. J. Smith

A widespread Asian species, *Robiquetia spathulata* is known from northeast India to Borneo. Long, densely flowered, pendent racemes in the summer bear flowers that are heavily marked with brown except for their white centers and spurs. Because of the relatively large plant size and pendent inflorescences, *Robiquetia spathulata* should be suspended to show the flowers to best advantage.

Rodriguezia leeana

Rodriguezia batemannii Poepp. & Endl.

This species occurs from Venezuela to Peru and Bolivia at the base of the Andes. The leaves are narrowly elongate and rigidly leathery. The flowers reach seven centimeters in diameter. The sepals and petals are pinkish white densely flecked with red. The lip is white flushed with rose and speckled with red. The lip is much broader toward the apex than at the base.

Rodriguezia bracheata (Vell.) Hoehne

This species occurs in southeastern Brazil. It was previously known as *R. fragrans*. The leaves are thick and elongate. The flowers are white with a yellow callus and reach a diameter of five centimeters. The callus of the lip has two erect keels.

Rodriguezia decora (Lem.) Reichb.f.

Rodriguezia decora occurs in southeastern Brazil. The pseudobulbs are separated on the elongate, slender rhizome by up to 30 centimeters. The flowers reach 3.5 centimeters in diameter. The sepals and petals are yellow-white with dark red-purple spots inside. The lip is white with red keels on the disc located on a long, oblong claw.

Rodriguezia lanceolata Ruíz & Pavón

This species occurs in Panama, the West Indies, and from Venezuela to Bolivia, Brazil, and Guyana. The leaves are leathery, narrow, sharp at the apex, and V-shaped in cross-section. The flowers reach 2.5 centimeters in diameter and are rose-red with the base of the lip white.

Rodriguezia leeana Reichb.f.

This species occurs from Venezuela to Ecuador and Brazil at lower elevations. The leaves are leathery, elongate, sharp at the apex and are V-shaped in cross-section. The flowers reach four centimeters in diameter and are yellow-white flushed with red-brown.

Rodriguezia venusta

Rossioglossum grande

Rodriguezia venusta (Lindley) Reichb.f.

This species occurs in Brazil. The leaves are elongate, sharp at the apex and V-shaped in cross-section. The flowers reach three centimeters in diameter and are white with a golden yellow disc on the lip. The callus has eight to ten keels.

ROSSIOGLOSSUM Garay & Kennedy
ross-ee-oh-GLOS-um
Tribe: Cymbidieae
Subtribe: Oncidiinae

Etymology: After Ross, a collector for Barker; Gr. *glossa*, tongue

This is a genus of six species native from Mexico to Panama. The genus is distinguished by the roundish, compressed pseudobulbs of a single internode with two or three thick leaves at the apex; the erect inflorescences with four to eleven large flowers produced from the sheaths at the base of the pseudobulb; the sepals and petals spreading, yellow, barred with red-brown; the fiddle-shaped, yellow lip with a brown margin; the column spreading from the lip; and the two hard pollinia on a stipe with a small, round viscidium.

The species are epiphytic in wet cloud

Rossioglossum insleayi

Sarcochilus fitzgeraldii

forests from 600 to 1,500 meters. They can be cultivated under intermediate conditions with cool night temperatures in pots with well-drained media. They benefit from a short rest period after completion of new growths.

Rossioglossum grande (Lindley) Garay & Kennedy

This species occurs from Mexico to Honduras. The flowers reach thirteen centimeters in diameter. The sepals are yellow with bars of red-brown while the larger petals are bright yellow with the lower half red-brown. The lip is yellow-white, sometimes flecked with red-brown.

Rossioglossum insleayi (Barker ex Lindley) Garay & Kennedy

This species occurs in Mexico. The flowers reach seven centimeters in diameter and are very similar in shape and color to those of *R. grande*. The sepals and petals are pale yellow thickly blotched with red-brown, and the lip is yellow with a row of red-brown spots around the margin.

SARCOCHILUS R. Br.

sar-ko-KYE-lus
Tribe: Vandeae
Subtribe: Sarcanthinae
Etymology: Gr. *sarcos*, fleshy; *cheilos*, lip

About fourteen species are distributed in tropical, subtropical, and temperate regions. All but one are endemic to Australia. Most species are small epiphytes; however, three robust species grow on rocks, boulders, and cliff faces and may grow in extensive clumps. Growth habit is monopodial, and the slender racemes carry colorful, widely opening flowers which are long-lasting and often fragrant. All species have four pollinia attached via a narrow stalk to a viscidium. Small-growing species are best mounted on small slabs whereas the robust lithophytes should be grown in pots, slat baskets or saucers in a potting mixture of coarse materials. Bright light, humidity, and free air movement are essential. Some species are capable of withstanding cold periods to 3°C.

Sarcochilus falcatus

Sarcochilus hartmannii

Sarcochilus falcatus R. Br.

With its prominent white, orange-blossom-scented flowers and neat growth habit, this species is a firm favorite with orchid growers in its native country of Australia. It is a common species which grows on trees in moist forests, often where there is an abundance of air movement. Plants are best grown attached to a slab of weathered hardwood or cork. Flowering occurs from early winter to mid-spring.

Sarcochilus fitzgeraldii F. Muell.

This lithophyte forms extensive spreading clumps on boulders and cliff faces in moist, shady situations. Flowering clumps are very attractive with the long, slender, arching

racemes bearing showy white, crimson-centered flowers during the last two months of spring. Very easily grown in a shallow pot or saucer containing coarse potting material. Best in subdued light with high humidity and free air movement.

Sarcochilus hartmannii F. Muell.

One of the most popular Australian orchids which is valued for its ease of cultivation and free-flowering habit. Plants have proved to be long-lived and are ideal for specimen culture. In nature this species grows on large boulders, cliffs, and escarpments, frequently in situations exposed to considerable hot sun for much of the year. Plants form extensive clumps and are showy when in flower. Best growth is attained in

Satyrium carneum

saucers or shallow pots of coarse potting materials. Flowering occurs throughout the spring months.

SATYRIUM Sw.
sa-TEER-ee-um
Tribe: Diseae
Subtribe: Satyriinae
Etymology: Gr. *satyrion*, man orchid

This genus of over 100 terrestrial orchids occurs mainly in Africa, but five species are known in Madagascar and two in Asia. Some plants have leafy stems terminating in the inflorescence, and others have one or a pair of leaves on a separate sterile shoot adjacent to the flowering stem. The flowers are non-resupinate with the lip on the upper side of the flower. They are easily distinguished from all other genera by the pair of spurs at the base of the lip. The flowers come in a wide variety of colors, white, pink, red, yellow, orange, green, and purplish. Many species have proved rather difficult to cultivate, and the tubers are frequently lost through poor management during the dry season. They all need plenty of water and feeding while in active growth and dryness while dormant. Most species grow naturally in full sun. Temperatures required will vary according to the climate of the origin of each species.

Satyrium carneum R. Br.

This handsome species is endemic to the southwestern parts of the Cape Province of South Africa where it is now rare. The twin leaves are large and fleshy and pressed flat on the ground. The inflorescence arises

Satyrium coriifolium

between the leaves and bears pink flowers which are paler within, each supported by a large, attractive, green-veined bract.

Satyrium coriifolium Sw.

These robust plants are endemic to the Cape Province of South Africa where the species is widespread. Each plant has two to four leaves which are more or less upright and surround the base of the flowering stem. The flowers are rather large, yellow or orange often flushed with red, and borne on a purplish stem in a dense raceme.

Satyrium erectum Lindley

These robust plants are endemic in the south and southwest of the Cape Province of South Africa. They have two large leaves pressed flat on the ground between which the inflorescence arises. The flowers are pale to dark pink with darker spots on the petals and lip.

Satyrium pumilum Thunb.

The curious plants of this species form a rosette-like growth only just above the ground in a few places in the southwestern

Satyrium erectum

Satyrium pumilum

Cape Province of South Africa. There are three to five leaves surmounted by the large green and purplish flowers on a very short stem. The flower arrangement, coloration, and purplish spots and streaks create a resemblance to an asclepiad flower.

SCAPHOSEPALUM Pfitzer
skaf-o-SE-pa-lum
Tribe: Epidendreae
Subtribe: Pleurothallidinae
Etymology: Gr. *scaphosepalos*, with boatlike sepals

The 33 species of this genus are distributed through Central America, northern South America, and the Andes. They are characterized by thick to thin leaves that are often petiolate and borne by short leaf-stems. The inflorescence arises from low on the stem and produces a loose, often flexuous, successively flowered raceme. The flowers are non-resupinate. The lateral sepals are connate and variously caudate. A more or less triangular, thickened pad or cushion occupies the inner surface of both lateral sepals at the apex. The small, more or less violin-shaped lip is inconspicuous in the depths of the flower.
The species are easy to cultivate in moist, intermediate to cool-growing greenhouse conditions.

Scaphosepalum antenniferum
Rolfe

This remarkable species, locally but widely distributed in the Andes, is one of the giants of the genus. From the base of the stem of the broad, leathery, petiolate leaf the stout, erect, coarsely warty flower-stem arises. A

Scaphosepalum breve

continuously flowering, double-ranked raceme of grotesque flowers develops. The cushions are ovate and parallel, and the short tails of the lateral sepals curve downward like the fangs of a snake.

Scaphosepalum breve (Reichb.f.)
Rolfe

This species, variable and frequent across northern South America and the Andes, has been misidentified as *S. verrucosum*. The true *S. verrucosum* has been called *S. ochthodes*, a later name. *Scaphosepalum breve* is distinguished by the slender but

rough and rigid flower-stem. The successive, variously spotted flowers create a flexuous raceme that eventually exceeds the leaves in length. The cushions are triangular, and the tails of the sepals are slender.

Scaphosepalum gibberosum
(Reichb.f.) Rolfe

This narrow-leaved species, native to the Western Cordillera of Colombia, is noted for the transverse, narrowly triangular cushions from which long, straight sepaline tails stretch out from either side of the flower.

The flowers are produced over a long period in a loose, flexuous, continually lengthening and bending raceme borne by a rough stem.

Scaphosepalum grande Kränzlin

This species from the Western Cordillera of Colombia is distinguished by the broad, petiolate leaf and a smooth, erect flower-stem. The conspicuous floral bracts alternate in the raceme. The sepaline cushions are broad and transverse, creating a more or less arcuate, white band across the top of the flower, which is purple in the center.

Scaphosepalum microdactylum Rolfe

This small species is variable, frequent, and widely distributed in Central America and the western coastal areas of Colombia and Ecuador. The smooth flower-stem supports the continually lengthening raceme of alternating floral bracts. The middle sepal is conspicuously thickened, and the ovate cushions of the minutely tailed lateral sepals are sometimes not well developed.

Scaphosepalum ovulare Luer

Endemic to lowland eastern Ecuador, this little species produces tailless, ovoid flowers in a descending raceme. The sepals barely part, never exposing the cushions within the unopened flower, which may be either purple or yellow.

Scaphosepalum rapax Luer

Also endemic to lowland eastern Ecuador, this little species produces in a descending raceme a purple-spotted, gaping flower with narrow cushions and short, decurving, fanglike sepaline tails.

Scaphosepalum verrucosum (Reichb.f.) Pfitzer

Commonly called by its later name (*S. ochthodes*), this species is frequent in the Eastern Cordillera of Colombia. From the base of the thick, leathery leaf a tall, erect, warty stem produces a distantly flowered raceme of small, yellowish green flowers with ovoid cushions and very short sepaline tails.

SCAPHYGLOTTIS Poeppig & Endl.
scaf-ee-GLOT-is
Tribe: Epidendreae
Subtribe: Laeliinae
Etymology: Gr. *scaphe*, bowl; *glotta*, tongue; in reference to the concave lip

Scaphyglottis is a genus of 82 species found throughout much of tropical America. The genus is characterized by the slender canelike pseudobulbs superimposed at the

Scaphosepalum verrucosum

apex of previous pseudobulbs with two or three flat, often grasslike leaves at the apex; the subsessile one-flowered to shortly paniculate inflorescences terminal; the dorsal sepal and petals free, spreading; the lateral sepals often united with the column-foot forming a mentum; the lip three-lobed to obovate, obtuse to apiculate at the apex, attached to the apex of the column-foot, with or without a low callus; the column sometimes winged; and the four to six hard pollinia with caudicles (a few species have a viscidium).

The species are epiphytes or terrestrials on steep embankments and occur in wet tropical forest at elevations from sea level to 1,800 meters. The plants are easily cultivated under intermediate conditions on plaques or in pots.

Scaphosepalum gibberosum

Scaphyglottis amethystina (Reichb.f.) Schltr.

This species occurs from Guatemala to Panama and from Venezuela to Bolivia on the east side of the Andes. The leaves are narrow and thin, and the flowers reach one centimeter in diameter. The inflorescence is short with two or three flowers produced at a time. The flowers are pink, and the column is winged on each side.

Scaphosepalum microdactylum

Schoenorchis gemmata

Scaphosepalum rapax

SCHOENORCHIS Blume
shoan-OR-kis
Tribe: Vandeae
Subtribe: Sarcanthinae
Etymology: Gr. *schoenos*, reed; *orchis*, orchid

Schoenorchis comprises about 25 epiphytic and (rarely) lithophytic species distributed from Sri Lanka and India to the islands of the Pacific. Species of *Schoenorchis* have been previously included in a broadly defined *Saccolabium*. Their closest relative is probably the monotypic Indian *Xenikophyton*, which differs by having four globose pollinia, unlike the two cleft

Scaphyglottis amethystina

pollinia of *Schoenorchis*. The generic name refers to the terete leaves of the original species, *S. juncifolia*. A second group of

species bears more typical flattened leaves. All *Schoenorchis* plants have a large bifid rostellum, saccate spurs, and usually densely flowered, often secund racemes. Flowers range from white to purple. Most species of *Schoenorchis* are true miniatures and are shown to their best advantage when mounted on a slab. With care, however, they can be grown in small pots. All species prefer intermediate to warm temperatures and medium bright light levels. Terete-leaved species should be given even watering throughout the year. Broader-leaved species should be grown very dry with no water allowed to remain at the roots.

Schoenorchis densiflora Schltr.

This miniature species is native to New Guinea and Australia. It is very closely related to the widespread *S. micrantha* and may be conspecific. The tiny white flowers are secund, borne to one side like the bristles of a toothbrush. Plants freely produce lateral shoots, and plants of *Schoenorchis densiflora* quickly form attractive miniature clumps of needle-like foliage punctuated with multiple inflorescences. Flowers are produced in the summer.

Schoenorchis gemmata (Lindley) J. J. Smith

Schoenorchis gemmata is a miniature epiphyte native from Nepal and China through Indochina. The much-branched sprays of tiny flowers are white variously suffused with pink. The leaves, though linear, are not terete or needle-like. Flowering is in late summer.

SCHOMBURGKIA Lindley

schom-BURK-ee-ah
Tribe: Epidendreae
Subtribe: Laeliinae
Etymology: In honor of Richard
Schomburgk, German botanist, who
explored British Guyana during the
nineteenth century

This is a genus of seventeen species
distributed from Mexico to Brazil and
Bolivia. The genus is characterized by the
large plants with swollen, ribbed,
pseudobulbous stems of several internodes
and two or three flat, apical leaves; the
apical inflorescence elongate with a dense
cluster of several large flowers at the apex;
the sepals and petals free, spreading; the lip
connected to the column-foot; the column
concave on the underside, very narrowly
winged; and the eight hard pollinia with
caudicles united to a sticky viscidium.
The plants grow as epiphytes or lithophytes
on large boulders in the river in wet forest

Schomburgkia rosea

at elevations from 100 to 1,000 meters.
Members of this genus can be cultivated in
pots under intermediate conditions.

Schomburgkia rosea Linden ex Lindley

This species occurs in Venezuela and
Colombia. The floral bracts are five
centimeters in length and are pale pink. The
flowers reach four centimeters in diameter.
The sepals and petals are spreading and
evenly purple-red, and the lip is pink with
yellow keels on the disc.

Schomburgkia splendida Lindley

This species occurs in southwestern
Colombia and northwestern Ecuador. The
floral bracts are large, to nine centimeters in
length and are dark pink in color. The
flowers reach ten centimeters in diameter.
The sepals and petals are spreading,
undulate on the margin, and dark purple-
red. The lip is pale pink to dark rose with
yellow keels on the disc.

Schomburgkia superbiens (Lindley) Rolfe

This species is known from Mexico to
Nicaragua. The floral bracts are five
centimeters long and are brown. The
flowers are densely arranged on the apex of
the inflorescence. The flowers reach twelve
centimeters in diameter. The sepals and
petals are red-violet, and the lip has a red-
violet apical lobe with five yellow lamellae
on the disc.

SCUTICARIA Lindley

skoo-ti-KARE-ee-ah
Tribe: Maxillarieae
Subtribe: Maxillariinae
Etymology: L. *scutia*, a lash

Five species are currently known in
Venezuela, the Guianas, and Brazil. The
short pseudobulbs bear a long, cylindrical
leaf. Few-flowered racemes arise from the
base of the pseudobulb. About half the
species have a pendent growth habit
whereas the other half grow erect. All
species have four pollinia.
These grow best mounted on slabs of tree-
fern fiber or cork bark. Provide bright light,
intermediate temperatures (20°–25°C
during the day, 15°–20°C at night) and
plenty of water during periods of active
growth. Water sparingly after flowering.

Scuticaria steelei Lindley

This showy pendent species, found in
Colombia, Venezuela, the Guianas, and
Brazil, blooms in cultivation throughout the
year but especially from April to July.
Flowers are pale yellow spotted maroon
with a dark yellow callus at the base of the
lip.
Scuticaria hadwenii is another species
commonly found in cultivation.

Schomburgkia splendida

Schomburgkia superbiens

Sedirea japonica

Scuticaria steelei

Seidenfadenia mitrata

SEDIREA Garay & Sweet
se-DEER-ee-ah
Tribe: Vandeae
Subtribe: Sarcanthinae
Etymology: Anagram of *Aerides*

A genus of two epiphytic species native to China, Japan, and Korea. The genus was established for a species previously included in *Aerides; Sedirea* is *Aerides* spelled backwards. The flowers have a long nectar spur but lack a prominent column-foot and other technical features of *Aerides*. The fleshy flowers are reminiscent of *Hygrochilus* and are easily recognized by their forward-projecting petals, giving the flower a half-open appearance.

Plants may be grown in small pots or baskets with a compost that retains some moisture. Although they bear leathery leaves, plants of *Sedirea* lack pseudobulbs and appear to be easily prone to desiccation

in cultivation. Plants should be given medium bright light levels and intermediate temperatures.

Sedirea japonica (Linden & Reichb.f.) Garay & Sweet

This species is limited to Korea, Japan, and the Ryukyu Islands. The greenish white flowers are highlighted by a variously marked rose-colored lip. Although it is a miniature plant, the flowers are proportionately large and are prized for their strong, sweet fragrance during the summer.

SEIDENFADENIA Garay
si-den-fah-DEEN-ee-ah
Tribe: Vandeae
Subtribe: Sarcanthinae
Etymology: Honoring Dr. Gunnar Seidenfaden

This monotypic genus is native to Burma and Thailand. *Seidenfadenia* was previously placed in *Aerides* but differs from it by its semiterete leaves as well as technical characters of the flowers.

Seidenfadenia is adapted to an exposed habitat and a seasonally dry, monsoonal climate. Plants should be given bright light. As there are no pseudobulbs, most food and water storage takes place in the plant's massive, fleshy root system. Water abundantly when in active growth, and keep plants on the dry side when not actively growing.

Seidenfadenia mitrata (Reichb.f.) Garay

Long known as *Aerides mitrata*,

Seidenfadenia mitrata is prized for its white flowers with starkly contrasting cerise lip and strong candy fragrance. Some clones have sepals and petals suffused with varying amounts of purple. The springtime inflorescences are erect and rise above the pendent leaves. A distinctive feature of the flowers is the bilaterally flattened nectar spur, unlike that of related genera.

SERAPIAS L.
sir-RAP-ee-us
Tribe: Orchideae
Subtribe: Orchidinae
Etymology: Gr. *Serapis*, from Osirapis, an Egyptian deity

Serapias is essentially a Mediterranean genus, but several species have outposts farther north: *S. lingua* appears in central France, *S. vomeracea* in southern Swiss valleys, *S. cordigera* in Brittany, and, most surprisingly, *S. parviflora* has turned up in southern Britain.

In recent years, the measurement of "critical dimensions" of flower parts with detailed statistical analysis has led to a better understanding of the genus, which is now considered to comprise ten species.

As with *Ophrys* and *Orchis* there are tubers below ground (sometimes more than two). *Serapias* leaves are narrow, channeled and usually shiny. Flowers, comparatively few in number, are carried in a loose raceme. Flower structure is quite distinct with sepals and petals connivent to form a tubular galea. The labellum projects from this to form a "tongue."

Serapias plants are easy to grow in the alpine house using the basic "*Ophrys*" mix.

Serapias lingua

Sievekingia reichenbachiana

Serapias cordigera

They can also be established in a raised bed or frame provided it can be kept relatively frost-free.

Serapias cordigera L.

This species has between five and eight channeled leaves and stems from fifteen to 45 centimeters tall. The spike is fairly dense with between four and ten flowers, 20–35 millimeters long. Flower-bracts are usually shorter than the helmet but are colored the same violet-pink and veined longitudinally in deep maroon. The lip is heart-shaped, hairy, and colored deep maroon with fine blackish streaks. The two bosses at the labellum base are black, and the lateral lobes are partially hidden by the helmet. In the wild *Serapias cordigera* grows in both wet and dry grasslands, olive groves, and light woodland. It is found mainly in the western and central Mediterranean countries as well as north Africa, flowering in April and May. A well-established pan of *Serapias cordigera* can look magnificent, with numerous spikes of flowers persisting for a month or more.

Serapias lingua L.

This species has from two to five tubers, one of which is sessile, the others on short stolons enabling plants to multiply comparatively quickly. Plants are 10–30 centimeters tall with between two and eight well-spaced flowers in the spike. Each stands out nearly horizontal from the stem with the lip pointing vertically downward. Flower-bracts are shorter than or equal to the helmet in length and reddish violet or green in color. Sepals and petals forming the helmet are light pink or purple with distinct parallel veining in dark red or purple. There is a single dark boss at the lip base. The lip itself can vary in color from yellowish through light violet-pink to dark magenta. Partial albino forms with yellow lips are not rare. Flowers appear from April to May in damp meadows, marshlands, dune slacks, olive groves, and on drier hillsides in scrub. The distribution is mainly west and central Mediterranean, as far east as mainland Greece and Crete and north to the Dordogne in France.

SIEVEKINGIA Reichb.f.

siv-KING-ee-ah
Tribe: Cymbidieae
Subtribe: Stanhopeinae
Etymology: In honor of Dr. Sieveking, mayor of Hamburg, Germany, during the nineteenth century

Sievekingia is a genus of fifteen species distributed from Costa Rica to Bolivia. The genus is characterized by the ovoid pseudobulbs of a single internode with a single, petiolate, heavily-veined leaf at the apex; the sheaths surrounding the base of the pseudobulb nonfoliaceous; the pendent inflorescence with a dense cluster of flowers at the apex; the sepals and petals free, spreading; the lip simple to three-lobed with a fimbriate callus at the base or with the margin of the lip deeply lacerate-fimbriate; and the two hard pollinia attached to an elongate stipe connected to a round viscidium.
Plants of this genus grow as epiphytes in wet forest at elevations from 400 to 1,200 meters. The plants are best cultivated in baskets or on plaques, to allow the pendent inflorescences to emerge. They should receive abundant water throughout the year.

Sievekingia reichenbachiana
(Lehmann) Reichb.f.

This species occurs in southwestern Colombia and western Ecuador. The flowers reach a diameter of five centimeters. The sepals and petals are yellow, and the lip is yellow marked with orange and red-brown on the callus and base of the lip. The margins of the petals and the lobes of the lip are deeply lacerate-fimbriate.

Sigmatostalix minax

Sievekingia suavis Reichb.f.

This species occurs from Nicaragua to Colombia. The flowers reach a diameter of 2.5 centimeters. The sepals are yellow-orange, the petals orange, and the lip orange with reddish purple spots. The margins of all the floral segments are entire. The callus on the disk has three erect keels with the central keel prolonged.

SIGMATOSTALIX Reichb.f.
sig-mat-oh-STAY-lix
Tribe: Cymbidieae
Subtribe: Oncidiinae
Etymology: Gr. *sigma*, C-shaped; *stalix*, stake; in reference to the C-shaped, arcuate column

This is a genus of 35 species distributed from Mexico to Brazil. The genus is characterized by the presence of unifoliate or bifoliate pseudobulbs of a single internode subtended by distichous leaflike sheaths; the inflorescence paniculate with the branches short, each with single flowers produced in succession at coordinated time intervals, produced from the axils of the sheaths; the flowers without a spur; the sepals and petals free; the lip either entire or deeply lobed with slender projections; the slender column without a foot; and the two hard pollinia attached to a stipe connected to a viscidium.

The plants are epiphytes in very wet forest at elevations from 500 to 2,000 meters. The plants are easily cultivated under intermediate conditions in pots or on plaques.

Sievekingia suavis

Sigmatostalix graminea (Poeppig & Endl.) Reichb.f.

This species is known from Colombia to Bolivia on the eastern slope of the Andes. The pseudobulbs form dense mats, and the leaves are long and narrow. The inflorescence is shorter than the leaves, and the flowers are yellow, often with a longitudinal red-brown spot on each petal. In the middle of each petal a hooklike spur projects. The flowers reach eight millimeters in diameter.

Sigmatostalix minax Kränzlin

This species occurs in eastern Colombia and Ecuador. The pseudobulbs are clustered but not mat-forming. The inflorescence is elongate, and the flowers reach two centimeters in diameter. The sepals and petals are yellow to yellow-brown, and the lip is yellow. The lip is three-lobed with the lateral lobes spreading but curved inward toward the apices; the midlobe is elongate and oblong, with a large, protruding callus on the disc.

Sigmatostalix picta Reichb.f.

This species occurs in western Ecuador. The pseudobulbs are clustered but not mat-forming. The inflorescence is longer than the leaves, and the flowers reach 1.5 centimeters in diameter. The sepals and petals are yellow blotched with red-brown. The lip is red-brown with a yellow apex.

SMITINANDIA Holttum
smi-tin-AND-ee-ah
Tribe: Vandeae
Subtribe: Sarcanthinae
Etymology: Honoring Mr. Tem Smitinand

The genus *Smitinandia* consists of three epiphytic species distributed from the northwest Himalayas to Sulawesi. Previously placed in *Saccolabium* and *Ascocentrum*, *Smitinandia* differs by its short, saccate lip occluded by a backward-projecting callus and four pollinia. All species have small, fleshy flowers produced along a densely flowered raceme.
As they lack pseudobulbs, *Smitinandia* plants should be kept evenly moist. They prefer intermediate to warm temperatures and medium bright light levels. Small pots with a medium-grade epiphyte compost may be used, or the plants may be grown in small baskets. All species are easy to grow and readily produce lateral branches.

Smitinandia micrantha (Lindley) Holttum

Smitinandia micrantha is native from the northwest Himalayas to Indochina and Malaya. The pendent, fleshy racemes bear numerous small white flowers highlighted

Smitinandia micrantha

by a pink lip. Flower color is variable, from pure white to sepals and petals suffused with light pink. The flowers are long-lasting, and each inflorescence remains in flower for more than a month.

SOBENNIKOFFIA Schltr.
so-ben-i-KOF-ee-ah
Tribe: Vandcac
Subtribe: Angraecinae
Etymology: Named in honor of Schlechter's wife whose maiden name was Sobennikoff

This is a small genus of three species endemic to Madagascar. The plants are all robust, monopodial epiphytes, rarely terrestrial. They grow quite tall in time and have two rows of strap-shaped leaves. The inflorescences are axillary with five to fifteen white flowers. They can be distinguished from species of *Angraecum* by the three-lobed lip.
The plants require humid conditions under moderate shade and warm temperatures. They should be kept moist at the roots while a new leaf is developing and then somewhat drier until growth begins again.

Sobennikoffia robusta

Sobralia ciliata

Sobennikoffia robusta (Schltr.) Schltr.

This species comes from the western parts of Madagascar where there is a prolonged dry season. The plants are large and easy to grow. They usually bear several inflorescences at once with ten to fifteen flowers each. The flowers are large and showy with recurved sepals and petals, greenish on the outer surface. *Sobennikoffia humbertiana* has smaller flowers, and in *S. fournieriana* they are larger.

SOBRALIA Ruíz & Pavón
so-BRAL-ee-ah
Tribe: Arethuseae
Subtribe: Sobraliinae
Etymology: In honor of Dr. Francisco Sobral, Spanish botanist during the latter part of the eighteenth century.

Sobralia is a genus of 95 species distributed throughout tropical America. The genus is characterized by the canelike stems with thin, heavily veined leaves at the nodes; the inflorescence terminal or lateral from the axils of the upper leaves; the free sepals and petals; the large lip connected at the base of the column; the column slender, narrowly winged, with a falcate projection on each side of the operculate anther; and the soft pollinia.
These plants are epiphytes or terrestrials growing on embankments in wet forest from sea level to 2,000 meters elevation. The plants are easily cultivated in pots under intermediate conditions. They seem to flower best when the roots are cramped in smallish pots.

Sobralia candida (Poeppig & Endl.) Reichb.f.

This species occurs from Venezuela to Bolivia. The stems reach 40 centimeters long, and the leaves are narrow and grasslike. The inflorescence is apical and is formed of a bent, conelike structure with one flower produced at a time. The flowers reach three centimeters in diameter. The sepals and petals are straw colored with the lip yellowish brown marked with red on the disc.

Sobralia ciliata (Presl) C. Schweinf. ex Foldats

This species is known from Venezuela to Bolivia. The stems reach 2 meters tall, and the leaves are heavily veined. The inflorescence is lateral, produced opposite the nodes of the stem, and has several, evenly spaced flowers that open in succession with as many as two open at a time. The flowers reach four centimeters in

diameter. The flowers are bright magenta-red with a yellow callus.

Sobralia decora Batem.

This species is distributed from Mexico to Colombia. The stems are elongate, to one meter long, and branched beneath the inflorescence. The inflorescence is short and conelike with the flowers produced in successional pairs at intervals. The flowers reach seven centimeters in diameter. The sepals and petals are pale pink and the lip rose-purple with a yellow throat.

Sobralia dichotoma Ruíz & Pavón

This species occurs from Colombia to Bolivia. The unbranched stems reach three meters tall. The inflorescence is apical or lateral, dichotomously branched, and produces flowers simultaneously on each branch in succession at coordinated intervals. The flowers reach six centimeters in diameter. The sepals and petals are

whitish on the outer surface and reddish inside. The lip is white outside and red-brown inside with yellow lamellae down the midline.

Sobralia leucoxantha Reichb.f.

This species is known from Costa Rica to Colombia. The unbranched stems reach one meter in length. The inflorescence is short and conelike with the flowers produced at intervals, singly in succession. The flowers reach ten centimeters in diameter. The sepals and petals are white. The lip is white with a yellow throat.

Sobralia macrantha Lindley

This species occurs from Mexico to Costa Rica. The unbranched stems reach 2.5 meters in length and the inflorescence is short and conelike with the flowers produced at intervals, singly in succession. The flowers reach fifteen centimeters in diameter. The sepals and petals are pink. The lip is very large with a dark rose marginal area and is white inside with a tinge of yellow.

Sobralia macrantha

Sobralia leucoxantha

Sobralia candida

Sobralia rosea

Sophronitella violacea

Sobralia rosea Poepp. & Endl.

This species occurs from Colombia to Bolivia. The unbranched stems reach three meters in length. The inflorescence is produced at the apex and is elongate and zigzagged. The flowers are produced singly in succession. Sepals and petals are pink. The lip is pink with darker pink blotches and with a yellow throat.

Sobralia violacea Linden ex Lindley

This species is found from Venezuela to Bolivia in the lowlands at the base of the Andes. The stems are elongate, to one meter long, and branched beneath the inflorescence. The leaves are dark purple-red on the underside. The inflorescence is short and conelike with the flowers produced in successional pairs at coordinated intervals. The flowers reach seven centimeters in diameter. The sepals and petals are dark rose-purple and the lip darker rose-purple with a white throat.

SOPHRONITELLA Schltr.
sof-ron-i-TEL-ah
Tribe: Epidendreae
Subtribe: Laeliinae
Etymology: Gr. *sophron*, chaste, modest; diminutive of *Sophronia*

This is a monotypic genus of Brazil. The genus is characterized by the ovoid, tightly clustered pseudobulbs with a single leathery leaf at the apex; the short, one- to two-flowered inflorescence produced from the apex of the pseudobulb; the dark

Sobralia violacea

Sophronitis coccinea

reddish flowers; and the four flattened pollinia.

The plants are epiphytic in moist forests. Cultivation in well-drained material in pots, in considerable shade under intermediate conditions is recommended.

Sophronitella violacea (Lindley) Schltr.

This species occurs in Brazil. The flowers reach a diameter of 2.5 centimeters. The sepals and petals are spreading, dark rose-violet, and the lip is darker. The anther cap is dark purple-red.

Sophronitis cernua

SOPHRONITIS Lindley
sof-roe-NYE-tis
Tribe: Epidendreae
Subtribe: Laeliinae
Etymology: Gr. *sophron*, chaste, modest; diminutive of *Sophronia*

This is a genus of seven species distributed through southern Brazil, Bolivia and Paraguay. The genus is characterized by the cylindrical, jointed, tightly clustered pseudobulbs with a single, fleshy leaf at the apex; the inflorescence short, arising from the apex of the pseudobulb; one-flowered in some species, several-flowered in others; the brilliant red color of the flowers; the lip free from the column but surrounding it at the base; and the eight hard, flattened pollinia attached to caudicles.

The plants occur as epiphytes or lithophytes in wet forest at elevations of 500 to 1,000 meters. They are cultivated best in small pots with well-drained medium under intermediate conditions with abundant water supplied throughout the year.

Sophronitis cernua Lindley

This species occurs in Bolivia and Brazil. The inflorescence produces two to four flowers, and the flowers reach a diameter of

2.5 centimeters. The sepals and petals are usually orange-red with the lip orange-red with a yellow-orange base.

Sophronitis coccinea (Lindley) Reichb.f.

This species is found in southern Brazil. The inflorescence produces a single flower that reaches a diameter of 7.5 centimeters. The sepals, petals, and lip are scarlet-red, and the base of the three-lobed lip is orange-yellow.

SPATHOGLOTTIS Blume
spa-tho-GLOT-tis
Tribe: Arethuseae
Subtribe: Bletiinae
Etymology: Gr. *spatha*, spathe; *glottis*, tongue

A genus of over 40 species distributed from southern India to southern China through Malaysia to the Philippines and Indonesia and New Caledonia. Pseudobulbs arise from a creeping rhizome and bear a few deciduous, plicate leaves. The tall and slender raceme arises from the base of the pseudobulb and bears few to several

Spathoglottis ixioides

Spiculaea ciliata

medium-sized flowers of yellow or purple. Plants are widely grown as garden subjects in mild climates.

Cultivate in well-drained pots of garden loam, leaf mold, chopped sphagnum and sand, to which is added some bone meal. The plant should be potted with about one-fourth of the pseudobulbs covered with compost. Once new growth emerges, it benefits greatly from application of balanced fertilizer at frequent intervals.

Spathoglottis aurea Lindley

A warm-growing species distributed in the Malay Peninsula, Java, and Sumatra. Pseudobulbs are rather small and irregular with two or three narrow, lanceolate leaves. Flowers are gold-yellow with crimson spots on the midlobe of the lip and calli.

Spathoglottis ixioides (D. Don) Lindley

This elegant, cool-growing species is found in Sikkim and Nepal Himalaya and could prove hardy in temperate climates. In nature it grows on sloping hillsides on wet, moss-covered rocks. Between one and three large, golden yellow flowers are carried on a raceme that is shorter than the grasslike leaves. In culture plants should be treated as for *Pleione* and grown with pseudobulbs embedded in compost in a well-drained container. It flowers in June.

Spathoglottis plicata Blume

This species extends from Sri Lanka to the Pacific islands and blooms almost throughout the year. Flowers are usually deep purple-pink, often self-pollinating and variable in size and color with two deep

Spathoglottis plicata

yellow basal calli. It tolerates warm temperatures of 25–30°C and thrives as a garden plant in tropical areas.

Spathoglottis pubescens Lindley

Found from east of Bhutan to Vietnam and Hong Kong, this species produces racemes of three to eight yellow flowers with two triangular calli at the base of the midlobe of the lip. It favors intermediate temperatures and should be grown in a well-drained compost. Flowers appear during May–June.

SPICULAEA Lindley
spick-u-LEE-ah
Tribe: Diurideae
Subtribe: Caladeniinae
Etymology: L. *spiculum*, sharp point or sting

A single species is known. Its relatively small, greenish flowers have a fleshy insect-like labellum. Pollination is achieved when male thynnid wasps attempt to mate with the labellum.

Difficult to maintain in cultivation. Pot in a well-drained soil mix containing wood shavings and water when plants are in active growth (autumn to spring). Dry out as plants die down and keep dry over summer. Use fertilizers sparingly.

Spiculaea ciliata Lindley

A remarkable orchid which is restricted to Western Australia where it grows in winter-wet soils on and around the margins of granite outcrops. The ovate leaf is followed by a fleshy flower stem which contains water and stored nutrients. Completely independent of the tuberous root system, this stem withers upward from the base as flowering and seed production proceed. Flowers will continue to open after racemes have been picked. Even herbarium specimens have been known to continue flowering in a plant press.

SPIRANTHES Rich.
spy-RAN-theez
Tribe: Cranichideae
Subtribe: Spiranthinae
Etymology: L. *spira*, coil or spring; Gr. *anthesis*, flowering

This genus of terrestrial orchids has a cosmopolitan distribution with most of the species being tropical or subtropical (excluding Madagascar, South Africa, and tropical regions of America and Africa). Three species are found in Europe, some 20 in North America, and a few in temperate Asia.

The name *Spiranthes* refers directly to the spirally twisted flower-spike. Other

Spiranthes romanzoffiana

Spiranthes sinensis

Spiranthes spiralis

characteristics of the genus are: from two to six fleshy roots which are more or less tuberous; sepals united to form a tubelike hood; a lip as long as the other segments; and fragrant flowers with no spur. Most species can be container-grown in a woodland compost, and several are hardy enough to be established as garden plants.

Spiranthes cernua (L.) Rich.

This is essentially a North American species which has also become an established introduction on sand dunes in Holland. In stature and general appearance it resembles *S. romanzoffiana*, growing up to 50 centimeters in height. It has a tight double spiral of pure white flowers with flowers some nine to eleven millimeters long. These have a lip which is recurved toward the apex and has a pale yellow mark at its centre. Wet margins of lakes, stream banks with associated wet meadows, woods, and marshes form the natural habitat in North America and Canada. Plants can be pot-grown in an open loam/sand mix to which ample leaf litter and peat has been added. They can also be established in a peat bed by employing the same compost.

Spiranthes romanzoffiana Cham.

This can be a robust species. American plants reach 50 centimeters, whereas the European counterparts are a more modest twelve to fifteen centimeters. Flowers vary in number from twelve to 35, and are arranged in three distinct spiral rows. Perianth segments are longer than those of *S. aestivalis* or *S. spiralis* (around 12 millimeters) and converge to form a tubelike structure with the lip sharply

deflexed near its apex. Flowers have a green or cream tinge. Flowering takes place in late July or August, often, but not exclusively, in acid bogs and marshes. Plants can be pot-grown using the mixture suggested for *S. sinensis* below with additional peat; or, outdoors, in a raised peat bed with added loam and leaf mold.

Spiranthes sinensis (Pers.) Ames

This extremely pretty species is widespread in distribution and in cultivation. It just creeps into European Russia at the extreme west of its range but is found throughout tropical Asia (China, New Guinea, Japan) and Australasia (Australia, Tasmania, and New Zealand), flowering in July and August in wet meadows near lakes and rivers or in peat bogs. Each flower is four to five millimeters long with bright pink or rose-pink petals and sepals and a rolled white lip. *Spiranthes sinensis* is one of the few orchids to grow easily from seed. Plants grow well in a frost-free glasshouse in an open sandy mix with loam, leaf litter and the addition of a small amount of peat.

Spiranthes spiralis (L.) Chevall

This is the only true fall-flowering orchid species in Europe and is often overlooked, being frequently less than ten centimeters tall. In some Mediterranean pine woods, however, it can grow to 30 centimeters with up to 20 flowers in a single spiral row. By the time flowering begins the basal rosette has withered. However, the next year's rosette can then start to grow beside the stem. Flowers are tiny with perianth segments 6–7 millimeters long but quite exquisite in close-up. The lip margins curve upward to form a tube; its inner surface is

greenish and the apex crinkled. This species can be intentionally naturalized in short turf. In chalk and limestone regions it often simply appears on tennis courts or short lawns. Alternatively it can be pot-grown in the "*Orchis*" mix with added limestone.

STANHOPEA Frost ex Hook.
stan-HOPE-ee-ah
Tribe: Cymbidieae
Subtribe: Stanhopeinae
Etymology: In honor of Philip Henry, Fourth Earl of Stanhope, president of the London Medico-Botanical Society during the early part of the nineteenth century

Stanhopea is a genus of 55 species known from Mexico to Brazil. The genus is characterized by the ovoid, dark green pseudobulbs of a single internode with a single apical, heavily veined, petiolate leaf; the inflorescence produced from the base of the pseudobulb, pendent, two- to many-flowered; the dorsal sepal and petals free; the lateral sepals connate at the base; the lip usually with a hypochile, horned mesochile, and an epichile; the column winged; and the two hard pollinia attached to an elongate stipe and united to a cordiform viscidium.
The plants grow as epiphytes or, less commonly, as terrestrials on embankments in wet forest at elevations from 200 to 2,200 meters.
Cultivation of the species under intermediate conditions is recommended.

Stanhopea anfracta

Stanhopea annulata

They should be grown in baskets so that the pendent inflorescences may emerge through the bottom. More than normal sunlight and ample water throughout the year is beneficial. The plants should not be allowed to dry out excessively. The flowers are short-lived, seldom lasting more than two days in good condition.

The plant habit and characteristics are so similar from species to species that they cannot be used to distinguish them. The only reliable species indicators are the number of flowers produced; the characteristics of floral structure; and to a limited degree, the color.

Stanhopea anfracta Rolfe

This species occurs from Ecuador to Bolivia on the eastern slope of the Andes. Between seven and thirteen flowers are produced and they reach six centimeters in diameter. The sepals and petals are yellow-orange to orange, and the lip is orange, often with a red eye-spot on each side of the hypochile. The hypochile is sharply bent at the midpoint so as to form a "U" from the lateral view. The horns of the mesochile are thick, and the epichile is reflexed and thickened at the apex.

Stanhopea annulata Mansf.

This species occurs in western Colombia and Ecuador. Only two flowers are produced, each reaching four centimeters in diameter. The flowers are orange-yellow, and no horns are produced from the mesochile. A thickened ring surrounds the midpoint of the hypochile.

Stanhopea candida Barb. Rodr.

This species is found from Colombia to Bolivia and Brazil in the lowlands east of

the Andes. Normally two to four flowers are produced, each reaching six centimeters in diameter. The flowers are white with red lines on the upper side of the hypochile of the lip. The lip has a pair of erect, forward-curved horns at the base of the upper side of the hypochile on each side of the slitlike entrance to the cavity, and no horns on the mesochile.

Stanhopea cirrhata Klotzsch

This species is found from Nicaragua to Panama. Only two flowers are produced, each reaching 5.5 centimeters in diameter. The flowers are yellow-orange with the horns of the mesochile dark purple-red. The hypochile of the lip is saccate with a pair of short, thick horns produced from the sides of the mesochile.

Stanhopea costaricensis Reichb.f.

This species occurs from Guatemala to Panama. From five to seven flowers are produced, each reaching nine centimeters in diameter. The sepals and petals are yellow to yellow-white and are usually spotted with red-brown, and the lip is pale yellow, often with a red eye-spot on each

side of the hypochile and with small spots on the epichile. The hypochile is elongate and slender with a pair of swollen projections from the underside, clearly visible from a lateral view. The horns of the mesochile are terete and the epichile is broad.

Stanhopea ecornuta Lemaire

This species is known from Guatemala to Panama. Only two flowers are produced, each reaching six centimeters in diameter. Sepals and petals are white with red-purple spots at the base of each petal. The lip is yellow, becoming orange-yellow at the base and inside. The lip is fleshy, saccate, without horns on the mesochile, and with several tumor-like thickenings inside and on the apical margin.

Stanhopea florida Reichb.f.

This species occurs from Colombia to Peru on the eastern slope of the Andes. From five to eight flowers are produced, each reaching eight centimeters in diameter. Sepals and petals are yellow-orange to pinkish, and the lip is pale pink, often with a red eye-spot on each side of the hypochile, and flecked with red throughout. The hypochile is elongate and flattened from a lateral view. The horns of the mesochile are terete, and the epichile is broad.

Stanhopea grandiflora (Lodd.) Lindley

This species occurs in the West Indies and from Colombia to the Guianas and Brazil. Only two or three flowers are produced,

Stanhopea cirrhata

Stanhopea candida

Stanhopea costaricensis

each reaching fourteen centimeters in diameter. The flowers are white with red streaks on the hypochile of the lip. The hypochile has a pair of erect, forward-curving, short horns below the round cavity at the base on the upper side, and has no horns on the mesochile.

Stanhopea graveolens Lindley

This species is known from Mexico and Guatemala. From five to nine flowers are produced, each reaching eight centimeters in diameter. Sepals and petals are yellow-

Stanhopea grandiflora

Stanhopea ecornuta

Stanhopea florida

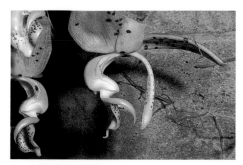

Stanhopea jenishiana

Stanhopea martiana

Stanhopea graveolens

orange to orange and the lip is orange, often with a red eye-spot on each side of the hypochile. The hypochile is bent at the midpoint and is nearly quadrate from a lateral view. The shoulders of the base of the hypochile do not have a teatlike projection. The horns of the mesochile are elongate, and the epichile is broad. The flowers produce a foul, feces-like odor.

Stanhopea jenishiana Kramer & Reichb.f.

This species occurs from Colombia to northern Peru. From five to eight flowers are produced, each reaching seven centimeters in diameter. Sepals and petals are yellow-orange to orange, and the lip is orange, often with a red eye-spot on each

side of the hypochile. The hypochile is elongate and slender with a smooth, unlobed underside from a lateral view. The horns of the mesochile are terete and the epichile is broad. The flowers smell of cinnamon.

Stanhopea martiana Batem. ex Lindley

This species is only known from western Mexico. From two to three flowers are produced, each reaching eight centimeters in diameter. The sepals and petals are white, heavily blotched with red, and the lip is white with a red-black eye-spot on each side of the hypochile. The hypochile is short and subtriangular from a lateral view;

Stanhopea saccata

Stanhopea oculata

Stanhopea pulla

produced, each reaching eight centimeters in diameter. The sepals and petals are yellow-orange to white, heavily blotched with red-black, and the lip is white with a red-black eye-spot on each side of the hypochile and heavily blotched throughout with red-black. The hypochile is elongate and subquadrate from a lateral view. The horns of the mesochile are terete and the epichile is broad.

Stanhopea saccata Batem.

This species occurs from Mexico to Costa Rica. From two to five flowers are produced, each reaching six centimeters in diameter. The sepals and petals are yellow-orange to orange and the lip is orange, often with a red eye-spot on each side of the hypochile. The hypochile is U-shaped from a lateral view. The horns of the mesochile are elongate and flattened, and the epichile is narrow and three-lobed at the apex. The flowers are fragrant of cinnamon.

Stanhopea tigrina Batem. ex Lindley

This species is known from eastern Mexico. Only two flowers are produced, each reaching eighteen centimeters in diameter. The sepals and petals are yellow-orange to white, heavily blotched with red-black, and the lip is white and heavily blotched

the mesochile has elongate, flattened horns with a curled spine at the apex; and the epichile is narrow and three-lobed at the apex.

Stanhopea oculata (Lodd.) Lindley

This species occurs from Mexico to Costa Rica and jumps to Colombia, Venezuela, and eastern Brazil. From five to eight flowers are produced, each reaching seven centimeters in diameter. The sepals and petals are yellow-orange to white. The lip is orange to white with a red eye-spot on each side of the hypochile and numerous blotches and specks of red on the petals and lip. The hypochile is elongate and slender with a pair of swollen projections from the underside, clearly visible from a

lateral view. The horns of the mesochile are terete and the epichile is broad.

Stanhopea pulla Reichb.f.

This species occurs from Costa Rica to Colombia. Only two flowers are produced, each reaching 2.5 centimeters in diameter. The flowers are yellow with a red-purple blotch on the sides of the lip. The lip is saccate and subtriangular from a lateral view. No horns are produced from the mesochile, and the epichile is fleshy-thickened.

Stanhopea ruckeri Lindley

This species is known from Mexico to Nicaragua. From four to seven flowers are throughout with red-black. The hypochile is triangular and flattened from a lateral view. The horns of the mesochile are elongate and flattened, and the epichile is narrow and three-lobed at the apex.

Stanhopea wardii Lodd. ex Lindley

This species occurs from Nicaragua to Colombia and Venezuela. From five to eight flowers are produced, each reaching seven centimeters in diameter. The sepals and petals are yellow-orange to orange, and the lip is orange with a red eye-spot on each side of the hypochile. The hypochile is bent at the mid-point and is nearly quadrate from a lateral view. The shoulders of the base of the hypochile have a teatlike projection. The horns of the mesochile are elongate, and the epichile is broad. The flowers produce a strong, pleasant, medicine-like odor.

STELIS Sw.
STEE-lis
Tribe: Epidendreae
Subtribe: Pleurothallidinae
Etymology: Gr. *stelis*, a mistletoe

This genus of over 600 species is widely distributed thoughout the American tropics. It is represented by as many diverse vegetative forms as are found in *Pleurothallis*, but the flowers are readily recognized by the short, thick, transverse petals and lip that form with the column a compact arrangement on the back wall of the center of the flower. The sepals are variously connate. Because of the superficial similarity of so many of the species, which

Stanhopea tigrina

Stanhopea wardii

Stelis argentata

are small-flowered, this genus has never been popular in cultivation. The column is short with an apical anther with two pollinia.

Most of the species are easy to cultivate in moist, intermediate to cool-growing greenhouse conditions.

Stelis argentata Lindley

This species is frequent and widely distributed from Mexico into Brazil. It has numerous, similar-looking relatives. The leaf-stems are shorter than the leathery, petiolate leaves. The simultaneously many-flowered racemose inflorescence emerges from the base of the leaf. The variously colored, equal-sized sepals create a triangular flower. The transverse lip has a

tiny, sharp point in the center. In common with many other pleurothallids, microscopic crystalline deposits can be seen in the floral parts, hence the specific name.

Stelis ciliaris Lindley

This attractive Central American species is distinguished by the drooping, congested, simultaneously many-flowered raceme of purple, long-ciliate flowers. The obtuse, triangular sepals create a broadly triangular flower. The lip is ovate and obtuse.

Stelis nexipous Garay

This species is frequent in southeastern Ecuador. The narrow leaf is about as long as the leaf-stem. The flowers are borne in a

Stenia pallida

Stenoglottis longifolia

Stenia calceolaris

congested, simultaneously many-flowered, two-faced raceme. Most unusual is the flat, "duck-footed" flower created by a deep union of the dorsal sepal with the lateral sepals, while the lateral sepals are nearly free from each other.

Stelis pardipes Reichb.f.

This Central American species has numerous close relatives in the Andes. From the base of the narrowly elliptical leaf, which is about as long as the leaf-stem, the longer, simultaneously many-flowered raceme emerges. The ovate dorsal sepal, nearly free from the lateral sepals, stands above the cup-shaped blade of the connate

lateral sepals. The tiny petals and lip are sharply pointed.

STENIA Lindley
STEN-ee-ah
Tribe: Maxillarieae
Subtribe: Zygopetalinae
Etymology: Gr. *stenos*, narrow; in reference to the long, narrow pollinia of the type of the genus

Stenia is a genus of eight species distributed from Trinidad, through Andean South America, to Bolivia. The genus is

characterized by the lack of pseudobulbs; the foliaceous, distichous sheaths forming a fanlike plant; the leaves lightly veined; the one-flowered inflorescences produced from the axils of the leaf-sheaths; the sides of the deeply saccate lip not surrounding the column; the lip acute at the apex; the shallow callus; and the four flattened, superimposed pollinia on a short stipe connected to a flattened, broad viscidium. The plants grow as epiphytes in very wet forest at elevations from 500 to 1,500 meters. They are easily cultivated under intermediate conditions in pots in well-drained media with abundant water supplied throughout the year.

Stenia calceolaris (Garay) Dodson & Bennett

This species is known from Ecuador and Peru. The flowers reach a diameter of 2.5 centimeters. The sepals and petals are green-white with roundish red-brown spots. The lip is whitish and deeply saccate.

Stenia pallida Lindley

This species is distributed from the West Indies to Bolivia and Brazil. The flowers reach a diameter of four centimeters and are white with yellow at the base of the lip with a few small red spots on the yellow. The lip is deeply saccate toward the base but the apical portion is laterally flattened.

STENOGLOTTIS Lindley
sten-o-GLOT-tiss
Tribe: Orchideae
Subtribe: Orchidinae

Stenoglottis fimbriata

Stenorrhynchus lanceolatum

Stenorrhynchus speciosum

Etymology: Gr. *stenos*, narrow; *glotta*, tongue

Three attractive species — *S. fimbriata, S. longifolia*, and *S. woodii* — grow as terrestrial and occasionally epiphytic herbs in southern Africa. Thick root tubers bear a basal rosette of leaves each year. Leaves are short or elongated, either light green or variously spotted purple-brown. Erect, unbranched inflorescences bear few to numerous small, white, pale or deep lilac flowers, sparsely to heavily spotted. Small petals enclose the column, and sepals are open. The elongated lip, variously lobed and spotted, is the striking feature. All species have two pollinia. The flowers continue to open over several months as the flower spike elongates.

Plants are of easy culture in a shallow pot or pan with a medium of coarse sand and leaf mould. Keep the plants well watered throughout the growing season, but provide a short, dry rest when leaves die. Feed with a dilute fertilizer solution and avoid build-up of salts. Allow semi-shade, cool to intermediate temperatures, good air movement and moderate to high relative humidity. Good clones selected for vigor and color make spectacular specimen plants.

Stenoglottis fimbriata Lindley

A rather variable species with a wide distribution from Natal to the eastern Cape, extending north to Tanzania. It can be found in forests and on rocks or in moss on tree-trunks from sea level to 1,800 meters. Leaf size and spotting are variable. The inflorescence may be up to 40 centimeters tall with 50 or more lilac flowers with heavy spotting. The lip is three-lobed with divided

Symphyglossum sanguineum

lateral lobes. Flowering is from March to May.

Stenoglottis longifolia Hook.

Closely related to *S. fimbriata, Stenoglottis longifolia* is from Natal. It is more robust, however, with longer leaves, an inflorescence up to 100 centimeters, and many more lilac-pink flowers (often over 100). The lip is five-lobed and between eight and twelve millimeters long. Flowering is from February to May.

STENORRHYNCHUS
Rich.
ste-nor-RHIN-cus
Tribe: Cranichideae
Subtribe: Spiranthinae
Etymology: Gr. *stenos*, narrow; *rhynchos*, snout. From the narrow rostellum on the column in the type material of the genus

This cosmopolitan genus generally has showy, bright-colored flowers. It was formerly considered a synonym of

Spiranthes with which it shares the general gestalt of the plant.

Stenorrhynchus lanceolatum
(Aubl.)
Rich. ex Sprengel

This is one of the first orchids to appear with the first rains in April, the spike bursting into flower when the surrounding vegetation is still brown and dry. The pink scapes and flowers often appear along roadsides. Leaves will appear only after the flowers have completely wilted. It grows in heavy clay and requires clear-cut wet and dry seasons, hot conditions, and full sun.

Stenorrhynchus speciosum
(Jacq.) Rich. ex Sprengel

This very attractive epiphytic species has its bright red flowers that are often in full bloom for Christmas. It grows in mixed woods, usually on oaks at elevations of about 1,800 meters, often with moss. It can be cultivated in a well drained pot with humus and/or moss. Keep moist throughout the year, but diminish water when the leaves wilt.

SYMPHYGLOSSUM Schltr.
simf-ee-GLOS-um
Tribe: Cymbidieae
Subtribe: Oncidiinae
Etymology: Gr. *symphyein*, to grow together; *glossa*, tongue; in reference to the lip united with the column

This is a genus of five species from Andean South America distributed from Venezuela to Peru. The genus is characterized by the

T

Tainia hookeriana

northwestern Peru. The inflorescence reaches one meter in length, and the flowers reach 2.5 centimeters in diameter. The flowers are dark pink with the base of the lip white. The lip has two oblong lamellae on the disc.

TAINIA Blume
TANE-ee-ah
Tribe: Arethuseae
Subtribe: Bletiinae
Etymology: Gr. *tainia*, fillet

About 40 terrestrial species comprise this genus which ranges from India to Malaysia, New Guinea, Australia, and the Solomon Islands. Small pseudobulbs bear plicate or fleshy leaves from the apex and racemose inflorescences from the base. Flowers have a mentum formed by the fusion of the bases of the lateral sepals and the labellum to the column-foot. There are eight pollinia. Most species are from tropical lowlands and should be given intermediate to warm temperatures, moderate shade, and a slight reduction in water on completion of new growth. Like many other genera in subtribe Bletiinae (*Phaius* in particular), tainias thrive in a peat/perlite compost with a small measure of processed manure either mixed in or added as a top-dressing.

Tainia hookeriana King & Pantl.

This species from India and Thailand has ovate pseudobulbs each bearing a long-petiolate, deciduous, plicate leaf up to a meter long. Flowers about five centimeters across are produced usually in March and

presence of unifoliate or bifoliate pseudobulbs of a single internode subtended by distichous leaflike sheaths; the inflorescence produced from the axils of the sheaths; the flowers without a spur; the petals united to the column at their base; the basal portion of the lip parallel to the column for more than half its length; the column without fleshy winglike lobes at the base and without a foot; and the two hard pollinia attached to a stipe connected to a viscidium.
The plants grow as epiphytes in wet forest at elevations from 1,000 to 2,500 meters. They are easily cultivated under intermediate conditions as provided for *Cattleya*.

Symphyglossum sanguineum (Benth.) Schltr.

This species occurs in western Ecuador and

Telipogon nervosus

April. Sepals and petals are yellow with reddish brown stripes. The labellum is white with a yellow callus, the apex of the midlobe flushed with red. There is a small brown spur.

TELIPOGON H. B. K.
tel-ee-POE-gon
Tribe: Maxillarieae
Subtribe: Telipogoninae
Etymology: Gr. *telos*, end; *pogon*, beard; in reference to the spiny end of the column

Telipogon is a genus of about 110 species distributed from Costa Rica to Bolivia. The genus is characterized by the presence of inconspicuous, cylindrical, flattened pseudobulbs with a single flat, apical leaf, or elongate, creeping stems that branch near the apex; the lateral or apical inflorescence; the flowers larger than two centimeters in diameter; the sepals and petals free; the lip sessile and surrounding the short, spiny column; and the four hard pollinia superimposed to form one pair attached to an elongate stipe united to a hooked viscidium.
The plants grow as epiphytes or terrestrials at elevations from 1,700 to 3,400 meters. These are among the most spectacular and interesting of orchids. The highly colored flowers are often larger than the whole mass of the plant that produces them. The column and callus of the lip often imitate the structures of spiny flies and thereby attract their pollinators.
Cultivation of species of the genus *Telipogon* has been considered to be

impossible, but some success has been achieved by persistent growers. One must remember that the plants grow in cold, wet habitats, with constant cloud effect at night, only in circumstances in which perfect drainage is available. They will not withstand temperatures above 25°C or below 2°C. Some species seem to die simply as a result of being moved to a different position on the same tree from which they were collected.

Telipogon nervosus (L. f.) Druce

This species is found in northern Colombia and Venezuela. The plants have long, creeping, unbranched stems and the inflorescence produces five to nine flowers that open in succession. The flowers reach three centimeters in diameter. They are pinkish brown with red-brown vein-lines and reticulations. There is no callus at the base of the lip. The column is covered with red-brown spines.

Telipogon pulcher Reichb.f.

This species is found in Colombia and northern Ecuador at high elevations. The plants have clustered stems and the inflorescence produces three to five medium-sized flowers. Most of the flowers are open simultaneously. The flowers reach five centimeters in diameter. The white flowers have heavy red-brown vein-lines that terminate about three-fourths of the way to the margin and a large red-brown spot occurs on the disc of the lip. There is no callus at the base of the lip. The column is elongate and covered with red-brown spines.

TETRAMICRA Lindley
tet-ra-MY-kra
Tribe: Epidendreae
Subtribe: Laeliinae
Etymology: Gr. *tetra*, fourfold; *micros*, small; referring to the four small compartments in the anther cap

Tetramicra is a genus of six species distributed in the West Indies with one occurrence reported in Florida. The genus is characterized by the pseudobulbs small or lacking, clothed with fans of distichous, fleshy, stiff leaves usually separated by elongate rhizomes; the erect, terminal inflorescences; the flowers, several, opening successively over considerable time; the lip erect, separate from but appressed to the column; and the four hard pollinia on well-developed caudicles.
These are scrambling terrestrial plants in sandy areas or on rocks. Cultivation is best on plaques with abundant water throughout the year.

Tetramicra canaliculata (Aubl.) Urban

This species occurs in Florida and the West Indies. The flowers reach five centimeters in diameter with greenish sepals and petals that are flushed with purple. The three-lobed lip has rose-colored lateral lobes and a darker pink midlobe with violet-purple stripes.

Tetramicra eulophiae Reichb.f.

This species occurs on the island of Cuba. The flowers reach 1.2 centimeters in diameter with grey-red sepals and petals.

Telipogon pulcher

Tetramicra canaliculata

The rose-purple, three-lobed lip has earlike lateral lobes.

THELYMITRA G. Forster & Forster

thee-lee-MY-tra

Tribe: Diurideae
Subtribe: Diuridinae
Etymology: Gr. *thelys*, female; *mitra*, cap or hat

About 45 species comprise this genus of colorful terrestrial orchids distributed mainly in Australia and New Zealand, with a widespread species extending to New Guinea, New Caledonia, and the Philippines. They are deciduous terrestrials with subterranean tuberoids and a solitary, narrow, usually erect leaf. Slender racemes bear few to many flowers, the segments of which spread widely only on warm, sunny days, closing at night and remaining closed during cool weather. Many species have blue flowers, but other colors include yellows, reds, pinks, and browns, with some having mixed colors in striking combinations. Pot in a well-drained soil mix containing wood shavings. Keep moist when in active growth (autumn to late spring), dry out as plants die down, keep completely dry and repot over summer. Use fertilizers sparingly.

Thelymitra crinita

Thelymitra nuda

Thelymitra carnea

Thelymitra carnea R. Br.

The small, bright pink to reddish flowers of this species open widely only during hot, humid weather. In the absence of these conditions the flowers self-pollinate without opening at all. A native of eastern Australia, this species flowers there from September to December. It can be difficult to maintain in cultivation, although seedlings are easily raised by sprinkling seed on the surface of the compost around the base of the parent plants.

Thelymitra crinita Lindley

One of the prettiest of the Western Australian terrestrials, this species develops racemes to 75 centimeters tall, with individual flowers expanding to four centimeters across. These brilliant blue flowers have an interesting column, the upper part of which is covered with narrow black, orange, and yellow calli. The flowers open freely in warm, sunny weather, and each lasts for several days. Adapts well to cultivation.

Thelymitra nuda R. Br.

Widespread in eastern Australia, this colorful species is found in a range of open habitats. Tall multiflowered racemes appear from late winter to the end of spring and carry blue, fragrant flowers each to four centimeters across. The petals and sepals expand widely on sunny days, with each flower lasting several days. Easily grown in temperate regions.

Ticoglossum krameri

TICOGLOSSUM R. Lucas
Rodriguez ex Halbinger
tee-co-GLOS-sum

Tribe: Cymbidieae

Subtribe: Oncidiinae

Etymology: Tico, the familiar name by which Costa Ricans are known in Latin America, and Gr. *glossa*, tongue, in reference to *Odontoglossum*, the genus under which this group of species was formerly known. This small genus of two species is endemic to Costa Rica and western Panama. It can be recognized by the short column and the bunch of trichomes located behind the fleshy callus.

Ticoglossum krameri (Reichb.f.) Lucas Rodríguez ex Halbinger

The plants have light green, lentil-like, flattened pseudobulbs, and the flowers are pink, but a white variety has also been described. They grow at the base of trees at the top of the Cordillera Central in Costa Rica in cloud forest, and should be grown in intermediate to cool, wet conditions.

Ticoglossum oerstedii

Trichocentrum tigrinum

Trichocentrum pulchrum

Ticoglossum oerstedii (Reichb.f.) Lucas Rodríguez ex Halbinger

The dark green, globose, small pseudobulbs are characteristic, with the delicate white flowers. The plants can be seen growing on fence-posts and small trees at intermediate elevations, in cloud-forest conditions in Costa Rica. Grow in cool, well-ventilated conditions, as with *Masdevallia* species, but with good light.

TRICHOCENTRUM Poeppig & Endl.

try-koe-SENT-rum
Tribe: Cymbidieae
Subtribe: Oncidiinae
Etymology: Gr. *tricho-*, hair; *kentron*, spur; in reference to the slender spur of most species

This is a genus of 31 species distributed from Mexico to Bolivia and Brazil. The genus is characterized by the presence of small, unifoliate pseudobulbs of a single

internode subtended by distichous sheaths; the leaf flat, thick, and fleshy; the inflorescence produced from the axils of the sheaths; the flowers with a spur; the sepals and petals free; the lip not deeply saccate and immersed in the ovary; the base of the lip with an elongate, single, hollow spur; the column with a foot; and the two hard pollinia attached to a stipe connected to a viscidium.

The plants grow as epiphytes in wet forest or seasonally dry forest at elevations from 300 to 1,400 meters. They are best accommodated in pots in well-drained media with water supplied throughout the year.

Trichocentrum candidum Lindley

This species occurs from Mexico to Costa Rica and is probably erroneously reported from Brazil. The flowers reach 3.5 centimeters in diameter. The sepals and petals are white, and the lip is white marked with red on the base of the lip and column. The lip is truncate at the apex and has a saccate spur at the base that is two centimeters long.

Trichocentrum pfavii Reichb.f.

This species is found from Costa Rica to Panama. The flowers reach four centimeters in diameter. The sepals and petals are white with a basal red blotch. The lip is wedge-shaped and white with a reddish blotch near the base. The spur at the base of the lip is short.

Trichocentrum pulchrum Poeppig & Endl.

This species occurs from Venezuela to Peru. The flowers reach a diameter of six centimeters. The sepals and petals are pink to white with small red spots. The lip is pink spotted with red, quadrate, and has an elongate spur projecting from the base of the lip that is longer than the lip.

Trichocentrum tigrinum Linden & Reichb.f.

This species is found in seasonally dry portions of western Ecuador and northern Peru. The flowers reach a diameter of six centimeters. The sepals and petals are yellow with large, red-brown blotches, and the lip is white with a large red blotch on each side near the base. The lip is quadrate

Trichoceros muralis

Trichoglottis philippinensis

lobes of the lip are round and red-brown. The column is covered with red-brown spines.

TRICHOGLOTTIS Blume
trick-oh-GLOT-tis
Tribe: Vandeae
Subtribe: Sarcanthinae
Etymology: Gr. *thrix*, hair; *glotta*, tongue

Some 60 species are known to occur in east Asia, Malaysia, the Philippines, Polynesia, and adjacent islands. These are epiphytic herbs with leafy, monopodial stems that are climbing or pendulous. The small, fleshy flowers can make solitary, sessile appearances in the axils of leaves, or on many-flowered racemes. All species have four unequal pollinia in two pairs. Species requirements range from shady to bright sun. Temperatures must not drop below 15°C. The plants require high humidity and ample water.

Trichoglottis brachiata Ames

This attractive species from the Philippines has been regarded by several authors as a variety of *T. philippinensis* Lindley. It is distinguished by the broader petals and sepals of the flowers, their rich dark maroon, and the shape and red-purple of the lip. The star-shaped, mildly fragrant, and long-lived flowers occur individually at each leaf-axil. Since several flowers open simultaneously on each stem, a well-grown specimen, with multiple stems branching from the base, can make for a striking display. Optimal growth is obtained with the same conditions provided for tropical vandas.

with a bilobed apex. The callus is yellow marked with red, and the spur at the base of the lip is short.

TRICHOCEROS H. B. K.
try-kos-SIR-os
Tribe: Maxillarieae
Subtribe: Telipogoninae
Etymology: Gr. *tricho-*, hair; *cheilos,* lip; referring to the pilose midlobe of the lip

Trichoceros is a genus of about five species distributed from Ecuador to Bolivia. The genus is characterized by the elongate rhizomes between obvious pseudobulbs with flat, distichous leaves; the lateral inflorescence elongate, racemose; the sepals and petals free; the lip three-lobed, sessile and surrounding the short, spiny column; and the four hard pollinia superimposed to form one pair attached to an elongate stipe united to a hooked viscidium.

These are scrambling terrestrial plants on steep hillsides at elevations from 2,500 to 3,200 meters. The aspect of the flowers is of a spiny fly seated on a small leaf; male flies attempt to mate with it, thereby pollinating the flower.

The species are easily cultivated on plaques or in well-drained media in pots when provided with abundant water throughout the year. They should be given cool treatment but will withstand intermediate conditions.

Trichoceros antennifer (H. & B.) H. B. K.

This species occurs from Ecuador to Bolivia at high elevations in the Andes. The flowers reach two centimeters in diameter. The sepals and petals are green with red-brown stripes, and the lip is red-brown, often greenish toward the apex. The lateral lobes of the lip are narrow and elongate and are barred with red-brown. The column is covered with red-brown spines.

Trichoceros muralis Lindley

This species occurs in central Ecuador at high elevations. The flowers reach a diameter of two centimeters. The sepals and petals are green with red-brown stripes, and the lip is completely red-brown. The lateral

Trichoceros antennifer

Trichopilia fragrans

Trichoglottis philippinensis
Lindley

Widely distributed in the Philippines, this species is more variable than *T. brachiata* Ames. The sepals and petals are narrower, greenish to yellow-brown, and outlined with yellow to white margins. The lip is also narrower, and predominantly white. Its fragrant flowers are produced singly in leaf-axils which are spaced farther apart than those of *T. brachiata*. It flowers in spring and summer.

Trichopilia marginata

TRICHOPILIA Lindley
trick-o-PIL-ee-ah
Tribe: Cymbidieae
Subtribe: Oncidiinae
Etymology: Gr. *tricho-*, hair; *pilos*, felt; in reference to the ciliate or fimbriate margin of the hood over the clinandrium

Trichopilia is a genus of 29 species distributed from Mexico to Bolivia and Brazil. The genus is characterized by the presence of unifoliate, flattened pseudobulbs of a single internode subtended by distichous, non-foliaceous sheaths; the inflorescence produced from the axils of the sheaths; the flowers without a spur; the sepals and petals free, spreading; the lip surrounding the column for most of its length; the column without a foot; and the two hard pollinia attached to a stipe connected to a viscidium.
The plants grow as epiphytes or terrestrials

on embankments in wet forest at elevations from 500 to 2,000 meters. Cultivation is relatively easy under intermediate conditions in pots with well-drained media and abundant water throughout the year.

Trichopilia fragrans (Lindley) Reichb.f.

This species occurs in the West Indies and from Colombia to Bolivia and the Guianas. The flowers reach a diameter of seven centimeters. The sepals and petals are greenish white with undulate margins. The lip is white with a yellow blotch in the throat. The apex of the lip is bilobed.

Trichopilia marginata Henfr. ex Moore

This species is found from Guatemala to Colombia. The flowers reach ten

centimeters in diameter. The sepals and petals are reddish with paler, undulate margins. The lip is white on the outer surface, and the inner surface is dark red with a white margin. The margins of the lip are crisped or undulate.

Trichopilia suavis Lindley & Paxt.

This species occurs from Costa Rica to Colombia. The flowers reach a diameter of ten centimeters. The undulate sepals and petals are white or cream-white, sometimes spotted with pink or red. The very large lip is white heavily spotted with red, and the throat is yellow or orange. The margins of the lip are crisped, and the disc has a prominent, erect keel.

Trichopilia tortilis Lindley

This species is distributed from Mexico to Costa Rica. The flowers reach twelve centimeters in diameter. The sepals and petals are twisted and are red-brown to lavender with an irregular yellow-green border. The large lip is white spotted in the yellow throat with red or brown. The margins of the lip are crisped-undulate.

Trichopilia turialbae Reichb.f.

This species occurs from Nicaragua to Colombia. The flowers reach seven centimeters in diameter. The sepals and petals are undulate and white. The lip is tubular and white with pale orange lines in the throat. The disc of the lip has an elongate, central keel.

Trichopilia turialbae

TRIDACTYLE Schltr.

try-DAK-ti-lee
Tribe: Vandeae
Subtribe: Aerangidinae
Etymology: Gr. *tri*, three; *daktylos*, finger

About 42 species have been described in this monopodial genus, all from Africa and mostly from tropical regions. They are mostly epiphytic, but several species do well as lithophytes at high elevations or near the southern end of their range. The

Trichopilia suavis

Tridactyle bicaudata

Trichopilia tortilis

plants have upright or pendent stems with fleshy or leathery leaves in two rows. The small flowers are mostly in shades of green or ochre, and a few are white. They are all distinguished by a three-lobed lip, sometimes with additional auricles toward the base on either side of the slender spur. Many of the species are easily maintained in cultivation in bright light and cool, intermediate or warm temperatures depending on their origin in the wild. They need plenty of water and feeding while a new leaf is growing and a dry period thereafter.

Tridactyle bicaudata (Lindley) Schltr.

This is probably the most widespread of all epiphytic orchids in Africa, and it is still a common plant at widely ranging elevations. The flowers are greenish brown in long inflorescences. The side lobes of the lip apex are minutely fringed.

Tridactyle gentilii (De Wild.) Schltr.

This species is also widespread in the warmer forests of west Africa, extending eastward and south to Mozambique and

Tridactyle gentilii

Trigonidium egertonianum

Trisetella triaristella

South Africa. The flowers are white, pale green or yellowish and are among the largest in the genus with conspicuous fringing on the side lobes of the lip.

TRIGONIDIUM Lindley
trig-oh-NID-ee-um
Tribe: Maxillarieae
Subtribe: Maxillarinae
Etymology: Gr. diminutive of *trigonos*, three-cornered

Fifteen to 20 species are currently known in tropical America, ranging from Mexico to Bolivia and Brazil. One-flowered scapes, covered with tubular bracts, arise from the base of the pseudobulbs. A gray, dark maroon or iridescent blue thickening in the tip of the petals is most characteristic. All species have four pollinia.
Follow growing instructions for warm-growing *Maxillaria* species.

Trigonidium egertonianum
Bateman ex Lindley

This showy species, found from Mexico to Ecuador, blooms in cultivation throughout the year but especially from February to July. Flowers vary from greenish yellow to pinkish tan, with or without maroon veining. The tips of the petals have a glandular, bluish thickening.

TRISETELLA Luer
tri-see-TEL-la
Tribe: Epidendreae
Subtribe: Pleurothallidinae
Etymology: L. *trisetellus*, with three little bristles

This genus of small plants, native to much of the American tropics, contains 20 species. The leaves are borne by short stems. A very slender peduncle bears a congested, successively flowered raceme of proportionately large flowers. The sepals are connate basally into a shallow sepaline cup. The short, broad dorsal sepal is terminated by an erect tail that may be long, short, or clavate. The lateral sepals are connate (with one exception) into an oblong lamina with tails that emerge from the apex or from the sides of the apex. The column-foot of the cylindrical column fits into a cleft at the base of the little, simple lip. Two pollinia are present.
The species are relatively easy to cultivate in moist, intermediate to cool-growing greenhouse conditions.

Trisetella triaristella (Reichb.f.) Luer

This species is similar to *T. triglochin*, except that the peduncle is warty, and the flowers are a little larger with longer, slender tails.

Trisetella triglochin (Reichb.f.) Luer

The concept accepted as *Trisetella triglochin* is a species-complex of several very closely interrelated taxa that are difficult to define. The clustered leaves are narrow. The peduncle is smooth and hairlike. The dorsal

sepal is yellowish to brownish, and the connate lateral sepals vary from purple to purple-brown. The tails of the lateral sepals usually emerge from the sides of the synsepal below the tip. They are sometimes slightly thickened toward the apex.

TRUDELIA Garay
troo-DEEL-ee-ah
Tribe: Vandeae
Subtribe: Sarcanthinae
Etymology: Honoring Mr. Trudel, a Swiss horticulturist

Trudelia is a genus of six species native from Nepal to Thailand, with one species extending to Indonesia. Species of *Trudelia* were formerly included in *Vanda*, as *Vanda* section *Cristatae*, a position maintained by some authors. All are characterized by having few-flowered racemes of waxy white to greenish yellow flowers with contrasting maroon stripes or markings on the lip.
Plants of *Trudelia* should be grown in pots or small baskets in bright light and intermediate temperatures. Lacking pseudobulbs, *Trudelia* plants have leathery leaves that can withstand periodic drying out but will do best when kept frequently watered throughout the growing period. All *Trudelia* species flower in late spring.

Trudelia alpina (Lindley) Garay

Endemic to northeast India, *Trudelia alpina* is the smallest-flowered species in the genus. The yellow-green flowers with a dark maroon lip are unusual for being partially closed when in flower. The several, one- to

Trisetella triglochin

Trudelia cristata

Tuberolabium quisumbingii

two-flowered racemes, produced from upper leaf-axils, are much shorter than the leaves.

Trudelia cristata (Lindley) Senghas

Trudelia cristata, native from Nepal to Bhutan, is most frequently encountered under the name *Vanda cristata*. The pale green flowers, with contrasting white lips marked with maroon, are variable in size, flower count, and lip morphology. Normally producing one- to two-flowered racemes, plants consistently bearing three- to five-flowered inflorescences are known as var. *multiflora*. The lip terminates in two prongs, which vary from parallel to widely divergent.

Trudelia pumila (J. D. Hook.) Senghas

Native from the northwest Himalayas and China to Sumatra, this species bears white flowers with longitudinal purple stripes on the lip. The flowers are unusual in *Trudelia* for having a pronounced nectar spur, similar to that of *Vanda*. The flowers, produced in few-flowered racemes shorter than the leaves, are extremely variable in size.

TUBEROLABIUM Yamamoto
too-ber-oh-LAY-bee-um
Tribe: Vandeae
Subtribe: Sarcanthinae
Etymology: L. *tuber*, tuber; *labium*, lip

This genus, of about six epiphytic species from southeast Asia to Taiwan and the Philippines, is closely related to and perhaps includes *Trachoma*. *Tuberolabium* species have a column-foot and bear

inflorescences with persistent flowers that open simultaneously, while *Trachoma* species lack a column-foot and bear ephemeral flowers in periodic pulses. All are small monopodial orchids with saccate lips and fleshy, densely flowered inflorescences.

Tuberolabium plants should be grown in small pots or baskets with a compost that retains moisture. While tolerant of periodic drying, they grow best when kept evenly moist, like *Phalaenopsis*. The plants prefer medium to medium bright light and evenly intermediate to warm temperatures.

Tuberolabium quisumbingii (L. O. Williams.) E. A. Christ.

This species is native to the Philippines and is usually exported under the synonym *Saccolabium quisumbingii*. The species has been confused with *T. kotoense* from Taiwan. These easily grown plants produce multiple, fleshy, lax inflorescences bearing numerous, fragrant, white flowers with sharply contrasting red-and-purple lip markings. When not in flower the plants are almost identical to those of *Amesiella*.

VANDA Jones
VAN-da
Tribe: Vandeae
Subtribe: Sarcanthinae
Etymology: Sanskrit name for *Vanda tessellata*

The genus *Vanda* comprises about 50 species distributed from Sri Lanka and southern India to New Guinea and Australia, and north to China, Taiwan, and the

Philippines. It is a highly confusing genus taxonomically, and several groups of species have been treated as separate genera with varying degrees of agreement. These include: (1) *Euanthe*, based on *Vanda sanderiana* from the Philippines; (2) *Trudelia*, based on a small group of mostly Himalayan species; (3) *Holcoglossum*, based on a group of semiterete species from Indochina and China; and (4) *Papilionanthe*, for a series of species generally called terete-leaved vandas in horticulture.

Vanda plants are generally large monopodial orchids, usually with stout, short, leafy stems. They have lent their name, as the adjective "vandaceous," to describe other large monopodial orchids such as *Aerides*, *Arachnis*, *Rhynchostylis*, and *Renanthera*. The leaves characteristically have erose, unevenly cut tips. The flowers are generally large and most commonly yellow-brown with brown markings. All species have a stout column, a saccate spur, a three-lobed lip and generally a midlobe that deflexes to some extent. Most species are strongly day-fragrant.

Vandas are most commonly grown in baskets, with or without compost, so that their large, ungainly root systems can hang exposed to the air. Small-growing species can be accommodated in a pot. Suspended to receive maximum air movement, the plants should be given extremely bright but not direct sunlight, intermediate to warm temperatures, and regular watering. Provided that the plants have a healthy root system, watering should be daily under most circumstances. The single most important feature of *Vanda* culture is providing *even* conditions on a day-to-day

Vanda Rothschildiana

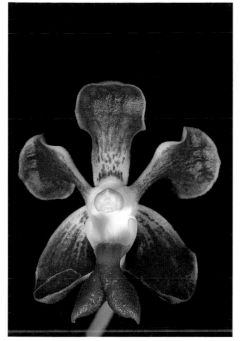

Vanda denisoniana

Vanda coerulea

Vanda merrillii

basis. Fluctuation of any environmental condition results in loss of lower leaves and an unpleasing depauperate stalk crowned by a few leaves.

Vanda coerulea Griffith ex Lindley

This native of northeast India, China, Burma, and Thailand is unusual in *Vanda*, and indeed the orchid family, for its glorious blue flowers marked with deeper blue tessellation. Coveted by local growers and Western horticulture, wild populations of *Vanda coerulea* were decimated for the horticultural trade. Select seed-raised plants have supplanted wild-collected material. Native to higher elevations than most *Vanda* species, *Vanda coerulea* should be grown intermediate to cool during the winter months. An unusual feature of this species is its habit of producing branched inflorescences, a characteristic transmitted to its hybrids, including the famous *V. Rothschildiana*. Flowers are produced in the winter.

Vanda coerulescens Griffith

Native to China, Burma, and Thailand, *Vanda coerulescens* is the other blue *Vanda*. Unlike *V. coerulea*, however, *Vanda coerulescens* is a miniature species with tiny blue flowers. Unlike most species with their short, broad spurs, *Vanda coerulescens* has a long, narrow spur. In this feature it is similar to *V. lilacina*, a white-flowered species with which it has produced natural hybrids. Also native to higher elevations than other vandas, *Vanda coerulescens* should be grown under intermediate temperatures and never subjected to consistently warm conditions.

Vanda coerulescens

The species flowers in late spring and early summer.

Vanda dearei Reichb.f.

This species is endemic to Borneo. One of the largest species in the genus, *Vanda dearei* produces large, strongly fragrant, pale yellow flowers periodically throughout the year. They are unusual because of their pure color, devoid of spots. The species is in the genealogy of most modern yellow hybrids. Unlike most *Vanda* species, *Vanda dearei* is intolerant of cold and should be kept consistently warm.

Vanda denisoniana Benson & Reichb.f.

Native to Burma, Thailand, and China, *Vanda denisoniana* is unusual in *Vanda* for its waxy greenish white flowers produced in the spring. A form with dark brown markings, var. *hebraica*, is known. The very flat flowers have been much utilized in hybridization. Unlike most *Vanda* species, which are fragrant during the middle of the day, *Vanda denisoniana* is fragrant during the early evening.

Vanda lamellata Lindley

Native to the Philippines and Borneo, *Vanda lamellata* is a variable species with several formally recognized varieties. The typical species has yellowish green flowers heavily marked with brown on the lower half of the lateral sepals. The var. *boxallii* has more brightly colored flowers that are nearly white with more purple markings. The species is adapted to extremes in nature and has proven a durable horticultural subject. Flowering is in the winter and periodically throughout the year.

Vanda luzonica

Vanda luzonica Loher

Vanda luzonica is native to the Philippines. The large white flowers have a few purple spots and a diffuse rose border. The petals are strongly clawed. Very similar to *V. tricolor*, *Vanda luzonica* differs by its markings and lack of fragrance. Like *V. tricolor*, it is one of the largest species of the genus. Flowers appear in the spring.

Vanda merrillii Ames & Quisumbing

Vanda merrillii is native to the Philippines and is closely related to *V. hindsii* from New Guinea and Australia. The springtime flowers are yellowish with variable amounts of reddish brown markings; some individuals appear solid red. The remarkable features of the flowers are the glossy, lacquered sheen and their strong, spicy fragrance.

Vanda Rothschildiana

Vanda Rothschildiana is a primary hybrid made by crossing *V. coerulea* with *Euanthe sanderiana*. The hybrid combines the finest qualities of both parents — blue flowers on branched inflorescences from the Himalayan *V. coerulea*, and full flower shape and flat floral segments from the Philippine *Euanthe sanderiana*. *Vanda* Rothschildiana exhibits hybrid vigor (heterosis) and is much more satisfactory in cultivation than pure *V. coerulea*. Most hybrid blue vandas have *V.* Rothschildiana in their ancestry.

Vanda tricolor Lindley

This species is endemic to Java although dubiously reported from other countries. The plants are frequently found under the name *V. suavis*, a later synonym. *Vanda tricolor* is closely related to the Philippine *V. luzonica* and differs by its bold spotting and strong fragrance. The purple-spotted white flowers with dark purple lips are

Vanda lamellata

notable for their strongly reflexed segments and long pedicels and ovaries. *Vanda tricolor* usually flowers in the fall and winter.

VANDOPSIS Pfitzer
van-DOP-sis
Tribe: Vandeae
Subtribe: Sarcanthinae
Etymology: *Vanda*, a genus of orchids; Gr. *opsis*, resemblance

The genus *Vandopsis* comprises five epiphytic, lithophytic, and terrestrial species native from Nepal to the Philippines. They are characterized by large plant size, elongate fleshy lip bent like a knee, and two deeply cleft pollinia. The taxonomy of *Vandopsis* is complex, and many plants previously considered *Vandopsis* have been relegated to other genera, including *Arachnis*, *Hygrochilus*, and *Sarcanthopsis*. *Vandopsis* should be given culture similar to other large monopodial orchids. They prefer heavy, uniform watering throughout the year, warm temperatures, and very bright light levels. The plants can be grown in large pots or baskets. Slow-growing, the

Vanda tricolor

plants should not be disturbed more frequently than is absolutely necessary.

Vandopsis gigantea (Lindley) Pfitzer

Native from Burma through Indochina, China, and Malaya, *Vandopsis gigantea* is a massive epiphyte. The large, round flowers are pale yellow with large brown spots that appear as rings with lighter centers. The inflorescence is relatively short, and the flowers are borne near the center of the plant during the late spring. *Vandopsis gigantea* is particularly cold-sensitive, a feature it transmits to hybrids.

Vandopsis lissochiloides (Gaudich.) Pfitzer

Vandopsis lissochiloides is native to Thailand, Laos, the Philippines, and New Guinea. Unlike other species in the genus, it is a terrestrial. The plant size is equally massive and it is not uncommon to find plants with stems to several meters in length. The summer flowers are a rich golden yellow with dark purple spots and a purple lip. Some plants have flowers with white outer surfaces, while others have flowers with rich purple outer surfaces. *Vandopsis lissochiloides* will tolerate full sun.

VANILLA Sw.
va-NIL-luh
Tribe: Vanilleae
Subtribe: Vanillinae
Etymology: Sp. *Vainilla*, little pod

Over 50 species are currently known

Vandopsis lissochiloides

Vandopsis gigantea

throughout the world's tropics and subtropics. The plants are vinelike, sometimes reaching 30 or more meters in length, bearing fleshy leaves (rarely scalelike) and roots, opposite the leaves, in each node. The short, few-flowered racemes also arise at the nodes from the leaf-axils. The flowers, showy but very short-lived in most species, are produced in succession. Vanilla essence is extracted from the fleshy fruits of several species of *Vanilla*, making it the only orchid group used for commercial purposes (other than for their ornamental value). In all species pollen is soft and mealy, not divided in distinct pollinia.

Most species grow well if the basal roots are potted in well-drained clay containers packed with the medium recommended for *Cyrtopodium*. However, due to their growth habits, all species need support for their long vines. Provide bright light, keep plants evenly moist and fertilize frequently. Most species, however, will not bloom until they have reached a large size.

Vanilla phaeantha Reichb.f.

This showy species, found in Florida, the West Indies, and Trinidad-Tobago, blooms in cultivation from December to July. Sepals

Vanilla planifolia

Warmingia eugenii

Warrea warreana

and petals are pale green, the lip cream-white with yellow veining.

Vanilla planifolia Andrews

This showy species, found originally in the West Indies and in Central America but now cultivated throughout the tropics as a source of vanilla essence, blooms in cultivation throughout the year but especially from January to May. Flowers are pale green to yellowish green.

Vanilla pompona Schiede

This showy species, found in the West Indies and from Mexico to Bolivia and Brazil, blooms in cultivation from January to May. Flowers are yellowish green, the lip white to orange-yellow.

the column which is shorter than the sepals and parallel to the axis of the inflorescence; and the two hard pollinia attached to a stipe united to a viscidium.

The plants grow as epiphytes in wet forest at elevations from sea level to 1,000 meters. They are best cultivated on plaques under intermediate conditions where the pendent inflorescences can emerge.

Warmingia eugenii Reichb.f.

This species occurs from Bolivia to Brazil. The flowers reach a diameter of three centimeters. The flowers are white with a yellow callus at the base of the lip. The lateral lobes of the lip are quadrate and lacerate on the margins. The apical lobe is narrowly ovate and has an erose margin.

form one pair attached to a short stipe united to a viscidium.

The plants grow as terrestrials in the shade of wet forest at elevations from 600 to 1,200 meters. Cultivation of members of this genus should be under intermediate conditions in a well-drained medium with abundant water supplied.

Warrea warreana (Lodd. ex Lindley) C. Schweinf.

This species is distributed from Colombia to Bolivia and from Brazil to Argentina. The inflorescences reach 70 centimeters tall and produce four to ten flowers. The flowers reach seven centimeters in diameter. The sepals and petals are white with yellowish margins. The tubular lip is white marked inside with purple and yellow. The lip has a three-lamellate callus at the base.

WARMINGIA Reichb.f.
war-MING-ee-ah
Tribe: Cymbidieae
Subtribe: Oncidiinae
Etymology: In honor of Eugene Warming, Danish botanist and explorer during the nineteenth century

This is a genus of three species distributed from Brazil to Ecuador. The genus is characterized by the presence of unifoliate pseudobulbs of a single internode subtended by distichous leaflike sheaths; the pendent inflorescence produced from the axils of the sheaths; the white flowers; the lateral sepals spreading, not forming a tube at the base; the apical lobe of the spurless lip elongate, slender, concave; the lateral lobes large, forming a cavity under

WARREA Lindley
WAR-ee-ah
Tribe: Maxillarieae
Subtribe: Zygopetalinae
Etymology: In honor of Frederick Warre, British plant explorer during the nineteenth century

Warrea is a genus of four species distributed from Mexico to Brazil. The genus is characterized by the pseudobulbs of several nodes surrounded by the bases of thin, heavily veined leaves; the erect, lateral inflorescences; the sepals and petals free; the lateral sepals united at the base to form a mentum with the column-foot; the lip with a basal callus of three to five lamellae united to the column-foot; the beaked anther; and the four hard pollinia united to

XYLOBIUM Lindley
zi-LO-bee-um
Tribe: Maxillarieae
Subtribe: Bifrenariinae
Etymology: Gr. *xylon*, wood or log; *bios*, life

Twenty or 25 species are currently known in this genus that ranges widely from Mexico to southeastern Brazil but is most diverse in the Andean countries. The plants are caespitose with spherical to cylindrical pseudobulbs topped by one-to-four plicate leaves. Relatively short, few- to multiflowered racemes arise from the base of the pseudobulbs. Flowers are cream-in 10–20-flowered racemes. Perianth segments are creamy green or yellow-green, the labellum with dull orange-ochre nerves. Flowering occurs November-January. Culture is easy in the warm or intermediate greenhouse.

Xylobium squalens (Lindley) Lindley

One of the most commonly cultivated species, this taxon has until recently been called *Xylobium variegatum,* a name that applies to a very different species. *Xylobium squalens* is known from Costa Rica southward to Brazil at elevations of 200–1,000 meters. Flowers are produced in September-November in short, dense racemes. The segments are dull white-pink to dull maroon with darker nerves; the midlobe of the labellum is very dark. Cultivation is easy in the warm or intermediate greenhouse.

ZOOTROPHION Luer
zo-o-TRO-fee-on
Tribe: Epidendreae
Subtribe: Pleurothallidinae
Etymology: Gr. *zootrophion,* a menagerie

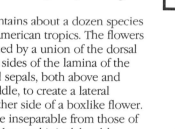

This genus contains about a dozen species native to the American tropics. The flowers are characterized by a union of the dorsal sepal with the sides of the lamina of the connate lateral sepals, both above and below the middle, to create a lateral window on either side of a boxlike flower. The flowers are inseparable from those of *Cryptophoranthus,* and it is debatable whether, in spite of vegetative differences, the species should be included in *Cryptophoranthus.* The petals, lip, and

Xylobium foveatum

colored to purplish. All species have four pollinia.

Provide bright light but not direct sun for most species along with warm to intermediate temperatures (15°–25°C at night). Keep plants evenly moist when in active growth, but water less frequently once pseudobulbs have developed. Most species are vigorous and of easy culture, but the systematics of the genus are confused and many of the names used for the cultivated species are incorrect.

Xylobium foveatum (Lindley) Nichols

A common and widespread species ranging from Mexico and the West Indies to southeastern Brazil, usually at elevations of 100–1,000 meters. The flowers are produced

Zootrophion dayanum

column are hidden within the flower. There are two pollinia.

The species are relatively easy to cultivate in moist, intermediate to cool-growing greenhouse conditions.

Zootrophion dayanum (Reichb.f.) Luer

This robust species, native to the Andes of Venezuela, Colombia, and Ecuador, is characterized by a large, elliptical, leathery leaf borne by a stout stem enclosed by a series of loose, inflated sheaths. The flower, dark purple-brown and more or less bristly on the outside, is large with wide open windows, created because only the tip of the dorsal sepal is connate to the tip of the lamina of the lateral sepals. Inside, the lamina of the lateral sepals is convex and orange.

ZYGOPETALUM Hook.

zy-go-PET-a-lum
Tribe: Maxillarieae
Subtribe: Zygopetalinae
Etymology: Gr. *zygon*, yoke; *petalon*, petal or sepal; in reference to the callus yoking the floral segments together

This is a genus of sixteen species from South America. The genus is characterized by the approximate pseudobulbs of several nodes surrounded by the bases of flat leaves; the erect, lateral, multiflorous inflorescence; the sepals and petals free; the three-lobed lip with a basal fan-shaped callus; and the four hard pollinia united to form one pair attached to a viscidium. The plants grow as terrestrials or epiphytes in wet forest at elevations from 300 to 1,500 meters. They can be cultivated in pots in well-drained media with abundant water supplied throughout the year.

Zygopetalum crinitum Lodd.

This species occurs in Brazil. The inflorescences are somewhat spreading, reaching 45 centimeters tall, and producing three to ten large flowers. The flowers reach eight centimeters in diameter. The sepals and petals are green, blotched with red-

Zygopetalum maxillare

brown. The white lip is large and frilled on the margin with radiating, branching, red vein-lines.

Zygopetalum graminifolium Rolfe

This species is found in Brazil. The pseudobulbs are often separated on the rhizome. The erect inflorescence reaches 45 centimeters tall and produces six to ten crowded flowers. The flowers reach five centimeters in diameter. The sepals and petals are green mottled and blotched with greyish red. The lip is blue-purple with radiating, branched vein-lines of darker blue, and a white blotch at the apex.

Zygopetalum mackayi Hook.

This species is known from Brazil. The inflorescence reaches one meter tall and produces five to ten large flowers. The flowers reach eight centimeters in diameter. The sepals and petals are yellowish green with red-brown blotches. The petals are shorter than the sepals. The lip is white with branching, bluish red vein-lines radiating from the base. The column is glabrous on the underside. This species is very close to the more commonly cultivated *Z. intermedium* Lodd., which differs by having petals of about the same length as the sepals and the column pubescent on the underside.

Zygopetalum crinitum

Zygopetalum mackayi

Zygosepalum lindeniae

Andes. The flowers reach eight centimeters in diameter. The sepals and petals are red-brown, and the oblong to semi-cordiform lip is white with branching, radiating vein-lines.

Zygosepalum tatei (Ames & C. Schweinf.) Garay & Dunsterv.

This species is found in Venezuela and Brazil. The flowers reach five centimeters in diameter. The sepals and petals are yellow-green blotched with red. The kidney-shaped lip is white with a red claw at the base.

Zygopetalum maxillare Lodd.

This species occurs in Brazil and Peru. The pseudobulbs are separated on a creeping rhizome. The inflorescence reaches 30 centimeters in length and produces five to eight flowers. The flowers reach seven centimeters in diameter. The sepals and petals are light green, washed with red-brown. The petals and dorsal sepal are ascending, and the lateral sepals are downcurved. The purplish blue lip is three-lobed with the lateral lobes erect and narrowly oblong united to the nearly round apical lobe. The lunate, fleshy crest is purple.

ZYGOSEPALUM Reichb.f.
zy-go-SEE-pal-um
Tribe: Maxillarieae
Subtribe: Zygopetalinae
Etymology: Gr. *zygon*, yoke; *sepalum*, sepal; in reference to the basally united sepals

This is a genus of seven species known from Colombia, Venezuela, Peru, and Brazil. The genus is characterized by the elongate rhizome with pseudobulbs of a single internode with one to four leaves at the apex; the foliaceous sheaths surrounding the base of the pseudobulbs; the leaves plicate, heavily veined; the inflorescence arising from the axils of the foliaceous sheaths with one to three large flowers; the flowers resupinate; the sepals and petals free spreading; the lip three-lobed, entire on the margin; the callus at the base fan-shaped; the anther cap with an elongate, hornlike projection from its apex; and the four hard pollinia superposed in two pairs, attached to a quadrate stipe.
The plants grow as epiphytes in lowland forest at elevations from 100 to 500 meters. Cultivation of the species is best on plaques because of the elongate rhizomes. They should be grown under intermediate conditions with liberal applications of water throughout the year.

Zygosepalum lindeniae (Rolfe) Garay & Dunsterv.

This species occurs from Venezuela to Peru and Brazil at lower elevations east of the

ZYGOSTATES Lindley
zy-go-STAY-teez
Tribe: Maxillarieae
Subtribe: Ornithocephalinae
Etymology: Gr. *zygostates*, weigher, balance; in reference to the projections from the base of the column which resemble a balance

Zygostates is a genus of seven species from central and southern Brazil. It is characterized by the equitant, fan-shaped plants without pseudobulbs — the leaves dorsiventrally flattened and imbricating at the base, with a line of dehiscence near the base, or by the presence of pseudobulbs with leaf-bearing sheaths surrounding their base; the inflorescence lateral from a leaf-sheath; the sepals and petals free, spreading; the lip free; the column stipitate, usually with an extremely elongate rostellum and anther; the stigma at the base on the underside; the pair of clublike projections from each side of the column at the base; and the two hard pollinia on an

extremely elongate stipe united to a small viscidium.
The plants grow as epiphytes in moist forest. Cultivation is best accomplished under intermediate conditions on plaques with abundant water throughout the year.

Zygostates alleniana Kränzlin

This species occurs in Brazil and Peru. The pseudobulbs are provided with an apical leaf and one or two leaf-bearing sheaths surrounding the base. The flowers are white with green markings on the base of the petals and on the lip. The rostellum of the anther is relatively short.

Zygostates grandiflora (Lindley) Cogn.

This species is found in Brazil. The leaves are equitant and form a fanlike plant. The sepals are white, and the petals are white with a green basal claw. The lip is white with a green callus. The rostellum of the anther is extremely elongate. This species is often treated as a member of the genus *Dipteranthus.*

Zygostates grandiflora

GLOSSARY

acuminate: referring to an apex (leaf, sepal, etc.) which tapers to a fine point

acute: referring to an apex that is broadly tapered

adnation (adj. *adnate*): fusion of unlike parts, e.g. labellum with column; contrasted with connation

anther: the pollen-bearing portion of the stamen

apicule (adj. *apiculate*): a short, sharp point

auricles: ear-like lobes, often paired, as on the labellum or column

axil (adj. *axillary*): the angle formed by a petiole and stem or, on an inflorescence, pedicel and rachis

bifid: two-lobed

bifoliate: two-leaved

bifurcate: forked

bract: a leaflike organ

caespitose: tufted; growing in small clumps

callus (pl. *calli*): a waxy or fleshy protuberance, as on a labellum

capitate: appearing in heads, as some inflorescences

capitulum: a dense head of flowers

capsule: a dry fruit splitting along one or more sutures; the fruit type in the orchid family

cataphyll: scale-like leaf, as on a rhizome or base of a stem

caudate: having a "tail" or narrowed, apical extension, as some sepals and petals

caudicle: extensions of tissue derived from the anther and connected to pollinia in many orchids

ciliate: fringed with cilia or tiny hairs

clavate: club-shaped, sometimes said of some pseudobulbs and pollinia

claw: a long and narrowed basal portion of a sepal or petal (including labellum)

clinandrium: the portion of the column that supports the anther

column: the organ of the orchid flower representing the fusion of stamens, styles, and stigmas

column-foot: a basal extension of the column to which the labellum is attached, often flexibly

column wings: paired protuberances or winglike flanges on the column

conduplicate: folded once longitudinally down the middle

connation (adj. *connate*): fusion of like parts, e.g. sepal with sepal; contrasted with adnation

conspecific: belonging to the same species

cordate (*cordiform*): heart-shaped

coriaceous: having a leathery texture

corm: a condensed stem, usually underground

corymb (adj. *corymbose*): a broad, flat-topped inflorescence in which the outermost flowers open first

deflexed: bent backward or downward

dentate: referring to a toothed margin, the teeth pointing perpendicularly

disc: an elevated region of the labellum, usually the midlobe, distinguished by color and/or accessory features such as calli, keels, or lamellae

distichous: in two ranks or rows on opposite sides of an axis

echinate: having prickles, as some orchid ovaries and capsules

entire: smooth and continuous; said of the margin of a leaf or leaflike organ

epichile: the apical portion of the labellum in some orchid genera, e.g. *Stanhopea*

epiphyte: a plant growing on another

equitant: with leaves overlapping and arranged in two ranks or rows

erose: referring to the irregular margin of a leaf or leaflike organ which appears to have been chewed

facultative: not restricted to a particular way of life

falcate: sickle-shaped

fimbriate: finely fringed, as the margin of the labellum

foliaceous, foliose: leaflike

fugacious: withering away early; ephemeral

fusiform: spindle-shaped, as some pseudobulbs

galea: a hood or "helmet" formed by the dorsal sepal or fusion of dorsal sepal and petals in some orchids

glabrous: lacking hairs

glaucous: covered with fine white hairs or powder

glomerate: densely clustered

hypochile: the basal portion of the labellum in some genera, e.g. *Stanhopea*

imbricate: overlapping, as the scales on a snake

imperfect (flowers): having only male or female parts; unisexual

internode: the region of an axis between two successive nodes

keel: a fleshy ridge, as on a labellum

keiki: a vegetative offshoot ("plantlet") formed at a node, as on an inflorescence

labellum (lip): the median, modified petal of an orchid flower

lacerate: appearing torn, as the margin of a sepal or petal

lamella (pl. *lamellae*): raised, membranous outgrowths on the labellum, as in *Coelogyne*

lamina: the blade (of a leaf, sepal, petal, etc.)

lanceolate: lance-shaped

lateral lobes: the two lobes to either side of the midlobe of a three-lobed labellum

ligulate: strap-shaped

lip (see *labellum*)

lithophyte: a plant which grows on rocks

maculation: spotting or marking

mentum: a "chin" on some orchid flowers, formed by the fusion of the lateral sepals and the column-foot

meristem: in plants, undifferentiated tissue which retains the ability to provide new cells

mesochile: the middle portion of the labellum in some genera

midlobe: the middle lobe of a three-lobed labellum, usually brightly colored and furnished with calli, keels, and/or lamellae

monopodial: referring to a growth habit in which new leaves develop from the same meristem or growing point

mycorrhiza: a nutritional relationship between certain fungi and the roots and seedlings of orchids (as well as other plants)

node: the region on an axis (stem, rhizome, etc.) to which other plant parts (e.g. leaves) are attached

non-resupinate: referring to orchid flowers which do not twist 180 degrees during development or which twist a full 360 degrees, with the result that the labellum is uppermost

obligate: restricted to a particular way of life

obovate: egg-shaped, the broader end above the middle

orbicular: circular, spherical

osmophore: a gland, usually floral, which produces fragrances that attract pollinators

ovary: the part of the pistil which contains ovules

ovate: egg-shaped, the broader end below the middle

ovule: the unit of the ovary which contains the egg cell and becomes the seed

panicle: a branched raceme

papillae (adj. *papillose*): a rounded projection from a portion of an epidermal cell; a small bump or protuberance

pedicel: the stalk of an individual flower in an inflorescence

peduncle: the stalk of a solitary flower or an entire inflorescence

perfect (flowers): having both male and female parts; bisexual

perianth: the sepals and petals of a flower

petal: the whorl of flower parts just inside the sepals, usually colorful; the median petal of orchids, the labellum, is often differentiated in form and/or function

petiole: the stalk of a leaf

pilose: densely haired

pistil: the female portion of the flower, consisting of the stigma, style, and ovary with ovules

plicate: folded or pleated

pod (see *capsule*)

pollinarium (pl. *pollinaria*): a functional unit in orchid pollination, consisting of two or more pollinia, stalk or stipe, and viscidium

pollinium (pl. *pollinia*): a mass of pollen grains

pseudobulb: the variously thickened portion of an orchid stem

pubescent: covered with fine hairs

quadrate: square or rectangular

raceme (adj. *racemose*): an unbranched inflorescence of stalked flowers

rachis: that portion of an inflorescence, above the peduncle, bearing flowers

ramicaul: the leafy stem of some sympodial orchids such as those in subtribe Pleurothallidinae; distinguished from the rhizome

reniform: kidney-shaped

resupinate: referring to orchid flowers which twist through 180 degrees during development, with the result that the labellum is lowermost

retuse: notched at the apex (of a leaf or flower part)

rhizome: the indeterminate axis of many plants (such as sympodial orchids) which successively gives rise to new shoots and flowers; often horizontal or underground, but not necessarily

rostellum: part of the median stigma lobe of orchid flowers

rugose: referring to a rough or wrinkled surface of a plant part

saprophyte (adj. *saprophytic*): a plant which derives its nourishment, in whole or in part, from dead organic material

scape: a leafless peduncle; commonly, the leafless stalk of an entire inflorescence

scarious: dry and papery, often said of bracts

sectile: referring to pollinia in loosely coherent "packets"

secund: to one side, as flowers on an inflorescence

sepal (adj. *sepaline*): the outermost whorl of flower parts

serrate: referring to a toothed margin, the teeth pointing forward

sessile: lacking a stalk

spathe: a bract surrounding or subtending an inflorescence

speculum: the shiny, colored region of the labellum, as in some *Ophrys* species

spicule (adj. *spiculate*): a small, sharp point

spike: an unbranched inflorescence with sessile flowers; commonly used in lieu of inflorescence, as "a flower spike"

spur: a saccate or tubular extension of the labellum (or other floral parts) in many orchid species, often bearing nectar

stamen: the male portion of the flower, consisting of the pollen-bearing anther and filament

staminode: a sterile stamen

stigma: that portion of the pistil that receives the pollen

stipe: the stalk connecting pollinia and viscidium in a pollinarium

style: the elongate portion of the pistil between stigma and ovary

subtend: to insert below, as a bract below a flower

sulcate: furrowed lengthwise, such as pseudobulbs

sympodial: referring to a growth habit in which new shoots arise successively from axillary buds of a rhizome

synsepal: a floral part formed by the partial or complete fusion of two or more sepals

terete: pencil-like; round in cross-section

tessellation: a checkered pattern

trichome: a plant hair

tridactylate: literally, three-fingered, with three narrow lobes

triquetrous: three-angled; three-winged

truncate: with one end squared off

tuber: a thickened, usually underground storage organ consisting of stem tissues; commonly ascribed (incorrectly) to orchids

tubercle: a small, wartlike protrusion, as on the callus on an *Oncidium* flower

tuberoid: a thickened, underground storage organ with stem and root tissues

umbel: a more or less flat-topped inflorescence in which the pedicels arise from the same point, much like an umbrella

undulate: wavy, as the margin of a sepal or petal

unguiculate: having a claw; commonly said of a perianth segment

unifoliate: one-leaved

velamen: the outermost tissue of roots of many orchids, dead at maturity and capable of absorption and short-term storage of water and nutrients

verrucose: with a warty or bumpy surface

viscidium: the sticky portion of the rostellum which is connected to pollinia

Bibliography

GENERAL WORKS

ARDITTI, JOSEPH [ed.]. 1977. *Orchid Biology: Reviews and Perspectives, I.* Cornell University Press, Ithaca, New York.
————. [ed.]. 1982. *Orchid Biology: Reviews and Perspectives, II.* Cornell University Press, Ithaca, New York.
————. [ed.]. 1984. *Orchid Biology: Reviews and Perspectives, III.* Cornell University Press, Ithaca, New York.
————. [ed.]. 1987. *Orchid Biology: Reviews and Perspectives, IV.* Cornell University Press, Ithaca, New York.
————. [ed.]. 1990. *Orchid Biology: Reviews and Perspectives, V.* Timber Press, Portland, Oregon.

BECHTEL, H., P. J. CRIBB, and E. LAUNERT, 1986. *Manual of Cultivated Orchid Species.* 2nd ed. MIT Press, Cambridge, Massachusetts.

DARWIN, CHARLES. 1862. *On the Various Contrivances By Which British and Foreign Orchids Are Fertilised By Insects.* John Murray, London.

DRESSLER, ROBERT L. 1981. *The Orchids: Natural History and Classification.* Harvard University Press, Cambridge, Massachusetts.
————. 1986. Recent advances in orchid phylogeny. *Lindleyana* 1: 5–20.
————. 1990a. The Neottieae in orchid classification. *Lindleyana* 5: 102–109.
————. 1990b. The Spiranthoideae: grade or subfamily? *Lindleyana* 5: 110–116.

HAWKES, ALEX D. 1965. *Encyclopaedia of Cultivated Orchids.* Faber and Faber, London.

PIJL, L. VAN DER, and C. H. DODSON. 1966. *Orchid Flowers: Their Pollination and Evolution.* University of Miami Press, Coral Gables, Florida.

PRIDGEON, ALEC M. 1987. The velamen and exodermis of orchid roots. Pages 139–192 *in* J. Arditti [ed.], *Orchid Biology: Reviews and Perspectives, IV.* Cornell University Press, Ithaca, New York.

REINIKKA, MERLE A. 1972. *A History of the Orchid.* University of Miami Press, Coral Gables, Florida.

SCHULTES, RICHARD EVANS, and ARTHUR STANLEY PEASE. 1963. *Generic Names of Orchids: Their Origin and Meaning.* Academic Press, New York.

SHEEHAN, TOM, and MARION SHEEHAN. 1979. *Orchid Genera Illustrated.* Van Nostrand Reinhold, New York.

STEWART, JOYCE. 1988. *Orchids.* Royal Botanic Gardens, Kew, England.

VEITCH, JAMES AND SONS. 1887–1894. *A Manual of Orchidaceous Plants.* 2 vols. Reprinted 1963. A. Asher & Co., Amsterdam.

MONOGRAPHS

BOCKEMÜHL, LEONORE. 1989. Odontoglossum: *A Monograph and Iconograph.* Kurt Schmersow, Hildesheim.

CRIBB, PHILLIP. 1983. *A Revision of* Dendrobium *Section* Latouria. *Kew Bull.* 38: 229–306.
————. 1986. The 'Antelope' Dendrobiums. *Kew Bull.* 41: 615–692.
————. 1987. *The Genus* Paphiopedilum. Royal Botanic Gardens, Kew, England.
————, and Ian Butterfield. 1988. *The Genus* Pleione. Timber Press, Portland, Oregon.

DRESSLER, ROBERT L., and GLENN E. POLLARD. 1974. *The Genus* Encyclia *in Mexico.* Asociación Mexicana de Orquideología, Mexico City.

DU PUY, DAVID, and PHILLIP CRIBB. 1988. *The Genus* Cymbidium. Christopher Helm, London.

LUER, CARLYLE A. 1983–. *Thesaurus Masdevalliarum.* Helga Königer, Munich.

————. 1986–1989. *Icones Pleurothallidinarum I–VI.* Missouri Botanical Garden, St. Louis, Missouri.
————, with Rodrigo Escobar R. 1988–. *Thesaurus Dracularum.* Missouri Botanical Garden, St. Louis, Missouri.

REEVE, T. M., and P. J. B. WOODS. 1989. A revision of *Dendrobium* section *Oxyglossum* (Orchidaceae). *Notes RBG Edinburgh* 46: 161–305.

SWEET, HERMAN R. 1980. *The Genus* Phalaenopsis. Orchid Digest Inc., Pomona, California.

VERMEULEN, J. J. 1987. A Taxonomic Revision of the Continental African Bulbophyllinae. *Orchid Monographs,* vol. 2. E. J. Brill, Leiden.

WITHNER, CARL L. 1988. *The Cattleyas and Their Relatives. Vol. 1. The Cattleyas.* Timber Press, Portland, Oregon.

FLORAS

AMES, O., and D. S. CORRELL. 1952–1953. Orchids of Guatemala. *Fieldiana (Bot.)* 26: 1–727.

CASE, FRED. 1987. *Orchids of the Western Great Lakes Region.* Cranbrook Institute of Science, Bloomfield Hills, Michigan.

CLEMENTS, M. A. 1989. Catalogue of Australian Orchidaceae. *Austral. Orchid Res.* 1: 1–160.

COMBER, J. 1990. *Orchids of Java.* Royal Botanic Gardens, Kew, England.

CRIBB, P. 1989. *Orchidaceae (Part 3).* Flora of Tropical East Africa. A. A. Balkema, Rotterdam.

DAVIES, PAUL, JENNE DAVIES, and ANTHONY HUXLEY. 1983. *Wild Orchids of Britain and Europe.* Chatto & Windus, Hogarth Press, London.

DODSON, C. H., and DAVID E. BENNETT. 1989. *Orchids of Peru. Icones Plantarum Tropicarum, Series II.* Fascicles 1, 2. Missouri Botanical Garden, St. Louis, Missouri.
————, and Roberto Vasquez Ch. 1989. *Orchids of Bolivia. Icones Plantarum Tropicarum, Series II.* Fascicles 3, 4. Missouri Botanical Garden, St. Louis, Missouri.
————, and Piedad Marmaol de Dodson. 1989. *Orchids of Ecuador. Icones Plantarum Tropicarum, Series II.* Fascicles 5, 6. Missouri Botanical Garden, St. Louis, Missouri.

DUNSTERVILLE, G. C. K., and L. A. GARAY. 1959–1976. *Venezuelan Orchids Illustrated.* 6 vols. Andre Deutsch, London.
————, and ————. 1979. *Orchids of Venezuela: An Illustrated Field Guide.* Botanical Museum, Harvard University, Cambridge, Massachusetts.

ESCOBAR, RODRIGO R. [ed.]. 1990–. *Native Colombian Orchids.* Editorial Colina, Medellín.

GARAY, L. A., and H. R. SWEET. 1974. *Orchids of the Southern Ryukyu Islands.* Botanical Museum, Harvard University, Cambridge, Massachusetts.

HÁGSATER, ERIC, and GERARDO O. SALAZAR. 1990. *Icones Orchidacearum, Fascicle 1. Orchids of Mexico.* Asociación Mexicana de Orquideología, Mexico City.

HAMER, F. 1974. *Las Orquideas de El Salvador.* 2 vols. Ministerio de Educacion, San Salvador.

HOLTTUM, R. E. 1964. *Flora of Malaya. Vol. I. Orchids of Malaya.* 3rd ed. Government Printing Office, Singapore.

JOHNS, JOHN, and BRIAN MOLLOY. 1983. *Native Orchids of New Zealand.* A. H. & A. W. Reed, Wellington.

JONES, DAVID L. 1988. *Native Orchids of Australia.* Reed Books, Frenchs Forest, New South Wales.

LEWIS, B., and P. CRIBB. 1989. *Orchids of Vanuatu.* Royal Botanic Gardens, Kew, England.
————, and ————. 1991. *Orchids of the Solomon Islands and Bougainville.* Royal Botanic Gardens, Kew, England.

LUER, CARLYLE A. 1972. *The Native Orchids of Florida.* New York Botanical Garden, New York.

————. 1975. *The Native Orchids of the United States and Canada (Excluding Florida).* New York Botanical Garden, New York.

MCVAUGH, R. 1985. *Orchidaceae. Flora Novo-Galiciana, vol. 16.* University of Michigan Press, Ann Arbor, Michigan.

PABST, G. F. J., and F. DUNGS. 1975–1977. *Orchidaceae Brasilienses.* 2 vols. Kurt Schmersow, Hildesheim.

SCHLECHTER, R. 1982. *The Orchidaceae of German New Guinea.* English transl. Australian Orchid Foundation, Melbourne.

SEGERBÄCK, L. B. 1983. *Orchids of Nigeria.* A. A. Balkema, Rotterdam.

SEIDENFADEN, GUNNAR, and TEM SMITINAND. 1958–1965. *The Orchids of Thailand: A Preliminary List.* The Siam Society, Bangkok.

STEWART, JOYCE, H. P. LINDER, E. A. SCHELPE, and A. V. HALL. 1982. *Wild Orchids of South Africa.* Macmillan, Johannesburg.

TEO, CHRIS K. H. 1985. *Native Orchids of Peninsula Malaysia.* Times Books International, Singapore.

VERMEULEN, J. J. 1991. *Orchids of Borneo. Vol. 2.* Bulbophyllum. Bentham-Moxon Trust, Royal Botanic Gardens, Kew, England.

WILLIAMS, LOUIS O., and PAUL H. ALLEN. 1980. *Orchids of Panama.* Missouri Botanical Garden, St. Louis, Missouri.

CULTIVATION

BIRK, LANCE A. 1983. *The* Paphiopedilum *Grower's Manual.* Pisang Press, Santa Barbara, California.

CRIBB, PHILLIP, and CHRISTOPHER BAILES. 1989. *Hardy Orchids.* Christopher Helm, London.

FERGUSON, BARBARA [ed.]. 1988. *All About Growing Orchids.* Ortho Books, San Ramon, California.

HILLerman, FRED E., and Arthur W. Holst. 1986. *An Introduction to the Cultivated Angraecoid Orchids of Madagascar.* Timber Press, Portland, Oregon.

HOLMAN, RALPH T. 1976. Cultivation of *Cypripedium calceolus* and *Cypripedium reginae. Amer. Orchid Soc. Bull.* 45: 415–422.

KOOPOWITZ, HAROLD, and NORITO HASEGAWA. 1989. *Novelty Slipper Orchids: Breeding and Cultivating* Paphiopedilum *Hybrids.* Angus & Robertson, North Ryde, New South Wales.

NORTHEN, REBECCA T. 1990. *Home Orchid Growing.* 4th ed. Prentice Hall Press, New York.

PRIDGEON, ALEC M. [ed.]. 1988. *Handbook on Orchid Culture.* American Orchid Society, West Palm Beach, Florida.
————. [ed.]. 1990. *Handbook on Orchid Pests and Diseases.* American Orchid Society, West Palm Beach, Florida.

RITTERSHAUSEN, BRIAN, and WILMA RITTERSHAUSEN. 1985. *Orchid Growing Illustrated.* Blandford Press, Poole, Dorset, Great Britain.

WHITLOW, CARSON E. 1977. Growing temperate cypripediums in containers. *Amer. Orchid Soc. Bull.* 46: S23–S25.

CONSERVATION

KOOPOWITZ, HAROLD, and HILARY KAYE. 1990. 2nd ed. *Plant Extinction: A Global Crisis.* Christopher Helm, London.

LIGHT, MARILYN H. S. 1990. Doing your part for conservation. *Amer. Orchid Soc. Bull.* 59: 786–793, 897–903, 1014–1022.

PRANCE, G. T., and T. S. ELIAS [eds.]. 1977. *Extinction Is Forever: The Status of Threatened and Endangered Plants of the Americas.* New York Botanical Garden, New York.

PRITCHARD, H. W. [ed.]. 1989. *Modern Methods in Orchid Conservation.* Cambridge University Press, Cambridge.

THOMPSON, P. A. 1980. *Orchids From Seed.* Royal Botanic Gardens, Kew, England.

CONTRIBUTORS

ALEC M. PRIDGEON PH.D., F.L.S.

Alec Pridgeon was born in 1950 in Dallas, Texas, and received his Ph.D. in biology from Florida State University, his specialty being the anatomy and systematics of orchids. He is now working at the Royal Botanic Gardens, Kew, and also serving as a Visiting Research Fellow at the Australian National Botanic Gardens in Canberra.

In orchid circles he is perhaps best known as past Editor of the *American Orchid Society Bulletin* and founding Editor of the scientific orchid journal, *Lindleyana*. However, he has written or co-written over twenty scientific articles and book chapters and 80 popular articles, co-written and co-directed five video-tapes, and edited seven books, all on orchids.

He has been an invited speaker to three World Orchid Conferences as well as symposium chairman and speaker at the 14th International Botanical Congress in Berlin in 1987.

Dr. Pridgeon is a member of the International Orchid Commission, Fellow of the Linnean Society of London, and Associate of the Oakes Ames Orchid Herbarium of Harvard University.

ERIC A. CHRISTENSON PH.D.

Eric Christenson is an orchid taxonomist with a keen interest in horticultural taxonomy. Long-term research projects include the coordination of the orchid treatments for the *Flora of the Guianas* and *Flora Mesoamericana* as well as the study of Asiatic monopodial orchids and orchid bibliography.

GERMÁN CARNEVALI

Germán Carnevali is the major contributor to the orchid treatment for the Flora of the Venezuelan Guayana Project. He is now pursuing a doctorate at the University of St. Louis in association with the Missouri Botanical Garden. His main area of interest is the systematics of tribe Maxillarieae.

PAUL HARCOURT DAVIES
M.A. (OXON.), M.SC.(LONDON)

Although he is a theoretical physicist by training, a lifelong love of the natural world and a mania for orchids have led Paul Davies to a career as an author and photographer. He was senior editor of a standard work in 1983, *Wild Orchids of Britain and Europe*; has written and illustrated numerous articles on orchids, conservation and photography for European and American journals; has co-authored three further books; and has acted as consultant editor for two others.

CALAWAY H. DODSON PH.D.

Dr. Dodson is an authority on the orchids of the western hemisphere, with particular

emphasis on the orchids of Ecuador. Formerly Professor of Botany at the University of Miami and Founding Director of the Marie Selby Botanical Garden, he is presently Senior Curator of the Missouri Botanical Garden and Honorary Director of the National Herbarium of Ecuador.

ERIC HÁGSATER

Eric Hágsater has dedicated 30 years to research in the orchids of Mexico and the Neotropics, in particular the genus *Epidendrum*. He is currently contributing to various floras of the New World and maintains an extensive live collection together with the herbarium of the Mexican Orchid Association.

DAVID L. JONES B.SC.

David Jones is a research scientist at the Australian National Botanic Gardens, the Chairman of the Research Committee of the Australian Orchid Foundation, and a Life Member of the Australian Native Orchid Society. He has studied the biology of orchids, particularly those of Australia, for 30 years, and has published numerous articles and books, including *Climbing Plants in Australia, Australian Ferns and Fern Allies, Ornamental Rainforest Plants in Australia* and *Native Orchids of Australia*.

CARLYLE A. LUER, M.D.

Dr. Luer, Research Associate of Missouri Botanical Garden, is recognized as one of the world's authorities on orchids in the subtribe Pleurothallidinae as well as the North American orchid flora. His ongoing generic monographs — *Thesaurus Masdevalliarum, Thesaurus Dracularum,* and *Icones Pleurothallidinarum* — reflect almost twenty years of exploration in the New World tropics.

DR. HENRY F. OAKELEY
M.B. B.S., F.R.C.P., M.R.C.PSYCH.

A consultant psychiatrist, Dr. Oakeley has been growing Lycastes and Anguloas as a hobby for 35 years and now holds the United Kingdom National Collection for these genera with 170 different species and hybrids.

UDAI CHANDRA PRADHAN B.SC. (AG.)

Udai C. Pradhan graduated with Gold Medal from Allahabad Agricultural Institute in 1971 and studied orchids at the Royal Botanic Gardens, Kew, for one year. After studying orchids in Europe, he introduced tissue and seed culture techniques of orchid propagation in India, and runs a private commercial laboratory in Kalimpong. He has contributed to many orchid magazines, and published a two-volume work, *Indian Orchids: Guide to Identification and Culture*, in 1976 and 1979. He is Founder Editor of *Himalayan Plant Journal* and an elected member of

Orchid Specialist Group of the Species Survival Commission of the International Union for Conservation of Nature and Natural Resources.

T. M. REEVE

Tom Reeve spent twelve years working for the Department of Primary Industry in Papua New Guinea, and established the Highland Orchid collection at Laiagam. With a special interest in *Dendrobium*, he has published some twenty papers on New Guinea Orchids, including a major joint study on section *Oxyglossum* with Paddy Woods of Edinburgh.

GUSTAVO A. ROMERO

With a background in ecology and evolutionary biology, Gustavo Romero focuses his work on the orchids of southern Venezuela. He spent six years in this region before going to Harvard University where he curates the Oakes Ames Orchid Herbarium. Gustavo is currently conducting monographic studies on several genera of subtribes Catasetinae and Cyrtopodiinae.

JOYCE STEWART M.SC., F.L.S.

Since 1985 Joyce Stewart has been the Sainsbury Orchid Fellow at the Royal Botanic Gardens, Kew, where she is involved in research and conservation. She is an authority on African orchids and their cultivation, having worked in Kenya from 1960–71 and at the University of Natal in South Africa 1971–82.

DR. KIAT W. TAN

Director of Singapore Botanic Gardens, Dr. Tan is the author of scores of scientific and popular articles on orchids and other plants. He served as editor of the *Proceedings of the 11th World Orchid Conference* and is currently a member of the Editorial Board of the *Malayan Orchid Review*.

WALTER T. UPTON

Walter T. Upton is the author of *Dendrobium Orchids of Australia* and *Growing Orchids*. He regularly writes articles for orchid journals and gives talks in Australia and overseas. He is a well-known breeder and hybridizer of orchids and has received the Award of Honour of the Australian Orchid Council.

LOUIS VOGELPOEL M.D., F.R.C.P.

Louis Vogelpoel is a specialist physician and a keen horticulturist, orchidist and photographer. He is an accredited orchid judge and Director of the South African Orchid Council and the Disa Orchid Society of South Africa, of which he is a Founder Member. He has been growing and hybridizing Disas for over twenty years and has lectured and published extensively in this field.

ACKNOWLEDGEMENTS

AUTHOR'S NOTE
The contributors chosen for this truly international undertaking, all of them well-known authors and experts in certain genera or regional floras, must be thanked beyond measure: Germán Carnevali, Eric A. Christenson, Paul Harcourt Davies, Calaway H. Dodson, Eric Hágsater, David L. Jones, Carlyle A. Luer, Henry F. Oakeley, Udai C. Pradhan, Tom Reeve, Gustavo Romero, Joyce Stewart, Kiat W. Tan, Walter T. Upton, Louis Vogelpoel. We are fortunate to have their authoritative text and outstanding photography combined in one reference.

I offer profound thanks also to a few other photographers who supplied slides of very many species at a moment's notice, particularly Charles Marden Fitch, Mark A. Clements and Rudolf Jenny. Mark Clements was also kind enough to read and comment on a draft of the opening sections of the book. Rosie Sayer helped in compiling the bibliography.

Murray J. G. Corrigan was kind enough to invite me to serve as General Editor of this project. Cheryl Hingley, Managing Editor of Weldon Publishing, had the drive, enthusiasm, and patience to maintain the momentum of production and manage the international cast. Director Roger Hnatiuk and the staff of the Australian National Botanic Gardens in Canberra graciously offered facilities and hospitality during production.

This work was made possible in part by the Australian Orchid Foundation; Nell and Hermon Slade Foundation; Royal Botanic Gardens, Kew; Australia-Pacific Science Foundation; and Papua New Guinea Biological Foundation.

The publisher would like to express gratitude to the following for contributing photographs.

FRONT COVER
Top left, Paul & Jenne Davies; bottom left and top right, Calaway H. Dodson; centre, Louis Vogelpoel; bottom right, Mark Clements.

BACK COVER
Eric Hágsater

ENDPAPERS
Charles Marden Fitch

PAGES 1–291
Page numbers only are given where a photographer has supplied all the photographs for a particular page. Where necessary, column numbers (1,2,3,4) are also given, and letters (A,B,C,D) indicating position in the column from the top down.

A. Andreetta   24:2A, 65:2A, 146:2, 146:3, 186:1, 186:2, 187, 188:1, 189, 191:1, 196:1, 199:3A, 200:1, 201:2A, 258:1, 277:3, 279:1, 280:1

G. Allikas   274:1

Bergold   116:1

Lloyd Bradford   90:1B, 91:2, 93:3A

Andrew Brown   9:2B

Eric A. Christenson   27:2, 28:1, 28:2A, 28:3A, 34:2, 34:3, 80:2, 110:2, 115:3, 133:2A, 146:1, 156:3, 157:2A, 176:3A, 177:1, 226:3A, 227:3, 238:2, 239:3, 245:2, 248:3, 249:1, 259:1B, 259:2, 285:3A, 286:2

Mark A. Clements   9:1B, 9:3A, 10:3A, 11:1, 12:1A, 12:1B, 20:4, 21:3, 23:2, 23:3, 24:1, 34:1, 44:3, 46, 47, 48, 49:1, 60:3, 61:1, 61:2, 69:2B, 73:3, 74:1, 75:1, 75:3B, 85:3B, 106:3, 110:1, 114:1, 117:1, 133:2B, 133:3, 162:1, 162:2, 239:1, 241:2, 242:3,

243:1B, 243:2, 243:3, 244:1, 244:2, 248:2B, 253:1, 253:2A, 266:3, 276

J. B. Comber   88:1

Jim Cooks   87:1B, 88:2B, 95:1A

Dorothy Cooper   242:2A, 243:1A

Paul & Jenne Davies   3, 37, 58:2B, 59:1, 59:2A, 67:2, 71:1, 86, 87:1A, 87:2, 87:3, 128:3, 155:3, 183:3, 184:3B, 193:1, 205:2, 205:3, 206:2, 206:3A, 207:1, 208:2, 209:1, 260:1A

Paul Harcourt Davies   22:2, 23:1A, 24:3B, 29:1, 32:3, 41:1A, 43:1A, 49:2, 52:2B, 54:3, 56:2, 68, 69:2A, 79, 83, 84:2, 97:2B, 117:2A, 118:2, 128:1, 129:3, 133:1, 135:2B, 136:1, 138:2, 140:1, 141:2, 143:1A, 151:1A, 152:2A, 155:1, 155:2, 163:3B, 164:1, 165:2B, 166:3C, 170:2C, 178:1, 181:2B, 184:3A, 192:3, 203:2A, 206:1, 206:3B, 207:2, 207:3, 208:1, 208:3, 215:1A, 215:2, 215:3A, 216:1B, 216:2, 217:1, 218:3B, 219:2A, 219:3, 220:3B, 221:1A, 221:2, 221:3A, 224:1, 224:3B, 229:3A, 252, 253:2B, 260:1B, 267:1, 267:2, 267:3A, 271:1, 272:3, 285:2A, 286:1

Calaway H. Dodson   21:1B, 24:2B, 32:1, 32:2A, 35:2, 38:2, 39:2C, 40:2C, 40:3B, 21:1C, 41:1C, 41:2, 50:3B, 55:1B, 57:1C, 58:2A, 60:1, 60:2, 62:3A, 64, 65:1, 65:2B, 66:2A, 67:1B, 70, 72, 73:1, 76:2A, 77:1A, 77:3A, 105:1, 107:1, 115:1A, 117:2B, 134:2, 135:2A, 139:3, 141:1B, 141:3, 142:1A, 144:3B, 145:1B, 145:2, 147:1, 151:3B, 152:1, 156:2, 157:1, 173:1, 179:2, 180:1A, 180:2, 180:3A, 183:2, 188:2, 193:2B, 194:2A, 195:2A, 195:3B, 196:3B, 197:2, 199:1A, 199:2A, 201:2A, 201:3A, 203:1B, 204:1, 210:1, 210:3, 211:1, 223:1B, 223:2, 228:2A, 229:2B, 229:3B, 236:1, 237:3A, 241:3A, 250, 251:1, 251:2B, 261:2, 263:2A, 263:3, 264:1B, 267:3B, 268, 269, 270:1, 271:2, 272:1, 273:2B, 274:2, 275:1, 278, 279:2B, 281:1B, 288:3

T. Dodson   36:2, 199:3B, 200:2B

R. Dressler   36:3A, 40:2B, 55:1A, 62:1, 195:3A

G. C. K. Dunsterville   53:1A

Charles Marden Fitch   18, 25:3, 27:3, 29:2, 31:2B, 39:2B, 40:2A, 42:1, 44:1, 45:1B, 53:2B, 55:2B, 57:1A, 61:3, 63:1B, 66:2B, 69:1A, 69:3, 71:3, 78:2B, 82:2, 89:1A, 92:1, 94:2B, 98:1B, 103:2B, 103:3, 111:3B, 114:2, 135:3, 143:3, 150:1A, 153:1B, 154:1A, 154:3, 163:1, 163:3A, 164:2, 164:3B, 166:1, 166:2A, 166:2C, 167:2, 168:1A, 168:2B, 169:1, 170:3A, 175:2A, 176:1, 176:2, 178:2, 179:1A, 179:1C, 180:2B, 182:2A, 183:1, 184:1, 185:1, 185:2, 186:3, 191:2, 194:1, 197:1B, 198:2A, 199:2B, 200:3, 201:2B, 202:3, 203:2B, 205:1B, 213:3B, 214:1, 214:3, 215:1B, 216:1A, 217:2B,, 218:1, 218:2B, 218:3, 219:2B, 222, 225:1, 225:2B, 226:1B, 227:3A, 228:2B, 230:1, 232, 233:2, 246:3B, 248:1, 251:2A, 256:3, 264:3, 265, 281:2, 283:1, 284, 287:2, 288:1, 290, 291:1

E. W. Greenwood   33:2B, 39:2A, 136:2, 143:1B

Eric Hágsater   28:2B, 33:2B, 38:3, 39:1, 84:1, 119, 120, 121, 122:3, 123, 124, 125, 126, 127, 139:1, 192:1, 192:2, 222:1, 273:2A, 273:3, 277:1, 277:2

M. Harrison   90:3

Jim L. Henderson   63:3B, 77:1B, 203:1, 288:2

A. Hirtz   141:1, 151:2, 179:1B, 242:2B, 260:2, 261:1, 262:3, 263:2B

Jack Jannesse   95:2B, 100:1A, 101:2A

Rudolf Jenny   24:2A, 33:1, 36:1B, 40:3A, 51:3, 76:1, 80:1, 104:1, 131:1A, 132:2, 134:3, 140:3, 145:3A, 147:2B, 152:2B, 164:2A, 165:3A, 167:1, 174:1A, 176:3B, 177:2, 180:1B, 181:1, 190, 209:2, 209:3, 213:1, 213:2, 215:3D, 222:3, 223:3, 227:1, 231:2A, 236:3, 246:1B, 246:2B, 256:2, 257:3, 259:1A, 270:2, 275:3, 279:2A, 281:1A, 282:3, 283:2, 283:3, 285:2B, 285:3B, 289:1

R. Jimenez   122:1A

G. Kennedy   36:1A, 36:2B, 39:3, 49:3, 50:3A, 51:1B, 52:3, 53:2, 78:2A, 85:1B, 116:3, 130:2, 138:1, 147:2A, 147:3, 148, 149, 150:1B, 151:1, 154:1B, 157:2B, 172, 173:2, 174:1B, 174:2, 174:3, 175:2B, 182:2B, 185:3, 193:2A, 194:3, 194:2B, 196:2, 196:3A, 197:1A, 197:3, 198:1, 198:2B, 201:3, 203:3, 204:2, 204:3, 205:1, 210:2, 211:2, 212:1, 214:3B, 215:3C, 217:3, 219:2C, 221:3B, 235:1, 241:1B, 241:1C, 266:2, 285:1, 287:1

M. Kindlmann   224:1A

L. B. Kuhn   139:2, 220:3A, 225:1B, 225:2A, 226:2, 226:3B, 227:2A, 227:2C

Marcel Lecoutle   262:2B

Macchoro   122:2

R. D. Mackay   89:3A, 95:1A

Marie Selby Gardens   106:1, 262:2A, 291:3

Sylvia Maunder   158:2B

Bruce Mulholland   162:3

T. Neudecker   212:2B

Henry F. Oakeley   157:3, 158:2A, 158:2C, 159, 160, 161

F. Paget   50:2B, 50:3C, 52:1, 52:2A

K. Peterson   42:2

Udai C. Pradhan   32:2B, 129:1, 230:2, 266:1

Alec M. Pridgeon   1, 7, 8, 9:1, 9:2, 10:1, 10:3B, 11:2, 12:1B, 12:2B, 13, 16, 17, 18, 20:2, 20:3, 21:2, 23:1B, 30:1, 31:3A, 35:2B, 38:1A, 41:1B, 42:3, 43:1B, 43:3, 44:2, 44:3, 45:1A, 45:2, 53:3, 54:1, 54:2, 55:1C, 55:2A, 56:1, 56:3, 57:1B, 57:1D, 57:2, 59:2B, 63:1A, 63:3A, 67:1A, 69:1B, 69:1C, 77:3B, 99:2A, 99:3A, 101:2B, 103:3B, 105:2, 111:1, 111:2, 111:3A, 112, 113, 115:1B, 117:3, 118:3, 135:1, 138:3, 153:1A, 153:2, 153:3A, 165:1, 165:2A, 165:3B, 166:2B, 166:3B, 167:2B, 168:1B, 168:2A, 168:3, 169:2, 170:1, 170:2A, 170:2B, 170:3B, 171, 172:2D, 202:1, 212:1A, 213:3A, 214:2A, 216:3, 217:3A, 218:2A, 219:1, 220:1, 221:1B, 223:1A, 226:1, 228:1, 229:2A, 231:2B, 231:3, 233:1, 233:3, 234, 235:3, 240, 241:1A, 246:1A, 246:2A, 246:3A, 247, 248:2A, 249:2A, 255:2B, 257:1, 280:2, 289:2

Tom M. Reeve   94:1B, 94:2A, 96:3B, 97:1, 98:1A, 99:1, 101:3A, 103:1B, 106:2

K. Rinaman   291:2

Gustavo A. Romero   22:1, 23:2B, 38:1B, 50:1, 50:2A, 51:1A, 51:2, 62:3B, 74:3, 75:3A, 76:2B, 82:3, 85:2A, 94:3, 98:2B, 98:3A, 118:1, 131:1B, 132:1, 134:1, 142:1B, 145:1A, 153:2B, 174:1B, 175:1, 181:2A, 195:1, 195:2B, 199:1B, 241:3, 242:1, 257:2, 258:2, 259:3, 264:1B, 282:2

A. M. Romo   28:3B

Joyce Stewart   25:1, 26, 27:1, 29:2B, 29:3, 30:2, 30:3, 31:1, 31:2, 31:3B, 40:1, 78:1, 81:2, 81:3, 85:1B, 104:2, 104:3, 109:3, 131:2, 136:3, 137, 144:1, 144:2, 144:3A, 181:3, 182:1, 231:1, 235:2, 237:1, 237:2, 237:3B, 238:1, 238:3, 244:3, 245:1, 254, 255:1, 255:2A, 281:1C, 282:1

Walter T. Upton   88:2A, 89:1A, 89:3B, 90:1A, 90:2, 91:1, 91:3, 92:3, 93:1, 93:3B, 94:1A, 95:2B, 96:1, 96:3A, 97:2A, 97:3, 98:1A, 99:2B, 99:3B, 100:3, 101:1, 101:2C, 102:1, 103:1A

Louis Vogelpoel   107:3, 108, 109:1, 109:2, 273:1

Mark Webb   88:3, 101:2B, 102:2

Babs & Bert Wells   21:1A

Mark Whitten   15

Jack Wubben   158:3

INDEX